China and Japan in the Late Meiji Period

The first war between China and Japan in 1894–95 was one of the most fateful events, not only in modern Japanese and Chinese history, but in international history as well. The war and subsequent events catapulted Japan on its trajectory toward temporary hegemony in East Asia, whereas China entered a long period of domestic unrest and foreign intervention. Repercussions of these developments can be still felt, especially in the mutual perceptions of Chinese and Japanese people today. However, despite considerable scholarship on Sino–Japanese relations, the perplexing question remains as to how the Japanese attitude exactly changed after the triumphant victory in 1895 over its former role model and competitor.

This book examines the transformation of Japan's attitude toward China up to the time of the Russo–Japanese War (1904–05), when the psychological framework within which future Chinese–Japanese relations worked reached its completion. It shows the transformation process through a close reading of sources, a large number of which are introduced to the scholarly discussion for the first time. Zachmann demonstrates how modern Sino–Japanese attitudes were shaped by a multitude of factors, domestic and international, and, in turn, informed Japan's course in international politics.

Providing a nuanced interpretation of the shifting power dynamics between China and Japan in late Meiji times, this book is essential reading for students and scholars interested in getting to grips with the complexities of this key East Asian bilateral relationship.

Urs Matthias Zachmann is Assistant Professor at the Japan Centre of the University of Munich (LMU).

Routledge/Leiden Series in Modern East Asian Politics and History

Series editors: Rikki Kersten, Christopher Goto-Jones and Axel Schneider.

Through addressing ideas about history and politics in the modern period, and by encouraging comparative and inter-disciplinary work amongst East Asian specialists, the Leiden Series on Modern East Asian History and Politics seeks to combine Area Studies' focus on primary sources in the vernacular, with a distinct disciplinary edge.

The Leiden Series focuses on philosophy, politics, political thought, history, the history of ideas, and foreign policy as they relate to modern East Asia, and will emphasise theoretical approaches in all of these fields. As well as single-authored volumes, edited or multi-authored submissions that bring together a range of country specialisations and disciplines are welcome.

1. **Political Philosophy in Japan**
   Nishida, the Kyoto school and co-prosperity
   Christopher Goto-Jones

2. **The Left in the Shaping of Japanese Democracy**
   Essays in honour of J. A. A. Stockwin
   Edited by Rikki Kersten and David Williams

3. **Re-Politicising the Kyoto School as Philosophy**
   Christopher Goto-Jones

4. **Ideology and Christianity in Japan**
   Kiri Paramore

5. **China and Japan in the Late Meiji Period**
   China policy and the Japanese discourse on national identity,
   1895–1904
   Urs Matthias Zachmann

China and Japan in the Late Meiji Period

China policy and the Japanese discourse on national identity, 1895–1904

Urs Matthias Zachmann

Routledge
Taylor & Francis Group

LONDON AND NEW YORK

First published 2009
by Routledge
2 Park Square, Milton Park, Abingdon, Oxon OX14 4RN

Simultaneously published in the USA and Canada
by Routledge
270 Madison Ave, New York, NY 10016

Routledge is an imprint of the Taylor & Francis Group, an informa business

Typeset in Times New Roman by
Taylor & Francis Books
Printed and bound in Great Britain by
CPI Antony Rowe, Chippenham, Wiltshire

British Library Cataloguing in Publication Data
A catalogue record for this book is available from the British Library

Library of Congress Cataloging in Publication Data
Zachmann, Urs Matthias.
China and Japan in the late Meiji period : China policy and the Japanese
discourse on national identity, 1895–1904 / Urs Matthias Zachmann.
    p. cm. – (Routledge/Leiden series in modern East Asian history and
politics)
  Includes bibliographical references and index.
  1. Japan–Relations–China. 2. China–Relations–Japan. 3. Sino–Japanese
War, 1894–1895. I. Title.
  DS849.C6Z25 2009
  327.5105209′034–dc22
                        2008036870

ISBN 978-0-415-48191-5 (hbk)
ISBN 978-0-203-88158-3 (ebk)

To my parents

Contents

chapter
origin
explained
(p.5)
↓

Acknowledgements

Writing this book would have been impossible without the help of many people and institutions. It is my great pleasure to acknowledge this fact and to extend my heartfelt thanks, first and foremost to my advisor for the original PhD thesis, Professor Wolfgang Schamoni (Heidelberg), who has encouraged me on my way with unstinting support, good advice, and never-flagging enthusiasm. I am also greatly indebted to Professor Akira Iriye (Harvard University) for a wonderful half-year of research in Harvard, his willingness to act as the second reader for my thesis and his generous advice and support throughout.

Research for this book has been conducted in various places, and during my progress, I have encountered much help and advice, for which I am greatly indebted to: Professor Rudolf Wagner (Heidelberg) for his help in the initial phase of my PhD; Professor Irmela Hijiya-Kirschnereit (Freie Universität Berlin) for being my host at the German Institute for Japanese Studies (DIJ), Tokyo, and providing me with ideal working conditions and kind support; Professor Yasumaru Yoshio (Hitotsubashi University) for his wise advice in comments and conversations during and after his seminar at Waseda; Professor Andrew Gordon (Harvard) for accepting me into an inspiring seminar during my stay in Harvard; Professor Obinata Sumio (Waseda University) for repeatedly acting as my advisor at Waseda and generously sharing his profound knowledge with me; to Professor Wolfgang Seifert and Professor Gotelind Müller-Saini (Heidelberg) for their kind co-operation in the last phase of my PhD and their help and encouragement; and, finally, to Professor Klaus Vollmer and my colleagues in Munich for their great patience and goodwill while I was still busying myself with this book. To all I extend my heartfelt gratitude.

I am also greatly indebted to Professor Paul A. Cohen (Fairbank Center for Chinese Studies, Harvard University) and Professor Watanabe Hiroshi (Tokyo University), who have kindly read the manuscript and given me their very helpful comments and criticism. I also thank the two anonymous readers for Routledge for their comments. Needless to say that, for all the remaining errors, I take sole responsibility.

The following institutions have made this book possible through grants and fellowships: Studienstiftung des deutschen Volkes, Deutsches Institut für

Japanstudien (Tokyo), Alexander von Humboldt-Stiftung, Japan Society for the Promotion of Science. I thank these institutions for their generosity as well.

Most important of all has been the constant support of my parents, Dieter and Brigitte Zachmann, to whom I dedicate this book with immense gratitude.

A short note on conventions: Japanese and Chinese names are rendered in their usual order, with the family name preceding the given name. Chinese names and words are transcribed according to the Pinyin system. Translations are my own, if not otherwise indicated.

Munich, December 2008

Abbreviations

FYZ   *Fukuzawa Yukichi zenshū* (The collected works of Fukuzawa Yukichi), Keiō gijuku (ed.), 22 volumes, Tokyo: Iwanami shoten, 1969–71.

GSN   Kokusai nyūsu jiten shuppan iinkai, Mainichi komyunikêshonzu (eds), *Gaikoku shinbun ni miru Nihon* (Japan as seen through foreign newspapers), 10 volumes, Tokyo: Mainichi komyunikêshonzu, 1989–93. (Note: numbers refer to the volumes with the original texts.)

KKZ   *Kuga Katsunan zenshū* (The collected works of Kuga Katsunan), Nishida Taketoshi *et al.* (eds), 10 volumes, Tokyo: Misuzu shobō, 1968–85.

Numbers after the abbreviations refer to volume and page numbers, respectively; e.g. 'KKZ 6:223' means '*Kuga Katsunan zenshū*, Vol. 6, p. 223.'

Introduction

 very useful

Sino–Japanese relations throughout history, although culturally enriching, have seldom been without their tensions. In modern times, the memory of the second Sino–Japanese War (1937–45) looms large, and the legacy of history still burdens the relations between both countries. However, if the second war was certainly the most painful, more fateful and lasting in its consequences was the period that spanned the first Sino–Japanese War (1894–95) and the Russo–Japanese War (1904–05). Within a mere decade, China's and Japan's positions in international politics, their relations to each other and toward the Western powers underwent a fundamental change, the consequences of which can still be felt, especially in the mutual perspectives of Chinese and Japanese in the present. *1895– 1905*

Defeat in the first Sino–Japanese War hurtled China down a slope of foreign greed, domestic turmoil and financial distress. The Boxer Incident and the following Protocol of 1901 is generally seen as the unprecedented, or even all-time, low of China's international status in modern history, although during the Russo–Japanese War China arguably found itself in no better position.[1] The Sino–Japanese War and its consequences reduced China from a sovereign empire of relative strength in East Asia to a 'powerless power,' subject to the whims of international politics. Despite valiant attempts at progress and reform, the Qing Empire suffered its eventual demise in 1912, barely seven years after the Russo–Japanese War, and the tumultuous years of Republican China began.

Japan, on the other hand, thrived. The brilliant victory over China catapulted Japan on its trajectory toward status as a great power, which – after some difficult years of adaptation to the new situation – was finally achieved through another victory over Russia in 1905. Within a decade, Japan had made its way from a regional power in the shadow of China and Russia to the status of the new key power in East Asia.[2] The achievement was paralleled by the completion of Japan's internal development as a modern, centralized state and the beginning of a second phase of modernization in line with similar efforts of the Western powers. By 1905, Japan was accepted into the hitherto all-Western club of 'civilized' great powers, albeit with considerable reservations.[3] However, although Japan's ascent to power during this era is often seen as a singular success story, it should be noted that the geostrategic thinking that developed during this time, and the decisions it motivated, also created the problems that sent Japan, fewer than three decades later, into another war with China and, finally, to defeat at the hands of the United States and its allies.

The period between the Sino–Japanese War and the Russo–Japanese War was not only a watershed for China and Japan (and Russia, of course), but also for international politics in general. The historian William Langer has observed that of all the issues that confronted European governments between 1890 and 1904, the 'Far Eastern Question' was the most serious and most complex; especially from 1895 until 1905, the problems connected with China stood at the center of the powers' attention and came to dominate the course of international relations.[4] The European contemporaries were well aware of the gravity of East Asian affairs, although they often misjudged the dimension of the changes and the breathtaking speed at which this transformation took place. Thus, as late as 1895, the British prime minister Archibald Rosebery declared: 'We have hitherto been favoured with one Eastern question, which we have always endeavoured to lull as something too portentous for our imagination, but of late a Far Eastern question has been superadded, which, I confess, to my apprehension is, in the dim vistas of futurity, infinitely graver than even that question of which we have hitherto known.'[5] Little did the speaker know that these 'dim vistas of futurity' contracted into a mere ten years of time.

Considering the momentousness of the events, it is hardly surprising that scholars have lavished their attention on the various factual aspects of the transformation of Sino–Japanese relations within the international context of the time. And yet, despite these efforts and the rich knowledge it produced, we are still left with some important questions, mainly pertaining to the intellectual background of the transformation. Thus, one would expect that the momentous shift of power relations was accompanied by an equally dramatic revision of mutual perceptions. However, for the Japanese side, there seems to exist a remarkable disagreement about what the Japanese attitude actually was after the decisive victory, and how it developed over time. Thus, on the one hand, we find the more traditional assurance that the war almost instantly transformed the Japanese attitude from respect and friendship for the former cultural model to scorn and contempt for the defeated.[6] On the other extreme, it is argued that such an assessment is tainted by hindsight of what Japanese imperialism had in store for China in the following decades, and that, on the contrary, Sino–Japanese relations between the war and the fall of the Qing had been surprisingly harmonious and constructive, constituting something of a 'Golden Decade' of Sino–Japanese relations.[7]

Such statements are, of course, conscious generalizations which are subject to modifications by their authors when discussing their chosen aspect of Sino–Japanese relations in more detail. In fact, one could argue that the generally negative or positive tendency of portraying Sino–Japanese relations is actually a choice of focus: whether to concentrate, for example, on the Japanese public attitude during and immediately after the war of 1894–95 and thus reach the conclusion of a decidedly negative view of China among the public; or whether to concentrate on the flurry of interactions that ensued between China and Japan after a cooling-off period in 1898 and thus be able to give a more cheerful and constructive view of Sino–Japanese relations, although the question of motivation for these activities remains.

What is necessary, then, is to add a broader and more general view of Japanese attitudes toward China, in terms of the time span covered as well as the perspective studied. Hence the subject of this book, which is the Japanese public's attitude toward China during the period between the Sino–Japanese War 1894–95 and the Russo–Japanese War 1904–05. The purpose of this study is twofold: first and foremost, to provide a general background, not only for understanding Japan's formal and informal contacts with China on the level of actual interactions, but also to situate the motivations of these actors in the Japanese military, the Foreign Ministry, in the Japanese education system, the economy and even at the fringes of Chinese revolutionary activities in the broader context of the opinions and attitudes of the society in which they acted.[8] Likewise, this broader background highlights even more clearly the unique characteristics and achievements, but also the more-or-less popular political agenda of modern Japanese Sinology, the development of which began around that time.[9] Finally, the popular Japanese attitude towards China helps to explain why Chinese overseas students, who came in great numbers to Japan during the period, thought so badly of their own government, reacted with increasing fury against their Japanese surroundings, and brought this attitude back to their motherland, for further dissemination and cultivation.[10] On a second level, albeit quite outside the scope of this study, the Japanese attitude towards China in the late Meiji period is the starting point for understanding subsequent developments in Sino–Japanese attitudes, permutations of which may be traced in popular attitudes in both countries even today.

A study such as this is inevitably confronted with methodological problems, most prominent of which are the choice of angles from which to look at Japanese popular attitudes toward China, and the selection of sources to make a valid judgement on the subject. To begin with the former: discussing the Japanese public's attitude toward China is not a simple affair. Many factors play into the relations between two countries, and can be fully understood only when considering both domestic and global factors.[11] The same holds true for Sino–Japanese relations, but discussing its intellectual representation is made even more complex by the multitude of perspectives and motives that mix into it. Thus, what the Japanese public saw in China may at times tell more about Japan's self-awareness, domestic troubles or relations with a third party than about China itself.

Japan between 1895 and 1904 advanced from a regional power in the shadow of China to great power status among the concert of the Western powers. The Japanese image of China reflected this progress as an 'ideological mirror' and thereby acquired the image of an enemy of civilization, a dying country or, later, of a weak, but docile protégé of Japan.[12] However, Japan's transition was not an easy one either, as victory over China only attracted much more powerful competitors and led to a second phase of modernization that wrought havoc on domestic politics, finances and the economy.[13] The acute sense of crisis that pervaded the interwar years manifested itself domestically in a continuous lamentation on the political stagnation of the time and an almost obsessive concern with 'social problems' (*shakai mondai*);[14] in international matters, it showed in an equally obsessive concern with the 'Chinese Question' (*Shina mondai*) and – especially among advocates of a strong foreign policy (*taigai kōha*) – in constant political agitation to overcome domestic stagnation by 'stimulation' in foreign politics. Thus factors contributing to the image of China held by the Japanese public often had nothing to do with China at all.

Forming an attitude in bi-national relations is neither a one-way nor a wholly isolated process. To some extent, it is also the reflection of the (assumed) other perspective. Japanese before the war minded very much the seemingly condescending attitude of Chinese toward Japan, and reacted to it with aggression. After the war, however, Japanese began to woo the Chinese elite for 'friendship,' but now assumed an air of unassailable cultural superiority themselves. Thus, this study also has to consider the interactivity of Sino–Japanese perspectives. However, probably even more powerful in determining the Japanese perspective of China was the assumed gaze of the 'civilized powers' fixed on Japan. After all, what measured Meiji Japan's progress in the world was the (European) 'standard of civilization,' and Japan, by consciously and conscientiously trying to fulfill the 'standard' in the eyes of the Western powers, internalized this standard.[15] Thus, *bunmei*, 'civilization,' was the identificatory keyword of the time and, as we shall see in Chapter 1, the declaration of Japan as the 'vanguard of civilization in East Asia' or as the 'only civilized nation in East Asia' assumed a mantra-like quality during the interwar years.

The Western perspective, of which Meiji contemporaries were acutely aware, affected Sino–Japanese relations in various ways. Firstly, Japanese contemporaries came to see China through Western eyes, and measured Japan's progress not only by the closing gap with the Western powers, but also – in a polemical way – by the growing distance from the image of China. Secondly, simultaneously with the evolving standard of civilization, there emerged the notion of race in political theory which, as it were, countermanded the universality of the standard.[16] Although Meiji contemporaries, for obvious reasons, rejected the notion of race, Western racist fears imposed severe limitations on a Sino–Japanese rapprochement. Thus pan-Asianist concepts such as 'same race, same culture' were invoked only in informal interactions with Chinese, but avoided in public. Instead, the Japanese government held China at arm's length and pretended to regulate its neighborly relations strictly by the book of international law.[17] Finally, with the standard of 'civilization,' Japan also adopted its missionary quality.[18] Soon after the Sino–Japanese War, Japan assumed the 'moral responsibility' to lead China on the path of civilization. For most Japanese commentators, educating China also implied the use of force or direct intervention, and may have appeared as arrogant paternalism. This, however, was not an aberration from the standard, but was a corollary of Japan's self-definition as a 'civilized power.'

Having clarified the problems of perspectives, the question remains as to what source basis the argument should be built on, as with this kind of study, truth lies in the selection of sources. Considering that neither the author nor the reader is granted unlimited time and energy to pursue the 'presumptuous attempt' of discussing even such a fraction of late Meiji life as the attitude towards China in its totality, one has to make a choice that is meaningful and still representative.[19] Thus, on a more technical level, we have decided to discuss the Japanese attitude through comments on major China-related events in the period between 1895 (Chapter 2, including comments in the Sino–Japanese War) and 1904; especially the Far Eastern Crisis 1897–98 (Chapter 3), the Hundred Days Reform in China 1898 (Chapter 4) and the Boxer expedition 1900 and its aftermath (Chapter 5, likewise including comments on China's position in the Russo–Japanese War).

This still leaves us with the question of what is the Japanese 'public' whose comments we are looking at. Here, too, a choice must be made, and since newspapers constituted the prime medium of political discourse in the late Meiji era, we have eventually decided on six major metropolitan newspapers, the systematic evaluation of whose comments and their presentation in a meaningful pattern forms the backbone of this study: the *Tōkyō nichinichi shinbun*, *Chūō shinbun*, *Kokumin shinbun*, *Jiji shinpō*, *Nippon* and *Yorozu chōhō*, as well as the most popular general magazine at the time, the *Taiyō*. This does not preclude the use of other sources, but these are subject to a less systematic evaluation.

The above newspapers represent a wide spectrum of political outlooks and temperaments in the late Meiji era.[20] The *Tōkyō nichinichi shinbun* stoutly defended the policy of the Meiji oligarchs and supported the politician Itō Hirobumi, although in later times, it switched allegiances to Katsura Tarō. The *Chūō shinbun*, a newspaper with a large readership, was also pro-oligarchic and came to support Itō Hirobumi in 1898, a decision which caused Kōtoku Shūsui to leave the newspaper for the rabidly anti-Itō newspaper *Yorozu chōhō*.[21] The *Chūō's* owner, the politician Ōoka Ikuzō (1856–1928), accompanied Itō Hirobumi to Beijing in 1898. In general, the newspaper was one of the best informed in Japan about Chinese affairs. The *Jiji shinpō* and the *Kokumin shinbun* were both presided over by two of the most prolific intellectuals at the time, Fukuzawa Yukichi (1835–1901) and Tokutomi Sohō (1863–1957). Although of a different generation and, initially, of a wholly different political outlook, they and their newspapers both had in common that they took a rather opportunistic course after the Sino–Japanese War, generally oriented towards those in power.[22] For this, both were criticized rather harshly by their contemporaries, the *Kokumin shinbun* to the extent that it was burnt down during the Hibiya riots in 1905. The *Jiji shinpō* had close ties into the Foreign Ministry (among other circles) and high-ranking diplomats such as Hayashi Tadasu were publishing in its pages.[23] Moreover, the *Jiji shinpō* was notorious for its 'China bashing,' but at the same time was also read in Chinese reformist circles after the Sino–Japanese War, at which point the newspaper became somewhat more conciliatory towards China, as we shall see.[24] The *Nippon* was owned and led by Kuga Katsunan (1857–1907).[25] Although the newspaper had a relatively small circulation and was, in any event, an economic failure, it carried disproportionate political weight through the personal network behind it. Thus Kuga Katsunan, who will appear somewhat more often in the following pages than other intellectuals, was very much a mover behind the scenes (Tokutomi somewhat enviously remembered him as a 'tactician who loved schemes'[26]) and had ties into the high bureaucracy as well as being connected with almost every important strong foreign policy movement during his time.[27] The *Yorozu chōhō*, on the other hand, was a commercial success due to the shrewd management of Kuroiwa Ruikō (1862–1920), and is famous for having attracted, for a time, such intellectuals as Kōtoku Shūsui, Uchimura Kanzō and Taoka Reiun. In 1899, the *Yorozu* had the largest circulation of all metropolitan newspapers, but it was ignored by many smaller newspapers as being of a dubious, 'popular' character (only the *Taiyō* often feuded with the *Yorozu* on matters of religion). Indeed, the *Yorozu* often was radical, sensationalist, and did not necessarily heed its own high moral standards and thus was constantly busy defending itself against libel suits.[28]

Despite the wide range of these organs, and despite the fact that, in this study, they stand to represent 'the public,' it is patently clear that this is but a (necessary) fiction for several reasons: firstly, although these newspapers reached a wide readership, the Meiji world of publications was so much more varied than this. Moreover, Ōsaka newspapers are not included, nor are newspapers of other regions such as Niigata, the Tōhoku, etc., which probably had an even more critical view on the domestic and foreign policy of the central government. But more fundamentally speaking, there is always the general question as to what extent Meiji newspapers really represented public opinion, or rather tried to create a new opinion trend. The *Nippon*, for example, had a very strong sense of mission, and even proclaimed in its founding manifesto that its aim lay in 'raising the national spirit.' This it often did in a very manipulative way, as we shall see, along with most of the other newspapers, which had all more-or-less strong affiliations or sympathies for certain political agendas. However, since these were publicly known, or made known by competing newspapers, Meiji contemporaries generally could read between the lines.

It is with these severe limitations in mind that the words 'public opinion' are used in the following pages. These limitations, if properly understood, do not speak against the project of this study. After all, in China politics, as in most other topics at the time, there was only a certain range of positions to take and, within this range, the statements become repetitive and vary merely in individual modes of expression. The newspaper and magazine sources chosen here cover most of the diverse political positions, and their eventual convergence, despite their diversity, on a common China policy is the most conspicuous indicator of a general tendency of the Japanese public attitude toward China in the years between 1895 and 1904.

1 China in the Tokugawa and early Meiji period

The Sino–Japanese War of 1894–95 and its aftermath led to a fundamental reversal of power relations in East Asia and lastingly changed Japan's attitude toward China and the world. The energies that fuelled the shock-like transformation did not spring up spontaneously, but had accumulated over centuries in a gradual and complex process, the beginnings of which reach back into the pre-modern condition of Sino–Japanese relations. On the Japanese side, the relations betray an ambiguous and complex attitude towards China, in both its cultural and its political dimension. Already during the Tokugawa period (1603–1867), the two dimensions were separate, and the gap became even wider during the frist decades of the Meiji period (1868–1912), when Japan modernized along Western lines and openly challenged China's political role in East Asia. This chapter gives a brief outline of Sino-Japanese relations from the Tokugawa period until the eve of the Sino–Japanese War, and describes the complex and ambiguous process by which Chinese culture could maintain a high social status in Japan, while China's political role gradually changed from studiously ignored neighbor-empire to Japan's open rival in the East and enemy of civilization *per se*.

China's political and cultural role in Tokugawa Japan

China had two very different presences in the Tokugawa world. As a political rival, the Chinese empire was consciously excluded from Japan's own self-centered 'international order.'[1] As a cultural function, however, Chinese civilization was central in the intellectual world of Japan. This double role of China continued into the Meiji period, although adoration for Chinese culture became superimposed by the adoption of 'practical' Western civilization, and political China was declared the 'enemy' of civilization (and thus Japan's enemy) in East Asia.

Politically, Toyotomi Hideyoshi's disastrous campaigns against Korea in the 1590s marked a historical low in Japan's relations with China. The campaigns upset the whole balance of power in Northeast Asia and eventually contributed to the downfall of the Ming (1368–1644) and the rise of the Qing dynasty (1644–1912).[2] However, Toyotomi's successor Tokugawa

Ieyasu was eager to restore good relations with Japan's neighbors for reasons of domestic authority as well as of commercial expediency. Already in 1607, the Shōgun welcomed the first embassy from Korea. With China, however, the negotiations, begun only half-heartedly, soon reached an *impasse*.[3] Diplomatic and commercial relations in the traditional framework of the 'Chinese world order' would have required that the Shōgun submit to the authority of the Chinese throne and thereby ritually acknowledge China's political (and cultural) superiority.[4] Yet neither Ieyasu nor his successors were ready to do so. On the contrary, the Tokugawa rulers persistently sought to establish international relations that would guarantee Japan's sovereignty and security and the Bakufu's legitimacy, all of which was incompatible with Japan's integration into the Sino-centric order. Thus the Tokugawa rulers established their own 'international order' in the shadow of the Chinese political sphere, and when this order reached its perfection in the 1630s, China was conspicuously absent from it. In the new order, Japan had diplomatic relations (*tsūshin*) with the 'foreign countries' (*ikoku*) Korea and the Ryūkyū kingdom, but not with China. Merely individual Chinese merchants dealt with Japanese officials in Nagasaki on a commercial level (*tsūshō*), in the same way as the Dutch merchants who had remained after the expulsion of the Portuguese. Moreover, there was contact with the 'foreign region' (*iiki*) of the Ainu in Hokkaidō through the liaison of the Matsumae-han. Thus, in the 'Tokugawa international order,' we find China, the 'Central Kingdom' of East Asia, excluded (like the Portuguese), and its nationals treated like Dutch or even Ainu 'barbarians.'

Even so, China was present in the 'Tokugawa international order' in more than one way: structurally in the fact that the Japanese 'international order' constituted a miniature copy of the Chinese order, born of the same defensive dogma that informed the latter until the middle of the nineteenth century: 'That dogma asserts that national security could only be found in isolation and stipulates that whoever wished to enter into relations with China must do so as China's vassal … It sought peace and security, with both of which international relations were held incompatible.'[5] However, whereas China expected formal submission as a vassal, the Bakufu only demanded acceptance of its own norms of international behavior, most importantly the diplomatic protocol which guaranteed that the Japanese sphere remained an exclave from the Chinese tributary system.[6]

Yet, for all the care and the money that was spent to create an autonomous order of foreign relations (for example by subsidizing Tsushima), this could hardly disguise the fact that the small sphere was *not* exclusive and that it was overshadowed by the much bigger sphere of Chinese tributary relations. Thus, whereas Korea and the Ryūkyū kingdom sent envoys to Japan only sporadically, Korea sent tributary missions to China every year, and the Ryūkyū kingdom every other year, with only few exceptions. It is not accidental that the two countries at the intersection of the Chinese and Japanese order became the bones of contention in the early Meiji period.

Moreover, informed Japanese during most of the Tokugawa period viewed China as the strongest power in East Asia, stronger even than the Western powers, and much more so than Japan.[7]

If China's political presence was powerful but hidden in the Tokugawa world, its cultural influence was all the more obvious and omnipresent. All fields of human culture, such as ethics, law, ideology, religion, literature, the arts, etc., in Tokugawa times were felt to be indebted to the Chinese model.[8] The Chinese classics and poetry lay at the core of the education of the samurai elite and of affluent, culture-conscious urban classes as well. But it was not only 'old' Chinese culture that informed the Edo society. Recent Chinese trends, brought to Japan in person by exiles and migrants from China, or through the medium of books, gave new impulses to the Tokugawa culture as well.[9] The scope and content of China's cultural influence has already been the subject of a number of studies and need us not concern here. Let it suffice to indicate the *intensity* of the influence by quoting Marius B. Jansen's conclusion that Chinese culture in the Tokugawa world 'assumed an importance that was religious in nature.'[10]

Although China's cultural influence was strong, its hegemony did not go uncontested. It has often been observed that even those who, by profession, were the most susceptible to Sinophilia, the Japanese Confucianists, sought to break this cultural hegemony of China by dissociating the civilization from its original locale of production.[11] They applied various strategies of argumentation, all of which eventually aimed at universalizing the Confucian Way, or even 'naturalizing' it and thereby elevating Japan's cultural position *vis-à-vis* the 'original.' Thus some of the Confucianists argued for parallel convergence – that the essence of Confucianism in a naive way had existed in Japan even before the advent of Confucianism in Japan.[12] Others argued that, since Confucianism was a universal way, the cultural center could be wherever its ideals were realized most fully.[13] Some even positively declared Japan the current center of civilization, since it had preserved the original Confucian rituals and institutions more faithfully and realized the cardinal virtues more truly than did China, which, since its golden days, had gone into steep decline and now suffered 'barbarian' rule under the Manchurians.[14] Consequently, Japan could claim to be the real 'central kingdom' of the present.

Thus Japanese Confucianists (and the Japanese elite in general) showed a strong competitive spirit towards China and were eager to best the former model by its own standard of civilization. However, one wonders whether this 'game of one-upmanship' (as Kate Wildman Nakai calls it) was not a rather one-sided and also desperate affair.[15] Firstly, Ming and Qing China did not take much notice of Japan except as a political or piratical threat.[16] Otherwise, in Chinese descriptions of civil Japan, it was merely seen as a minor but distant subvariation of China itself.[17] Secondly, the Japanese assertion that China under Manchurian rule had gone into steep decline and thereby lost its claims of cultural centrality to Japan is quite extravagant.[18]

After all, the Qing rulers, beginning with the Kangxi emperor (r. 1661–1722), were eager to appear as sage rulers in the Confucian sense by training themselves in the Chinese classics and also widely promoting cultural projects which were aimed at co-opting the Chinese intellectual elite.[19] In fact, so successful was their patronage of learning and culture that Jonathan Spence describes its success as a 'flowering of Chinese culture' in the later seventeenth century, despite the recent imposition of alien rule.[20] Consequently, the behavior of illustrious Japanese intellectuals when meeting Chinese exiles or migrants in person contradicts their assertions of superiority, as the standard reaction on the Japanese side was ready submission to the authority of the Chinese (or, more often, Korean) guests' erudition and refinement, thereby acknowledging *a priori* that contemporary China was still the arbiter in matters of civilization.[21]

Of course, not everybody shared the excessive Sinophilia of Japanese Confucianists, or even the more moderate veneration of the elite. It is well known that the school of 'national learning' (Kokugaku) rejected Chinese civilization altogether by taking recourse on a pristine Japanese culture that was supposed to have existed before the 'contamination' through foreign influences.[22] However, their strong Sinophobia, too, has to be understood with qualifications. Firstly, inasmuch as the Kokugaku thinkers used China as a generic term for everything odious (cleverness, artificiality, empty rationality, etc.) in order to let the Japanese 'golden age' shine forth in an even brighter, purer light, it is obvious that China was little more than an ideological function.[23] Moreover, the very fact that the image could be exploited in that way testifies to the immense authority and polarizing power which Chinese culture had in the Tokugawa society. Thus one could describe the Kokugaku really as the radical exception to the rule of Chinese learning in these days.

In the Meiji period, the dominant position of Chinese learning in Japanese society certainly underwent a significant change, as we shall see presently. However, for all the changes, there were also continuities, most of all in the strategies through which the Japanese sought to maintain equality, or even claimed superiority in matters of civilization. Thus we will find the same strategies of 'universalization' applied to Western civilization – the argument that, if Western civilization was universal, Japan could be as 'civilized' as the European nations. After the Sino–Japanese War 1894–95, people even began to assert Japan's superiority as a 'truly civilized nation' in contrast to some Western nations. At the same time, there was a tendency of denouncing the ills of excessive Westernization, although this, too, must be understood as a tribute to the immense authority of Western civilization rather than a viable alternative.

The foreign politics of the early Meiji period

The great event of Bakumatsu foreign politics (1853–67) was the advent of the Western powers seeking direct diplomatic contact with Japan. The Japanese government at first grudgingly, and after the Meiji Restoration (1868) quite proactively, accepted the proposition and entered into diplomatic relations with the Western powers on the legal basis of the European system of states. This led to a paradigm shift in Japanese thought on international relations.[24] Henceforth, the Japanese leaders sought to emulate the Western powers with the object of attaining equality *vis-à-vis* the Western powers, or even hegemony in the East Asian region. The paradigm shift consequently destabilized Sino–Japanese relations. The co-existence of the two overlapping political spheres could only work as long as both were intrinsically defensive in nature. However, as soon as Japan switched to the more competitive Western state system, co-existence with China became untenable and Japan began to actively break up China's political sphere.

Japan's relations with the Western powers

The advent of the Western powers thoroughly dislodged the Tokugawa international order. In March 1854, Japan concluded with the United States the 'Treaty of Amity' and, in July 1858, the 'Treaty of Amity and Commerce.' Ten more treaties of the latter kind were concluded by the Bakufu (the 'Ansei Treaties') and three more by the new Meiji government. The treaty with Austria-Hungary (1869) was among the last, and since it contained all elements of the preceding treaties and some additional, it is sometimes called the 'definite edition of the unequal treaties.'[25] The treaties were called 'unequal' since they unilaterally granted the Western powers consular jurisdiction and also fixed Japan's tariffs, thus depriving it of its tariffs autonomy. In particular, consular jurisdiction soon became a powerful symbol in popular discourse of an alleged discrimination against Japan on the grounds of civilization, race or religion.[26]

Although discrimination on racial or religious grounds certainly played a role, civilization was the central argument for the Western powers' unwillingness to yield jurisdiction over its citizens, or to grant full international status in general to any non-European country in the nineteenth century. A renowned German expert on international law in 1889, for example, defined the minimal preconditions of international intercourse as follows: 'International relations require certain preconditions, especially a higher level of civilization, the ability of and the reliability in international relations.'[27] The 'higher level of civilization' for long remained an implicit set of requirements. However, the Western powers' protracted negotiations with Japan over its full acceptance eventually led to the evolution of a more explicit standard of 'civilization,' which included as its basic requirements the protection of basic rights, an efficient organization of the state (including the capacity for self-defence), adherence to international law, and the maintenance of diplomatic relations.[28] This was the standard for Japan's 'integration process,' to which all domestic reforms and its foreign policy were subjected during the Meiji period.

This subjection to a heteronomous integration process in itself may seem unfair, since the relations with Western powers had been forced upon Japan and arguably against the norms of Western international law, too.[29] However, it should be noted that, although the specific composition of the standard, especially at its margins, was contentious in Japan (as much as it was in Europe), and although there was considerable discussion by the Japanese public as to how to modernize and, especially, how fast, there was eventually little protest against the fact that Japan should modernize at all and become a strong and rich member of international society. On the contrary, the policy of 'proactively opening up the country' (*kaikoku shinshu*) was one of the very founding myths of Meiji Japan, which united people within and legitimated Japan's position abroad. Thus it bolstered Japan's claims as the 'single civilized country in East Asia' against China during the early Meiji period, as we shall see presently. But even after the Sino–Japanese War, we find Japan eager to demonstrate its stunning progress on the path of civilization on any given occasion, as we shall see, although by then the Western powers remained the sole addressee of such demonstrations.

Moreover, when discussing Japan's relations with the Western powers in the early Meiji period, it should be kept in mind that the treaties were not wholly 'unequal.' After all, the privilege of consular jurisdiction was counterbalanced on the Japanese side by severe restrictions on the freedom of movement, residence and property for foreign citizens (although in practice these restrictions may have been handled with less strictness). In contrast, China, in its treaties with the Western powers, for example, had to yield even the freedom of movement to the Western powers.[30] Thus 'mixed residence' (*naichi zakkyo*), which lifted the restrictions for foreigners in Japan, always remained the bargaining position in the treaty negotiations. It eventually came into effect in 1899 and, at the same time, consular jurisdiction was abolished.

Incidentally, the introduction of 'mixed residence' symbolically coincided with the end of Japan's relatively sheltered existence and the beginning of direct confrontation with the Western powers in East Asia. Thus, after the initial dramatic incidents which led to the conclusion of the Ansei treaties, Japan's relations with the Western powers during the early Meiji period remained rather static. Leaving aside the treaty negotiations (which remained inconclusive until 1894) and the odd skirmish with Russia about Sakhalin or with the United States about Hawaii, interactions with the Western powers remained fairly uneventful. This changed only with the end of the Sino–Japanese War, which placed Japan in direct rivalry with the Western powers. In fact, during the early Meiji period, it was really Japan's competition with China that dominated the dynamic part of Japan's foreign relations.

Japan's relations with China

After Japan had been forced to discard its 'international order' and accept the framework of the Western system of states, it proactively sought to establish similar relations with China, and aggressively challenged China's position in East Asia. The conflict that ensued between the two nations ran along the fault lines that had formed the intersection of the Tokugawa and the Chinese international order. In the following, I give a short overview of the course of this conflict between 1871 and 1894 and, while doing so, highlight some aspects significant for the later discussion.

In 1871, Japan concluded a Treaty of Amity with China.[31] It was the first 'modern' treaty (made on the basis of Western international law) that Japan concluded with an East Asian country, and it was also an *equal* treaty. However, the equality was due more to Japan's lack of power than to anything else. The Japanese delegation, led by Date Munenari (1818–1892), initially proposed an unequal treaty in favor of Japan, which was modeled on the Prussian treaty with China.[32] Yet such aspirations to superiority had no factual backing, and the resulting treaty eventually was based on the draft of China's representative, Li Hongzhang (1823–1901).

Japan's treaty with China raised considerable suspicion among the Western powers. It should be noted that China's willingness to enter a treaty with Japan at all was motivated in part by the fear that Japan would otherwise seek the military assistance of a Western power. Ironically, the Western powers feared just the opposite, namely that the Sino–Japanese treaty would result in a military alliance between the two nations against the West. Thus it is recorded that when Date Munenari left Tokyo, some foreign ministers inquired 'whether his mission was to form an alliance with China. Minister Date laughed at this and told them that they would know the truth when they saw the finished treaty.'[33] Obviously, the overconfident Date assumed that he would succeed in pressing his version of an unequal treaty upon China. However, the finished treaty was not only an equal one, but also included – on the insistence of Li Hongzhang – a mutual assistance clause in the case that a third country (a Western power) would treat either country 'unfairly.' Not surprisingly, the representatives of the Western powers in Japan protested vehemently against this potentially menacing clause. The suspicion even affected treaty revisions with the Western powers. Thus, State Secretary of the United States Hamilton Fish, when discussing the revisions with Iwakura Tomomi in Washington in 1872, also raised the question of a Sino–Japanese alliance.[34] The Japanese foreign ministry, eventually, could allay Western fears by securing the assurance from the Chinese that 'mutual assistance' in the treaty did not mean 'military assistance.'[35] However, it had learnt its lesson well that, although the Western fears were wholly unfounded, even the suspicion of too close an association with China could affect Japan's relations with the Western powers. Thus open cooperation with China was never really an option.[36] This circumstance certainly did not help to assuage the conflict between Japan and China that ensued in the following decades.

The first incident was the so-called Taiwan expedition of 1874, which showed Japan's first attempt to extend its influence not only to the Ryūkyū kingdom, but to Taiwan as well.[37] Soon after the Restoration, the new Meiji government placed the Ryūkyū kingdom into the responsibility of the new prefecture Kagoshima. In 1872, officials of the prefecture went to the Ryūkyūs and informed the king of the change. During their stay, they learned that Ryūkyū inhabitants had been stranded on Taiwan in December 1871, and most of the shipmates had been slain by Taiwanese people. Thereupon, the Japanese government planned to send an expedition force and retaliate for the murder of their 'own people.' This was done upon the consultation of an American legal advisor, who argued that Japan could punish the Taiwanese and claim the island because the Chinese government was obviously incapable of exerting jurisdiction over Taiwan.[38] In April 1874, orders were given to Saigō Tsugumichi, the leader of the expedition, to 'pacify' and 'civilize' the aborigines. However, due to protest from China, Britain, and the USA, the Japanese government soon stopped the expedition. In October 1874 a compromise with China was reached, and the plenipotentiaries signed a treaty in which China accepted the 'righteousness' of Japan's cause and the payment of an indemnity to compensate for the death of the Ryūkyūans.

China's signing the treaty regarding Taiwan naturally demonstrated to the Japanese side that it acknowledged Japan's rights on the Ryūkyūs.[39] Of course, no such thing was the case. China still claimed the Ryūkyū king as its vassal, and the Ryūkyūan king still sent tributary embassies to China.[40] Thus the double status of the Ryūkyūs continued. For both China and Japan, Ryūkyū was a matter of prestige, being, besides Korea, the most important vassal state of China and, by the same token, a most coveted prize for Japan. Moreover, from early on the island group was considered to have strategic value for Japan's expansion to Taiwan and the Pescadores. Thus Japan at first tried to sever ties between the Ryūkyū kingdom and China by threats, and finally decided to solve the double status by means of force. In March 1879, Japanese troops surrounded the residence of the Ryūkyū king and led him off to Tokyo. In April 1879, Japan formally abolished the 'Ryūkyū-han' and turned it into the prefecture of Okinawa.

Japan's high-handed action could not fail to incense the Chinese. In 1877, China had sent He Ruzhang (1838–1891) as the first Chinese minister to Japan, especially with a view to settling the Ryūkyū question. After the annexation, minister He warned Li Hongzhang that if China now remained inactive, Korea, too, would eventually be lost, and then China would have common borders with Japan, and Taiwan and the Pescadores would be threatened, too.[41] The Japanese consul in Tianjin and the Japanese minister in Beijing reported that Li Hongzhang believed that, if China remained inactive now, Japan would attack Korea next, and finally Beijing.[42] However, both parties were unwilling to fight a war at that moment. China at the time was involved in another territorial conflict with Russia. Thus influential politicians recommended that China should wait until the conflict was solved, and in the meantime prepare for war with Japan.[43] Japanese diplomats and politicians, on the other hand, warily eyed China's growing military strength since the Tongzhi Restoration (1861–75), and the military leadership from 1879 onwards began to survey China's capabilities of war with Japan.[44] Thus both parties decided to negotiate for the time being, with former president of the United States Ulysses Grant as a mediator. However, the Korean conflict soon drew all attention away from the Ryūkyū business.

The Sino–Japanese rivalry over Korea was a matter of prestige as well as a security issue. Of all its tributary states, China regarded Korea as the most important. Moreover, the 'hermit kingdom' had an important function as a strategic shield. Thus Japanese military strategists often referred to Korea as Japan's 'line of interest', or as a 'knife dangling over the head of Japan' if under the influence of a third nation.[45] The third nation was, of course, at first China, but also Russia, moving southwards at the time. Conversely, Korea fulfilled the same function for China. Already in 1875, Li Hongzhang saw Korea as a 'protective fence,' and this function became even more important after Japan's seizure of the Ryūkyūs.[46]

Since the Sino–Japanese rivalry over Korea has been the subject of a number of studies already, we will let it suffice here to outline the basic stages of the conflict: In 1876, Japan pressured Korea into a Treaty of Amity (Kanghwa Treaty), using the same display of military power and demanding the same conditions as the Western powers had done towards Japan. However, at the same time, it solicited the diplomatic help of the Chinese government which, after some hesitation, complied and encouraged the Korean government to sign the Treaty.[47] Henceforth, Japan sought to extend its influence informally by assisting Korean reforms. However, in 1882 an anti-Japanese uprising (the so-called Imo mutiny) occurred, in which one Japanese military advisor was killed and the Japanese legation in Seoul burnt down. China immediately sent troops and quelled the mutiny. In the same year, the Korean government signed the Treaty of Chemulpo, which gave Japan the right to keep soldiers in Seoul to guard the legation. Although Japan's Korea policy and the Ryūkyū conflict caused much irritation in China, the Chinese leadership again decided against war and in favor of armament expansion.[48] At the same time, China pushed forward its influence in Korea, to the extent that some historians see a decided shift of China's Korea policy towards imperialism whereby Korea was turned into a 'semi-colony' of China.[49]

Finally, in late 1884 the Japanese Minister to Korea, with his legation guard, openly supported a coup d'état of the pro-Japanese Korean 'enlightenment faction' (Gaehwapa) led by Kim Ok-kyun. Again, Chinese troops quickly put down this coup at the request of the ousted Korean government and, in doing so, successfully fought the Japanese soldiers who supported the other side. As was to be expected, the Japanese public at home was furious about the shame of being defeated by China, and even in government circles there was a faction that called for war with China. However, the Japanese leadership again opted against war. Instead, Prime Minister Itō Hirobumi (1841–1909) went with full powers to Tianjin to settle the issue with Li Hongzhang. In April 1885, they signed a treaty (Li-Itō Convention or Tianjin Treaty) in which both agreed to withdraw their troops and, in case of further disturbances, send them only upon notification of the other party. For Japan, the treaty was a diplomatic success, as it placed Japan and China (at least theoretically) upon a basis of equality in Korea.[50]

After the Kapsin debacle, Japan pulled out of Korea for a while, as it had other matters to tend to. Since 1885, the Japanese government again became busy in its efforts to revise the treaties with the Western powers. Moreover, there were the preparations for the promulgation of the Constitution in 1889 and the opening of the Diet in 1890. Thus Japan did not once object to Chinese influence in Korea or anything China did in Korea.[51] On the contrary, it cooperated at times quite closely with China to keep Russian influence in Korea at bay.

Thus, in 1885, China and Japan had found a solution for the *status quo* in Korea, and war was not a foregone conclusion. Nor was the Korean problem deemed insoluble, although realistic proposals that transcended mere power politics seemed to have been scarce. One of the most popular, albeit eventually inconsequential, solutions among Chinese and Japanese politicians was the idea of gradually internationalizing or neutralizing Korea, thereby creating a buffer state in East Asia impenetrable to the interference of one single foreign power. Thus the Chinese reformer Huang Zunxian (1848–1905), in his famous treatise *Chaoxian celüe* (*A Strategy for Korea*) of 1880, developed the idea of internationalizing Korea and thereby protecting it against the encroachments of Russia and Japan.[52] This idea, which was quite influential among Korean and Chinese politicians, formed the background of Li Hongzhang's subsequent encouragement of the Korean government to enter relations with Western powers, especially with the United States.[53] On the Japanese side, Councilor Inoue Kowashi (1843–1895) argued similarly in an opinion paper of 1882 that Korea's weakness inevitably attracted the interference of a third country, and the only solution possible therefore was to declare Korea a 'neutral state' like Belgium or Switzerland, and have its neutrality guaranteed by China, Japan, the United States, Britain and Germany (the powers with which Korea had established formal relations so far).[54] Under the influence of the Kapsin Incident, Inoue seemed to have lost hope of solving the problem peacefully.[55] Thus he quoted Li Hongzhang's belief that Japan's strategy was military power (*Nihon ni okeru seiryaku wa heiryoku ni ari*) and solely pursued the doctrine 'to make peace with the West and wage war on the East' (*sei ni wa shite tō ni tatakau*).[56] However, even after 1885, the 'neutrality' option remained influential, as can be gathered from an opinion paper of Yamagata Aritomo (1838–1922) in 1890, in which he developed the idea of a Korea under joint Sino–Japanese tutelage and committed to 'permanent neutrality' like Switzerland or Belgium.[57] Although, with hindsight, this option seems utopian, at least its existence proves that war with China was not deemed inevitable.

This, on the other hand, did not prevent the Japanese leadership from intensifying the military build-up of Japan's forces. By 1886, military expenditure had risen to 25 per cent of Japan's annual budget; by 1890, to 31 per cent.[58] The chief hypothetical enemy of Japan's military preparations was, of course, China. Likewise, China's military program since the Ryūkyū dispute in 1879 was directed against Japan.[59] To give a sense of proportion of the military build-up (although sheer numbers can be deceiving, as we shall see): at the time of the Sino–Japanese War, the Japanese navy consisted of 28 warships and 24 torpedo boats with a total tonnage of 59,106 tons; the combined Chinese fleets, on the other hand, consisted of 82 warships and 25 warships with a total tonnage of 85,000 tons.[60]

The cohabitation of Chinese and Western knowledge in the Meiji period

Western civilization

If Chinese culture had been the prime foreign stimulus and reference standard of civilization for Japan during most of the Tokugawa period, this role was completely taken over by Western civilization in the Meiji period.[61] However, Chinese learning still retained its high status and significance. In fact, despite the conflicts described above, at least in the cultural realm, 'modern' Western knowledge and classical Chinese learning co-existed peacefully, albeit for different purposes and functions.

Western civilization in the Meiji period constituted the technocratic knowledge necessary to qualify as a 'civilized nation' and be accepted as an equal by the Western power. In this respect, Western knowledge fulfilled the same function as Chinese knowledge had done *vis-à-vis* China and Korea in Tokugawa times. Thus it is significant that the word *bunmei*, when used without further specification in the Meiji period, now invariably came to refer to Western civilization. Moreover, like Chinese culture before, Western civilization was now considered as being universal and therefore essentially transferable to Japan. Benedict Anderson once argued that the European idea of the nation after 1820 became 'modular,' – capable of being transplanted to a great variety of social terrains, such as Japan.[62] If this is true for the nation as a cultural 'module,' it is even more so for the concept of European civilization in Japan in general.[63]

One of the most famous examples for such a modular or universalist understanding is Fukuzawa Yukichi's *Outline of a Theory of Civilization* (*Bunmei-ron no gairyaku*) of 1875.[64] However, to quote a less well known but nonetheless representative example: in 1884, Hinohara Shōzō (1853–1904), a close associate of Fukuzawa, was stationed as a bank's representative in the world's financial capital, London. From there, he contributed reports and articles to Fukuzawa's newspaper, one of which appeared in November 1894 under the title 'Japan must not be an Oriental country.'[65] On the occasion of the Sino-French War, Hinohara explained to his readers the European view of Asia, and especially insisted that the concepts of 'Europe' and 'Asia' were cultural rather than geographical ideas and thus universal, quoting the hypothetical example of the Ottoman empire:

Generally speaking, Europeans call all countries in the East [*Tōyō-koku*], without distinction, 'Oriental' [*'Orientaru'*] and they call its people Orientals [*Tōyōjin*]. When they draw a clear line between themselves and the others and establish boundaries, they do not rely on the nomenclature of natural geography, but they speak of 'Western countries' or 'Oriental countries' according to the characteristics of man-made society. [...] Therefore, what people today call 'the Orient' is not the geographic Orient, but refers to the Orient of international relations. It is not an entity defined by natural geography, but it is called Oriental because all institutions of man-made society in a uniquely singular way differ from Europe. [...] Therefore, supposed the Turkish Empire would change all things of their society, from the political system, law, religion, science etc. down to everyday clothing, food, housing, and transform everything into the European style, there is no doubt that nobody would consider it Oriental anymore, and that from that day on [Constantinople] would be added to the capitals of the great countries in Europe.[66]

Thus Hinohara argued that 'Europe' was wherever a society conformed to its standard, much in the same way as Tokugawa intellectuals located 'China' wherever a society met the standards of the Chinese civilization. Consequently, Hinohara in his article never leaves a doubt that Japan, by adopting European ways, could become part of civilized and strong 'Europe.'

Hinohara's argument, especially his example of the Ottoman empire, strikes the reader as oversimplistic and even outright naive, mostly because it does not consider the limitations that racism and religious prejudice imposed on the 'modularity' of Western civilization and the upward mobility of non-European nations (this, after all, was the function of discrimination in international relations). Hinohara, of course, could not have missed this aspect. After all, he was reporting from London at the height of British jingoism (the British public at the time was greatly agitated by the Sudan Crisis), and at home the Japanese public was vehemently denouncing the Western powers' unwillingness to accept Japanese jurisdiction over foreigners as discriminatory.

In fact, Hinohara's seemingly naive optimism must be seen as a rather deliberate act of denial so typical for the Japanese stance at the time. Thus, whenever racial or religious prejudice threatened Japan's position, this was routinely countered by an even stronger insistence on the universality of civilization and followed by an even greater effort to show off Japan as a civilized nation. We will observe this especially after the Sino–Japanese War, when Japan became a conceivable threat to the Western powers and thus increasingly the object of racialist invective. The rationale behind Japan's insistence on universality was, of course, to forestall any attempts to disqualify Japan on grounds which were outside its power and ensure that Japan had at least the theoretical chance of reaching equality or even attaining superiority in the 'competition of civilization' (*bunmei kyōsō*).

Already, at this point, it should be made clear that the Western powers, although setting the standard of universal civilization, were not considered to be Japan's direct competitors, yet. This was rather a development of the postwar years, as we shall see presently. In fact, if there was a competitor in the 'race of civilization' during the early Meiji, it was China, which had its own 'self-strengthening movement' (*ziqiang yundong*), and showed signs of progress as well, although this was mainly concentrated on military fortification.[67] Of these, Japanese contemporaries were well aware. Thus Japanese newspapers throughout the 1870s repeatedly warned their readers lest they underestimated China's strength or potential of modernization, and betrayed a certain insecurity as to Japan's advantage in the race. On the occasion of a Chinese warship's visiting the port of Nagasaki in 1875, the *Tōkyo nichinichi shinbun* clearly presented China as a worthy rival whose potential was virtually unknown. The *Yūbin hōchi shinbun* in 1878 impressed the same warning on its readers, adding the observation that the sluggishness of China's modernization also meant that China was saving up its energies, whereas Japan's rapid reforms ultimately remained shallow.[68] Finally, a similar morale can be gathered from a caricature in the popular satirical magazine *Marumaru chinbun* in 1879, entitled (in English) 'Walking Match of Civilization.'[69] The picture shows a race track inscribed with the English word 'civilization' on which swift small Japan is nimbly running ahead, while big, burly and awkward China has troubles to follow. Of course, Japan is way ahead and the spectators are cheering for Japan while jeering at China. However, the comments also show the concern that Japan, at this speed, may trip and take a fall.[70] Thus, until the Sino–Japanese War, there was still some insecurity as to the outcome of the 'walking match.'

Chinese learning

While Japan was in the pursuit of 'modern' civilization, Chinese culture in the meantime did not lose its significance, either. However, its function changed from the formerly 'modern education' to 'classical accomplishments.' Chinese ethics also became the repository of a set of 'classical' values for the education of the good Meiji citizen.

Donald Keene has observed that literature proved the medium that preserved much of Japan's reverence for Chinese culture in Meiji times.[71] Erudition in classical Chinese language and literature, especially the ability to produce good Chinese poems (*kanshi*), remained a sign of high cultural accomplishment. It has been observed that 'probably never since the Nara Period had there been such a vogue for composition in that language.'[72] Moreover, it was a vogue not limited to literary circles: newspapers, especially the extra large issues around New Year, abounded with *kanshi* on all sorts of subjects. People of a surprising variety were highly erudite in Chinese literature or turned out to be real *kanshi* aficionados. The most popular *kanshi* were written by the politician Saigō Takamori and General Nogi Maresuke.[73] Nakamura

Keiu (Masanao), the translator of Samuel Smiles' *Self-Help*, became Professor for Chinese literature at the Tokyo Imperial University in 1880. Itō Hirobumi was an impassioned *kanshi* dilettur. The influential journalist Kuga Katsunan, who will figure prominently in the following chapters, is known for his *kanshi*, and the famous *kanshi* poet Kokubu Seigai contributed to his newspaper *Nippon*.[74] Finally, the novelist Natsume Sōseki is considered as the 'outstanding *kanshi* poet of the Meiji era.'[75]

As in Tokugawa times, Chinese *belles-lettres* continued to serve as a medium for international communication. Thus members of the Chinese embassies since 1877 were fêted and lionized by the Sinophile Meiji society.[76] The conversation between the Japanese hosts and their honored guests was in Chinese, but on paper, the so-called 'brush-talk' (*hitsudan*). In this sense, the 'same culture' (*dōbun*), which was so often invoked in Sino–Japanese conversations to conjure up a spirit of solidarity, *did* have a reality in the 'same writing' they used for communication. However, as we shall see presently, above and beyond this, the spirit of solidarity remained a somewhat tenuous concept and often stood in stark contrast to the Japanese sentiments betrayed toward the real China or to Chinese permanently residing in Japan.

Chinese learning was not only an elegant pastime of the elite, but also the subject of regular education. Margaret Mehl, in a recent study on private academies for Chinese learning in the Meiji period, has shown that the Chinese academies in the early Meiji period even had 'something of a heyday' and that they went into decline only in the 1890s, with the consolidation of the modern education system that stressed Western knowledge.[77] However, even afterwards, Chinese learning retained an important function in education. Already in 1881, the bureaucrat and future minister of education Inoue Kowashi proposed to promote Chinese studies in education to instill 'the Way of loyalty to ruler, love of country, and allegiance.'[78] Later, Inoue and the Confucian scholar Motoda Nagazane played a major role in drafting the Imperial Rescript on Education (promulgated in October 1890), which is seen as the most prominent expression of the neo-conservative tendencies since the late 1880s.[79] Not surprisingly, the Rescript had a strong emphasis on Confucian morality, especially the cardinal virtues of loyalty and filial piety. Thus Chinese ethics was reinstituted as the vehicle of moral education for the 'good' Meiji citizen and became an island of Chinese universality within the sea of Western 'universal' knowledge.

Thus Chinese learning, despite the massive adoption of Western knowledge, retained a relatively high standing in Meiji society. It is sometimes argued that, in the late Meiji period, this combination was enlarged by a third strand of Japanese nationalism. Kenneth B. Pyle observed a neo-conservative trend among 'the new generation' of Meiji intellectuals, such as *Nipponjin* editors Miyake Setsurei (1860–1945) and Shiga Shigetaka (1863–1927), who, during the treaty revisions debate 1889–94, advocated the 'preservation of the national essence' (*kokusui hozon*); and Takayama Chogyū (1871–1902) who, among others, after the Sino–Japanese War propagated the concept of

'Japanism' (*Nippon-shugi*).[80] However, it would be wrong to understand these nationalist expressions as a challenge to Western or Chinese learning. Firstly, they were limited in personal scope and intention (to a particular political issue or to a certain group). Secondly, they were diffuse in content and had neither the philosophical depth nor breadth to constitute a 'Japanese' alternative to Western or Chinese learning. But most of all, they did not aspire to do so. As we have seen above (and as the following chapters demonstrate), the majority of the Japanese public saw Japan firmly grounded in a universalistic frame of 'civilization' which did not allow for any anti-Western tendencies, did not exclude Chinese learning either, but certainly did not want to situate Japan uniquely outside the universalist frame. Any attempt to do so met fierce public censure and was hastily aborted. Thus Meiji nationalism should be understood not as a challenge, but rather as an expression within the framework of knowledge that constituted Meiji universalism.[81]

The 'real China' in early Meiji popular experience

The bifurcation of China's image – the cultural and the political – which existed in the Tokugawa period became even more extreme in the early Meiji period. Thus, whereas the cultural image remained generally positive, China's image as a country and a collective deteriorated the more the Japanese were confronted with both in real life. The Japanese political experience of 'real China' was twofold: domestic, as in the question of how to treat the small but possibly growing community of Chinese immigrants in Japan; and international, in the rivalry of both countries in East Asia as described above.[82] In both cases, rivalry elicited professions of enmity of sometimes shocking intensity, especially in the 1880s, when the immigration question as well as Sino–Japanese relations became critical. Moreover, in the latter case, enmity, or the wish to distance oneself from China, was considerably amplified by the assumed gaze of Western powers on Sino–Japanese relations, as well as a reaction to Chinese Sinocentrism.

Domestic politics

With more than 5000 people, the Chinese constituted the largest foreign community in Japan shortly before the outbreak of the Sino–Japanese War.[83] However, the Sino–Japanese Treaty of Amity of 1871 stipulated that Chinese, like other foreigners, reside in the designated treaty ports. Within this circumscribed radius of action, the Chinese maintained a self-governing community, although there existed some degree of integration through intermarriage, unofficial liaisons and adoption (of Japanese children).[84] Most of the Chinese residents were laborers, although the rich merchants, who controlled much of Japan's trade with Asia before the Sino–Japanese War, also busied the public imagination.

Considering the relatively small and contained number of Chinese in Japan, the degree to which their presence was problematized in the 'mixed residence' debate seems to be out of proportion and irrational. Yet it was one of the most controversial subjects in the debate during the 1880s and 1890s, which continued well after all other issues had been resolved.[85] The debate reflects very well the popular attitude towards Chinese at the time. Of course, one argument for the majority's resistance against Chinese residing in the interior of Japan may have reflected merely non-specific xenophobia, as Chinese constituted the archetype of the foreigner since Tokugawa times.[86] Secondly, the country's image as a backward, 'oriental' nation on the whole certainly reflected on its citizens, and gave rise to the usual array of prejudices such as lack of hygiene, poverty and stinginess, lack of education and morals etc. and, specifically Chinese, the 'filthy habit' of opium smoking.[87] However, an even more powerful motive for rejection was fear aroused by the alleged strengths of the Chinese, with which the average Meiji citizen felt the Japanese could not compete. Thus, as late as 1898, the journalist and politician Hara Takashi (1856–1921) in his guide book *Preparing for the Implementation of the New Treaties* named as the principal concerns of the people about 'mixed residence' with Chinese that, in the event, cheap Chinese laborers would flood the Japanese market and drive out the Japanese, and that Chinese businessmen, with their shrewd sense and unscrupulous practices, would eventually monopolize and take over the Japanese economy.[88] The *Jiji shinpō*, too, opposed 'mixed residence' with Chinese on the same grounds, likening it – in the newspaper's accustomed predilection for strong similes – to 'letting a cat loose in a fish market.'[89]

From this, it becomes apparent that the Japanese popular attitude toward Chinese was not merely condescension, as is so often claimed, but also concern about not being able to stand the competition.

International politics

The same sense of competition also pervaded the early Meiji outlook on international politics. Generally, political thought in the early Meiji period was dominated by the belief that strife in international affairs was inevitable.[90] Thus the journalist Kuga Katsunan in 1893 began his *Treatise on International Politics* (*Kokusai-ron*) with the words:

> Man's world cannot be without fighting. Inevitably, nations or races will fight among each other. […] Domestic strife in any case is unethical [*michi ni arazu*]. However, the state cannot do much about competition which comes from outside the national borders. Since we cannot rely on it not to come, we must deal with it. This is the so-called fighting among nations.[91]

In viewing international relations as an arena of competition, Japanese political thinkers very much relied on the social Darwinism that was so popular in the 'civilized' countries in the late nineteenth century.[92] Thus Herbert Spencer (1820–1903), who at times was even directly consulted by Japanese politicians, has been called the most influential Western social and political thinker in Japan during the 1880s.[93]

However, although competition was the key concept in the political discourse of early Meiji Japan (as much as cooperation gradually came to be emphasized in the 'postwar' period, as we shall see), there were considerable differences in opinion about which position Japan should take in the competition. The 'realists,' the most outspoken representative of whom was Fukuzawa Yukichi, frequently quoted the phrase that the 'strong eat the weak' (*jakuniku kyōshoku*) as a simple fact that had to be accepted, and demanded that Japan necessarily must be on the side of the strong. The idealists, who were mostly found among the representatives of the People's Rights Movement and their intellectual successors, quoted the phrase too, but rather as an anathema to denounce the barbarism of power politics internationally and attack their opponents domestically.[94] Instead, and with much rhetorical bravado, they invoked the ideals of *liberté, égalité, fraternité* (*jiyū, byōdō, hakuai*) and demanded that Japan should use its newly acquired strength only in 'just wars' (*gisen*), fighting the strong and protecting the oppressed weak. More romantically inclined spirits described this attitude – in the tradition of the Bakumatsu braves (*shishi*) – as 'chivalry' (*gikyō*). The *Yorozu chōhō*, some of whose editors felt themselves the legitimate successors of the *shishi*, defined the 'spirit of chivalry', for example as follows:[95]

> In the feudal times of yore, people cherished justice, helped the weak and crushed the strong. If they saw somebody else in distress or danger, they shied away neither from fire nor water, but sacrificed their lives without regret.[96]

The same article criticized the blind egoism of the age as expressed in the phrases *jakuniku kyōshoku* and *yūshō reppai* ('the strong win, the weak lose') which betrayed a mean, 'merchant-like spirit' (*shōnin-teki kishitsu*) calculating on investment and return, whereas chivalry was the natural expression of the 'warrior-spirit' (*bujin-teki kishitsu*), which took to action not minding the danger nor possible reward. This attitude, irrespective of its label, was strongly rooted in the oppositional political thought throughout the Meiji period. However, it is evident that, despite the highfalutin rhetoric, the 'warrior-spirit' was of course as militant as – or, for lack of sobriety, even more dangerous than – the realist attitude. Thus, instead of power politics, many idealists came to advocate strong-arm politics, and it is no coincidence that the ranks of the 'strong foreign-policy advocates' (*taigai kōha*) swelled with them.[97]

As China was Japan's immediate competitor during the early Meiji period, not only politically but also in terms of 'civilization' (including military preparations), it is not surprising that Japanese intellectuals applied their respective credos towards China. The case of the realists is straightforward; in particular, Fukuzawa Yukichi's agitation for war is well known and needs no further discussion.[98] However, as in many other cases, the idealist stance did not lead to different results. Ironically, the 'chivalry' argument is often cited in scholarly literature as a source of Japanese pan-Asianist sentiment, imagining Japan as a leader of the oppressed Asian countries against the West.[99] This, however, overlooks the fact that, prior to the Sino–Japanese War, China was deemed to be the chief oppressor in East Asia, and thus an object of resistance. This was partly the case in the Ryūkyū conflict, but especially so in the case of Korea.[100] A famous incident of 'chivalrous' action is the so-called Ōsaka Incident in 1885, when Ōi Kentarō and other People's Rights partisans planned to help the ousted Korean politician Kim Ok-kyun by collecting money and weapons and setting off to Korea with a party of *shishi* to fight for Korea's 'independence' against China.[101] Later, in 1894, a secret group of Gen'yōsha-braves called Ten'yūkyō (the 'chivalrous men of heaven-sent assistance') again set off to Korea to support the Tonghak rebels, only to be ousted by Japanese police forces.[102] And, as we shall see presently, the Sino–Japanese War was popularly considered a 'just war' for the sake of Korea.

If competition and 'chivalry' made pan-Asianist solidarity with China difficult, an alliance with China seemed impolitic or even impossible the more intense the Sino–Japanese conflict became. Thus, in 1879, we can still observe instances of newspaper editorials advocating an alliance.[103] However, in the 1880s such a view became increasingly untenable. Former foreign minister Soejima Taneomi (1828–1905), for example, rejected the idea of a Sino–Japanese alliance in 1885 with the standard reference to the relentless competition in the international arena; Soejima rather advocated war: 'To wage war in order to make one's country strong is the highest justice and loyalty to country and ruler.'[104] In 1888, it was argued that Sino–Japanese friendship was possible only after a war had decided who the 'leader of the Far East' (*Tōyō no meishu*) would be.[105] In 1893, Tarui Tōkichi (1850–1922), an 'Asianist' who was involved in the Ōsaka Incident, in his *Daitō gappō-ron* ('On the merger into a Greater East Asia') *did* envision an alliance with China at some point in time, but only after Japan had merged with Korea to form a 'Greater East Asia.'[106] Thus neither hardliners nor 'Asian-minded men' considered China a likely alliance partner as long as the race was still on.

Competition, it was said, reached its temporary climax in 1884–85, when China fought a war with France over suzerainty in Vietnam on the one hand, and a Japanophile faction used the opportunity to stage a *coup d'état* in Korea, only to be ousted by Chinese soldiers a few days later. Japanese public agitation at the time likewise reached its maximum and seethed with ill-will against China. Public reactions to the Sino-French War functioned as an argumentative rehearsal, as it were, for Japan's own confrontation with China.[107] Thus many commentators defended France' actions and showed little or no sympathy for China's position.[108] France's position in Vietnam

was consciously likened to Japan's dealings with Korea, and China's somewhat belated claims of suzerainty over its 'tributary state' (*zokuhō*) Vietnam
were rejected with much vehemence, arguing that if China dared to do the
same in the case of Korea, this would mean not only going back on its word,
as it had already acknowledged Korea's independence, but also heaping
shame and insult on Japan.[109] Apart from this strategic identification with
France, commentators hoped for China's defeat for various other, even conflicting reasons: egoistically speaking, it would weaken China and thus slow
down the arms race with Japan.[110] On the other hand, it was altruistically
argued that defeat would teach China 'a good lesson' and spur it on to
modernize faster. This rather specious argument was ventured by Fukuzawa
Yukichi, and neatly summarized by the *North-China Herald* as follows:

> Little or no intellectual progress has been made by the Chinese for
> thousands of years, and we have hundreds of millions of people living
> like 'so many soulless automata,' as our writer puts it, and 'dreaming
> away their existence in careless oblivion of the great world just beyond
> the border.' This idea is enlarged upon with much skill, and we fully
> endorse the assertion, which follows, that the chronic conservatism of
> the Chinese will be incurable 'until they are made forcibly and unplea-
> santly aware of the irresistible power against which they are trying to
> stand.' And it is this to which, in the belief of the *Jiji Shimpo*, the Chinese
> are now gradually being brought.[111]

As we shall see in the following chapters, the same argument was conspicuously
absent when Japan actually fought China, but regained much currency in the
postwar years. Finally, and most importantly, China's weakness and defeat
only vindicated the politicized image of China and let Japan's virtues shine
forth even brighter.

'Oriental' China

Considering the above antagonism, it is only natural to assume that the same
would translate into a politicized image of China, which showed its greatest
contrast and brilliance in times when political tension was at its highest. And
as expected, the crisis years of 1884–85 saw the perfection of China's image
as the stereotypical 'political enemy.' In the following decade of relative
tranquility, this image receded somewhat into the background, but returned
with full vengeance in the Sino–Japanese War.

Carl Schmitt once famously described the political enemy as being 'simply
the Other, the Alien [*der Fremde*], and as to his characteristics, it is enough
that he is something different and alien in an especially intensive way, so that
in extreme cases conflicts with him are made possible which cannot be decided by a general normative provision in advance or by the arbitration of an
"uninvolved" and therefore "impartial" third party.'[112] This definition describes

very well the structure and strategic function of China's image in the course of the Sino–Japanese conflict. Thus commentators at the time invariably insisted on China being the complete opposite of what Japan was supposed to be, denouncing China as the archetype of oriental retrogression, whereas Japan assumed the *Lichtgestalt* of enlightened civilization and progress in East Asia.[113] The most famous example of this today is Fukuzawa Yukichi's editorial 'On leaving Asia behind' ('*Datsua ron*'), which appeared in March 1885. In the editorial, Fukuzawa vilified China and Korea as lawless autocracies, its people infatuated and completely adverse to (scientific) progress, mean, shameless and cruel.[114] Illustrations in the *Jiji shinpō*, incidentally, carried the same message.[115] However, it should be mentioned that, although the *Jiji shinpō* was more constant than other newspapers in 'bashing' China, Fukuzawa's characterization was hardly excessive if seen in the context of the time. Uchimura Kanzō (1861–1930), for example, who had a worldview completely different from Fukuzawa's, described China's and Japan's role with the following strong words: 'We interfere with Korea because her independence is in jeopardy, because the world's most backward nation is grasping it in her benumbing coils, and savagery and inhumanity reign there when light and civilization are at her very doors.'[116]

Three aspects of the process of fashioning China into the stereotypical 'political enemy' deserve our special attention: firstly, the antipodal portrait of China and Japan strikingly ignores the competition going on between the two and the fact that Japan's victory in the 'match of civilization' was not yet an established fact. However, such images were cherished not for their veracity, but for their emotive quality, and they drew considerably on wishful thinking at the time. Secondly, the image of China and Korea shows a striking resemblance to 'orientalist' disourses in the West. If we compare, for example, the above image with the image of Egypt as it appeared in Sir Evelyn Baring's (1841–1917) description *Modern Egypt*, there, too, the Egyptian is shown as being irrational, weak, dishonest, cruel, etc., in short, everything opposite to the alleged qualities of the Anglo-Saxon race.[117] However, this, too, is not so surprising. After all, Western 'orientalist' discourse was known well enough in Japan. Articles such as Hinohara Shōzō's 'Japan must not be an Oriental country' or Fukuzawa's 'On leaving Asia behind' (which must be seen as a short version of Hinohara's article[118]) are troubled accounts of these. And although China may have had a negative image in Japan even prior to the introduction of this image, the Meiji period certainly saw a synchronization of this image with Western 'orientalist' discourse.[119] After all, Western ideological images of the 'Orient' had the same structure and strategic function *vis-à-vis* Asian countries.

Finally, Japan's image of China most strikingly illustrates how profoundly the presence of a Western spectator affected Japan's attitude towards China in substance. Thus the main concern of Fukuzawa's 'On leaving Asia behind' actually is not Japan's relations with China, but with the West, and the danger that Japan and China in 'the eyes of the civilized Western people' (*seiyō bunmei-jin no me*[120]) looked too similar, which in turn would greatly disaffect Japan's relations with the Western powers. This was not a mere illusion, as we have seen in the instance of Western protest against the Sino–Japanese Treaty of Amity 1871, and as we shall see recurrently in the following chapters. Thus it must be seen as a *leitmotiv* in Japan's China policy to draw a line between itself and China in the eyes of the West, and self-consciously to distance itself from its neighbor. Already in 1884, Hinohara spelt this out with almost staggering aggressiveness:

> Now, I want to change the direction of the argument and ask the reader this: do you wish to remain in the position of an Oriental [*Tōyōjin*] for a long time and in the future forever suffer the shameful subjugation and reign of the Europeans? Or do you wish, *if that was possible*, to leave the boundaries of Asia, join the ranks of Europe and America, and thereby evade all future sorrows? Some people may say: 'The principles of freedom are gradually being practiced in the world, the idea of universal brotherhood and equality of all countries will soon become reality [...] Therefore, even if we are located in Asia, why should we fear of suffering unreasonably at the hands of the Europeans? Bending the rules of justice by the use of brute force and oppressing the meek by military force, such are the practices of barbarian countries of the distant past and is not likely to happen in these days of the nineteenth century.' Alas, what blindness! Even if we accept the fact that liberalism is practiced in the world, that a plan for a Peaceful Congregation of Nations does exist, that among scholars there are not a few who propagate the theories of universal brotherhood and the equality of nations and so forth, this liberalism, this Peaceful Congregation of Nations, this universal brotherhood and equal rights of nations is carried out solely within the realms of Europe and does not yet apply to other regions. [...] Therefore, we must be aware that, as long as we are content to be counted among [the countries of] the Orient or Asia, we will suffer at the hands of the Europeans. Are you, honored readers, aware of this fact? [...] I hear that there are people who for some unfathomable reason have founded a Raising Asia Society [Kōa-kai],[121] and plan to ally with the countries of Asia to resist Europe at any cost. Why must I revive Asia and resist Europe? Whether the whole Asian continent, is crushed, shattered or goes to ruins has nothing to do with us. We have to maintain the independence of our country Japan and ensure the welfare of our people. Even if the Chinese Empire is taken over by France and the Indian natives enslaved by the British, as long as Japan does not share the same fate, there is nothing to be sorry about. [...] I hope that in opposition to the Raising Asia Society, somebody will establish a Leaving Asia Society [*Datsua-kai*].[122]

Thus the fear of being bundled together with China (whether as a common threat or a common prey for the Western powers) certainly did not help to ease the tensions with China. In fact, it has been repeatedly argued that the Sino–Japanese War was, apart from its strategic objectives, also consciously designed as an 'advertising campaign' to demonstrate to the Western powers the real and substantive difference between China and Japan.[123] Japan's participation in the Boxer expedition had a similar rationale, as we shall see, although by then the difference between China and Japan was already taken for granted and China, actually, did not matter any more.

Japan's double inferiority complex: cultural condescension East and West

On top of the above factors, the negative and even hostile image of China may have been reinforced by China's attitude towards Japan, which, incidentally, was quite similar to the attitude of the Western powers towards Japan at the same time. China's attitude towards Meiji Japan, despite the latter's modernizing efforts and pretensions at civilization, did not differ considerably from Tokugawa times, a fact that must have galled Japanese observers considerably. Except for a very small number of well informed politicians and diplomats, the Chinese elite before the Sino–Japanese War hardly thought Japan worth the bother.[124] Knowledge about Japan in China up until the 1870s was extremely scanty and based on outdated hearsay.[125] Even after entering formal diplomatic relations, the situation did not improve much, except for the very few who actually went to Japan.[126] The image of Japan in China was not necessarily unsympathetic, but was extremely self-centered insofar as descriptions of Japan rated its people according to their ability to live up to the Chinese standard of civilization.[127] Thus to the Chinese, the Japanese appeared 'quaint, amusing, possibly clever, but never to be taken very seriously,' and deviations were registered as 'evidence of their failure to model themselves upon the Chinese more perfectly.'[128]

Such condescension, even if mitigated by personal contact and friendships of diplomats and intellectuals on the individual level, was not likely to elicit much sympathy in Japan in general. Thus foreign minister Mutsu Munemitsu (1844–1897), who was relatively immune to jingoism and usually viewed Sino–Japanese relations with cool detachment, described the mutual representations at the time of the Sino–Japanese War as follows:

> Japanese students of China and Confucianism were once wont to regard China with great reverence. They called her the 'Celestial Kingdom' or the 'Great Empire', worshipping her without caring how much they instulted their own nation. But now, we look down upon China as a bigoted and ignorant colossus of conservatism. She, in turn, mocks us as a tiny island of barbarians who have recklessly and impudently rushed forward in a mad effort to imitate the external trappings of Western civilization.[129]

Mutsu's observation hints that no small portion of the 'argument' was motivated by the resentment of the 'small island-barbarians' against the alleged condescension of China towards Japan. This explains the glee during the Sino–Japanese War that Japan had 'castigated' proud China, which was expressed in many war ditties, such as the following: 'China was wise of old / China is wise no more / Back into darkness has rolled / For all her sages and lore. / She may boast as the Kingdom of Heaven, / Her barbarous heart is of hell, / What light to the East shall be given / Till wisdom her darkness dispel?'[130]

Even Japanese intellectuals who were sympathetic towards China and pursued a Sino–Japanese rapprochement after the war openly blamed Chinese condescension as a cause for the conflict. Thus when the Sinologue and journalist Nishimura Tenshū in late December 1897 visited the Chinese governor-general Zhang Zhidong (1837–1909) with a group of Japanese military officials to sound out the possibilities for a rapprochement, he presented Zhang with a memorial that clearly spelt out that the Sino–Japanese War, although being merely a 'quarrel between brothers,' had been caused by China treating the Japanese as 'island barbarians', which eventually forced Japan to disprove the insult by fighting its 'brother.'[131]

However, it should be cautioned that Chinese condescension towards Japan was hardly typically 'Chinese.' If we study Western comments on Japan, especially before the Sino–Japanese War, we find the same condescension with the same characteristics, namely the tendency to describe 'our rapidly developing protégé'[132] as quaint, amusing, possibly clever, but never to be taken very seriously, and the tendency to define the quaintness as Japanese failure to model themselves upon the West more perfectly, or – and this was, of course, a Western peculiarity – as endearing exoticism. Both variants were unwelcome in Japan. Many modern-minded Meiji contemporaries loathed the exoticist view of Japan as a 'beautiful Oriental garden of mountains and water' or of 'birds and butterflies,' as in effect it seemed to tell them that they were 'pretty weaklings.'[133] On the other hand, they were very well aware of being ridiculed by Westerners for copying the West. Thus, when in 1899 the President of the House of Peers, Konoe Atsumaro (1863–1904), gave a speech to the British gentlemen of the Japan Society in London, he once departed from his manuscript and defiantly acknowledged to his audience that the Westerners may ridicule Japan as 'Oriental monkey' (*Tōyō no saru*) for aping the West; this, however, would not keep Japan persevering in its endeavor to acquire the culture of superior countries.[134]

Consequently, Japanese observers until the Sino–Japanese War felt themselves sandwiched between the Western powers and China, the latter being Japan's direct rival in East Asia, and both of which bathed Japan in the same condescension of cultural superiority. The early Meiji period saw a continuation of the solitary 'game of one-upmanship' which Japan had pursued in the Tokugawa period. With respect to China, however, this would change profoundly in the Sino–Japanese War.

2 The Sino–Japanese War, the Tripartite Intervention, and Japan's 'postwar management'

The Sino–Japanese War of 1894–95 finally ended the mutual acquiescence that had lasted for so long between China and Japan and, for the first time in modern history, sent masses of Japanese soldiers to the continent. As such, the event was monumental enough. However, it was also a watershed, not only of Japanese and Chinese modern history, but of international history in general. As the diplomatic historian William Langer observed, the war 'marked the transition of the Far Eastern question from a state of quiescence to one of extreme activity. From 1895 until 1905 the problems connected with China and her future demanded the untiring vigilance of the European powers. More and more they came to dominate the course of international relations.'[1] Although one could argue that, on the Sino–Japanese side, the state had been far from quiescent before the war, the scope and extent of its repercussions certainly excelled everything experienced before in East Asia.

The factual side of the Sino–Japanese War and its immediate aftermath has been the subject of a number of detailed studies already, and for our purpose only the briefest outline will suffice:[2] At the beginning of June 1894, on the occasion of the Tonghak riots, the Korean government requested China to send military assistance and quell the uprising. China complied and, after notifying Japan to this effect (as stipulated in the Tianjin Treaty), dispatched its troops. However, Japan immediately responded by sending troops of its own, allegedly for the protection of its nationals and diplomatic personnel, although its size quadrupled the Chinese contingent.[3] After this, Japan's rather provocative actions in Korea and towards China relentlessly pushed the situation toward war. Finally, Japan declared war on China on 1 August 1894.

Although unexpected by most foreign observers, the development of the war soon turned out to be immensely successful for Japan. In mid-September 1894 the Japanese navy defeated China's Northern Fleet in the Yellow Sea and Japan's army won the battle of Pyongyang; in November Port Arthur on the Liaodong Peninsula fell; and finally, in February 1895, Weihaiwei on the Chinese coast was taken as well.

Already in spring 1895, representatives met, first in Hiroshima and then in Shimonoseki, to negotiate a peace treaty, largely on Japan's terms. On

17 April 1895, Li Hongzhang, Itō Hirobumi and Mutsu Munemitsu signed the Peace Treaty of Shimonoseki. The treaty stipulated China's acknowledgement of the independence of Korea, the payment of a large indemnity to Japan, the cession of Taiwan, the Pescadores and the Liaodong Peninsula, as well as a commercial section that granted Japan and the Western powers considerable commercial privileges and opened new treaty ports in China. Until full payment of the indemnity, Japan would keep its troops stationed in Weihaiwei. The commercial section of the treaty very much pleased Britain; the cession of Port Arthur, however, troubled Russia and Germany. Thus on 23 April 1895, less than a week after the Shimonoseki Treaty was signed, Russia, France and Germany intervened and gave the 'friendly advice' (*conseil amical*) that Japan retrocede the Liaodong Peninsula for the sake of peace and stability in East Asia. The Japanese government saw no other way than to accept the advice and to inform the public of the fact by imperial edict in mid-May. As a consequence of the Tripartite Intervention and the changed political situation in East Asia, the Japanese government started the so-called 'postwar management' (*sengo keiei*), at the center of which stood an ambitious armament program of 10 years' duration, and which had a considerable impact on Japan's foreign politics and domestic life in the decade after the Sino–Japanese War.

The popular interpretation of the war and its aftermath

War and the Peace Treaty

The Sino–Japanese War, in contrast to the Russo–Japanese War a decade later, was not the product of protracted public agitation. As observed in Chapter 1, after the peak years of public agitation in international politics in 1884–85, the frenzy subsided and there was a lull lasting for almost a decade. At the same time, and in close relation to this, the domestic stagnation in politics, which had peaked in the oppressive years of 1884–85, gradually subsided, and Japan was gearing up for constitutional and parliamentary politics. With this, Sino–Japanese relations lost much of their lure. The Japanese public seemed to have become so engrossed in the early chaos and confusion of parliamentary politics that as late as 1894, the Chinese minister to Japan, Wang Fengzao, is said to have reported to his superiors in Beijing that the Japanese were completely absorbed in internal squabbles and thus were not likely to become active externally, let alone fight a war.[4]

If one browses, for example, the 1894 issues of the *Jiji shinpō*, which seldom missed an opportunity to advocate war with China, one can hardly blame the Chinese minister for thinking so. To begin with, the traditional New Year's full-page illustration of 'Last Year's Events'[5] depicted, among the more important events, the dismissal of the Diet's president, the rapid drop of stocks, the suspension of the Diet, the schism within the Jiyūtō, and finally the dissolution of the Diet.[6] China does not feature, nor does Korea.

Even though the assassination of Kim Ok-kyun and the Tonghak riots featured in the newspaper in the following months, China remained relatively in the background. However, in June 1894, with the announcement of the Japanese government's decision to send troops to Korea,[7] the *Jiji shinpō* suddenly shifted gear and started again to viciously attack China for its high-handed and oppressive behavior towards Korea. The favorite target for its ridicule was Li Hongzhang, who featured in numerous rather vile caricatures. Moreover, the newspaper in mid-June started a series of illustrations of the '1884 riot in Seoul' (meaning the suppression of the Kapsin *coup d'état*), focusing exclusively on the various crimes that Chinese soldiers supposedly had perpetrated against Japanese civilians in Seoul at the time.[8] Thus the *Jiji shinpō* sought to bridge a 10-year gap in the public memory and rekindle public wrath against China.

The Japanese public quickly took up the subject, and by the end of July 1894 it was completely engrossed and prepared for war.[9] The rapidity with which the public frenzy was rekindled indicates, on the one hand, that the subject of Sino–Japanese rivalry had lain dormant in the public consciousness for a decade, but only in a light slumber. Moreover, one could argue that, exactly because of the mess in domestic politics, the politicians and the public were glad to avert their eyes and concern themselves with less tangled matters abroad.[10]

Considering the bare events directly leading up to the Sino–Japanese War, one is at first at a loss to see what exactly incensed the Japanese public about China's actions. But it was not so much the sending of troops itself that constituted the offence (as this was done within the limits of the Tianjin Treaty), as much as the accompanying notification that China would do so for the protection of its 'tributary state' (*zokkoku* or *zokuhō*) Korea.[11] This designation alone sufficed to convince the Japanese public that China was reneging on the Tianjin Treaty (which, according to the Japanese interpretation, acknowledged Korea's independence) and thus insulting Japan again, as it had done already in 1884.[12] Kuga Katsunan enumerated China's 'offences', one of which alone he thought sufficient to declare war, as follows: interfering in Korean politics and stationing troops there on the understanding that Korea was a tributary state; refusing to cooperate with Japan in upholding peace in East Asia; obstructing reforms in Korea under the guidance of Japan; and finally, sending troops to Korean soil and attacking Japanese ships in Korean waters.[13] Accordingly, Katsunan summarized the Imperial Declaration of War as follows: 'The Emperor of the Japanese Empire, in order to protect the rights of the Empire, establish Korea's independence and maintain peace throughout East Asia, hereby declares war upon China. You, my people, keep this faithfully in mind.'[14]

Although the Imperial Declaration set the tone, the public interpretation focused on two strands of legitimizing the war which are already familiar from the discussion of the Sino-French War and the Korean debacle in 1884–85, and therefore need only a brief discussion. For one, the war was seen as a 'just war' (*gisen*) or intervention on behalf of Korea. In this respect, Uchimura Kanzō's 'Justification for [*sic*] the Korean War,' written for a British public but being nonetheless representative, is the most famous example of this argument.[15] On the other hand, the war was, again, interpreted as a fundamental and therefore inevitable struggle between an old and a new civilization, or between civilization and barbarity.[16] Usually both arguments were harnessed together, as for example in Kuga Katsunan's justification of the war:

> It is being said that international relations have nothing to do with ethics, and yet do not the publicists of the whole world invoke ethics? Supposed international relations must be conducted upon ethics, would it be in the spirit of a civilized country to see the present situation of Korea and still do nothing about it? Would a civilized country consider China's cunning interference by exploiting Korea's weakness right? Would a civilized country consider Japan's well-meaning protection in order to save Korea from further deterioration as wrong? Giving this matter only a brief thought, every politician with a human heart will be able to judge right from wrong without so many words. If we consider the safety of the East and the balance of the great powers of the world, preserving the established order by helping troubled countries and subduing oppressive states is in the order of the truest sense. Who would dare to oppose such a thing?[17]

The case of 'chivalry' and civilization made here against China soon reappeared in the interwar years, when commentators began to take up Russia as the new enemy, thus indicating the change of guards that took place during the interwar years.

Interestingly, a third strand familiar from the Sino-French war, namely the altruistic argument that the war would only serve as a healthy shock for China, was conspicuously absent while the Sino–Japanese War lasted.[18] This argument became the dominating justification only in the postwar years when China's defeat was evident and irreversible, thus illustrating the general rule that Japan (as any other country) could afford to be generous towards a rival country only in retrospect. While the war lasted, China was still the enemy, and only by its defeat it could become a friend.

Although the public bristled with just indignation and called for war, it met the actual fighting with some initial apprehension. After all, even prime minister Itō Hirobumi and other Japanese leaders had their doubts as to whether the Japanese military was really a match for China.[19] Numerically speaking, there was ample reason for doubt: at the time of the Sino–Japanese War, China boasted a combined fleet of 82 warships and 25 torpedo boats against 28 Japanese warships and 24 torpedo boats. Moreover, the 240,000 Japanese men who were deployed during the war (including organizational units) met a Chinese army of 350,000 men, joined by another 650,000 recruited during the war.[20] Thus, in the first days of fighting, the public mood was far from exuberant, and Mutsu Munemitsu wryly observed that the public went jingoist only after the decisive battles at Pyongyang and the Yellow Sea in mid-September had been won.[21]

As the actual fighting showed, sheer numbers can be deceptive. Thus, since the combined Chinese fleet was not under unified command, only a fraction of it, 25 warships and 12 torpedo boats, actually met the Japanese fleet in fighting. Moreover, in sea battle speed was of the essence, and in this respect the Japanese mode of fighting far excelled the Chinese in terms of both equipment and formation.[22] Likewise, although the Chinese army eclipsed the Japanese in numbers, mobilizing those numbers throughout the vast empire and concentrating them on the battleground posed an almost insurmountable logistical problem. It has been argued that, since the Chinese army was basically an army of mercenaries, it was inferior to the Japanese conscription army in terms of both drill and fighting morale.[23] Whatever the reasons, the vast superiority of the Japanese army showed in the drastic disparity of numbers of casualties: in the battle of Tianzhuangtai in March 1895, for example, 1000 Chinese soldiers died whereas Japanese casualties amounted to 16.[24]

In total, too, the number of Japanese casualties was exceedingly low: until November 1895 only 1132 of the 174,017 soldiers who had gone abroad died in battle, most victims (11,894 soldiers) suffering death from indirect causes such as infections or diseases, in the shadow of the public attention.[25] In the light of these facts, it is hardly surprising that after the first successes the Japanese public exulted and declared that 'the actual war was easier than drill maneuvers' (*jissen wa enshū yori mo yōi*).[26] The impression was amplified by a stream of newspaper extras incessantly heralding new victories to the public. Thus the war brought a windfall to the newspaper business, as circulation numbers rose in equal proportion to the high tide of nationalist wartime frenzy.[27] The most colorful expression of this mood is found in the immensely popular woodprints (*nishiki-e*) of heroic battle scenes.[28] They conveyed a feeling of almost superhuman power and invincibility, translating the actual casualty ratio into pictures of, for example, five Chinese soldiers falling to one Japanese soldier merely drawing his sword, and of whole Chinese cities literally blown away by a single Japanese soldier.[29] Thus Mutsu Munemitsu observed, with some detestation: 'the entire Japanese populace now would heed no voice other than one that called for advancing further'.[30] The public cheered the army on to advance *Pekin made*[31] – 'to Beijing' – and conclude a 'peace treaty at the gates' of the enemy (*jōka no mei*).

Once the Japanese public had come to know the 'excitement' of war, it did not want it to end so soon. Thus, when the plenipotentiaries of China and Japan met in Hiroshima in February 1895, and again in Shimonoseki in late March to negotiate a peace treaty, there was the prevailing sentiment that peace was still premature.[32] Consequently, when peace was concluded in Shimonoseki – not at the 'gates of the enemy' – on 17 April 1895, the public was *not* elated. The Belgian minister to Japan, Albert d'Anethan, described the atmosphere at the time as follows:

> The news of the peace was received with very little enthusiasm in Tokyo. There seems to be a general feeling of disappointment that Japanese victories were not crowned with a triumphant entry into Peking. The government was forced to suppress most capital newspapers, nearly all of which contained articles condemning 'the weakness of the negotiators.' When successes had been announced, the entire city had displayed flags, and joy and animation had lit up all faces. Since yesterday there is not a banner in the streets; all flags were removed at once. [There are] no festivities; no rejoicing! Instead of cheerfulness which would seem natural; [there is] a despondency which assumes the proportions of national mourning.[33]

Thus the premature timing of the Peace Treaty severely disappointed the Japanese public and left it pining for the consummation of its hopes – a treaty at the gates of Beijing.

Public exuberance during the war was also manifested in heightened expectations for the content of the Peace Treaty. Immediately after the first decisive battles in mid-September 1894, a discussion began about the terms of peace and what demands Japan should make of China. Although suggestions varied widely, one recurring theme was the idea that the terms should humiliate and cripple China, thereby humbling it and at the same time preventing it from ever becoming a rival again.[34] Moreover, the decisiveness of the victories and the accompanying sense of power soon gave rise to dreams of material gain which very much ran counter to the initial argument of a 'just war' solely fought for altruistic motives. More idealistically minded men such as Uchimura Kanzō and Naitō Konan (1866–1934) soon regretted having justified the war on these grounds, and Uchimura famously called the Sino–Japanese War in retrospect an 'avaricious war.'[35] However, material gains, too, could be justified in political terms. Kuga Katsunan, for example, in a very early contribution to the discussion, argued that claiming reparations was based on regular precedence in international law and served three functions: as punitive damages excelling the actual expenditure for the war by about ten times; as a subsidy to expand one's own military preparations; and finally as a measure to prevent future aggression by weakening the enemy country. However, Katsunan repeatedly stressed that China's notorious unreliability and arrogance, especially towards Japan, necessitated special 'securities,' such as the occupation of territories until all obligations had been met.[36]

The Tripartite Intervention

The terms of the actual Peace Treaty by and large fulfilled expectations, as they demanded a combination of reparations and territorial cessions so exacting that the London *Times* had little doubts 'that the Japanese intend at once to cripple and humiliate China.'[37] Thus the Tripartite Intervention, which forced Japan to retrocede the prize booty, the Liaodong Peninsula, to China, certainly came as a shock to the public and must have felt as humiliating as the cession had been supposed to be for China. The discrepancy between what could have been and what was now lost must have been felt all the more poignantly as most newspapers published the unaltered terms of the Peace Treaty on the same day, and often on the same page, as the imperial edict that informed the public of the Japanese government's decision to accept the 'friendly advice' of the three powers and to retrocede Liaodong.[38] However, it is difficult to gauge the reactions of the public, as the Japanese government immediately clamped down on the press and preventively suspended the publication of most oppositional newspapers, in some cases repeatedly and for 10 days or more.[39]

A good portion of the ill will the government sought to suppress was certainly vented against the intervening powers, especially Russia. Thus a traditional interpretation sees an almost inevitable link between the Tripartite Intervention and the Russo–Japanese War.[40] Yet we shall see presently that there were other voices that attributed the Intervention to Japan's newly acquired international status, and that the Intervention apparently did not disqualify Russia as possible alliance partner, if only to a minority.

In fact, much of the public wrath was directed against the Japanese government, either because it had given in to the intervention too easily, or because it had misjudged the international situation and could have spared Japan the humiliation. Tokutomi Sohō, as an example of the former kind, remembered in his autobiography that his first reaction to the news of the Intervention (which he received when boarding the ship from Port Arthur back to Japan) was ill will not against the Tripartite Powers, but rather against Itō Hirobumi and his cabinet, who had given in too easily.[41] On the other hand, Kuga Katsunan in late July and August 1895 famously feuded with *Tōkyō nichinichi shinbun*'s pro-oligarchic editor Asahina Chisen (1862–1939) about the 'question of responsibility' (*sekinin mondai*), attacking the government for its short-sighted foreign policy.[42]

The misunderstanding as to the primary object of public discontent is also reflected in the interpretation of the slogan *gashin shōtan* – 'sleeping on firewood and licking bile.' This slogan, which recalls a famous tale in the Chinese classic *Shiji* of sweet revenge after a long period of hardship and perseverance, has come to represent the whole interwar period, and is often seen as the motto of hardliners calling for revenge against Russia and the other Tripartite Powers.[43] This interpretation may have been influenced by later uses of the motto in Japanese history. However, in the interwar period, in the same way as revenge was not the primary concern of the public, this motto, too, had quite the opposite meaning.

The *locus classicus* for the slogan in the context of the Intervention is often, but erroneously, seen in the first installment of Miyake Setsurei's article 'Licking bile, sleeping on firewood' ('Shōtan gashin') on 15 May 1895.[44] However, even prior to that, the *Kokumin shinbun* on 10 May, several days before the public was actually informed of the Intervention, prepared its readers for the bad news with the following ominous lines:

> Sleeping on firewood and licking bile
> The policy of our nation in the future must be to wholeheartedly adopt the spirit of a defeated.
> Do not be content with a small victory, do not be content with a small success, let us strive anew for greater victories and greater successes in another day!
> To wait for the day to arrive while sleeping on firewood and licking bile, that is the great resolution of our nation.[45]

The intention of this comment is ambiguous, as it could be read either as an admonition not to relax and move on to even greater goals, or – seen in the light of the Intervention, of which journalists already knew – as an exhortation to stay calm and endure. Whatever the intentions here, supporters of the government soon appropriated the phrase primarily in the latter sense, trying to defuse public wrath against the government. Thus, when the publication ban on the *Nippon* was finally lifted after 10 days and Miyake Setsurei could publish the second installment of his article 'Shōtan gashin' on 27 May 1895, he closed it with the note that he would discontinue the article since, in the meantime, the slogan had become a 'good pretext to salvage the blunder [of the government] in foreign policy' (*gaisei no shitsu wo kyūjo suru no ryō-kōjitsu*).[46]

In the following decade, the slogan continued to be used in defense of the oligarchs' policy of armament expansion (when this had become unpopular again), the several rounds of tax raises which the expansion necessitated, and the cautious, non-provocative foreign policy of the postwar management until 1902. When the politician Ōkuma Shigenobu (1838–1922) in 1898 gave a speech to the members of the Tōhō kyōkai (among whose members were many advocates of a strong foreign policy), he jocosely cited the slogan as follows:

> There are at present phrases in Japan such as 'postwar management' [*sengo keiei*] and 'sleeping on brushwood and licking bile' [*gashin shōtan*], and I am not so sure *what* these phrases actually say, but something like 'Please, kindly put up with everything!' (Laughter.) We had to put up with a lot, and this year's budget shows the evils of it, too, and, frankly, I am quite in a sweat. (Laughter.)[47]

Thus, whatever the uses of this phrase in the later course of Japanese history, in the decade after the Sino–Japanese War it was not used to call for an aggressive foreign policy but, on the contrary, to defend the government's rather cautious policy. Hardliners of the opposition, on the other hand, would cite the slogan ironically to attack the weak-kneed policy of the government.

The influence of the war on Japanese views of the world

Sino–Japanese relations

The public's war enthusiasm, as we have seen, once it had been roused, expressed itself in vilifications of the Chinese enemy with sometimes staggering aggressiveness. However, it would be quite naive to take these expressions of war jingoism at face value and as a sober judgment of Sino–Japanese relations. A closer look reveals that, immediately after the Sino–Japanese War, Japanese attitudes toward China remain far more ambiguous than expected.

There was, of course, the elated triumph of having defeated, against all odds, the big continental power China. Newspapers compared this historic event with Britain or Prussia defeating France, marveling that 'a nation of forty million people should be able to defeat a nation of four hundred million people seems to be completely illogical.'[48] Moreover, Japanese observers were quick to take up China's new nickname as the 'Sick Man of the Far East,' again paralleling China's case with the Ottoman empire.[49] During the war, both had been identified as the 'common enemies of the world' (*sekai no kōteki*).[50]

Not all sentiments expressed were inimical to China. For example, in January 1895, in the midst of the war, the Rikken kaishintō-politician Ozaki Yukio (1858–1954), who more than 10 years earlier had predicted the certain collapse of the Chinese empire, now argued in the inaugural issue of the magazine *Taiyō* for a Sino–Japanese alliance to be concluded after the war (albeit not quite on equal terms).[51] Moreover, China's perceived misery soon began to elicit first professions of condescending sympathy. Thus in June 1895 the *Nippon* declared that 'We must hasten to China's rescue.'[52] The article argued that Japan was a just and benevolent country which met courtesy with courtesy and impudence with 'exhortation.' China was a 'friend' (*yūkoku*) and repented its insolent behavior toward Japan. Japan should now exert its (newly found) strength and assist its friend in overcoming its problems. As we shall see, these professions of friendship in the course of postwar Sino–Japanese relations became more dominant the weaker and more irreversible China's international and domestic position became.

However, for the time being, the question of China's real strength remained somewhat elusive. True, the war had proven China's military power far inferior to Japan's. Yet the Tripartite Intervention, which some interpreted as a general breakdown of diplomacy, at least saw China in a winning position.[53] This created the impression that, while Japan had won in the battlefield, China had made good at the negotiation table, which somewhat redeemed the image of China as a worthy opponent. Miyake Setsurei, co-editor of the *Nippon*, wrote:

> Learn the skills of diplomacy from China!
>   That China's skills of warfare are poor, I have thought before, but that they are like that, I have not dared to think.
>   That China's skills of diplomacy are strong, I have thought before, but that they are like that, I have not dared to think.
>   'The *chanchan bōzu* of China is a rather weak fellow'
>   That is absolutely true, but:
>   'Li Hongzhang of China is a rather stupid fellow'
>   That is certainly a lie.
>   Thus, if we can teach them the skills of warfare, should we not learn from them the skills of diplomacy?[54]

Moreover, even the question of China's potential military power remained controversial. The renowned naval expert Alfred Thayer Mahan (1840–1914) in 1897 published the essay 'A Twentieth-Century Outlook' in the widely-read *Harper's Monthly Magazine*, in which he developed the apocalyptic vision of a final battle between Western and Eastern civilization.[55] Far from relegating China to the rear of the Oriental cohorts, Mahan argued that the newly awakened China with all its riches of people and resources had the potential to display an even greater vitality than Japan had yet shown.[56] Accordingly, in his vision of a final battle, Mahan granted China a role equal to Japan. Fukuzawa Yukichi, too, in 1898 acknowledged China's huge military potential and argued that Chinese made worthy enough soldiers if drilled and commanded by the right people.[57] Ironically, he developed from this a scenario that was quite the opposite of Mahan's, namely that the Western powers could use China's potential to build a huge army, produce arms and warships in China and thus threaten Japan.

Finally, even if people did not give much credit to such fantasies and believed that China as a state was doomed, in a sense this exacerbated the threat that the Chinese people continued to pose to the Japanese population domestically. As we have seen, the immigration of Chinese was one of the most controversial issues in the public debate about 'mixed residence.' The war had voided the Sino–Japanese Treaty of Amity in 1871, with the consequence that extraterritoriality of the Chinese was rescinded, but limitations on residence and movement remained in place according to new Japanese law.[58] Thus, even after the war and until 1899, the highly controversial question remained whether the Chinese alone of all foreign groups residing should be denied mixed residence. As Hara Takashi observed in his guide book *Preparing for the Implementation of the New Treaties*, a majority among the Japanese population in 1898–99 were still against it, and would rather do without the Chinese at all than integrate them, even under strict limitations (a view Hara did not share).[59] The fears of the population, which in many respects resembled anti-Semitic sentiments at the same time in Europe, were even increased by the perceived fragility of China as a state. Tokutomi Sohō, in a laudatory essay of 1899 on the qualities of the Chinese people, who were everything the Japanese were not, ended nonetheless with the following vision, turning all those qualities into a threat:

> If China is being divided up and effaced from the political map as the Chinese Empire, the influence of the Chinese race in the world from that time on will increase even further. Once the Chinese, like the Jews, will have lost their state, there is absolutely no doubt that, like them, they will become parasites in every country of the world and will exercise pressure and beneficence on the country where they temporarily reside, at times as workers, at times as financiers, and at times as traders.
>
> In any case, numerically speaking, they excel the Jews by fifty times. Not to speak of their racial characteristics which will set the world atremble![60]

The Japanese government eventually lifted the limitations on free movement and residence for Chinese in 1899, albeit with considerable exceptions for 'foreign workers' (meaning Chinese), who had to get an official permit to stay and work in the interior of Japan.[61]

The above should suffice to illustrate that, whether internationally or domestically, Japanese attitudes towards China and the Chinese, even after the war, remained ambiguous and, at least for some years, a mixture of triumphalism but also anxiety.

Japan's globalized status

The brilliant victories of the war fired hopes among many Japanese observers for the nation's future rise to global power. Thus, in the first edition of the *Taiyō* (New Year 1895), Nakanishi Ushirō envisioned for Japan the global status of what we may call today a 'superpower':

> Our duty as a nation lies nowhere else but that the whole nation united makes its own country the center of the great powers of the world [*sekai rekkoku no chūshin*], thus stimulate the vitality of the powers [*rekkoku no genki o katsudō shi*] and thereby maintain the peace among the great powers of the world; to crush those among them which are strong and violent and help those which are weak and small; and to lead those among them which are ignorant and to promote and advance those which are not yet enlightened, this is our duty.[62]

Although Nakanishi's visions may afford a wry smile for its naivety, there is no doubt that his contemporaries were tremendously aware of the 'stimulus' which the war had, domestically and abroad, and of the 'internationalizing' effects this entailed. The *Kokumin shinbun* in late March 1895 observed in its characteristically epigrammatic way:

A Vital Turn in Our Country's Fate
    The Chinese expedition in a single stroke has vitalized the state and infused the nation with self-awareness.
    This is the very moment, a watershed in our country's history. The greatest turn of our country's fate, it is now.[63]

Thus, although the Sino–Japanese War in retrospect was often imputed with having woken up China from its deluded opium dreams, in fact immediately after the war it was Japan that, through the war, was considered to have matured and become aware of its role in international politics. Uchimura Kanzō and other oppositionally minded people may have had their doubts about the indirect consequences of the war (in the sense that Japan, newly awakened, had instantly become as 'depraved' as the Christian powers). However, they, too, never denied the merits of the war as having finally opened up Japan to the world (and *vice versa*) for real. When looking back from five years' distance, the literary critic, Sinologue and journalist Taoka Reiun (1870–1912) judged the effects of the war as follows:

> The war of 1894–95, even if we would not have received Taiwan, or the huge indemnity, still had the use of making the world acknowledge us and, at the same time, of making our people, with their insular mindset, to broaden the range of their perspective and make it global [*sekai-teki*]. China, although the blow it received was bitter, *because* of this must now strive for self-strengthening and is aware that a [total] reform of its ways is unavoidable.[64]

Japan's globalized status also raised hopes for its maritime status after the war. Thus in January 1895, the President of the House of Peers Konoe Atsumaro argued that, given the inevitable and rapid spread of transportation networks into the remotest corners of the world, Japan now must use its natural geographical advantage and secure Japan's 'maritime rights in East Asia' (*Tōyō no kaijōken*):

> In the dawn of the future, when the Siberian Railroad will be fully connected, the completion of the Nicaraguan Canal[65] be announced and trade between the West and Asia will be flourishing more than ever, will not Japan be located exactly on the main fare of it? At that time, if we do not take the shipping rights of the Pacific, the Japanese Sea, and the Chinese Sea in our hands and if we do not make ourselves the maritime King of East Asia [*Tōyō no kaijō-ō*], this would be like throwing away the advantages which nature has bestowed on us and leave it to others to pick them up.[66]

Unfortunately, the Sino–Japanese War also broadened the range of the perspective of the Western powers, and their re-awakened ambitions in East Asia made them unwilling to yield power in East Asian (not to speak of dominance) to Japan too easily. The Tripartite Intervention was the first illustration of this. As we have said, probably influenced by the knowledge of later developments, the reactions of the public to this event have often been interpreted one-sidedly as an outcry against the injustice of the Intervention powers. However, the government, too, was heavily censured for its blunder, not least because it had fatally underestimated the internationalizing effects of the war. Kuga Katsunan in June 1895 saw 'international interventions' as the regular consequence of the globalization of power relations:

> International intervention in domestic politics is an irregularity, but in foreign politics we must say it is rather the rule.[67] In our times, where there are means of transport provided on land and on water, and the paths of trade span East and West, the interests of all countries of the world are naturally interrelated, and from these interrelations arise rights and obligations in a rather haphazard fashion. If the so-called proactive opening up of our country [*kaikoku shinshu*] really is to be our foreign policy, then we should be aware right from the start that we invite intervention by other countries in all matters. And if consequently we, too, intervene in the foreign affairs of other countries, is that not in the awareness that it is necessary for the extension of our national interest?[68]

Thus the Tripartite Intervention could also be viewed positively as proof of Japan's newly acquired status in the world and as another precedent for Japan's future claims to intervene in its own interests itself.

Alliance and cooperation

The 'globalization' of East Asia convinced many Japanese observers that Japan needed to leave its isolation and enter an alliance with a Western power. This was a fundamental change in public opinion. Hitherto, the idea of an alliance with a Western power had been toyed with only briefly and quickly discarded as unrealistic. The serious contemplation of an alliance after the war paralleled the gradual postwar abandonment of the idea of single-handed competition as too dangerous for Japan, but also reflected heightened awareness of Japan's risen status in the world.

Demands for an alliance were heard immediately after the Tripartite Intervention had been made known, and when the newspapers could publish again. The *Kokumin shinbun* on 29 May 1895 observed as a recent phenomenon that 'the people of our country cry we must enter an alliance.'[69] However, whether to do so, and with whom to enter an alliance, remained a contentious issue for some time. In August 1896, the *Tōkyō Asahi shinbun* described the debate as follows:

> We can divide the discussants of foreign policy in recent times broadly in two factions: there are the ones who advocate an Anglo–Japanese alliance,

and there are the ones who advocate a Russo–Japanese alliance. Since the retrocession of the Liaodong peninsula, many have realized that Japan cannot maintain peace in East Asia by its own powers and, therefore, are sure that Japan must cooperate with one of the strong powers. They differ in the selection of the partner, either Britain or Russia, but concerning the impossibility of walking alone and standing apart (*doppo koritsu*), one can say that they both share the same opinion. But are they not the kind of the people who continue to cry out in pain even after the illness has left them?[70]

The author of the *Asahi shinbun* in the rest of the article argued for the third, traditional option of 'walking alone and standing apart.'

From early on, a majority came to view Britain as the most advantageous alliance partner. However, it should be noted that, even among the most ardent advocates of an Anglo–Japanese alliance, there were still some reservations in the early postwar years, mostly based on perceived discrepancies in the level of civilization between the two countries. The *Jiji shinpō*, for example, consistently advocated the alliance and thereby supported influential advocates in the Foreign Ministry, such as Hayashi Tadasu (who himself wrote for the newspaper) or Katō Takaaki. However, Fukuzawa Yukichi made it very clear that an alliance with the superpower Britain was a hope for the future; as of now, Japan was not strong enough and therefore was not a suitable partner for Britain, which, of course, wanted to benefit from the alliance too.[71] Thus, according to Fukuzawa, Japan did not yet meet the standard of the 'most civilized' country in the world. The *Kokumin shinbun*, too, in July 1895 was still skeptical whether Britain could be Japan's alliance partner, and presented the opinion of a British author who answered the question in the negative.[72] However, in 1898 the *Kokumin* became one of the most ardent supporters of an Anglo–Japanese alliance due to the influence of the Far Eastern Crisis.[73]

Entering the real race of civilization

The somewhat conflicting self-image of Japan's strength and status, in a sense, paralleled the Western assessment of Japan after the war. On the one hand, Western observers retained their condescending attitude and did not acknowledge Japan's feat as equal to their ranks. On the other hand, the Japanese victory saw the rise of anti-Japanese racism in Europe which, however politicized and extraneous its motives were, betrayed some latent anxiety about Japan's recent ascent. Both attitudes, in turn, demonstrated to Japanese observers that the 'real race' of civilization had only begun and that Japan must try even harder to prove itself as civilized or, eventually, even more civilized than the European nations.

It has been argued that Japan's victory in the Sino–Japanese War caused the West suddenly to consider Japan to be 'one of them,' – one of the civilized countries and great powers of the world.[74] However, this means somewhat overstating the case. Although one might concede that parts of the Western public lavished effusive praise upon Japan in the glory days of its victories (which stood in stark contrast to the belittling and at times even hostile comments on Japan in the first days of the war), this does not mean that it accepted Japan as equally strong as the Western powers.[75] After all, Japan had merely 'won a race run with a lame man.' Such was the observation of the The *North-China Herald*:

> While, therefore, we may be and are perfectly ready to acknowledge that as an exhibition of strategic manoeuvring, and an object lesson as to the capabilities of an Eastern Power which thirty years ago could scarcely be considered emancipated from the thraldom of a most tyrannical feudal system, Japan has acquitted herself brilliantly; viewed as a conquest of such a country as China is at the present day it is certainly qualified. To conquer where no opposition is offered is but a conquest of a kind. To win a race run with a lame man may be a win, but it is hardly a victory calculated to bring a man glowing with pride and satisfaction to the winning-post for his laurels. This fact seems to be strangely overlooked by the home papers [...][76]

The *North-China Herald* was still rabidly anti-Japanese in these early days of the war, and much of its belittling of Japan's success could be attributed to this sentiment. However, even Alfred Thayer Mahan in retrospect showed himself not too impressed by the Japanese victory. In the article quoted above, he commented:

> The Japanese have shown great capacity, but they have met little resistance; and it is easier by far to move and to control an island kingdom of forty millions than a vast continental territory containing near tenfold that number of inhabitants.[77]

If an acknowledged authority such as Mahan voiced this opinion, we can be sure that many others followed.

On the other hand, the recent Japanese display of vitality led to the rise of racist sentiment against Japan in Europe in the form of the 'yellow danger' or 'yellow peril' scare.[78] This new development was well known in Japan from early on. The *Kokumin shinbun* in July 1895 already contained the following snippet of news:

> The Rise of the Yellow Race
>   ... really frightens a part of the people in Europe. General *Chuiiru*[79] also observes: 'Japan in twenty-five years has made the same progress as other countries in centuries. If, on top of that, China too awakes from its slumber, then Europe certainly cannot sleep safely anymore. Do the

European countries really have the time to sap each other's strength by internal fighting?'[80]

One of the most famous depictions of the 'yellow peril' is the so-called Knackfuss painting, which Kaiser Wilhelm II ordered in 1895 after his own design, copies of which were then sent to the rulers and politicians of Europe and Russia and displayed in German ships.[81] This painting, which bore the title 'Ye Nations of Europe, Defend Your Most Holy Goods!' was also well known in Japan from early on. The *Kokumin shinbun* presented its readers with a rough sketch of the Knackfuss painting as early as January 1896[82] (for comparison, the Russian czar received a copy only after September 1895, and Bismarck at Christmas 1895[83]).

Japanese observers, of course, did not agree to anti-Japanese racism, the implications of which we will discuss later in the context of Pan-Asianism. However, many Japanese commentators *did* share the view that to win the race against China did not mean to win the race of civilization, which had only just begun. Fukuzawa Yukichi warned his fellow men that they 'must not pride themselves in the vain glory of victory.'[84] Fukuzawa argued that the victory of China was 'no more than touching an old rotten thing and bring it down.' Even the modernization era after the Meiji Restoration was nothing to be too proud about. After all, foreign relations in the prewar era had been relatively simple, and Japan had been in a sheltered position then. This was different now, in the globalized era of East Asia, where Japan had to face the much more mighty opposition of the Western powers.

Japan's 'postwar management,' 1895–1904

Armament expansion and continental withdrawal

The changed international environment after the Sino–Japanese War had a lasting impact on Japan's security policy and, indirectly, on domestic politics and the economy as well. In order to compete better with the 'civilized' powers, soon after the war Japan entered a 'second phase of Westernization.'[85] The program of measures which the government introduced to this end was soon dubbed by its originators the 'postwar management' (*sengo keiei*).[86] At its core lay an ambitious armament expansion program that would bind all the nation's powers for the next 10 years.

Although the armament expansion, as it was decided upon in the summer of 1895, was the immediate reaction to the debacle of the Tripartite Intervention, victory in the Sino–Japanese War would have led to an expansion anyway, if only on a much smaller scale. Before the signing of the Peace Treaty in Shimonoseki, Yamagata Aritomo had already drawn up a plan that should guarantee Japan's capability of extending the 'lines of interest' (*riken-sen*) beyond the 'line of sovereignty' (*shuken-sen*) and eventually rise to become the 'leader of the East' (*Tōyō no meishu*).[87]

The altered international situation after the war forced the military leadership to shelve their dreams of becoming the 'leader of East Asia' for the
time being, and to envision scenarios of confrontation that necessitated an
even heavier military build-up than before. The army and navy expansion
programs each had different hypothetical enemies. The navy, observing the
advance of the Western powers into East Asia, planned to prepare for the
confrontation with either one of the powers Britain or Russia, in combination with one or two allied powers such as France or Germany.[88] In 1896 it
was estimated that Britain and Russia commanded in the Far East squadrons of roughly the same total tonnage (*ca.* 59,000 tons); France (29,000
tons) and Germany (23,000 tons) each commanded squadrons of less than
half the size.[89] Either combination would outmeasure Japan's fleet (with a
total tonnage of 59,106 tons in 1895) by far.[90] In July 1895, Minister of the
Navy Saigō Tsugumichi proposed to the cabinet a 10-year navy expansion
plan, with 17 ships of the main fleet and 75 other ships to be newly built.[91]
The plan was accepted and, with the approval of the Diet in the next year,
even expanded somewhat. Between 1895 and 1904, Japan built 44 ships with
a total tonnage of 194,473 tons[92] – almost double the Russian, German and
French Far East squadrons of 1896 combined. Seen in the light of the past,
the navy's plan meant preparing to withstand another Tripartite Intervention
in the future. However, seen in the light of the present advance of the Western powers into the Far East, this was also meant to achieve a naval power
that would guarantee Japan's dominance in East Asia, and possibly extend it
southwards into the South Pacific, too.[93]

The enlargement of the army was undertaken primarily with a view to a
possible confrontation with Russia. In March 1896 the army decided to add
six more divisions to its existing seven, plus some extra units. In terms of
soldiers, this meant trebling the numbers from 50,000 to 150,000 soldiers in
peacetime, and from 200,000 to 600,000 in wartime. Enlargement to its new
peacetime size had already been accomplished by the end of 1898.[94]

The massive military expansion program could not fail to put a heavy
strain on state finances. Between 1896 and 1905 the total expenses of the
navy expansion amounted to 213 Mio Yen, the army in the same period cost
101 Mio Yen[95] (in comparison, the total national expenditure in the year
before the Sino–Japanese War, 1893, amounted to 85 Mio Yen[96]). The
reparations Japan received from China amounted to 360 Mio Yen. However,
only a part of it had been assigned to cover the costs of the actual expansion.[97] Thus the costs for army and navy very much weighed down the
yearly budgets. The budget plan for the year 1897 assessed the combined
costs of both, navy and army, as amounting to 139 Mio Yen. This commanded the lion's share of 58 per cent of the total budget, and the budget
was increasing yearly.[98]

It is this ratio that, compared with other Western powers, best illustrates
the early commitment of Japan to armament expansion. The arms race of
the European nations accelerated only in the new century, once more after

1911, and reached its peak in the year before the outbreak of the 'Great War.'[99] However, even during the peak years of 1913–14, none of the European powers invested more than 43 per cent of central and state government spending in defence.[100] Considering its size, already since 1895 Japan had pursued armament expansion with greater zest than the Western powers ever displayed until the eve of the First World War. With this in mind, one could argue that Japan in the postwar management years was not merely in its 'second phase of Westernization,' but actually among the *vanguard* of global development.

Considering the enormous strain which the armament expansion as the core of the postwar management program put on the national powers, it is not surprising that the Japanese leaders, while it lasted, were very cautious not to commit themselves to foreign adventures that would endanger its success. The foreign policy of the postwar management years was characterized by its utmost reserve. At least as long as Itō Hirobumi was in power, Japan did not venture abroad, nor did it strive for alliance partners, but resolved to 'walk alone and stand apart' (*doppo koritsu*), if only for the next 10 years. This neutrality we will see most typically illustrated in the government's reaction to the Far Eastern Crisis 1897–98.

However, it should also be mentioned that, apart from the self-imposed strain of the postwar program, the Japanese withdrawal was not wholly voluntary. In Korea, for example, Japan soon had to yield to Russia the ground that it had just contrived to snatch away from China, and thus made void the reason for going to war with China in the first place.[101] This was due to an incident that could be described as arguably the first instance of those unauthorized actions by 'men on the spot' that cost Japan so dearly in modern history. In October 1895 the Japanese minister to Korea staged a coup against the pro-Russian faction in Seoul, which tragically ended with the murder of the Queen Min and had the consequence of driving the surviving king into Russian hands.[102] On this, the *North-China Herald* commented smugly: 'What the unbiased had warned her [Japan] would happen when she attacked in order to secure the independence of Corea, has come to pass, and Russia now has established her protectorate over the Corean Court and Government. […] she has turned out China only, as she was forewarned, to let Russia in.'[103]

Taiwan was not exactly a success story in the beginning, either.[104] Already the occupation had cost more time and lives than originally envisioned, and guerilla warfare continued long after.[105] Mismanagement at first let Taiwan appear more as a liability than as an asset. Uchimura Kanzō, for example, scathingly attacked the government in a way that was very typical for the opposition:

> Of Satsuma [the government's] misrule in Formosa, it is all too painful for us to tell. The Land of the Virtuous in extending its 'virtuous rule' over its newly acquired territory, has converted it to a den of robbers

and extortioners. Formosa that was got as a guarantee of the peace in the East now proves 'a thorn in the flesh' of the nation that got it, and a fear of disintegration of the empire from which it was gotten.[106]

Foreign observers were skeptical, too. In 1900, the *North-China Herald* still referred to Taiwan as the 'lost dependency of Formosa.'[107] However, the *Herald* was wrong: things began to change after 1898 with the new Taiwan administration, and in due time, Taiwan became Japan's model colony.[108] Yet the strain which the Taiwan business put on Japan's administrative and financial powers, on top of others, was another reason for moving very cautiously in other affairs.

Finances, the economy and China's unattainable riches

It has been observed that the vast expenditures of the general armament race at the turn of the century generally required 'either higher taxes, or inflationary borrowing, or both.'[109] Japan was no exception to this observation in that it required both: old taxes were raised, new taxes introduced, and money borrowed on the international market when the domestic market was exhausted. On 28 March 1896, three days before the army made the decision to double its size, several new taxes were introduced in a first round of tax increases. The second round of raises took place in December 1898.[110] When even this was not enough to salvage the budget, the government, unable to raise any more domestic loans, had to go on the London market and raise foreign loans after a 22-year hiatus.[111] However, the period of heavy borrowing in London and other Western capital markets started in full only after 1902 and continued until the First World War, first to finance armament expenditures and later to pay up for the ruinous Russo–Japanese War.

Government expenditure for armament expansion also contributed to the decision to introduce the gold standard in 1897, as this facilitated the spending of large sums in gold-standard countries such as Britain, where most of Japan's navy ships were produced.[112] However, it should be noted that, apart from the considerations that the gold standard opened access to the European capital market, there was also the cultural prejudice that, as countries become more civilized, they would naturally progress from the silver to the gold standard.[113] Thus the Chinese indemnity, which was used for the shift, enabled Japan to progress to a higher rank of 'monetary culture.'

The above developments also seriously affected the Japanese economy. The decade after the Sino–Japanese War until the Russo–Japanese War can be divided into two phases of economic growth. In the first phase, spanning from the end of the Sino–Japanese War to the First Depression of late 1897 and early 1898, industry and other sectors grew rapidly. The prime cause for this revival is seen in the more generous credit policy which the Bank of Japan adopted shortly after the war in expectation of the Chinese Indemnity.[114] However, in late 1897 the financial situation became tighter, and combined with external factors to cause the First Depression. The economy in the second phase until the Russo–Japanese War did not recover, but stagnated and met a Second Depression in late 1899, lasting well until 1902. The prime causes for this development are seen in the repeated tax raises as well as the rigid monetary policy of the Bank of Japan, the result of state finances and the introduction of the gold standard, both of which were indirect results of the 'postwar management.'[115]

Given the above situation, it is understandable that in economic circles after 1897, the magic words were 'import of foreign capital' (*gaishi yu'nyū*),[116] and many an entrepreneur was impatiently expecting the era of 'mixed residence,' when foreign shareholdership would facilitate the import. In May 1898, a 'Society for the Introduction of Foreign Capital' (Gaishi yu'nyū no kiseikai) formed itself in Tokyo;[117] in June a high-ranking delegation, including among others Prime Minister Itō and Finance Minister Inoue, met with foreign financiers in Yokohama;[118] in the same month it was reported that Mitsui and Mitsubishi negotiated with Rothschild financiers about the 'import' of foreign capital.[119] Under these straightened circumstances, it was only to be expected that protest against the government's postwar management came not only from the opposition, but also from within economic circles, whose representatives from time to time called for armament retrenchment.[120]

However, probably the most important economic consequence within the scope of this study was the fact that Japanese economic expansion into the Chinese market remained far below existing opportunities. These had been greatly enlarged by the commercial chapter of the Shimonoseki Treaty of 1895. However, due to the notorious undercapitalization of the Japanese economy, the private sector could not live up to the opportunities, and almost all of Japan's economic ventures in China during the postwar management era (and even after) were heavily backed by government financial and organizational assistance, based on the so-called 'continental strategy' of the government.[121] This probably accounts for the fact that, although China loomed large in the economic imagination of the times, the economic exploits of China remained a minor and not-often-heard argument in the actual discourse on Sino–Japanese politics. Thus we can observe a certain fascination with the vastness of China, both in territory and in population, and an envious glance towards its richness of resources, the combination of which let China appear a promise and a threat: it made China the 'treasure house of the world' (*sekai no hōko*), which seemed to lure with limitless profits[122] (variations of such hopes existed in other countries as well[123]). On the other hand, China could also become the 'world's factory' (*sekai no seizōjo*) which, with limitless resources and cheap labour, could swamp the world market.[124] Moreover, especially after 1897, we do find the prophylactic assurance that Japan had no territorial, but great economic, interests in China.

However, despite these assurances, discourse on Sino–Japanese relations seldom dwelt longer than necessary on the specific details of how to realize these interests, but very quickly moved on to questions of a more strategic or ideological nature. The metropolitan newspaper *Chūō shinbun*, for example, which more than others supported Japanese business in China, complained that because of this tendency, economic relations with China even three years after Shimonoseki had not improved greatly:

> Our well-informed betters have the bad habit that they like idle talk, but do not strive to make it real, that they delight in splendid words and big phrases, but in coming up with tangible profits and gains, they are inconsequential. This is the misfortune of our country. [...]
>
> Demands that we must expand our national interests or that we must raise the national prestige, especially the gentleman in the political world put forth in speech and writing with gallant bravery. With gusto they attack the government and, at their own permission, think themselves patriotic and concerned men of high aspirations [*shishi*]. However, the fact that the private business abroad [*taigai mingyō*], which must be the fundament of expanding the national interests and raising the country's prestige, consists in starting businesses overseas and in appropriating railways, mines, and other profits, of this these people seem to be totally ignorant.[125]

Of course, other factors played into this relative reticence on economic matters as well. For one, it was not in the spirit of the times to dwell on economic arguments in general. In international politics, power was the paradigm of the age, and economic arguments played only a secondary role (at best) when contrasted with the overriding importance of strategic arguments.[126] Moreover, strategic and ideological arguments tended to mobilize the interest of people rather more than economic aspects. However, the fact that the private economy simply did not have the *means* to expand into China certainly did not make it a fashionable topic either.

Domestic politics during the interwar period

The resolution of the Meiji oligarchs to enter the 'real race of civilization' and meet the standards of the Western powers (and their military capacities) through an ambitious program of armament expansion and administrational reform was not accompanied by a similar determination to reform the political system. Nonetheless, the financial consequences of the program forced the oligarchy into closer cooperation with the Diet, which opened new political vistas for the parties, but also initiated a phase of transition and tumult in domestic politics with many changing cabinets, party splits and mergers, and ups and downs of politicians and partisans. It is not within the scope of this study to follow the wounded way of Japanese domestic politics in the years 1895–1904 in all its vicissitudes.[127] However, one aspect which deserves our attention is the most intimate relationship between foreign and domestic matters during the postwar management years. Meiji political discourse on foreign matters is only half understood without its dimension of domestic politics, and *vice versa*.

The extent to which foreign policy was a ground for political compromise and a means for political attack became apparent immediately after the Tripartite Intervention. Soon after the Sino–Japanese War, the Second Itō Cabinet (August 1892–September 1896) and the Jiyūtō made a secret agreement which secured the latter's informal participation in cabinet decisions.[128] In return, the Jiyūtō publicly declared in July 1895 (the same month the cabinet made the decision for its naval expansion program) that it would stop criticizing the government for its responsibility in the Tripartite Intervention. It argued that the parties with their incessant demands for tax relief and their protest against armament expansion before the war had a joint responsibility in the affair. The nation should now focus on the immediate domestic tasks ahead (*naichi yūsen-ron*) and make a determined effort at armament expansion, if necessary financed by a rise in taxes.[129] At the same time, members of the Shinpotō (among them Ozaki Yukio and Shiga Shigetaka) started a vicious attack on the government, with the government's responsibility in the Intervention (the *sekinin-ron*) as the main weapon.[130] The government tried to suppress the attacks (and even had Ozaki sentenced to prison for some months), but to no avail. The attacks found wide support throughout the country (and especially in the Shinpotō-dominated regions of the *ura Nihon* such as Niigata or the Tōhoku). The Korean debacle added to the pressure. In February 1896, Itō only barely deflected a motion for impeachment by the Kokumin kyōkai.[131] However, in September 1896 Itō stepped down and made way for the Second Matsukata Cabinet, which lasted until January 1898.

Domestic instability reached its peak in 1898, which witnessed a total of four succeeding cabinets (Matsukata, Itō, Ōkuma, Yamagata). The fall of the first two Itō cabinets was invariably linked to the issue of the second round of tax rises. However, in the case of the Third Itō cabinet (January–June 1898), this was combined with immense pressure in matters of foreign policy. In April 1898, prominent Shinpotō members (among them Ozaki Yukio, again), formed a Taigai dōshi-kai, a 'society of like-minded fellows in foreign affairs' which attacked the government for its lenient position in the Far Eastern Crisis (discussed in more detail in Chapter 3). When the Shinpotō failed with its motion of non-confidence on this point, it cooperated with the Jiyūtō and brought the Itō Cabinet down in tax matters. The cooperation led to a merger of the two parties in June 1898. Soon after, the leaders of the new Kenseitō, Ōkuma Shigenobu and Itagaki Taisuke (1837–1919), were entrusted to build the first 'party cabinet' in history (June–November 1898). Not surprisingly, most of the important activists of the Taigai dōshi-kai-days received minister portfolios or high-ranking positions in the government. However, the foreign policy of the new cabinet did not differ significantly from the old one, although the briefness of the cabinet makes it difficult to tell. The Ōkuma cabinet lasted for a little more than four months. Internal jealousies and fighting, as well as lack of support by the emperor, the oligarchs and the administration, soon wore the cabinet down. The ministers resigned, and the Kenseitō split again. The new cabinet was headed by Yamagata and lasted somewhat longer (November 1898–October 1900). Its composition already showed a strong leaning towards the military, as half of its members came from the army or the navy. Thus Kuga Katsunan famously dubbed the cabinet the 'saber cabinet' (*sâberu naikaku*).[132] Itō led a cabinet one more time (October 1900–June 1901), but then his (and Yamagata's) active role in government was over and younger (less prudent) leaders came into power. Katsura Tarō (1847–1913) as prime minister and Komura Jutarō (1855–1911) as foreign minister led Japan into and out of the Russo–Japanese War.

The 'Chinese' dullness of the people

The above should suffice to give a rough picture of the main features of the *sengo keiei* period. Considering this, one might momentarily think that public life, in a way, had retrogressed into its prewar routine, with its domestic confusion, its endless squabbles over political affairs and its relatively constricted radius of action in international affairs.

Yet not only were the postwar problems different in scope, the Japanese public by now had also learned to think of Japan as an empire, with all its seeming possibilities. And this is probably how the *sengo keiei* period is best characterized: as a transitory phase in which the reality did not live up to these apparent opportunities, internationally and domestically. Although Japan had acquired global status, necessities of strategy and prudence required it to withdraw; although economic opportunities beckoned abroad, they could not be realized; and although domestic politics seemed to indicate reform and the end of *hanbatsu* regime, party politics proved no alternative either. Thus, despite the apparent 'ease,' Japan's success in the war and all it entailed was taking its toll on the 'national strength' (*kokuryoku*) and did not immediately pay off in a more glorious way of national life, but was more burdensome than the public might have expected.[133]

Under these circumstances, it is not surprising that the *sengo keiei* period was an era pervaded by a deep sense of melancholy and, at the same time, restlessness. 'Weariness,' 'exhaustion,' 'disintegration' and 'decay' were frequent words in public discourse, which combined with a rising critique of social reality and civilization in general.[134] The late Meiji period may have been a 'time of settlement,' as Carol Gluck calls it,[135] but for many Meji contemporaries it was also a time of unbearable stagnation.

A typical diagnosis of this state can be seen in an editorial which the young Kōtoku Shūsui (1871–1911) wrote in 1897 on 'The paralysis of the nation.'[136] Shūsui found his fellow-citizens to have sunk into a strange state of exhaustion. Two years after the war, in which the Japanese so gloriously had manifested their pluck and patriotism, the people stood by passively while the political elite (*hanbatsu* and party politicians alike) corrupted the nation, so that 'a civilized country suddenly is about to turn into a barbaric region.'

> In general, the corruption of our political world, the economic instability, and the moral decay is becoming more and more extreme with each day. All of these factors are pushing the state towards a dangerous course. And yet, our people seem to be cool and almost without sensation. Our people have reached a state of paralysis. Rome of old has fallen like this, and China today will fall like this. [...]
>
> Now, if people take a stimulant [*kōfun-zai*] in too great a dose, the mood becomes excited at once and slightly disoriented, after a while there is confusion, faintness, and a loss of sensations. If the person finally awakes from this state, it is as if a mental absence or a spell had gone. In our case, the people have become too excited in the Sino–Japanese War and afterwards suddenly fell into a state of utter exhaustion and, sleeping the sleep of the utterly exhausted, do not know what is going on. Meanwhile, thieves plunder your coffers and fiends are scheming to take your life, but you are oblivious in your paralysis and idly dream of rising stocks.[137]

The observation that the people had lost their former 'alacrity' was a common notion. Kōtoku's article was merely concerned with the 'inner dangers' (*hanbatsu* politics and party corruption), but advocates of armament expansion used the same arguments with regard to Japan's 'external dangers,' especially in the discussion about armament retrenchment in November 1897. The causes for the 'dulling' of the senses were seen either in the excessive joy about the victory (Fukuzawa[138]), in the long, debilitating peace of two years (*Kokumin shinbun*[139]), or – similar to Kōtoku – as a consequence of the sudden expansion of the empire, which brings exhaustion and the danger of disintegration to nations (*Taiyō*[140]).

However, whatever the different explanations were, all commentators were equally at a loss when it came to advising a feasible method of how to rid the 'patient' of his dullness. Thus it is not surprising that many people saw no other way than craving for more 'stimulus' (*shigeki*, another watchword of the time) from the same place as it had come from before – foreign politics. The first round of this kind of stimulus after the Sino–Japanese War came with the shock of Germany's occupation of Jiaozhou in late 1897 and the beginning of the Far Eastern Crisis.

3   The Far Eastern Crisis of 1897–98

While Japan was turning inward and became absorbed in the vicissitudes of the postwar management, the Western powers continued their expansion into China and Korea. Until the end of 1897, Russia and France pursued an active policy of 'peaceful penetration' in China, aimed at securing railway and mining privileges in the areas they had chosen as their respective 'spheres of influence,' while Britain and Germany, although with the greatest commercial interests in China, played a merely secondary, defensive part.[1] However, all this changed with the Far Eastern Crisis of 1897–98 when, in a chain reaction set off by Germany's occupation of Jiaozhou Bay, the Western powers one by one secured territorial leases on the Chinese coast.[2]

In the history of Western imperial politics towards China, the Far Eastern Crisis 1897–98 was an important landmark, as it signalled a decided shift from a more restrained policy of negotiating concessions on the basis of international law to a policy of establishing *faits accomplis* by force first, and letting diplomacy and law follow after.[3] The new shift was not uncontroversial, and the often erratic and, in the case of Britain, rather opportunistic behaviour of the actors involved shows considerable insecurity in the face of the new situation.

For the Japanese government, the new development had the reverse effect of acting as a catalyst for a restrained East Asian policy that sought to keep Japan out of the continental embroglio as best as possible, while pursuing its interests there by less formal and more unobtrusive ways. This also meant not siding with any of the Western powers, but 'standing alone and walking apart.' With the single exception of the Boxer expedition, Japan's policy of neutrality kept in place until 1902, when it was discarded for an Anglo–Japanese alliance against Russia. On the other hand, the Far Eastern Crisis marked the beginning of a rapprochement between China and Japan which the Japanese side, however, considering its official policy and the neuroticism of the Western powers, consciously sought to keep on a merely informal level.

For the Japanese public, the Far Eastern Crisis led to a heated discussion about China's future and Japan's responsibility to ensure it, which, despite some participants' bitter protest to the contrary, generally followed the government's China policy. Previous scholarship has described the discussion rather statically as juxtaposition between the realist argument of a partition of China (*Shina bunkatsu-ron*) and the idealist advocacy of protecting China's integrity (*Shina hozen-ron*) or even 'Asian solidarity' against the Western powers (*Ajia rentai-ron*).[4] However, a discussion of Konoe Atsumaro's and Takayama Chogyū's positions at the time will show that 'Asian solidarity,' especially on the ground of 'same race, same culture,' was a highly contentious idea in the public, but well employed in public diplomacy towards China.[5] Moreover, a discussion of Fukuzawa Yukichi and Kuga Katsunan will demonstrate that the static juxtaposition misses the really significant part of the discussion, which was a dynamic convergence of seemingly antagonistic positions in the idea of protecting China, by which one adopted elements of the other and both eventually became undistinguishable except for different modes of expression. The convergence of positions may have been due to the specific circumstances of Japan in international politics, which led to a certain homogenization of world views, more than their proponents would probably have liked to acknowledge. Yet the blending of realist and idealist positions could also be seen as a phenomenon not restricted to Japan, but a general tendency of imperialist thought at the time.

The Far Eastern Crisis

The Far Eastern Crisis began with the forceful arrival of Germany in the Far East. Germany needed a naval and coaling station on the Chinese coast in order to be independent from its rival in the Chinese trade, Britain, and as a prerequisite for its new aspirations in *Weltpolitik*.[6] Although the Chinese court protested that the ensuing race among the other powers for similar privileges would eventually threaten China's integrity, the Kaiser persisted in his plans. In the summer of 1897, the decision fell on the Bay of Jiaozhou in Shandong province. On 1 November 1897, two German catholic missionaries were killed in the province of Shandong. This gave the German government the pretext to occupy the bay. On 14 November 1897, Admiral von Diedrichs led the East Asian Cruiser Squadron into the bay and took possession of the Qingdao Fort. On 6 March 1898, Germany obtained Jiaozhou as a lease from China for a period of 99 years.

The German action provoked a chain reaction among the other Western powers and led to a complete reversal of Russia's and Britain's China policy. Until then, Russia favored in China, as well as in Korea, a policy of peaceful penetration that would leave its territorial integrity untouched and that eventually promised influence undivided.[7] However, Germany's action, and China's refusal of Russian access to the Yellow Sea, finally led the Russian government (albeit with much inner protest) to discard this policy. On 15 December 1897, Russian warships anchored in Port Arthur and Dalian Bay (Russia, too, in March 1898 signed a lease of Port Arthur and Dalian for a period of 25 years). This, in turn, raised the opposition of Britain, which traditionally championed China's integrity as it served Britain's commercial interests in the region best (80 per cent of the foreign trade in China was British). There were reasons to fear that Russian ports would not remain free and open to other nations, and that Russian presence in Port Arthur would eventually close off the whole north of China as an exclusive Russian sphere. The crisis reached its peak when Britain, in January 1898, with the consent of the Chinese government, sent warships into Port Arthur to anchor side by side with the Russian ships. At the same time, a member of the British government publicly declared that Britain would, even at the cost of war, seek to guarantee that Chinese territory remained open to commercial penetration, and 'that the door should not be shut against' Britain.[8] Both events incited a war fever in the British press, whose most strident attacks, however, were directed against Germany, so much so that when the crisis died down, the Queen advised the newspapers to be more moderate.[9]

By the end of March 1898, the Crisis de-escalated. On 25 March 1898 the British government decided that China's integrity was not worth the war, and that the best solution would be to secure a lease of Weihaiwei, opposite of Port Arthur, as a counterweight. Britain's 'surrender' might be explained in the fact that Britain had no allies in the Far East (Japan having turned down the suggestion), and was therefore in a militarily weak position against Russia. Moreover, since 1895 most Western China experts predicted the division of China, which might have weakened the resolution to uphold an eventually untenable position.[10] The British government, too, discarded its integrity policy and on the Queen's birthday, 24 May 1898, a British squadron stepped ashore at Weihaiwei.[11] France leased the bay of Guangzhou on 10 April 1898 and took possession of it on 22 April 1898. The US Naval Department in February 1898 considered establishing a naval base in China as well, but nothing came of it.[12]

The response of the Japanese government

The decision for Japan's 'neutrality' in the Far Eastern Crisis fell in the first days of the Itō Cabinet, in January 1898. Until then, the domestic turmoil that accompanied the demise of the Matsukata Cabinet had made a decision impossible. However, on 10 January 1898 the emperor summoned the six leading *genrō* – Itō Hirobumi, Yamagata Aritomo, Kuroda Kiyotaka, Saigō Tsugumichi, Ōyama Iwao and Inoue Kaoru – into his presence to discuss Japan's future East Asia policy.[13] At the conference, Itō presented a memorial that analyzed Japan's difficult position in the crisis. Following the traditional scheme of *gaikan naiyū* ('dangers without and troubles at home'), Itō started out with a most dramatic description of the Far Eastern situation:

> I think that the general situation of East Asia, where greedy powers are pushing ahead, is on the brink of chaos. Today, it is no longer merely the issue of Korea's independence, but now, China's independence, too, is in

grave danger. The powers may begin to divide China at any moment
now. Under these circumstances, the paramount and imperative goal our
country must pursue is this: to place our own country in the position of
unbridled independence [*dokuritsu fuki*], so that we cannot be touched
by anyone.[14]

With urgent words, Itō argued for a policy of non-involvement and warned
against hastily choosing alliance partners. In the second half of his memorial, Itō proceeded to outline the domestic troubles that had beset the country
lately: the disintegration of the political sphere due to constant feuding
between the factions had reached its limits; parties ignored the welfare of the
state in the pursuit of their petty interests. The bureaucracy and the people
were confused by the constant change of cabinets and had lost direction. The
economy, bound to experience a tremendous boost in the postwar years,
lacked capital and saw no other way than to import foreign capital in order
to survive. Society on the whole was torn by conflict and mutual envy, so
that the state eventually lacked all the essentials for cohesion and unity.

Itō's plea to neutrality was thus motivated by two factors: the explosive-
ness of the international situation right in front of Japan's doorstep, and the
political and social instability at home. Conspicuously absent from the discussion were the burdens of the 'postwar program' which, as we have seen,
contributed much to the instability – but then the program as such was a
given and not subject to political calculation. Moreover, it is worth men-
tioning that, in Itō's analysis of the situation, we do not find any concerns on
the relative morality or legitimacy of the Western powers' actions in China
and how Japan should react to *that*, nor, for that matter, any further thought
wasted on China's fate, especially what Japan should do about it. This is less
noteworthy in itself, as one could hardly expect an inveterate power-politician
such as Itō to do so, but stands in stark contrast to the often emotional,
moralistic and – with regard to China – increasingly 'altruistic' discussion in
the Japanese public and among oppositional politicians at the same time.

The imperial conference unfailingly adopted Itō's recommendation of neutrality and immediately put it into practice. As a consequence, Japan did not
reciprocate when Britain suggested an Anglo–Japanese alliance against Russia
in March 1898.[15] This, in return, paid off in better relations with Russia and
resulted in a preliminary agreement over Korea that acknowledged the equal
strategic position of both countries and Japan's overriding commercial interests
in Korea.[16] With respect to Chinese territories, Japan remained seemingly
passive, too. The only positive action that Japan took was to secure the
relatively inoffensive promise of the non-alienation of the province Fujian,
across Taiwan, on 22 April 1898. This echoed a similar agreement between
Britain and China with regard to the Yangtze basin (where British commercial
interests were concentrated) in January 1898. However, in contrast to Britain,
the non-alienation did not go hand-in-hand with a privileged position in
Fujian (such as railway or mining concessions).[17]

One of the less immediately discernible, but all the more important, consequences of the Far Eastern Crisis was the gradual rapprochement between China and Japan. The Far Eastern Crisis brought a reversal of the pro-Russian attitude among Chinese leaders, which in turn led to a cautiously cooperative stance toward Japan. Japanese leaders were quick to discern this change of attitude, or the possibility of it, and encouraged it in their own interests.[18] Thus, soon after the beginning of the Far Eastern crisis, a flurry of activities ensued, the initiative coming both from the Japanese military, which even prior to the Far Eastern Crisis had looked for opportunities to approach China, and from the foreign ministry. In December 1897 General Kawakami Sōroku (1848–99) sent a group of officers and one journalist to China in order to visit high-ranking Chinese officials such as Zhang Zhidong and Liu Kunyi (1830–1902), both governor-generals in regions of strategic and economic importance to Japan, and to sound out the possibility of a closer cooperation with China.[19] Kawakami, who was soon to become Chief of the General Staff, thus started a tradition of Japanese military training and advice in China. The Japanese minister in Beijing, Yano Fumio (1850–1931), in April and May 1898 invited large numbers of Chinese students to Japan on the Japanese government's expenses and initiated a phase of Japanese teachers going to China and Chinese students coming to Japan in large numbers.[20] On the economic level, the government, too, tried to implement its 'continental strategy' of state-supported expansion acting *in lieu* of private entrepreneurs who lacked the capital (in 1902 foreign minister Komura Jutarō affirmed this policy as the common policy for both China and Korea). Between 1898 and 1899, the Japanese government, for example, tried to monopolize the management of iron ore mining in Hubei province (Hanyang and Dayeshan) to feed its newly built Yawata Steelworks (but lost out in the competition with other Western powers).[21] As we shall see, Itō Hirobumi himself in July 1898 went on a tour through Korea and China, especially to visit the newly opened ports in China and observe the possibilities of Japan's economic expansion in China.

The flurry of activities in the wake of the Far Eastern crisis finally developed into what Douglas R. Reynolds has called the 'golden decade' of Sino–Japanese cooperation, which extended to almost all fields of public life and state governance.[22] Whatever the quality of the decade, it should be cautioned that this cooperation remained purely pragmatic and never assumed the quality of an official 'friendship.' With respect to Western suspicions, Japanese leaders were scrupulous in avoiding any impression that Japan had a special relationship with China that was closer than its relationship with any Western country. Thus, if Kawakami's envoys may have invoked 'same culture, same race' (*dōbun dōshu*) when trying to ingratiate themselves with Zhang Zhidong, among Japanese leaders we seldom hear such words spoken in public.[23] On the contrary, numerous instances are known when Japanese politicians of all factions clearly decided or spoke against a closer formal relationship with China. When the reform-minded Guangxu emperor (1871–1908) in September

1898 proposed to send a special plenipotentiary to Tokyo, Ōkuma Shigenobu's minister in Beijing, Hayashi Gonsuke, replied very cautiously that this would need time and consultation with Britain and Russia first.[24] And again, in May 1899, Yamagata Aritomo commented on the arrival of a special envoy from Beijing that, if the intention was an alliance, Japan should politely reject it, arguing as follows:

> On the present occasion, we should treat the envoy so as not to hurt the feelings of China and maintain the close relationship of our countries. If there is an opportunity to expand our line of interest [*waga rieki-sen*] we should always pay attention not to lose it. However, if our country and China entered a relationship which would exceed the degree of closeness and arouse the suspicion among the Western powers of a Sino–Japanese alliance against Europe, this would not only eventually result in a battle of races [*jinshu no arasoi*], but it is difficult to tell if this would not also have consequences which would prove detrimental to our interests in the present Hague Peace Conference [1899]. Moreover, even if our financial, political, and military power would allow it, I believe that to cooperate with China for the independence of East Asia is a poor strategy [*sessaku*]. China, as I have said before, like the Jewish race will continue as a race, but it will not long maintain its state as a whole. This is already the fixed opinion of the experts. Even if it can maintain its state, it will not be able to maintain it with the present territory. It will save only a small fraction, and the rest will be divided among the powers. In East Asia, the only country which will be able to maintain its independence is our empire.[25]

This 'arm's length'-policy remained in place as long as the Qing dynasty lasted, and the Japanese government, as we shall see presently, was intent to broadcast the fact to the Western powers, lest any doubts should arise that Japan firmly adhered to the (Western) standard of civilization.

Reactions of the Japanese public to the Far Eastern Crisis

First responses

The new crisis forcefully reminded the Japanese public of Japan's internationalized environment after the Sino–Japanese War and roused bad memories of the Tripartite Intervention. The first reactions also reveal an acute sense of vulnerability, which people felt despite, or because of, the fact that Japan now was an extended empire.

News of the occupation of Jiaozhou reached the Japanese public around 20 November 1897, via Reuters' cables.[26] Commentators apparently needed some time to digest the momentous news, as substantial commentaries started to appear only a week later. By then, however, the *fama* had made its way from Shanghai to Japan that the German occupation was only the beginning of a second Tripartite Intervention, which would cost Japan its precious colony Taiwan. Anxiety was especially fired by a dispatch reported by the *Jiji shinpō* on 3 December 1897 according to which, France, Russia and Germany had conspired to seize territory in East Asia.[27] Kuga Katsunan recorded and ridiculed the hysterical reactions of the people:

> Suddenly, a telegram arrives from Shanghai which says that Russia has interests in Korea and North-China, and France in Taiwan and Fuzhou. This has now practically turned into the rumour that Europe, led by two or three powers, will come upon Japan, China, and Korea. The talk about the division of China has made a full turn and has now become a discussion of the division of the whole Far East. The hopes that Japan sooner or later would enter the rows of those who would do the dividing, has undergone a complete transformation, and it is now being said that Japan soon will be reckoned, like China, among those being divided.[28]

Considering the triumphant sense of invincibility which the Japanese public boasted during the Sino–Japanese War, this reaction, indeed, was a reversal of extremes, and grossly exaggerated in the light of the facts. On the one hand, the hysteria seems to indicate that Japanese observers, despite the recent triumph, still felt deeply insecure *vis-à-vis* the Western powers. At the same time, and not necessarily in contradiction to this, one could interpret the hysteria also as the regular reaction to a new threat of a newly risen imperial power with extended frontiers. After all, now that Taiwan had become part of the empire, the latter had become all the more vulnerable, and might be forced to expand even further in order to protect what it already had. Fukuzawa Yukichi's first reaction pointed in this direction:

> Although it is said that the fire is on the other side of the shore, that shore is separated from us only by a small strip of water. That means, now that Taiwan has become already our territory, we must defend it like our mother country and must not lose one inch of our land. Since olden times, our country has been cherished as 'golden jar, without a blemish.'[29] However, in our modern times to keep this greatly expanded 'golden jar' without a blemish, it may not do just to defend it. Depending on the case, we may be forced to attack, as well. Because it is a rule that if you want to protect a hundred per cent, you will have to have a hundred-and-thirty or hundred-and-fifty per cent. Thus, we must be prepared that, if we want to protect Taiwan, we might have to move forward and protect territory outside of the island.[30]

Thus, in a sense, the somewhat unbalanced first reactions to the Crisis could be also seen as a proof that the Japanese public by then had already settled into the imperialist mode, along with its somewhat neurotic siege mentality.[31]

Further reactions in the acute stage of the Crisis (until the end of March 1898) can be divided into two basic patterns, and generally along political fault lines. Pro-government organs such as the *Tōkyō nichinichi shinbun* and the *Chūō shinbun* tended to support the official policy of neutrality by systematically playing down the Crisis and its effects, refraining from any comments as to the legitimacy of actions, and – especially – from demonstrating any particular sympathy towards China. To give a few examples: when Russian warships entered Port Arthur and Dalian in December 1897, the *Tōkyō nichinichi* studiously tried to appear untroubled and argued that this might be merely for wintering the Russian fleet, since Jiaozhou Bay was now occupied by the Germans.[32] In February 1898, when the majority opinion in a heated debate was in favor of extending the deadline for China to pay the last installment of the war reparations (and thus keep Weihaiwei as security occupied), the *Nichinichi* was against it, despite its own amazement two weeks earlier at China's scandalous indebtedness.[33] Now it argued that the question of payments affected more countries than just China and Japan (in fact, Britain and Russia at the time were arguing about who would become China's next creditor), and therefore the Shimonoseki Treaty could not be amended at one's own whim.[34] Finally, when the opposition in April 1898 attacked the government for its 'weak policy' against Russia and Germany, and demanded that Japan stay in Weihaiwei despite full payment of the indemnity, the *Chūō shinbun* made a counterattack with the argument already discussed above, that the people should rather concentrate on the commercial exploits of the privileges Japan already possessed in China.[35]

The other pattern of reaction was moral indignation at the 'barbaric' way in which Germany and Russia 'robbed' and 'extorted' land from China. Even Fukuzawa was impressed by the brashness of Germany's actions: 'To seize land without any preliminary negotiations is like extortion, posting oneself with a bare knife at the head of the debtor's bed. It is a most outrageous and violent behaviour, which on the grounds of international etiquette is absolutely not permissible.'[36]

Reminded of the Tripartite Intervention, the German emperor's racist antics again became the object of indignant ridicule. On the occasion of the Far Eastern Crisis, the *Tōkyō nichinichi* printed another drawing taken from the Knackfuss painting,[37] soon to be followed by satirical variations on the theme taken from the German satirical magazines *Ulk* and *Kladderadatsch* (for example, 'Ye nations of Europe, grab the most holy territories in China!').[38] Kuga Katsunan decried the German emperor's pompous gesture when sending off his royal brother as a 'stage act', which would do well in a Kabuki-drama set in the Sengoku era but did not befit the monarch of a modern nation.[39] As was to be expected, the indignation was especially strong among those who traditionally championed the virtue of 'chivalry' in foreign affairs – the opposition and especially the strong foreign policy advocates close to the Shinpotō.

Intermezzo: German-Japanese perspectives

Although oppositional observers vehemently attacked Germany and Russia for their wrongful deeds, protests were usually not expected to be heard in those countries. However, late Meiji Japan was not always on the receiving end of information, and, as we shall see more frequently in these chapters, its rising status in the world increasingly led to the intentional or accidental projection of Japanese opinions to the outside. A rather curious example of this is the recorded dialogue that took place in Heidelberg in the winter of 1897–98 between a Japanese and a German law professor about the legitimacy of German's actions and imperialist politics in general.

At the time of the Far Eastern Crisis, the young law professor Nakamura Shingo (1870–1939), protégé of Konoe Atsumaro and later a famous advocate of war with Russia, was on his grand tour through Europe, studying law in Heidelberg.[40] There he attended the lecture on international law by Hermann Strauch.[41] During one of the accompanying tutorial classes (which only he and another German student attended), Nakamura presented an essay on the 'Jiaozhou question.'[42] The specific subject of Nakamura's presentation was the question whether Germany's occupation and lease of Jiaozhou was legitimate according to international law, especially whether the occupation was a form of legitimate 'reprisals' (*Repressalien*) for the murder of the two German priests. However, the technical question, which Nakamura answered in the negative, made only the smallest part of the essay, of which the bigger part was devoted to a harsh critique of the ruthless expansion policies of the Western powers in general, and of Germany in particular, much to the displeasure of Strauch. Thus Nakamura lambasted the world-conquering ambitions of the powers:

> And it will be always incomprehensible why the states today, especially the European states, despite the great progress in international law, still try to emulate Napoleon, Alexander, and Charles the Great. As long as such an idea is prevalent, a complete development and realization of international law will remain impossible.[43]

On hearing this, Strauch protested vehemently: 'What nonsense is that?! Firstly, not one of the European states today plans to conquer the world. This applies to Germany, as well. It does not plan to conquer the world, on the contrary, Germany is in constant fear of being attacked by another country. If you would think seriously about the matter, you would come to find that you are quite mistaken.'[44] However, Nakamura proceeded to attack Germany and Russia for doing the same thing that they had considered 'illegal' three years ago, in the Tripartite Intervention, and advocated an Anglo–Japanese alliance for the protection of China.

The discussion that ensued was rather controversial, as could be imagined. Strauch argued that law was not identical with morals and, in his opinion, the case of Jiaozhou constituted a case of legitimate reprisals. Moreover, the territory was eventually gained on a contractual basis. Japan, on the other hand, had acted much more immorally towards China in the Sino–Japanese War. Had Japan not attacked China to sack Korea, and to take Liaodong and Taiwan, as well? To this, Nakamura replied that Japan only wanted to help Korea's independence and that the beginning of the Sino–Japanese War was China's fault. This, however, Strauch rejected as talk for 'amateurs.'[45]

Thus Nakamura's protest against Germany's actions met equally harsh censure of Japan's policy in East Asia. It is conspicuous that both sides, while criticizing each other, take recourse to much the same arguments and accusations. Eventually, Nakamura's and Strauch's differences seem more the product of political contingency rather than of conflicting *Weltanschauungen*. Were it not for the fact that both countries had conflicting interests in East Asia, their two rather typical representatives would probably find each other's political outlook quite congenial. Thus, although a comparison of public discourses lies beyond the scope of this study, one could venture the hypothesis that the globalization of power politics in the late nineteenth century also led to a certain convergence of political mentalities. The Japanese domestic protest, too, would then constitute but an instance of a series of similar agitations among the public of imperialist powers around the globe.

Later reactions

After the Far Eastern Crisis de-escalated by the end of March 1898, and after Britain had secured its lease of Weihaiwei, the public debate changed significantly: Firstly, oppositional commentators shifted their attention away from the wrongdoings of the powers back to those of the Japanese government, attacking it for abetting the East Asian situation. This shift was clearly motivated by domestic politics. A typical, and arguably the most notorious, example was the founding of the 'Society of like-minded fellows in foreign matters' (Taigai dōshi-kai) in April 1898. This society, founded by strong foreign policy advocates close to the Shinpotō, demanded that the government must 'protest' (*kōgi*) against the occupation of Russia and Germany, or otherwise stay in Weihaiwei or step down altogether.[46] They issued manifestos and sent delegations to the prime minister, thus setting the pattern for the anti-Russian agitation only a few years later (and it is no coincidence that several leading members of the 'Society' played a leading role in the anti-Russian movement as well).[47]

Most oppositional newspapers supported the campaign with often devious commentaries of their own. Thus, when the Shinpotō newspaper *Hōchi shinbun* argued in April 1898 that Japan should seek in Weihaiwei a compensation for the lease of Port Arthur to Russia (blissfully disregarding the fact that Britain had just obtained a lease), and included in the article a draft of the right kind of dispatch to China, the *Japan Weekly Mail* commented on this draft with ironic admiration:

[...] we are bound to say that the language of the document belongs to an exalted rank of diplomatic speciousness. [...] the gist of the whole thesis [of the dispatch] is that Japan, commiserating China's weakness, and appreciating the danger of disruption that threatens her, advises her to hand over some important points [including Weihaiwei] to be guarded by her neighbour, so that the two Powers may act in concert to stem the eastward set of the tide of Occidental aggression.'[48]

According to the members of the Taigai dōshikai, the declared objective of the campaign was to 'shatter the delusions [*meimu*] of the people, who were just indifferent towards foreign politics, and to administer one big stimulus [*shigeki*] to the authorities.'[49] However, the obviously quixotic nature of the demands shows that the 'stimulation' was motivated more by domestic politics rather than by concern for foreign politics. Consequently, although the movement soon faltered, the 'stimulation' was carried on in the Diet by the Shinpotō, which relentlessly attacked the government for its foreign policy and pushed as far as a motion of non-confidence. However, when the old cabinet finally fell and the same people who had so viciously attacked it came into power, their foreign policy did not differ considerably from the old one.

Apart from these more domestic concerns, the debate after the acute phase of the Crisis saw a decided shift towards advocating more and more Japan's responsibility to help China in the face of adversity, thus echoing with a certain time lag the overtures of Japanese military and diplomatic circles for informal Sino–Japanese cooperation. However, as the discussion of individual positions will presently show, the arguments in the public debate stressed more the aspect of forcible education and guidance of a protégé or dependent, rather than cooperation between equals.

The growing concern for China, genuine or not, was clearly motivated by the perceived increase in signs of China's deterioration in 1898, not only through foreign pressure, but also through domestic unrest. An illustration of the latter was the so-called 'Shashi outrage' in China, which put Japan to the test. On 9 May 1898, a mob of disgruntled Chinese in the newly opened port of Shashi in the province of Hubei attacked (among other locations) the British and Japanese consulates, and burned them down. The Japanese consul barely escaped on the seaway.[50] The moment the news reached Japan, it was obvious it constituted an even better pretext for intervention than the murder of the two German missionaries.[51] However, the Japanese government kept to its policy, and settled the affair by negotiation. The public, too, remained calm, and no one advocated following the 'heroic example' of Germany any more. The incident even caused a large part of the public to 'appreciate' China's difficulties and postulate Japan's duty of civilization to help China on its way to progress. Thus Ōkuma Shigenobu, in an interview with the Shinpotō-newspaper *Hōchi shinbun*, voiced the popular sentiment as follows:

But the heart of the nation would oppose anything of that kind [reprisals]. Japan never forgets that she is the pioneer of civilized progress in the East, and that it is her duty to set an example of moderation and justice in her dealings with foreign Powers. She ought to be able to appreciate China's difficulties.[52]

However, as we shall see presently, this appreciation of China's difficulties had certain limits and expressed itself in sometimes quite peculiar notions of assistance.

China policy: the positions of Konoe Atsumaro, Takayama Chogyū, Fukuzawa Yukichi and Kuga Katsunan

The following case studies explore the limits and the specific development of sympathies for China which began on the occasion of the Far Eastern Crisis. The example of Konoe Atsumaro shows that advocating too close a relationship with China, especially when founded on the notion of 'same race, same culture,' was highly contentious and rather to be avoided by the late Meiji public. However, such professions were well employed in public diplomacy towards China when addressing and wooing Chinese intellectuals and the public. As the case of Takayama Chogyū shows, in the complex mirroring of opinions that ensued, even Japanese observers occasionally became confused. Finally, the changing positions of Fukuzawa Yukichi and Kuga Katsunan demonstrate the high volatility of political discourse at the time, which left few points of creed untouched and often saw a *volte-face* within a couple of months due to considerations of political expediency. However, both individuals, who clearly saw each other as opponents, also indicate a remarkable convergence of positions in the idea of protecting China's integrity (*Shina hozen*). This process blurred the boundaries between realist and idealist worldviews even more – if they had ever been clearly defined. Consequently, the China policy that eventually became generally accepted was a mixture of both, justifying power politics as a means of realizing Japan's mission towards China.

Konoe Atsumaro

The forceful arrival of Germany and Russia in East Asian waters led some Japanese observers to believe that Japan and China must reconcile in order to ward off the new danger. Thus, the *Kokumin shinbun* in December 1897 argued for the possibility of a Sino–Japanese rapprochement:

In former times, Prussia and Austria-Hungary have waged war, but as a result of the war, is it not recorded that they have become much better friends? Could it be similar between Japan and China? Indeed, it is now the time that Japan expresses its goodwill towards China.

Nationas are much like individuals: it is not a rare instance that, for having once fought with each other, their relation becomes all the better after. Because, since they fight with each other, they also can understand each other's real intentions best.[53]

The improving Austro-Prussian relations after the war of 1866 became a popular analogy in 1898 when arguing for a Sino–Japanese rapprochement.[54]

A few commentators went even further, and advocated a fully fledged alliance with China, like Taoka Reiun in the *Yorozu chōhō*, who envisioned a 'Great alliance of East Asia' – an alliance between Japan, China and Korea against the 'white race.'[55]

However, the most radical proposal in this line, and certainly the one that received the widest attention, was an article by Konoe Atsumaro which the magazine *Taiyō* published in its New Year edition of 1898, entitled 'A same race-alliance and the necessity of studying the Chinese Question' ('*Dō-jinshu dōmei, tsuketari Shina mondai kenkyū no hitsuyō*').[56] Today this essay is generally viewed as a manifesto of Konoe's individual pan-Asianist convictions, and as a 'classical' document of Japanese Pan-Asianist feelings in general at the time.[57] However, this assessment is highly problematic, as we shall see presently.

The wide attention the text received was due partly to its provocative content, but probably even more to its exalted authorship.[58] Konoe Atsumaro was the scion of one of the most illustrious lineages of Japan, closest to the emperor, and for this reason received the active protection and support of the emperor. In fact the emperor deliberately groomed Konoe for prime ministership, which Konoe might have easily attained if death had not intervened prematurely. In 1898, Konoe was both president of the House of Peers (*Kizokuin*) and principal of the prestigious Peers' School (*Gakushūin*), despite his relatively young age of 34.

Politically, Konoe Atsuamaro kept aloof from the *hanbatsu*-oligarchs and party politicians alike. Konoe considered the oligarchs as *homines novi*, and party politicians he viewed even less favorably. Konoe followed the concept of an elitist model of non-partisan politics.[59] However, in political contents, Konoe was close to the strong foreign-policy advocates, whose figurehead Konoe eventually became in 1900. Konoe had strong 'Asianist' interests: he founded the Dōbun-kai (Common Culture Association) in June 1898, and in November 1898 became head of the Tōa dōbun-kai (East Asia Common Culture Association), a semi-governmental society for fostering Japanese interests on the continent.[60]

The text that Konoe dictated to the pen of *Taiyō* editor Toyabe Sentarō (Shuntei) at the beginning of December 1897[61] was but a short one, comprising only six short paragraphs. In the first four paragraphs, Konoe expounded the idea of an alliance with China and other Asian countries against the Western powers, developing the following apocalyptic vision:

As I see it, East Asia in the future inevitably will become the stage for a contest between the races [*jinshu kyōsō no butai*]. Even if momentary considerations of foreign policy should produce a different setting, this will be but of fleeting existence. The final destiny will be a contest between the yellow and the white race [*kōhaku ryō-jinshu no kyōsō*], and in this contest the Chinese people and the Japanese people will be placed in the same position, being both considered as the sworn enemy of the white race [*hakujinshu no kyūteki*]. Those who are considering a long-term strategy do well to consider these facts.[62]

The last two paragraphs contained a much more sober and pragmatic exposition of the necessity to gather intelligence and conduct public diplomacy in China. This was common sense, and was soon implemented by the founding of the above 'Asianist' societies.[63]

However, with the suggestion of a 'racial competition' and the proposal of a racial pan-Asianist alliance, Konoe broke with a received notion and hit on a taboo subject: for one, he contradicted the stout belief of Meiji citizens in the universal standard of civilization and the 'race of civilization' (see Chapter 1); and secondly, his pan-Asianist fantasies could not fail to rouse fears in the West of a 'yellow peril.' And in fact, Konoe's vision could be seen (and was seen at the time) as a mere variation on the 'yellow peril' theme.

Curiously enough, the subject of a pan-Asianist alliance does not seem to have come to Konoe naturally. His private secretary, Ōuchi Chōzō (1874–1944), remembered that in August 1897, having returned from his studies at Columbia University in New York, he had a job interview with Konoe in which he tried to impress Konoe with the new ideas he had brought back from his studies, and thus predicted a 'race antagonism' (*rêsu antagonizumu*) in the Pacific.[64] Ōuchi even had written an essay on the subject, which he wanted to publish. However, to his surprise, Konoe warned that such a thing must not be published and insisted on the common sense, that there was only a 'competition of civilization,' arguing:

> You are mistaken if you think it is a racial competition. There is no such thing as a racial competition. But there does exist a competition of culture [*bunka no kyōsō*[65]]. Those who are superior in culture are not being subjugated by those who are inferior in culture. You think that the Westerners are pressuring the yellow race in a race competition, but that is because we lack in culture. Because of the lack of culture, such a competition arises. Therefore, if you say that, in order to beat them culturally, we must exert ourselves much more, that makes a lot of sense. But to claim out of the blue that this is a racial competition or a *race antagonism*, is not something a sensible person should do.[66]

Why Konoe should change his mind within four months and publish the idea of race antagonism under his own good name in January 1898, remains somewhat mysterious. However, the harsh reactions in Japan and abroad were such that he soon changed his mind again and recanted every notion of a pan-Asianist alliance.

In Japan, Konoe's proposal of a 'race alliance' was met with scorn and derision. In February 1898, for example, an editorial of the newly founded journal *Tenchijin* critically reviewed Konoe's article under the title 'The appropriateness and merits of an alliance of the yellow race'.[67] The editorial started out with the observation that the question of China's future had always been an important issue for the powers, especially for Japan. The central question was whether China would go to pieces and Japan should consider a strategy for its division, or whether China would survive and Japan should consider relief measures. However, after considering China's retrograde obstinacy and the recent actions of the Western powers, the author eventually concluded that the demise of the 'Central Efflorescence' (*Chūka*) was imminent, and therefore also that of the theory about China's division (*Shina bunkatsu ron*), which had spread lately, not without reason. However, what with China's splendid role in history, its ancient and singular culture, its vast spaces and multitudes, some people could not help feeling overwhelmed by 'poetic sentiments' (*shika-teki kangai*) when thinking that an empire of 3000 years would go down in a morning, all the more as it was a neighboring country of the same race. Thus it was not accidental that there had been recent talk about a racial alliance in Japan, and that a person like Konoe would raise his banner high.

The author proceeded to quote Konoe's text at length and praised it as a 'bold article.' However, he ventured to analyze Konoe's thesis considering the following questions: Was race necessarily the criterion of an alliance? Or if it was civilization, could Japan and China form an alliance on the basis of civilization? The author bluntly answered the above questions in the negative: to enter an eternal alliance with one race while wholly ignoring the aspect of cultural superiority was contrary to the principles of evolution and paved the road to certain demise. 'And who is superior? Is it not he who casts away the old ways [*kyūtai o datsu shi*], transcends its cognates and transforms himself to someone more superior?'[68] Thus not racial, but cultural competition was the watchword. The author, without hesitation, credited the white race with having the superior civilization at present:

> The crucial point is merely that, even though we belong to the yellow race, we exert ourselves to study as best as we can the strong points of the white race, make use of its conveniences and thereby surpass all races around us and become someone superior [*yūshō-sha*]. What does that mean, a 'fellow man'? Is it preordained by nature that we must associate with the Chinese? The only thing that *is* necessary is that we align ourselves with the civilization of the European Christian nations. Just look, are not the examples of those who refused it and invited their downfall numerous and right before our eyes?[69]

If not on racial grounds, Japan could not form an alliance with China on the basis of civilization, either. Rather than pulling China upwards, an association with China would invariably drag Japan down into the abyss of oriental retrogression (*Nihon o hiite Shina no gotoki Tōyō-teki bunmei no kōchū ni ochiirashimezaru bekarazu*).[70] Japan would have to induce China to make fundamental reforms and completely change the nature of its civilization. However, this was like (quoting Mencius) 'crossing the bay of the Bohai carrying Mt. Tai under one's arm,' in other words, utterly impossible.

This was the gist of the writer's critique of Konoe. Although the magazine seemed to be close to the oppositional parties, the author's 'realist' stance very much resembled the realist stance of the *Jiji shinpō* at the time. It is therefore no surprise that the writer ended his article by quoting extensively – *quasi* as an antidote to the lengthy quotes from Konoe's article – from two recent 'excellent articles by the esteemed Mr Fukuzawa,' which he recommended for their relentless sharpness of insight.[71] We will discuss these two articles in the context of Fukuzawa Yukichi's position later.

Even Ōkuma Shigenobu, whose views otherwise were close to those of Konoe Atsumaro, called the proposal of a racial alliance a 'stupid idea' (*guron*). This was in an interview in the same issue of the *Tenchijin*, on his views on East Asian politics.[72] Ōkuma argued that, in international politics, alliances were formed usually without regard to religion or race. Talking now of a 'racial alliance' therefore was extremely thoughtless and ignorant (*ukatsu futsū*). If an alliance was to be considered at all, this would have to be on the grounds of civilization and benefits (*bunmei to rieki no ue ni*), that is, 'we should merely strive to align ourselves with the civilization that is likely to win.' At the beginning of the interview, Ōkuma had discoursed long and favorably about the option of an alliance with Britain, and it is obvious that Ōkuma thought an Anglo–Japanese alliance much more advantageous in terms of 'civilization and benefits' than a Sino–Japanese alliance. And this, in fact, became the majority opinion early in 1898: that, instead of a Sino–Japanese alliance, an alliance with Britain in favor of China (China's integrity) would be the best.

Thus even the *Taiyō* finally rejected Konoe's idea, and in May 1898 published an article on the 'true meaning of a Sino–Japanese alliance,' which ran very much along the lines of Ōkuma's views, arguing that, if there were to be an alliance between China and Japan at all, it would be a strategic one to save China and maintain the *status quo* in East Asia, but certainly not a racial or culturally justified alliance. It was open to any country that shared the same goals, as Britain did, and the United States.[73] The number of reactions indicates how contentious the idea of a Sino–Japanese alliance *à deux* was among the Japanese public. In fact, a majority were rather against it, favoring an alliance with Britain instead.

However, Konoe's article did most of its damage in Europe. To begin with, Russian diplomatic circles deviously employed the article as a weapon of public diplomacy, to forestall an Anglo–Japanese alliance by inciting racist fears and, at the same time, ideologically to bolster Russia's claims of East Asian domination instead. Thus, in April 1898, the *Japan Weekly Mail* syndicated an article in the British *Globe*, which contained the translation of an article in the *Novoe Vremya*, a conservative St Petersburg journal of great influence.[74] This Russian article 'by the well known Russian writer "Sigma" ' gave a rather accurate summary of Konoe Atsumaro's theses, stressing the fact that Konoe was the 'President of the Japanese House of Peers,' and adduced Konoe's theses as a proof that the Japanese leadership still pursued its long-term goal of East Asian domination through a racial alliance with China and Korea; the Sino–Japanese War had been a (failed) first attempt to 'wake up' the Chinese and Korean masses. Thus, the article implied, an Anglo–Japanese alliance could be but a temporary affair. Moreover, Russia had the 'natural mission' and capability to stop Japan from uniting the 'yellow hordes':

> It is but too clear that had only Japan become a continental Power of Asia [by keeping the Liaodong peninsula] she could have spread her wings widely over China and Korea. But Japan, having lost the basis for a future alliance of the whole yellow race, now enjoys the opportunity of carrying on the struggle by substituting for Asiatic allies those European powers – above all, England – whose interests suffer from the Siberian Railway. [...] Now, if Japan is striving to arouse the whole yellow race, Russia can at the same time play the old historic part: that is, of pacifying that race from the West, where in days of yore we pushed back from the heart of our kingdom the hordes of Polontzi, Petcheniegi, (Turkish Mongolian races), and of Tartars. Our action at Chifu and the Russo-Chinese loan are but a continuation of the policy of peaceful subjugation of those nations of the yellow race who inhabit the huge tract of country between the Volga and the Pacific, whose blood, besides, flows in our veins. There is no political sentimentality in this.[75]

Thus, suddenly, the Russians turned out to be half-Asian, too, providing just the right mixture of civilized distance and racial proximity to qualify as the perfect pacifiers of the 'half-barbaric' East.[76]

The reactions to Konoe's article in Germany and France were no less alarming. They were brought to Konoe's attention by his faithful protégé and employee Nakamura Shingo who, as we have seen, studied in Heidelberg at the time. In March 1898, Nakamura wrote Konoe a rather alarmed letter, observing that Konoe's article had provoked a controversy in all newspapers around Europe.[77] That afternoon, in the last session of his tutorial that semester, Professor Strauch had shown him the local newspaper, the *Heidelberger Tageblatt*, which carried on that day an article on Konoe's essay and the *Kokumin shinbun*-article mentioned above.[78] The professor commented on the article: 'There is somebody in Japan called Prince Konoe who is of the same opinion as you. Look at the newspaper!' Nakamura replied that he had read about it already in the *Frankfurter Zeitung* the day before, but said no more.

In his letter, Nakamura politely but urgently begged Konoe to refrain from similar statements in the future. After all, Konoe was not merely Prince Konoe of Japan, but Prince Konoe of the whole world, and in this age when international contact became ever more frequent, it was a formidable thing to attract such universal enmity. Especially now that mixed residence (*naichi zakkyo*) was about to become reality in Japan, and traffic with foreign countries became more and more extensive and intensive, the bigger part of what Konoe planned to do for his country would be frustrated because of this enmity. Even in Japan there might be people who expressed their absolute opposition to Konoe's thesis. How likely was it that foreigners would judge his thesis with calm and objectivity? People were unlikely to forget. In future, when Konoe would become an ambassador in Europe, minister of the Imperial Household, or prime minister, foreign people would still say that he was the one who advocated a Sino–Japanese alliance on racial grounds, and that he was opposed to a rapprochement between Japan and Europe. This would be most detrimental to Konoe's endeavors when in office.

As proof of how much Konoe's essay, once its contents had become known in the West, had intensified the suspicions of the West towards Japan, Nakamura copied an article he found in the *Frankfurter Zeitung* the very next morning (4 March 1898):

> A Conversation with the Japanese Envoy in Paris[79]
> [...] [Minister Kurino Shin'ichirō continued:] The suggestion of Prince Konoye (which has been taken notice of by the 'Frankfurter Zeitung' as well) of an alliance between Japan and China against the European nations is not to be taken too seriously. The Prince Honoye [*sic*], who actually does not belong to the imperial family, albeit he is the descendant of an indeed very illustrious aristocratic lineage, is, so the envoy said, *well known in Japan for the eccentricity of his political ideas.*[80] He is very young, *very fanatic*, has always sided with the opposition and *belongs to the small party of chauvinists who are hostile to foreigners.* For the very reason of his noble birth and his family ties, the government has always treated him with the utmost respect, and he is indeed President of the House of Peers. However, one should not, Mr. Kurino opinioned, overestimate his political influence. [...]

Apparently, the Japanese Foreign Ministry considered Konoe's article and the discussion in Europe so damaging that it saw no other way than to publicly disown Konoe and portray him as an incompetent radical. Considering that this was 'his majesty's' candidate for prime ministership, one cannot but call this a desperate measure.

Whether Konoe never sincerely believed in what he wrote, or whether he yielded to the pressure, in any case he soon, and repeatedly, recanted the idea of 'same race,' reverted to his former opinion, and advocated a pragmatic, interest-oriented China policy. Thus in December 1898, in the first number of the Tōa dōbunkai-organ *Tōa jiron*, Konoe wrote:

> Certainly the most urgent task today is to swiftly determine our national policy and unite public opinion. However, the most urgent task of all must be seen in defining our policy towards China. Today, I do not claim anymore that, because our empire and China share a common culture and a common race [*dōbun dōshu*], our empire should volunteer to shoulder China's fate itself. I say that we merely should consider our own empire's future fate, decide upon an urgent policy suitable to it, respond to the opportunities and watch the changes, act with swift determination and thereby secure today's advantages.[81]

For the president of the newly founded 'East Asia Common Culture Association' (Tōa dōbun-kai), to reject right away the notion of 'common culture, common race' (*dōbun dōshu*) was a rather remarkable thing to do. However, in September 1900, on the occasion of the founding of the Kokumin dōmei-kai, Konoe publicly reconfirmed his disavowal of the 'common race' idea.[82]

Instead of a Sino–Japanese Alliance, Konoe soon began to favor an alliance with Britain (like almost everyone else). In July 1898, the Meiji emperor told the new prime minister Ōkuma about his further plans with regards to Konoe: 'I secretly have expectations in Atsumaro. I wish that he is sent for a while abroad, so that he gradually cultivates his knowledge in diplomacy and in the future is closely entrusted with an important position of responsibility.'[83] The emperor had an ambassadorship in mind, but on Konoe's own request he was sent all around the United States, Europe and China to present himself (and, possibly, mend his reputation). Having returned to Japan in November 1899, Konoe soon became one of the most active advocates of an Anglo–Japanese alliance against Russia.

Takayama Chogyū

Among the few who supported Konoe's thesis, even after Konoe had recanted, was Takayama Chogyū (Rinjirō), editor of the *Taiyō* literature and arts section. Takayama belonged to the small circle of Meiji intellectuals who ardently believed in 'scientific racism,' racial homogeneity and the idea of race antagonism.[84] Thus, three weeks after Konoe's article on a racial alliance, Takayama, too, discoursed on the 'Far Eastern Question as seen as a racial competition.'[85] He 'scientifically' traced the development of the races of the world and came to the conclusion that the Far Eastern Crisis was the expression of another 'high renaissance' of the Aryan race at the end of the nineteenth century. Again, in March 1898, Takayama published a short commentary on 'alliances between different races' which was directed against the popular idea of an alliance with Britain or France. Tracing various incidents of world politics back to their racial origins, Takayama argued that the great trend of the nineteenth century was 'race nationalism.' Thus he warned his fellow-citizens against racially hybrid alliances: 'People, accept the historical fact that an alliance between different races is hardly maintained for long!'[86] Takayama remained faithful to the concept of racial competition long after and, unlike Konoe, did not yield to the Meiji common sense.[87]

Given Takayama's professed aversion against hybrid alliances, it is not surprising that, later in 1898, Takayama would register with considerable satisfaction a new tendency among the Chinese people to advocate an alliance with Japan. Thus he observed in July 1898:

> The tendencies of a Sino–Japanese alliance have gradually become stronger: a large number of students from abroad, the *Guowenbao*, the *Shiwubao*, and more recently the newly published *Yadong xinbao* [*sic*], none of them do not hint at this tendency. We must not lose this golden opportunity.
>
> The manifesto of the *Yadong xinbao* shows this especially clearly. It says: 'This newspaper has been founded solely for the purpose to convey the feelings and intentions of the idealistic and virtuous men of the two countries Japan and China. Therefore, its political articles view East Asia as one and consider the advancement of the yellow race as the central principle. Generally speaking, there exists some latent fear concerning [the concept of] the yellow race of East Asia in our two countries. However, the perusal of this [magazine] will hopefully render the changing times transparent and show what has to be done most urgently'.[88]

Takayama's eagerness to see a 'golden opportunity' realized is apparent. However, in his eagerness, he seems to have fallen prey to a delusion quite telling in its way. Thus, of the three Chinese-language newspapers Takayama cites for the new trend, only the *Shiwubao* was an independent Chinese news-paper run by reformist members of the Chinese gentry-*literati*.[89] Yet, even at the height of their enthusiasm for Japan, these reformers generally advocated a triple alliance together with Britain, something that Takayama would have rejected.[90] The *Guowenbao*, on the other hand, was founded in 1897 by Yan Fu (1853–1921) and other reform-oriented Chinese, but since March 1898 came to be published under the aegis of the Japanese consulate in Tianjin, and later even bought with money from the Japanese Foreign Ministry.[91] Finally, the *Yadong shibao*, which Takayama so enthusiastically quotes as proof of a new Chinese tendency, was in fact a Chinese-language newspaper of Japanese origin and agenda, albeit run with Chinese collaboration.

It has been observed that, in the course of modern Sino–Japanese relations until 1931, by far the greatest number of Japanese Chinese-language newspapers in China appeared in the late Meiji period. Within this period, the interwar years 1895–1904 constituted something of a golden age in the trade, when Chinese intellectuals welcomed Japanese newspapers and even cooperated in producing them. These newspapers, often short-lived and heavily subsidized by the Foreign Ministry, pursued, among other objectives, strategic ones such as the improvement of Sino–Japanese relations in general, the expansion of Japan's influence in China and, later, diminishing the influence of Russian propaganda in China.[92]

The *Yadong shibao*, too, was founded by the Itsubi-kai (The 1895 Society), a Shanghai-based society of Japanese entrepreneurs in the line of Arao Sei (1858–1896) to promote Japanese diplomatic and commercial interests in China. In fact, the newspaper was one of the official publishing organs of Konoe Atsumaro's Dōbun-kai.[93] Thus Takayama, who quoted the *Yadong shibao* as an example of a new trend in Chinese society, may have been fooled by a piece of Japanese public diplomacy in China. Chinese readers in Shanghai, on the other hand, certainly knew of the Japanese origin and agenda of the newspaper.

This somewhat bizarre situation throws considerable light on the general conditions of Pan-Asianism in late Meiji times.[94] Thus, as we have seen in the case of Konoe Atsumaro, professions of Pan-Asianist sentiment were not only heavily discouraged by the Japanese government, but also met with sharp criticism in the domestic debate. Yet, in informal interactions with the Chinese and for purposes of public diplomacy, pan-Asianist professions served as a convenient means of oiling the wheels of the 'Sino–Japanese friendship,' whatever both sides thought of their claims to truth and their true intentions. Thus one could argue that, contrary to its anti-Western bias in theory, Pan-Asianism in the political practice of late Meiji Japan was very much a necessary complement to Western-style power politics.

That is not to say that there existed no people who truly believed in the regional integration of China and Japan and attributed an affective value to Pan-Asianism that went beyond political expediency. Who would deny the romantically inspired 'continental adventurer' Miyazaki Tōten (1871–1922), for example, some sense of sincere belief in his mission?[95] However, as these people lived on the borderline of political and social respectability, and were rather conscious about their exceptional status and thinking, they certainly did not represent the political mainstream, nor did they strive to do so.[96]

Fukuzawa Yukichi

Fukuzawa's stance toward China is usually known by the short, but aggressive, leading article 'On leaving Asia behind' ('*Datsua ron*'), which we have already discussed in Chapter 1. However, during the Far Eastern Crisis, Fukuzawa's stance toward China underwent a remarkable change, converting his former aggressiveness within months into uncanny friendliness towards China.

Initially, the Far Eastern Crisis provided Fukuzawa with yet another opportunity to preach his accustomed gospel of power, according to which only the fittest nations would survive in the merciless struggle for domination (*jakuniku kyōshoku*).[97] Fitness, however, meant keeping abreast with progress and meeting the standards of civilization, which were decidedly Western, not Chinese:

> Generally speaking, it is a fundamental law of nature [*butsuri shizen no gensoku*] that that which makes no progress, retrogresses, and what does not retrogress, makes progress. The course of the world makes no exception from this rule, either. Today, when comparing East and West, it is said that the West refers to the countries of civilization and progress, whereas the East refers to the countries of obsolete customs and conservatism. […] China's position in the world of today is defined by its opposition to Western civilization with obsolete customs.[98]

China, having stopped progressing centuries ago, due to the snares of Confucianism, now was already dead.[99] Merely its body was still in good shape, and fair prey to the circling powers:

> If we look at the present state of China, its population is big, its produce is rich, and it occupies a vast territory. However, if we compare its lack of inner unity and its restriction of movement with the human body, then its blood circulation has stopped, and the nerves also have lost their movement. But still, the five parts of the body [*gotai*][100] are well nourished and magnificently plumb and are no different from a body which keeps its regular shape.[101]

In January 1898, Fukuzawa felt his constant predictions of China's imminent demise and division fully vindicated.[102] He pointed out that, 14 years ago in 1884, he had published an article entitled 'The Poland of the East' which had predicted the division of China.[103] At the time, he claimed, his prediction was being ignored as 'idle gossip' (*chawa*) and not taken seriously. However, the Far Eastern Crisis now seemed to justify his predictions. Triumphantly, Fukuzawa republished the central part of the 14-years-old article: a fictitious future 'Plan for the Partition of the Chinese Empire' for the year 1899, which predicted remarkably well the real situation in 1898 (although, apart from Shandong, this was not too difficult). As is well known, a Chinese translation of the 'Plan' appeared in March 1898 in the Chinese reform newspaper *Zhixinbao*.[104]

Fukuzawa argued that, under these circumstances, anyone would be a fool who would not let Japan have its proper share of China (Fujian, preferably). He especially lambasted the 'romantic idealism' of the opposition who, insisting on the empty words of international law, attacked the actions of Germany and Russia:

If one judges the action superficially, then this anger is not unreasonable. However, what the world today calls International Law [*bankoku kōhō*] or International Conventions [*kokusai reigi*] generally are no more than sham courtesy and empty words [*kyorei kyobun*] which merely embellish the surface. If one looks at the real state of things, the so-called survival of the fittest [*jakuniku kyōshoku*] is the true face of international intercourse, and the only thing reliable is military power. […] it is essential that we, too, are determined at the bottom of our heart to immediately shed off those empty conventionalities ourselves and get a share of the juice. To harangue others for their actual impropriety in the everyday categories of benevolence and revenge is the height of boorishness and cannot avoid the scorn of the world.[105]

Fukuzawa not only argued that Japan was entitled to a share, but even claimed that Japan, in fact, would be the perfect ruler for China, more than any other nation.[106] When it actually came to the division of China, Fukuzawa argued, it would show that the Western nations were unfit for ruling China. All they had succeeded in, so far, was 'domesticating' mere barbarians. Yet China was not so simple a matter, as it had been a fully fledged empire with a long history of civilization for thousands of years. Of this, the Western powers knew nothing. Japan, on the other hand, was familiar with China's tradition and situation, and had proven its ruling abilities already in the case of the Ryūkyū kingdom. Thus Fukuzawa concluded:

Therefore, when it finally comes to the division of the Chinese empire and the question arises as to the relative abilities to rule it, a comparison of the Western people and the Japanese should produce great concerns for the skills of the former. On the other hand, the application of the specific abilities of the Japanese people to the task will guarantee terrific results. This, I venture to say without the least doubt.[107]

However, the end of March 1898 saw an almost full conversion of Fukuzawa's image of China. Instead of dividing China and ruling the Chinese, Fukuzawa suddenly denied any territorial interests in China and proclaimed that 'we must befriend the Chinese.'[108] As before, Fukuzawa maintained that 'self-interest' was the driving force in international relations, but there was no more talk about 'the strong eating the weak' and much about mutual benefits through friendly commercial relations:

Generally speaking, the Japanese are certainly not without interests of their own. It is not that they do not demand great things from China. However, what they demand is not territory, but solely trade and commerce, nothing else. Their sole intention is but to profit themselves and, at the same time, let the other side profit. But to achieve this object we must get acquainted with the people of the other country as much as possible and, through the spirit of partnership, befriend each other.[109]

Likewise, there was no more talk about the Chinese as a dull and demented people. On the contrary, the Chinese had finally awoken to the truth of where China's real friends were:

> If we think about it, the Chinese are not stupid at all. Although it is evident that they saw and understood the general interests themselves, at the time [of the Tripartite Intervention, 1895], it was a situation of emergency, and they could not afford to consider what would come after. Merely to master the crisis at hand, they must have accepted foreign intervention as their chance and relied on it as their rescue. This might have been inevitable, but now, after the passing of only three or four years, what has come of it, eventually? The former Buddha [the Tripartite Powers] has suddenly turned into the Lord of Hell [*Emma*]. The demands [of the powers] are huge, and if we look at what has been granted so far, the Liaodong Peninsula is nothing against it. […] It is a rather disagreeable business, and today, they must have realized that it might have been the better strategy to give the Liaodong Peninsula to Japan. In fact, the Chinese recently do feel that they must fear the foreigners [the Western powers] and have developed sympathies for Japan. This is exactly what a telegram from Peking says, i.e. that the ruler and the subjects of China in general have come to trust in Japan. Moreover, according to news we have obtained from another source, among such people like Zhang Zhidong, there has been a great awakening recently. As part of this fortunate event, he has sent one of his men to make the passage for Japan, and according to the report [of this subordinate], he [Zhang Zhidong] will sent approximately one-hundred-and-fifty students to our country and let them study all sorts of matters. Even judging this kind of information suffices to discern more and more the recent tendency of the Chinese.[110]

And in this recent tendency, Fukuzawa bestowed great hopes. No more did Fukuzawa speak of China's demise and final partition, but instead declared that 'the Chinese must not lose hope.'[111] Suddenly, Fukuzawa found compassion for China's tribulations and assured that China was not lost. The occupation of some places at the Chinese coast merely meant 'a hair taken from among nine oxen'[112] and could do no harm to China. Although China might look ruinous on the outside, it was so big, and so 'well nourished' on the inside, that he had great hopes. These foreign tribulations may well be but the necessary rites of passages for the necessary changes, in the same manner as the Meiji Restoration had been triggered in Japan. China might still reach the same level as Japan today:

The future course need absolutely not let us lose hope. On the contrary, we can console ourselves that the tribulations are rather in the regular order of the process. From the Chinese perspective, the state of Japan today may probably arouse great envy. However, Japan has reached its present position by passing through what China is suffering today. The Chinese, too, must strive to pass through their present difficulties and become what Japan is today. I as a Japanese am especially sympathetic. That the time will come, if even one day earlier, this is my most fervent wish.[113]

Thus Fukuzawa concluded that if China would follow in the footsteps of Japan, all would be well.

Whereas the *Jiji shinpō* in January 1898 had been intent to demonstrate that it was best qualified to *rule* China, in May 1898 it very eagerly sought to persuade readers that it was best qualified to *teach* China. On occasion of the Shashi riot, the paper published an editorial entitled 'One must turn misfortune into one's blessings'[114] which assured that, of all foreign powers, Japan was the least interested in territorial possessions in China and cared the most about China's survival as a whole:

Japan's attitude towards China is motivated only by the wish to open the country and profit from trade with it. To show any ambitions with regards to occupying territory, it would not even dream of. As the old adage goes, if the lips crumble, the teeth are cold. If it comes to the worst, will China become the second Poland? Japan in its dealings with the European powers has acutely felt the difficulties of maintaining its position as a state. Therefore, it considers the protection of China's independence [*Shina no dokuritsu o hozen suru*] as Japan's national policy.[115]

In 1884, Fukuzawa had entitled one of his editorials: 'There is no point in relying on the old adage of the cheekbones and the gums, the lips and the teeth.'[116] Now, suddenly, he became one of the most ardent champions of Sino–Japanese solidarity. To drive his point home, the *Jiji shinpō* was not even shy from invoking a special affinity because of cultural roots, something Fukuzawa would have abhorred only a couple of months ago:

Suppose even the Chinese *were* somewhat dim, if they see that their stubborn reactionarism time and again brings disaster over them, they must change their mind. However, once they have awakened to the necessity of reform, it is but the natural course that they will want to follow the precedent of Japan. The countries of the West from the beginning had a civilization which differed from China, and their customs and languages are altogether different. However, Japan, over a long time sharing the same civilization and adhering to the same religion [Buddhism] and moral precepts [Confucianism], by a sudden chance has moved forward alone and has thus achieved the wealth and power of today. Therefore, if China finally makes the effort to introduce civilization, it must necessarily move forward by following the footsteps of Japan. It will be essential that, in moving forward by following the footsteps of Japan, it will rely in all affairs on the guidance of Japan. Speaking from the point of experience as well as seen from the eagerness with which it strives for its independence, there is none better qualified to teach the old empire than Japan. To learn from the Westerners would be tantamount to being fostered by a stepmother, whereas being led by our people would be exactly like being raised by one's real parents. It goes without saying that between the two, there is a fundamental difference.[117]

Thus the *Jiji shinpō* tried to wean the Chinese suckling from its evil stepmother, the Western powers, and especially Russia (incidentally, a *Jiji shinpō*-caricature of February 1898 shows Russia as an evil-looking stepmother holding two children, China and Korea, in her arms, lulling them to sleep[118]).

How are we now to explain Fukuzawa's and his newspaper's sudden conversion from one of the most rabidly anti-Chinese stances to such zealous Sinophilia? The mercurial nature of Fukuzawa's thought has often been commented on, and has infuriated modern readers. To manage Fukuzawa, the concept of 'situational thought' or 'perception' (*jōkyō-teki shikō* or *ninshiki*) is often adduced as a panacea for the seeming contradictions in his statements.[119] However, genteel words aside, it should be noted that contemporaries of Fukuzawa and the *Jiji shinpō* considered the newspaper's meandering course as pure and simple radical opportunism. Especially the year 1898 saw three rapid switches of political allegiance (always to the one in power), which caused the *Tōkyō nichinichi shinbun* to devote a long and sardonic article on 'the suicide of the *Jiji shinpō*.'[120]

However, in its close ties to high government circles, especially in the Foreign Ministry, the *Jiji shinpō* remained constant, and in this light we should also view the conversion. It is certainly no coincidence that the newspaper's conversion occurred in May, at around the same time as Yano Fumio in Beijing suggested taking on Chinese students, an initiative that was ultimately backed by the Japanese Foreign Ministry.[121] Moreover, Fukuzawa himself mentioned, in March 1898, Zhang Zhidong's envoy and his willingness to send over Chinese students (see above).[122] Given Fukuzawa's welcoming of Korean overseas students in the 1880s, by which he sought to promote reform in Korea, this new interest in Chinese students is hardly surprising.

The wish to promote reform in China may also account for the wooing tone in some of the later articles, which seems somewhat out of place towards an exclusively Japanese public. However, as we have seen, articles of the *Jiji shinpō* and other Japanese newspapers received attention in China, especially among reformist circles.[123] Thus especially those articles that offered consolation in hard times and assured of Japanese friendship had a good chance of being disseminated by the Chinese press. This would parallel the attempts at public diplomacy we have already witnessed above in Takayama Chogyū's case, and gives an interesting new twist to Japan's awareness of the world: if in 1885 it was still 'the eyes of the civilized Western people' that exclusively mattered to Japan (at least to the *Jiji shinpō*, as we have seen), in 1898 the Chinese perspective became important as well. Of course, its importance was of a different character, as the *Jiji shinpō* expected the Chinese to view Japan rather in the way a student adores his venerable teacher. The *Jiji shinpō*, despite its conversion and concern for China's welfare, certainly did not renounce any claims of political dominance, much in the same way as the new Japanese policy of intellectual exchange was intended to foster Japan's influence in China.

Kuga Katsunan

In comparison with Fukuzawa Yukichi, Kuga Katsunan is often depicted as the more 'Asian-minded' and as a champion of protecting China's integrity.[124] However, in the same way as Fukuzawa seemingly departed from his purely realist stance and came to advocate the protection of China, Kuga Katsunan, too, moved towards Fukuzawa's initial position (while still viciously attacking Fukuzawa), and by May 1898 had integrated 'realist' power politics elements into his strategy for East Asia. Thus he began to advocate Japan's hegemony in East Asia and a 'shock therapy' for China.

Kuga Katsunan's double role as Asianist and advocate of strong foreign politics is, incidentally, well illustrated by the organizational role he played in 1898. Being very much an actor behind the scenes, he was one of the functionaries of the 'Society of like-minded fellows in foreign matters' (Taigai dōshi-kai) which was founded at the Kairaku-en in Nippon-bashi in April 1898.[125] At the same time, Katsunan was a prominent co-founder of the Tōa-kai, the 'East Asia Association', which later in the year merged with Konoe's Dōbun-kai. The founding of the Tōa-kai, too, took place in May 1898, also at the Kairaku-en and, to a large degree, with the same members as the Taigai dōshi-kai.[126] The identity of time, place and membership of both organizations shows how closely anti-Russian protest, anti-*hanbatsu* agitation and China politics were related, not only intellectually but also institutionally.

Being a central spokesman of the strong foreign policy movement, Katsunan typically reacted to the Far Eastern Crisis by first attacking Germany and Russia for their 'piracy' and 'blackmail' (*kyōhaku*) of China.[127] Their barbarous behavior heralded the advent of an age of conquest by 'brute force' (*juryoku*), which ran against all norms of international law and values of real civilization.[128] As motives Katsunan attributed to their actions: cowardice (the need to defuse the political situation in Europe by moving the conflict further away), social imperialism, in Germany's case the need to justify the costs of its new naval expansion program with desultory occupations,

and in Russia's case simple imperialist greed.[129] All this was cloaked by a
dubious 'new interpretation' of international law, and by blatant racism which
erected arbitrary obstacles to 'real civilization' and proved these Western
countries' interpretation of civilization a sham:

> The ideology of civilization [*bunmei no shugi*] says: 'Generally speaking,
> all the superior races of the world should encourage the unenlightened
> people and let them follow civilization. They should admonish countries
> in disorder and let them attain peace and order.' Europeans call them-
> selves civilized people. However, on grounds of racial otherness or dif-
> ferences in the national way [*kokufū*] they exclude others, and looking
> for an easy pretext, they pilfer property and rob territory or suppress
> their freedom or limit their independence. Thus, the so-called conveniences
> of civilization [*bunmei no riki*], have turned again into dangerous weapons
> of barbarism [*yaban no kyōki*].[130]

Thus the so-called 'civilized nations', by their own greed and cowardice, had
turned into the real 'barbarians.'

In the same vein, Katsunan attacked the champions of *bunmei-shugi* in his
own country (and thus Fukuzawa Yukichi prominently among them) who,
through their sole reliance on 'enriching the country and strengthening the
army' (*fukoku kyōhei*) were no better – or more civilized – than Germany
and Russia relying on brute force:

> [They say:] 'In the world of today, one cannot protect the country with
> empty words [*kūgen*], one must necessarily fight with real power [*jitsur-
> yoku*]. If there is not enough real power, one also will not be able to
> attain the independence and stability of one's country. Just look at China
> now! The powers of Europe have occupied its strategic points without
> hesitation, and this shows the truth that empty words are worthless.'
> Thus speak the advocates of civilization [*bunmei-ka*] and the vulgar
> people [*zokuhai*] in our country with a smug face. What these fellows
> call real power means military power and financial power, and one
> might say that it corresponds with what the Chinese from olden times
> always have called 'enriching the country and making the army strong'
> [*fukoku kyōhei*]. If one says *fukoku kyōhei*, it sounds quite majestic.
> However, when we carefully consider the truth [*shinri*] by which the
> world of man differs from the world of animals, at least in my opinion it
> runs counter to civilized thought [*bunmei shisō*].
> [...] The existence of Europe today, does it really originate from the
> [mere] animal aspect of humanity, or does it come from justice, freedom,
> and brotherhood [*seigi jiyū oyobi hakuai*]? This is what I would like to
> ask these self-styled advocates of civilization the first thing. And if we
> come to problems in international politics, it is just the same: The dip-
> lomats who despise justice, freedom, and brotherhood as empty words,

those who justify this survival of the fittest [*jakuniku kyōshoku*], do they still want to tell me that civilized diplomacy is like *this*?[131]

This finally led Katsunan to attack the government for sympathizing with Germany and Russia and abetting their deeds by simply looking away:

> The thought of the group around the clan politicians [*hanbatsu shuzoku*] in matters of foreign policy is either German-style or Russian-style. Therefore one must see it as the natural outcome that the group around the clan politicians not only does not consider the actions of Germany and Russia in our East Asia wrong, but, on the contrary, even has the tendency to glorify it.[132]

On the pretext that Japan was 'not yet ready', but was still in the midst of the postwar management program, the government would shirk its responsibility to protest against the Russian and German actions. However, the arms race would never stop, and Japan would not be able to catch up with the European powers.[133] Thus, on another occasion, Katsunan attacked this policy of expanding the army while not using it as a simple maneuver of the military elite to boost its power while being too inept to use it in foreign affairs:

> On the one hand they rattle with their sabers and demand the increased levy of taxes. On the other hand, they cower before the saber and just pray that everything will be fine on the other side of the coast [...][134]

For the sake of the 'true civilization' (*shinsei no bunmei*), which – as we have seen – Katsunan saw embodied in the French triad of justice, freedom and brotherhood (*seigi jiyū oyobi hakuai*), a 'truly civilized country' (*shinsei no bunmeikoku*) would always fight, regardless of the state of military preparations and the relative balance of powers:

> True advocates of civilization see the use of power [*jitsuryoku*] only in opposing barbarism, and if they saw a barbaric action, they would exhaust all their power at their present command to oppose it. To have power in abundance, but not make use of it arbitrarily towards other countries, that makes a real civilized country. To lack power and nonetheless oppose injustice, that too makes a real civilized country. In this point, I indeed differ from the self-styled advocates of civilization [*jishō bunmei-ka*]. After all, there is a difference between the laws of humankind [*jinrui no hōsoku*] and the laws of the rest of the living world.[135]

Thus Katsunan invoked the spirit of 'chivalry' (*gikyō*) which we have encountered earlier, although Katsunan – being the intellectual elitist that he was – would never use such a 'trite' word. However, his closeness to the *shishi*-bravado of his strong foreign policy associates is unmistakable.

Katsunan used the outbreak of the Spanish–American War in April 1898 to illustrate his ideal of a 'truly civilized country': a country that defended its principles, using both measures of diplomacy and powers, limited as they were, for the good cause of civilization.[136] Katsunan explained that the United States, being 'master' in North America, lately had extended its influence to South America (Monroe Doctrine) and thus had come into conflict with Spain over Cuba:

> In America, on the other side of the Atlantic, the United States is master [*shujin*]. However, from Middle America southwards, Spain even from a distance claims the Balance of Power, and presently there has arisen great talk about the problem of Cuba. […] The United States has no business in Europe […] But in America, it maintains its firm policy not to suffer any interference within its domain, and of late it has wanted to further include South America, too. […] In Central and South America, the United States of North America suppresses high-handed actions of the Europeans. Although it acts upon its Monroe Doctrine [*Monrō-shugi*], recently it also refers to it by the 'balance of power' [*kinsei*].[137]

For the sake of justice, freedom, and brotherhood 'within its domain,' the United States helped the Cubans against their Spanish oppressors, not minding the power imbalance, and thus fought a 'just war':

> America's opposition to Spain truly is founded on the wish to free the Cuban people from their fetters. Not heeding its insufficient military preparations, it dared to declare war upon Spain, and what is more, even plans to come to the Southwest Pacific in aid of the Philippine people. *That* is a just war in the realm of humankind [*kore jinrui-kai ni okeru shinsei no tatakai nari*].[138]

Of course, in reality, it was Spain's military preparations which were pathetically insufficient. However, what Katsunan needed was the Western precedent of a militarily weak, but still hegemonic power that would fight any unjust intrusions on behalf of even weaker countries in the region as an analogy of what he had in mind for Japan's role in East Asia.

The first hints of Katsunan's idea that Japan should claim its right as natural leader or 'master' (*shujin*) of East Asia appeared in an editorial on 8 May 1898 calling for 'a reform in foreign policy thinking.'[139] The editorial attacked the two great parties, Shinpotō and Jiyūtō, arguing that, if they wanted to remain true to the values for which they professedly stood – progress (*shinpo*) and freedom (*jiyū*) – they should do so in foreign policy as well, and not acquiesce to the indolent policy of the cabinet. They should take the 'virtuous, civilized' powers of the West as an example, namely the United States, Britain and France. If the world powers Britain and France had failed to take action in East Asia as decisively as one could wish for, this was also because East Asia was far away and the Western 'civilized powers' were not genuinely responsible for East Asia in the first place:

> However, the East Asian continent is, geographically speaking, distant to these countries, and their race is not the same, either. Consequently, if one or two powers perpetrate some unjust action and the others do not protest [*kōgi*], this compares with the fact that our empire does not concern itself much about the Cuban problem. In the Far Eastern situation, Japan should be master [*shujin taru beki mono*]. Silently watching the actions of Germany and Russia is tantamount to throwing away this privilege of being master [*shujin taru kenri*].[140]

Thus the parallels and the identical wording (*shujin*, 'master,' for both the US position in the Americas and Japan's envisioned position in East Asia) strongly suggest that Katsunan envisioned a 'Monroe Doctrine' for Japan in East Asia as well. It should be noted that this led to a conspicuous re-evaluation of the divisive factors of geography and race. Katsunan in February 1898 had viewed these factors as 'obstacles to world civilization' (*sekai bunmei no shōgai*)[141] and attacked the Western powers for establishing artificial barriers between Europe and East Asia. Now, in May 1898, Katsunan relied on the same categories to justify Japan's position as 'master' in East Asia. A similar ambivalence toward the functions of race and geography was inherent in many visions of Japan's primacy in East Asia. Katsunan was not the first to develop the idea of a Japanese Monroe Doctrine, but was certainly an early example (Konoe Atsumaro being another prominent one).[142]

On occasion of the Shashi riot on 9 May 1898, Katsunan finally declared that Japan, of all civilized countries, had the principal responsibility to solve the Chinese Question, which lay at the heart of the Far Eastern Question. In an essay entitled 'Our duty to encourage domestic reforms in China: on occasion of the Shashi outrage',[143] Katsunan argued:

> The East Asian Question [*Tōa mondai*], although its manifestations may be infinite and the matter extremely involved, if we put a conclusion to it, it all comes down to the first cause that China has not been able to become a 'modern state' [*'kuni' taru o ezaru koto*] in response to the currents of this century. Supposing China would eventually be able to build a 'state,' the bigger part of the East Asian Question would probably go away by itself. [...][144]

For Katsunan, there were eventually two parts to the solution of the Chinese Question: one was to restrain the territorial ambitions of the Western powers in East Asia, especially the 'barbaric' powers Germany and Russia, and thereby guarantee China's integrity. Thus Katsunan argued in June 1898:

Therefore, it is a matter of course that our empire, which has to solve the problem of China, in accordance with the Rescript on the Retrocession of Liaodong [of May 1895] sooner or later must impose the appropriate constraints on the actions of Germany and Russia. Today, we must not limit ourselves to merely protecting the balance of power by busying ourselves with a strip of the Chinese coast, but for the sake of peace in the East, nay, of the world, we insist on the preservation of China's integrity [*Shinkoku no hozen*]. In another step, it is the duty of our empire, due to neighborly friendship but also to what is reasonable in international intercourse, to render effective assistance to internal reforms of this country.[145]

Besides checking the 'selfish' powers Germany and Russia, domestic reforms in China constituted the other part of the solution. Thus, on the occasion of the Shashi outrage, Katsunan proposed that Japan, in concert with other 'truly civilized powers' (Britain, the United States and France), should undertake to lead China onto the path of reforms. The method of doing so, however, also included well meant 'threats' (*kyōhaku*):

I always say that, if there were two or three truly civilized countries and they could work together, they should put pressure on the Chinese government and let it reform the fundamental structures of its political system. Unfortunately, the powers without exception only heed their immediate interests and do not care for real, lasting peace. On the contrary, they even promote chaos and disaster on the East Asian continent and privately seem to consider it disadvantageous if the Chinese empire reformed itself. However, most of the powers have their countries far, far away, and if they see order or chaos in East Asia, it is as if we would view some incident in the Mediterranean. Their sense of involvement is not very strong, and consequently, it is only natural that the intensity with which they desire for peace in East Asia is so much weaker than ours. Therefore, although I absolutely do not think the powers to be uncivilized countries, I do not want to blame them too much for not attempting a fair and square solution of the East Asian problem at its roots. The one who must take the lead and apply itself to the solution, is that not our Japanese Empire?

The Japanese empire, in fact, is Master in the East [*Tōdō no shu*],[146] and since we are so lucky that every power comes as a guest here [to East Asia], is it not possible then that our empire, when receiving those guests, appeals to them to exert their powers for the foundation of peace in East Asia? The foundation of peace in East Asia lies in letting the Chinese empire become a real state in this world of today [*Shina teikoku o shite konnichi no yo ni okeru shinsei no kuni tarashimuru*] and the way to let it become a 'state' is to threaten [*kyōhaku*] the government in Beijing as the responsible institution. If I say 'threaten', it is not with any bad intentions, but because I think that if the situation of the government in Beijing does not receive some foreign threat, nothing can be done. If our empire, as Master in the East, solicits the agreement of those powers which come as a guest, and voluntarily step forward to press the government in Beijing for domestic reforms, one could call this rather a procedure in international relations which answers to the requirements of the day [*konnichi no jigi ni ōzuru kokusai no reihō*].[147]

The 'therapy' which Katsunan proposed for China was based on the now familiar assumption that foreign pressure would induce a sovereign state to domestic reforms. Thus Katsunan in May 1898, like Fukuzawa, argued that what had been good for Japan in the Bakumatsu times must be good for China now as well.[148] China, unfortunately, was very slow to feel the 'threats and invitations' – ten times slower than Japan. It had already been more than 100 years ago that a British envoy had come to China (Katsunan refers to the Macartney Embassy, 1793), and people in South China were only gradually feeling the necessity of domestic reforms. Katsunan continued:

But the initial driving force for reform was still not enough to urge the implementation of the reform thought. Our war with China in 1894/95 for the first time produced some effects. But the persuasion which must come after the threat has not shown any results, yet. The knowledgeable people in China, still in the midst of hesitation, merely rely on the foreign stimulus [*shigeki*] to become even stronger. Japan as the advanced country [*senshin-koku*] in East Asia should take the lead ahead of the Western powers and undertake the responsibility. Has not the war of 1894/95 been already a prelude to this?[149]

Thus the shock therapy of the Sino–Japanese War set a precedent and gave rise to claims for Japan's further 'treatment' of China. It is important to note that this proposition entailed a remarkable re-evaluation of power, sovereignty and coercion. Whereas Katsunan had bitterly criticized the actions of Russia and Germany as 'barbarous' infringements on China's sovereignty and denounced their acts as 'piracy' and 'blackmail' (*kyōhaku*), Katsunan now likewise proposed to 'threaten' (*kyōhaku*) China into undertaking reforms. Moreover, he let the occupations of Chinese territory suddenly appear in the more positive light of stepping up foreign pressure.[150] Whereas, in the case of Russia and Germany, Katsunan had criticized the 'new interpretation' of international law to justify their infringement on Chinese sovereignty, he now declared that to pressure the Chinese government into undertaking reforms constituted 'a procedure in international relations which answers to the requirements of the day.' Thus we must conclude that 'barbarism' and 'civilization' were a matter not of means, but merely of ends, and only a hair's breadth away from each other.

This leads us to the conclusion of this chapter. While discussing the public reactions to the Far Eastern Crisis and its aftermath, we have witnessed a number of rather remarkable changes of opinion, often in the very opposite direction of where they were originally headed, or even performing a double *volte* in quick succession. Examples include Fukuzawa's Paulinian conversion to become a dedicated Sinophile, and Katsunan's vision of 'true civilized countries' bullying China into reforms. However, despite the frequent changes of direction, on the whole we can observe a gradual convergence of these diverse positions on a common China policy, which amalgamated power politics and professed idealism, and generally called for China's protection and its education, either by soft power or hard force.

The convergence of positions in late Meiji political thought on foreign relations has been often commented upon. Marius B. Jansen once stated that, in Meiji political thought, it was often difficult to 'separate the permissible from the aggressive, the promising from the demonic.'[151] Similarly, Banno Junji observed that both Western-style power politics and idealist ('Asianist') positions were indistinguishable in practice, and legitimized the same strategies, the one being no more (or less) inclined to expansionism than the other.[152]

Technically speaking, this convergence and lack of distinction (except for individual modes of expression) may be attributed to the fact that both positions, the realist and the idealist, operated with the assumption that the ends justified the means. Thus civilization became a matter of profession, as the means could be either 'brute force' or benevolent coercion, both being completely indistinguishable on the outside and depending solely on the profession of the agent as to their social meaning.

Seen in the wider context, one could argue that this ambivalence was nothing especially Japanese, but rather proof that Japan's perspective had widened and was becoming more and more 'globalized.' The historian Tōyama Shigeki once explained the convergence of positions by pointing out the common 'social practice' in a country that needed to modernize and protect its independence in the face of Western imperialism.[153] However, this probably stresses the antagonist aspect too much. Considering that Japan wanted to maintain its independence, but at the same time conform to the standard of 'civilization' and become part of international society, it is more likely that what seemed to Tōyama the common 'social practice' conformed rather to the common international practice of imperialist thinking and its ingredient, the 'civilizing mission.' After all, this concept likewise justified the means of its realization and accounts for much of imperialism's ambivalence.[154] Thus the formation of a common China policy in 1898 under the heading *Shina hozen*, could also be seen as another proof of Japan's synchronization with the world in the late nineteenth century.

4   The Hundred Days Reform, 1898

The Hundred Days Reform in China between mid-June and late September 1898 is one of the *causes célèbres* in the history of late imperial China. As in many cases of modern Chinese history, its interpretation is highly contentious.[1] Traditional Chinese interpretations (based on Maoist revolutionary premises) have interpreted the 1898 reform movement as the last and most progressive, but necessarily failing, reform attempt within the Chinese government before the revolution in 1911; 'revisionist' studies have de-emphasized the significance of the 1898 reforms, especially downplaying the role of the reformer Kang Youwei (1858–1927) in favor of the more moderate reform movement, which began under the Empress Dowager Cixi (1835–1908) after the failure of the Hundred Days and lasted until the end of the Qing Dynasty. The centennial of the 1898 reform movement in 1998 has demonstrated a markedly revived interest in the 'bourgeois' reform movement, partly in an effort to 'use the past to serve the present.'[2] However, Rebecca E. Karl and Peter Zarrow have pointed out that this revived interest could also be explained less ideologically as an understandable interest in parallel situations: the encounter of China with two globalizations, one at the end of the nineteenth century and the other at the end of the twentieth.[3]

Whatever the interpretation of its historical significance, Japan played an important role in the Hundred Days Reform, both as a model for modernization while it lasted, and as a safe exile for some of the reformers when it faltered. Previous scholarship has focused largely on comparing the Meiji Restoration with the Chinese reform movement, or on the role that the Meiji Restoration played in the Hundred Days Reform, especially in the reform proposals of Kang Youwei.[4] Thus it is not surprising that there remain some popular misunderstandings as to Japan's actual role and interest in the Reform, such as that the 'Hundred Days stirred great optimism in Japan';[5] that Japanese newspapers and magazines covered the reform movement in some detail, with special focus on Kang Youwei's memorials and the emperor's edicts;[6] and finally, that the Japanese government actively supported the Hundred Days Reform while it lasted.[7] However, none of these is true.

Naturally, considering how urgently Fukuzawa Yukichi, Kuga Katsunan and many others in Japan had called for reform in May and June 1898, one would expect them to greatly welcome the Hundred Days Reform. Yet this was not the case; on the contrary, a close study of the newspapers reveals that the Japanese public, for several reasons, did not acknowledge the Reform as such until it had actually failed, and then received the fact with (some) pity, but even more so with a 'we saw it coming' attitude, and probably also with elation. It is conspicuous that only *after* the failure of the Reform did professions of intimate 'friendship' pour forth, and even the most conservative government newspaper abandoned its neutrality and joined the chorus of *Shina hozen*, which thereby became the universally accepted China policy among the public. However, at the same time this policy changed in content: thus, after the failure of the Hundred Days and the Beijing riots, there is a marked move away from the idea of 'pressuring' the Beijing government into undertaking reforms towards the advocacy of direct intervention to aid and assist China, and this in concert with the Western powers. Thus, after the Reform, we see China's star as a sovereign state rapidly sinking and China increasingly becoming the mere object of Japan and the Western powers' joint care and 'protection.' Accordingly, discourse on China policy shifted its focus and increasingly became a discourse on Japan's relations with the *Western* powers concerning China.

The Japanese government, too, remained aloof while the Chinese Reform lasted. Far from actively supporting it, the short-lived Kenseitō cabinet under Ōkuma Shigenobu remained faithful to its predecessors' foreign policy and was unwilling to take sides. Itō Hirobumi's cautious reserve while meeting high officials and even the Guangxu emperor himself in Beijing during the last days of the Reform bespeaks a similar attitude, and must be seen as representing Japan's official China policy. Likewise, Ōkuma and Itō cooperated in the rescue of the reformers after the failure of the Reform, although new sources show that this was less due to special sympathy with the reformers (there seems to have been little of that), but more to fulfill the duty of a 'civilized nation,' together with Britain. The same rationale worked behind the joint intervention with the Western powers against the Boxers two years later.

The Hundred Days

In 1889, the Empress Dowager Cixi relinquished her rights as regent and retired to the newly built Summer Palace.[8] Emperor Guangxu formally assumed power and increasingly invested himself in reform projects to strengthen the country. As in Japan, the post-war administration was primarily directed at reinforcing the dynasty's defense capabilities.[9] An imperial decree in December 1895, for example, sent Yuan Shikai (1859–1916) to Tianjin to command the 'Newly Organized Army,' and expressly to follow German army regulations (the German army already had served as a model for the Japanese army).[10] Efforts at modernization were also made in the education and industry sectors. However, the Jiaozhou incident and following events demonstrated that these efforts were still not enough. On 11 June 1898, the emperor finally issued an edict that committed the throne explicitly to the cause of reforms. The edict observed a growing tendency among officials towards reforms, but also reluctance. The emperor called upon the people, high and low, to give up this reluctant attitude and actively to contribute to the effort of making the nation rich and powerful. While the 'essence' should remain traditional moral studies, the edict advocated extensive borrowing from Western learning (thus invoking the moderate *ti-yong* formula).[11] This commitment to reform is generally seen as the formal beginning of the Hundred Days.

Five days after the edict, on 16 June 1898, the emperor received Kang Youwei for an audience.[12] After the audience, Kang was promoted to the position of secretary of the Zongli yamen (the Chinese Foreign Ministry). At the beginning of September 1898, the emperor appointed Tan Sitong (1865–1898) as one of four additional secretaries to the Grand Council, with the assignment to assist him 'in matters of the new policies.'[13] Moreover, the emperor considered appointing Huang Zunxian ambassador to Japan.[14] These were the most visible signs that the emperor supported the 'radical' reformers. At the same time, the emperor also visibly embraced the thought of the 'conservative' reformers. On 24 July 1898, he ordered copies of the reform classic *Jiaobin-lu kangyi* ('Personal protests from the study of Jiaobin') to be printed and distributed inside the court bureaucracy for comments. Likewise, on the next day the emperor ordered the distribution of copies of Zhang Zhidong's *Quanxue pian* ('An exhortation to study') among the governor-generals, governors and directors of education in the provinces.[15]

Following the 11 June edict, the emperor initiated a considerable number of changes and new projects in the fields of education, the military, the economy and finance, as well as in government and administration. During the same period, Kang Youwei sent 21 memorials to the emperor with detailed proposals for reform, in the same fields and in the same sequence, although only a fraction of Kang's proposals were eventually realized.[16] Generally speaking, the reforms in education and the military started immediately after the edict, whereas changes in the economy and government followed later, by the end of August 1898.

Some of the more 'spectacular' measures were as follows: On 15 June 1898 an edict announced that the emperor would accompany the empress dowager to review a maneuver of the Northern armies in Tianjin. On 19 June, the emperor ordered that, henceforth, army drills should be conducted in the Western style, taking Yuan Shikai's and Zhang Zhidong's armies as models. On 23 June, the cumbersome eight-legged essay (*bagu wen*) as mandatory format of the examination system was abolished.[17] On 21 August, a Central Bureau of Agriculture, Commerce, and Industry was established. At the end of August, sinecure positions were abolished and the court bureaucracy cut down in size. Finally, on 8 and 10 September (allegedly) supernumerary positions in the administration of the provinces were rescinded, and the officials transferred to the new Bureau of Agriculture. More reforms were likely to follow, but on 21 September 1898, an imperial edict announced to the astonished public that, for reasons of health, the emperor had requested the empress dowager to 'tutor' him in government affairs.[18] Thus ended the reform period of the Hundred Days under the Guangxu emperor (actually after 103 days). However, the Empress Dowager Cixi, soon after resuming the regency (which she kept until her death in 1908), initiated another phase of moderate reforms which, again, was cut short by the revolution in 1911.

Japanese perspectives of reform in China

If we systematically browse the Japanese newspapers in the period from June to September 1898, we will find that most Japanese newspapers acknowledged a distinct reform *movement* only as late as 22 September 1898, if at all.[19] Even an avid observer of Chinese affairs such as Naitō Konan began to comment on the reforms as late as mid-September, and this with a (typically) ambiguous attitude.[20] Some newspapers acknowledged the Hundred Days as a reform program for the first time on 25 September 1898, at the same time announcing the failure of the program.[21] Thus the Hundred Days certainly did not stir great optimism in Japan, but did not excite much grief either, as we shall see.

The peculiar inability, or even reluctance, to acknowledge reforms in China was conditioned by several factors. One reason lay in the nature of the medium – the often erratic and rather eclectic news coverage of foreign affairs, which tended to focus on the spectacular and on big names. Another was the view of the political China immediately prior to the Hundred Days, so disastrous that no-one would expect a Chinese reform even possible; nor did the general image of Kang Youwei and his followers inspire much hope. However, behind all this lay the even more profound cultural bias that China could not, and should not, reform too quickly and, especially, too independently. And finally, parallels with the political situation in Japan show that most contemporaries thought rapid political change neither possible, even in modern Japan, nor really desirable. Thus, arguing *a fortiore*, if a 'Second Meiji Restoration' was impossible in Japan, there was even less reason to hope for even a first one to happen in China.

The settings of the Japanese perspective: problems of information density

One of the reasons why the Reform came into the Japanese focus so late was certainly the material conditions of news reportage at the time. In general, the Japanese public was not worse or better informed about developments in China than the rest of the global public. As has been explained above, through Reuter's news agency, Japan in the 1890s had access to the information pool which provided the world globally and exclusively with information on East Asia.[22] Moreover, the Japanese newspapers, like Western newspapers, had their own special correspondents on the spot to supplement information. In 1898, the *Jiji shinpō,* for example, had *tokuha-in* stationed in Peking, Shanghai, Seoul and Incheon. From there, the correspondents sent 'special telegrams' (*tokuden*) containing *short* news items on the current situation.

However, both Reuters' news as well as the *tokuden* had a problem of focus: they usually covered only the 'simple and spectacular,' that is, only what had already been established as relevant. In 1898, this was the Far Eastern Crisis and the scramble for concessions, but not the Hundred Days. If we browse the London *Times* (or the *New York Times,* for that matter), we will probably find that news of the Hundred Days reached the British or American public at about the same time as the Japanese public, when it was almost or already over.

Detailed analysis of the situation at hand was sent in by mail as so-called 'special reports' (*tokuhō*) or just 'news' (*tsūshin*) by the special correspondents on the spot. However, whether special correspondents were employed, and at what intervals they sent reports, often seems to have been a subject of chance. The *tokuhō* of the *Jiji shinpō,* for example, appeared quite erratically; *tokuhō* in the *Yorozu chōhō* appeared often in June and July 1898 from Beijing, and afterwards from Yingkou, which was due to the itinerary of a Japanese China-traveler (Shiga Sukegorō) whose *tokuhō* we will discuss in some detail below. The *Tōkyō nichinichi shinbun* received *tokuhō* from Beijing or Shanghai regularly, one at the end of each month. In the case of the Hundred Days, this meant three times, until the project faltered. However three times hardly makes for a movement.

Yet it has been claimed that Japanese newspapers and magazines covered the reform movement in China 'quite in detail,' with a special focus on Kang Youwei's memorials and on the emperor's edicts.[23] One could argue that, if one assumed an omnivorous reader who pieced all fragments of the regular news, *tokuden,* and *tokuhō* of several major Japanese newspapers together, this reader might have received a fair picture of all major developments of the Hundred Days: the emperor's inviting critique and advice on state affairs;[24] the death of Prince Gong in May;[25] the reform edict of 11 June;[26] the dismissal of Weng Tonghe (1830–1904) on 15 June and other personnel reshuffles;[27] the audience of Kang Youwei with the emperor on 16 June;[28] the subsequent appointment of Kang Youwei as secretary of the Zongli yamen;[29] the abolishment of the eight-legged essay, the revision of the examination system, and the institution of the Imperial College;[30] important edicts on the founding of a mining and railway bureau; on the promotion of agriculture, trade and commerce; and on matters of administration;[31] finally, the spectacular dismissal of Li Hongzhang on 7 September.[32]

As to Kang's memorials, these with few exceptions were not made public until Kang Youwei himself published an edition of his memorials in 1911.[33] Moreover, the person of Kang Youwei appeared only late in the media, and with mixed reputation, as the following two examples of Japanese foreign correspondence about China will show.

China prior to the Hundred Days: Kawasaki Shizan's analysis

An example of how Japanese 'China experts' viewed the chances of reform in China prior to the Hundred Days is found in a series of 12 articles which the newspaper *Chūō shinbun* published in April 1898 under the title 'China after the war' (*Sengo no Shina*). The author, the journalist Kawasaki Shizan (1864–1943), had been stationed in Peking at the beginning of 1898, and the series of articles was the fruit of his observations.[34] Kawasaki later elaborated the parts that concerned the political situation in Peking and republished them in August and September 1898 in the *Taiyō*.[35] Moreover, on 22–24 September 1898, Kawasaki republished a portion in the *Chūō shinbun* under the title 'The situation in China is about to change.'[36] As the *Chūō shinbun* was the metropolitan newspaper with the third largest circulation at the time, and the *Taiyō* the most popular general magazine at the time, Kawasaki's opinions on China reached a wide readership.

In the first three installments of the initial *Chūō* series, Kawasaki described the rise and fall of the Qing imperial government. Although we cannot discuss this in detail, it should be mentioned that Kawasaki here very much relied on an analogy with Japan's history and saw present China in the same state as Bakumatsu Japan. Thus he described the present Qing state as a 'closed and isolated world without relations to foreign countries' (*rekkoku no kankei naki sakoku koritsu no tenka*), whose central power had been weakened through the debilitating effects of a long peace and the snares of Confucianism.[37] Most of the power had gone to the provinces, where the governor-generals ('vice-roys') reigned.[38]

The Bakumatsu parallel was a popular one, as we have seen in the previous discussion of Fukuzawa Yukichi and Kuga Katsunan. Naitō Konan later used it as the standard pattern to describe the reform process in China.[39] The reformer Liang Qichao (1873–1929), even *before* coming to Japan, referred to it as well; it is said that he joined the Hunanese reform movement very much with the model of Satsuma and Chōshū in his mind.[40] However, contrary to most Japanese observers who used the Bakumatsu parallel to demonstrate that China's future, despite its gloomy aspect, was bright, Kawasaki in March 1898 saw *no hope* that China in its present state could reform and survive. He argued that one should not expect the Qing government to revive merely by importing Western material civilization. Some Chinese had said that 'China has been sleeping, but is now awake,' but this only pointed to superficial changes, as 'its spirit is not yet awakened' (*sono seishin wa sametari ni arazu*).[41] The weakness of the Chinese government had its cause not in the weakness of its army, navy or financial policy: 'it is, because the inner functions of the old empire are rotten, its structure and organs are weak, and the governing powers of the Manchu imperial family are already exhausted'.[42]

Kawasaki proceeded to describe the 'inner functions' of the empire in the remaining nine installments of his essay.[43] He identified the following four political factions: the reactionary faction (*shukyū-ha*) of court and government officials, the conservative Hunan-ha, the progressive Anhui-ha, and the 'revolutionary faction' (*kakumei-ha*).[44] It should be mentioned that, even in his discussion of these political factions, Kawasaki relied on the Bakumatsu model, using regional names for the political reform factions and describing them as *kōbu-ha* and *sonjō-ha*.

In his articles, Kawasaki painted a devastating picture of the Chinese political landscape. At the center of his critique stood the 'reactionary faction,' the imperial family and the palace and metropolitan officials, which he depicted in the style of an oriental despot's court. In this context, his portrayal of the empress dowager Cixi is especially interesting. Kawasaki acknowledged Cixi as an able enough person, but of doubtful morality:

> A Western diplomat once praised the empress dowager as 'the most enlightened ruler since the Qianlong emperor [r. 1736–96].' However, for over more than twenty years of her regency on behalf of the Tongzhi and Guangxu emperors,[45] she has secluded herself deep in the inner recesses of the palace, and did no more than rule as regent according to the old statutes. And isn't it a fact that she hasn't met a foreign representative even once? The various talents and accomplishments of the empress dowager: if she takes a brush, delicate landscapes and calligraphy, birds and flowers flow from it. Every day she invites her favorites and, with soft song and slow dance,[46] spends endless nocturnal banquets as she likes. She abuses the donations she receives from her subjects of the capital and the provinces (although, depending on her inclination, she might bestow high offices or academic degrees in return) and squanders them in unrestrained luxury. She is sharp and quick-witted, she is watchful and, deeply distrustful, conceals herself from the people. All this is just in the style of the former Korean Queen Min. And just as the Korean Queen did not have one speck of moral authority among the common people, it is obvious that the empress dowager, too, has no moral authority among her Chinese subjects.[47]

One would think that some of Cixi's alleged predilections (slow dances, nightly Bacchanalians) would befit an infatuated Tang emperor better than a hexagenarian imperial dowager. Obviously, Kawasaki wanted to present the Manchu court as a slough of oriental stagnation, corruption and debauchery, even if this was at the cost of plausibility. In line with this picture, Kawasaki presented the Guangxu emperor as the perfect cliché of the degenerate princeling, a mere imperial presence and a puppet figure of mediocre talents, entirely dependent on the strong will of his formidable aunt, who was the real ruler of China.

Kawasaki's description of the power structure in Peking was, of course, inaccurate on several points. Cixi was not the sole ruler in 1898, and not totally opposed to modernizing reforms, as her subsequent reforms show.[48]

Guangxu was not a mere nonentity; in fact, in 1898 he was at the height of his power, of which the Hundred Days Reform was the expression.[49] Weng Tonghe, who Kawasaki described as an ultra-conservative grey eminence,[50] was certainly not that; in fact, after the Sino–Japanese War, Weng was one of Kang Youwei's patrons (until he withdrew his support at the beginning of 1898). Moreover, Weng's power base was not that unshakeable. After all, in June 1898 the Guangxu emperor dismissed him, with Cixi's approval.[51]

Nonetheless, Kawasaki's descriptions, especially his portrait of Cixi and Guangxu, are interesting, also with respect to the modern historiographical dispute mentioned above. Thus the 'revisionary' school claims that the same images were an invention of Cixi's malicious enemies Kang Youwei and Liang Qichao.[52] However, Kawasaki demonstrates that such images existed well before the Hundred Days.

Equally disconcerting was Kawasaki's analysis of the reform parties, the Anhui-ha (led by Li Hongzhang) and the Hunan-ha (dominated by Zhang Zhidong). He argued that Li Hongzhang's party had the skills for reform, but the disaster of the Sino–Japanese War had caused their fall from power.[53] Moreover, their closeness to Russia had raised distrust among the people of opportunism and corruption (as an illustration, the *Chūō shinbun* carried the news item that Li Hongzhang was being accused of having taken bribes from Russia[54]). Zhang Zhidong's party, on the other hand, was the most popular political group in China at the time. However, its power basis was in the provinces, and its voice was not heard in Beijing, where the 'reactionary' faction insulated the imperial family.[55]

Conspicuously absent from Kawasaki's political landscape was Kang Youwei and his group. In April 1898, Kawasaki provided a list for his readers which ranked more than 80 of China's most important reformers by name and official position.[56] Many high-ranking patrons and supporters of the Kang-Liang group were on it. However, neither Kang Youwei himself nor any of his associates are named. The reason for this may be simple: it has been argued that organized political action in China prior to 1900 concentrated on the bureaucratic community, whose reform-oriented members have been called the 'bureaucratic reform constituency.'[57] Kawasaki's list obviously focused on this important constituency of high-ranking office holders and automatically did not include the members of the Kang-Liang group. The latter held positions (if any) which were much too low to qualify for the 'constituency.' Kang Youwei, for example, held a lowly sinecure position in the Board of Works. The focus on those reformers who did count bureaucratically, in fact, was another setting of the perspective of all Japanese 'China watchers' at the time (and probably, of European ones, as well). This partly explains the prominence of Zhang Zhidong as a reformer in the Japanese press from very early on (the *Chūō shinbun* always paid close attention to Zhang Zhidong's life and opinions[58]) and the fact that Kang Youwei, when he appeared first on the radar of the Japanese press, did so very much as an 'annex' of Zhang Zhidong.[59]

Such was Kawasaki's analysis of the situation in April and late May 1898. A contemporary reader who would trust Kawasaki's authority as China expert would hardly expect a substantial reform in Beijing possible, or at least likely to happen in the near future. However, it should have become apparent that Kawasaki was not altogether objective in his observations. Thus it seems that his sympathies rather sided with revolution instead of reform, and therefore with the fourth political faction, the revolutionists (*kakumei-ha*). He predicted that unless the fundament of government, the structure and organs, were not reorganized (*kaizō*), the Manchu dynasty would not revive. Even if the Qing government was incapable of such changes (which Kawasaki believed), the importing of material civilization had made them inevitable: 'We have to be aware that the progress of these enterprises of civilization [*bunmei-teki jigyō*] will unwittingly produce a revolution of the people's minds [*jinshin kakumei*].'[60] Kawasaki saw it as inevitable that the Chinese would eventually 'overturn' (*keifuku*) the present Manchu-government and erect a new government.

It is therefore not surprising that Kawasaki until the end would not acknowledge a substantial reform movement in China. In 22 September 1898, one day after the end of the Hundred Days (not yet known to Japan), the *Chūō shinbun* published the first installment of another of Kawasaki's analyses, entitled 'The situation in China is about to change.'[61] However, since Kawasaki in the following series of articles analyzed the situation in exactly the same terms as he had done in April, this change obviously had nothing to do with the present situation. One day after the last installment of Kawasaki's analysis, news of the failure of the Hundred Days reached Japan.

Shiga Sukegorō's reports as an eyewitness of the Hundred Days

In spring and summer 1898, Shiga Sukegorō (1864–1918), a writer from Akita,[62] traveled through various parts of China (Beijing, Tianjin, Weihaiwei and parts of Manchuria) and recorded his observations.[63] In the months of May to July, Shiga was in Beijing and witnessed the first days of the Reform. About his impressions, he sent *tokuhō* to the *Tōkyō nichinichi shinbun* and the *Yorozu chōhō*, albeit under different pseudonyms.[64] This might have been necessary, as the two newspapers were of a wholly different (in fact, opposite) temperament and political outlook, and it is obvious that Shiga wrote the *tokuhō* with respect to these differences.

Initially, Shiga seemed to have come to Beijing with some hope for reform. In late May 1898, he reported about the enthusiastic activities of the 'new political societies' and of the censors (some of whom supported Kang Youwei):

> The enthusiasm of the reform party which rises high in the South [Hunan] is fairly evident. In Peking, too, there has been the founding of a Society for the Protection of the Nation [*Baoguohui*]. [...] The

memorials of the censors and others day by day continue to rally like-minded fellows for some purpose. This is all very agreeable. However, it is a pity to see how difficult it is to stem the raging torrents of decline with only one hand.[65]

In June, after the Guangxu emperor had issued the reform edict, Shiga commented the development by paying rather more attention to the reformers than to the edict itself:

The edicts and memorials pouring out daily now are almost invariably of reformatory contents. Especially edicts with passages such as 'The idle talk which, under the pretext of concern for the old and venerable country, noisily claims that one must resolutely preserve the old statutes and reject all new laws, is of no help' [...][66] naturally must make the faction of obstinates [*ganko-tō*] almost lose their mind. Consequently, the faction is not involved in the new measures to summon men who are knowledgeable in current affairs and not tainted by the habits and thereby provide [the state] with chivalrous men [*ninkyō*], and in accepting memorials from all directions with complaints about officials.[67] An edict has been issued to the effect that the emperor today [16 June] will receive Kang Youwei and the secretary in the Board of Rites Zhang Yuanji. A decree has been issued to summon Huang Zunxian, who has been to Japan and is known among Confucian scholars (now, he is salt intendant and judicial commissioner in Hunan). The Zongli yamen, by imperial command, is currently considering whether to employ Liang Qichao of the Shanghai *Shiwubao* (he is now here, being Kang's most brilliant disciple).

Moreover, it is also under deliberation to select and send princes of the imperial family on a study tour throughout the world. In short, it seems that the court is intent to carry out a major reform. But, alas, this is a little bit too late; actually, much too late.[68]

At this point, it should be noted that the more romantic, radically inspired authors of the *Yorozu chōhō* were very much inclined towards heroes and hero worship. Thus, if Shiga indirectly described Kang Youwei and his followers as 'chivalrous men,' this had an especially positive ring in the ears of the *Yorozu chōhō* reader, linking them with the venerable tradition of the Bakumatsu braves who, pure and untainted by petty politics, sacrificed their lives to change the nation. Around the same time, the *Yorozu* published a two-part 'Treatise on the spirit of chivalry' (*Kyōfū-ron*) in which the writer called for a renaissance of morality in all parts of Japan's corrupt society.[69] Moreover, 'chivalry' made the perfect reformer, because it enabled superior decisions and heroic resolve (*eidan*). Also in July 1898, the author of the chivalry article published an article on the new Ōkuma Cabinet entitled 'Reforms need bold decision.'[70]

However, Shiga soon became disillusioned with the political actors in Beijing in general and made it very clear that, although the times were ideal for a hero to appear, no such thing would happen. Thus, in another article only two weeks later, Shiga wrote disparagingly about the history of Chinese reforms:

> When you come to think of it, there are more than one or two instances in the past that the Chinese court has shown indications that it positively wanted to take action, start some new projects, instill a new spirit into the people, do away with bad habits, and start into a new direction altogether. But in some cases they rather made a mess of it, acting out a farcical play in helter-skelter fashion [*mekura meppō no kigeki*]. More-over, if the matter at hand finally passed and the danger gradually rece-ded, as a matter of rule, enthusiasm for reform instantly cooled off, too. One could use the simile of the frog leaving ripples in the water, but, of course, this is unacceptable as a regular policy for managing a state. Even as a cheap comedy [*chaban-teki kyōgen*], it had almost no interest.
>
> Most talk about reforms in the past was like that. And with the pre-sent talk about vigorous action, how should I think that it should be different?[71]

Shiga observed that, now that China's 'deep dreams' of greatness were shat-tered and 'the paralyzed nerves [*mahi seru shinkei*] generally are in a vague state of considerable stimulation and excitement [*shigeki kōfun*],'[72] it would be the ideal opportunity for an 'unusual man' [*hijō no hito*] to reform China 'with true words and deeds which penetrate metal and stone with sublime decision [*tenrai no eidan*].'[73] However, there was no such a hero, on the contrary:

> Most of those in power [in Beijing] cannot avoid being fellows of shal-low knowledge and limited understanding. When it comes to the middle ranks and below, even if in this ignorance and darkness there appeared Sâkyamuni himself, he would have troubles in saving them.[74]

In fact, in the *Yorozu chōhō*, Shiga made it clear that things even had gone from bad to worse *after* the personnel reshuffle that accompanied the begin-ning of the Hundred Days: 'In the times of Prince Gong and Weng Tonghe, there existed at least some action and behavior which looked like central government. But now Wang Wenshao and Sun Jianai, they are like the so-called 'walking dead and marching flesh' [*kōshi sōniku*]'.[75] Shiga, around the middle of July 1898, concluded: 'I am not afraid to state that, otherwise, there is absolutely nobody who is capable to gain the power of the govern-ment and the people, of high and low, and to shoulder the expanse of the 'nine districts of the King of Yu' [China]'.[76] This also applied to Kang Youwei and his followers.

Upon his return from China in September 1898, Shiga presented the fruits of his 'research' on the 'Chinese question' to the readers of the *Yorozu chōhō*.[77] The reforms received only fleeting attention. They appeared now as the somewhat erratic product of a reform-minded emperor who adopted the suggestions of some political 'outsiders':

> The present reform bills were originally not even the results of government planning, but two or three fellows outside government [*sōmō no hai*] have advocated them among the people. By chance, the emperor has adopted them and, wonderfully enough, some of them even have become reality.[78]

In Shiga's description, the Guangxu emperor seemed now completely isolated. If Shiga had scathingly criticized the government before, it was now the turn of the 'outsiders.' As 'item five' of his research results, Shiga stated:

> It is a scandal that the morale is so low. There is that person Kang Youwei. He is the leader of the reform-party. Conversations with him are lively and quite enjoyable. Among his disciples there is Liang Qichao, who has a singular perception of current events. [But] I have met the two often and come to understand that they are not the gentlemen of such great promise [as they profess to be].[79] To begin with, as Kang is being attacked from all sides, he has realized that he cannot bear it. He quietly has decided on the strategy to move south and thereby avoid the strikes of the enemy party.[80] He is planning to depart, but has not, yet. By chance he was summoned to the emperor, and that changed his life. In fact, this was due to the patronage of the censor Yang Shenxiu.[81] To sacrifice one's life for the affairs of the state [*mi o motte kokuji ni junzuru*] has always been a thing which a Chinese would never dream of. Thus, Kang Youwei to eighty or ninety percent is just someone who gathers the spittle of Westerners and takes delight in his own mindless chatter. And Liang Qichao, after all he is just some literary fellow, and it is not hard to see that the others are much of the same kind.[82]

Shiga's unusually harsh critique may be the result of personal disappointment. However, it should be noted that the critique he leveled against Kang essentially was the same which Kang had to suffer from his opponents in Beijing or in the Shanghai press, that Kang was a rhetorically brilliant, but vainglorious and irresponsible careerist who sought office through undue (and illegal) support of the censors, who were supposed to be impartial.[83] Moreover, Shiga was not alone in Japan in his negative assessment of Kang's personality. For example, Naitō Konan, Shiga's fellow editor at the *Yorozu chōhō*, shared his view of Kang, although he was impressed with Liang Qichao;[84] and the *Hōchi shinbun* criticized Kang, too, albeit not in such scathing terms.[85] The *Nippon-jin*, which was closely associated with the

Tōa-kai, initially showed much sympathy toward the reformers; however, this too changed when the Tōa-kai's successor Tōa dōbun-kai desperately tried to distance itself from the Kang-Liang group.[86]

Thus Kang was neither well known, nor, if known, necessarily well liked by the Japanese public. Ironically, it was the *failure* of the Hundred Days Reform which made him widely known, and through which he finally assumed a leading role independent of Zhang Zhidong in the Japanese eyes. Shiga's last critique of Kang appeared on the day when news of the failure reached Japan (25 September 1898) and on a page of the *Yorozu chōhō* bearing a portrait of Kang (after a photo taken in Shanghai) with the superscription 'The leader of the Chinese reform party, Kang Youwei.'[87] This status became gradually acknowledged by all newspapers in Japan, even before Kang reached Japanese soil.

At the beginning of this chapter, it was mentioned that 'revisionist' studies questioned Kang's role in the Hundred Days, arguing that Kang's contribution had been grossly overestimated in previous studies, and that much of this was due to Kang's and Liang Qichao's own fabrications after their flight to Japan.[88] This must be qualified in the light of the above. In fact, the reason why Kang was catapulted into his position of leadership in the Japanese press (and in the international press in general) even *before* Kang came to Japan was the fact that the Empress Dowager put six of Kang's associates to death, issued a warrant of arrest for Kang the day he fled, and pursued him mercilessly ever after, even more eagerly than the Qing government pursued Sun Yat-Sen (1866–1925).[89] Thus it seems that, ironically, it was Cixi who created Kang's high reputation abroad first (much as the Qing government had done in Sun Yat-Sen's case). That Kang sustained his role by later statements (whether exaggerated or not) is, however, an altogether different matter.

The relative speed of progress: Chinese time and Japanese time

Considering the fact that in April and May 1898, prior to the beginning of the Reform, many Japanese observers professed their hope that China would reform along Japanese lines, the indifference or even negative view of the heavily Japan-oriented Hundred Days needs some explanation. We would argue that, most likely, the same observers were also of the opinion that China could and *should* not reform too fast and without direct Japanese guidance (and control), and this opinion translated itself into a theory of the relative speed of Chinese and Japanese progress. This theory, in turn, precluded more active support among the Japanese majority for drastic change in China.

As we have seen in the previous chapters, Japanese attitudes toward China were ambivalent before the Sino–Japanese War and remained so until at least 1898, when the encroachment of the Western powers, and also particularly the repeated incidents of social unrest in China and the spectacular failure of the Hundred Days, changed the Japanese public's attitude towards China. Until then, the public eyed China warily with a mixture of pride and fear. Pride derived from the conviction (or dogma) that Japan, now that it had proved its valour in the war, was on a completely different level of development than China. Thus almost every newspaper defined Japan's position as singular in East Asia: for example, Japan was the 'pioneer in East Asia' (*Tōyō no senkusha*) or the 'steering wheel in East Asia' (*Tōyō no kaji*) – in short, a fully modernized state. China, on the other hand, was viewed as being still caught in a Bakumatsu situation, which meant that the international conditions were inductive for reform, but the domestic situation still had to develop. Thus the ideological difference between China and Japan was, speaking plainly, one between the dark Middle Ages and enlightened modernity. The *Nippon*, as late as September 1898, stressed the fundamental difference with the following words:

> In ancient times, the Chinese were more advanced in the sciences than our country. It has taken a while for our national polity to surpass China, and for our learning to earn the reputation of surpassing the teacher. In the sciences and in moral teachings, we have actually made China our teacher for almost two thousand years. Therefore, we certainly cannot say that our indebtedness to the Chinese in cultural terms is small. However, since the opening of our country, our country has actively adopted the sciences of the West, and just as it was in the case of the Chinese sciences in the old times, by now we have drawn even [with the West]. If we look back to the Chinese, they still stubbornly cling to their old views, exactly like the [proverbial] Meng from Wu [*Go-ka no A-Mō*].[90] However, as a result, we and they are in completely different positions, our relative strength is wide apart, and our fortunes are not the same.[91]

On the other hand, even after the Sino–Japanese War there remained a residue of lingering fear that the difference between China and Japan was not that fundamental and still could be bridged. As we have seen, foreign observers such as Alfred T. Mahan believed that China, despite its defeat, still had a high degree of military potential (not to speak of China's skills in outmanoeuvring Japan diplomatically), and even such a recalcitrant China skeptic as Fukuzawa Yukichi was inclined to see indications of this at the beginning of 1898 (see Chapter 2). Thus it was not unlikely that China, at some point in time, would revive and resume its course of progress.

This ambivalence translated itself into a theory of the different paces of progress of China and Japan. Many Japanese in the late Meiji period felt themselves as part of an 'accelerated generation.' It is not a mere accident that the train and the telegraph, those accelerating 'tools of civilization' (*bunmei no riki*), became the two most often-depicted emblems of progress in Japan in literature and the arts. Already during the Sino–Japanese War, foreign observers grudgingly acknowledged that '[w]hat Japan has accomplished in less than half a century – we might almost say within a quarter of a century – it has taken other countries many whole centuries to perform.'[92] Similarly, the European opinion that Japan, in 25 years, had made the progress of many Western centuries was proudly published in Japan.[93] Moreover, in 1898 the consciousness of the rapid progress of Japan since the Meiji Restoration was even more accentuated by the celebrations of the tri-decennial of the transfer of the capital (*tento*) to Tokyo (3 September 1868), an act that visibly marked the beginning of Japan's modern times. Many newspapers and magazines such as the *Taiyō* devoted whole sections of special issues to the happy event, with long overviews of the rapid progress in the past 30 years.[94]

Of course, the speed of Japan's progress also had its price, and led to symptoms of exhaustion. Natsume Sōseki, at the end of the Meiji era, in a famous speech on the 'civilization of present Japan', argued that with the stimulus (*shigeki*) of centuries of European development compressed into 50 Japanese years, the only thing that could be done was to keep Japan's speed of development at a certain level so as not to suffer from complete nervous exhaustion (*shinkei suijaku*).[95] However, despite this criticism of Japan's sore state, no-one would have denied that Japan's accelerated progress gave an unquestionable advantage in international competition, especially over China.

China had its own speed of progress, due to its size and mass of population.[96] Thus, in the *Marumaru chinbun* caricature of 1879 of the 'Walking Match of Civilization' (see Chapter 1), the spectators jeer at the slower competitor China with the words: 'His body is so big, he cannot walk at all, that's why he's been made fun of. Look at that, what a strange, piggy way [*butabuta to oka-Shina fū*] of walking!'[97] In March 1898, Fukuzawa wrote about China's natural inertia thus:

> If we look at those [Chinese] people in their everyday appearance, they may seem inert and lacking a certain spirit of sprightliness [*kappatsu no kifū*]. However, this is but for the reason that their country is big and not easily sets itself into motion. Once it has started moving, there will be, unexpectedly, quite astonishing things to happen. Therefore we must absolutely not view them as passive or procrastinating.[98]

Finally, Kuga Katsunan a month later explained the fact that Japan had reacted to 'foreign stimulation' long ago and swiftly, but China only recently and slowly, with the theory:

> Unfortunately, what with China's huge size, it is extremely slow in reacting to these threats and invitations. Maybe it is because its population is ten times bigger than ours that China needs almost a hundred years to react for what we need only ten years.[99]

The relative speed of reacting to the outer 'stimuli' (wars and foreign pressure), of course, made the gap between China and Japan ever-widening. For every one step China made in the 'walking match,' the theory said, Japan made ten steps.

Of course, some Chinese saw it exactly the other way round. Kang Youwei, for example, when persuading the Guangxu emperor to adopt the Japanese model, argued that China, due to its manpower and resources, could do in three years what Japan had done in 30 (and Europe in 300 years since the Middle Ages).[100] Thus Kang Youwei claimed that, if China made only three big steps (or should we call it a 'Great Leap Forward'), it could draw even with Japan.[101]

However, this is not what the Japanese observers expected or wished for in 1898. Comments in Japan on the Hundred Days are laced with insinuations and explicit verdicts that China could not (and should not) reform at a faster pace than was natural to China. Kawasaki Shizan only reluctantly acknowledged the Reform with the argument that this was only the sign of a *coming* reform in the future, that there was no reform *yet*; Shiga commented on the 'helter-skelter' fashion of some Chinese reform endeavors; and more succinctly, Konoe Atsumaro told Kang Youwei, when they met in November 1898, that the main reason why the Reform had faltered was because it had been too drastic, and should have been much more gradual:

> About the news since this spring of your emperor convening brilliant people in great numbers and carrying out reforms on all levels, I was happy, but at the same time worried. I was happy, of course, for your country that it was moving towards progress and enlightenment. But why was I worried? Because I was afraid that this reform might be too sudden and fail. Our Meiji Restoration has certainly not been carried out in merely two or three years. It has been long in the making and was the result of the sacrifice of many lives and the suffering of many changes. Your country in the present case is, in comparison to our Restoration, only in the beginning stage. Not to speak of the fact that the rashness of the reforms since this spring has deemed us as extremely dangerous, as your country, although it has international contact longer than we do, is of a conservative disposition [*hoshu-teki kokujō*] which still preserves the old state of things unchanged [*kyūtai o son suru*]. The present case, as I already said, is but one failure in reforms, and one certainly must not lose hope. However, for the future, I very much hope that you learn from the past and will adopt a much more gradual policy.[102]

Thus Konoe taught Kang Youwei about the right pace to reform China. Not surprisingly, the above attitude was also common to Konoe's Asianist society Dōbun-kai and to the majority of its successor's (the Tōa dōbun-kai's) members.[103] Shiraiwa Ryūhei (1870–1942), for example, China entrepreneur and key co-founder of the Dōbun-kai, from early on disliked the 'radical' reformers of low or no rank at all around Kang Youwei and favored the more gradualist Zhang Zhidong and his aide Wang Kangnian (1860–1911).[104] This attitude also facilitated the Tōa dōbunkai's severing its tenuous ties with the Kang-Liang group, when these began to endanger Japan's relations with the Chinese court and Zhang Zhidong.

However, it should be stressed again that this attitude itself was hardly exceptional, but rather was common sense, not only in Japan but also among European observers (not to speak of the Cixi-friendly Chinese press). The *Japan Mail* observed in October: 'It is believed in Peking that the Legations [in Beijing] had not much sympathy with Kang Yü-wei [*sic*] and the other reformers. They regarded Kang as a visionary who was hurrying the emperor along much too fast […].'[105] European newspapers, too, commented after the fact at the rashness and amateurishness of the reforms, albeit with much more open glee and *déja vu* than the Japanese papers.[106]

However, the parallel with Western opinion is even more revealing in a diachronic way. In fact, Konoe's exhortations towards Kang Youwei in 1898 strongly echo the opinion which the expert on social and political development at the time, Herbert Spencer himself, had voiced on Japan's development prior to the Sino–Japanese War. When Spencer, some time before 1890, was asked for counsel, he advised that political change in Japan should not be swift and radical, but slow and gradual. However, in 1892, after the pro-mulgation of the Constitution, Spencer was dissatisfied about its radical elements and the fact that his advice had not been heeded, and wrote to the politician Kaneko Kentarō:

> Probably you remember I told you that when Mr. Mori [Arinori], the then Japanese Ambassador, submitted to me his draft for a Japanese Constitution, I gave him very conservative advice, contending that it was impossible that the Japanese, hitherto unaccustomed to despotic rule, should, all at once, become capable of constitutional government.
>
> My advice was not, I fear, duly regarded, and so far as I gather from the recent reports of Japanese affairs, you are experiencing the evils arising from too large an installment of freedom.[107]

One wonders whether Spencer's skepticism, or that of Western commentators on Japan's progress in general, was not motivated by a similar ambivalence as Japanese skepticism towards Chinese reforms.[108] The respective reactions – the rise of anti-Japanese propaganda in the West after the Sino-Japanese War and, even more so, after the Russo–Japanese War, which proved that Japan's progress had been real; and the rise of 'friendship' towards China after the failure of the Hundred Days, which demonstrated that China's independent progress was a failure – point in the same direction.

Whatever the reasons, Spencer gave 'very conservative advice' to the Japanese, and so did Konoe Atsumaro to Kang Youwei. Despite Konoe's familiar critique that China was 'of a conservative disposition which still retains its old form,' it was the Japanese who had the much more conservative opinions about development in China.

Domestic parallels: a Second Meiji Restoration or a second Spain?

Finally, a similarly conservative bias also worked in Japanese domestic politics and let a rapid and radical political change appear to many political observers, despite protestations to the contrary, not only impossible, but also eventually undesirable. If the same observers did not think a 'Second Meiji Restoration' likely in Japan, how much less would they assume such an event possible in China?

At exactly the same time as China had its reform modeled after the Meiji Restoration, there occurred a 'Second Meiji Restoration' (*dai-ni ishin*) in Japan, or so some thought. In June 1898, the Itō Cabinet faltered, which gave sudden and unexpected rise to the cabinet formed by Ōkuma Shigenobu and Itagaki Taisuke, the informal heads of the new Kenseitō. The cabinet was formed largely by party members, and thus was almost a party cabinet. The dream of a 'responsible cabinet' (*sekinin naikaku*), which had been pursued by the parties at least since 1890, finally seemed to come true. However, the experiment failed utterly, and the Kenseitō Cabinet dissolved in late October 1898, deranged by the lack of support from (or even obstruction by) the emperor, the *genrō*, and the administration, and undermined by internal strife and jealousies. The 'Second Meiji Restoration' lasted little longer than the Hundred Days, and ended as miserably. And we see at work in the Japanese case the same pessimistic bias as observed in the case of the Hundred Days: apart from partisan Kenseitō papers, almost all newspapers right from the start showed the uneasy feeling that the new political development came too early, was too rash, and was not led by the right people. When the Kenseitō Cabinet faltered, there was as little surprise as when the Hundred Days failed.

During the time of transition, when the Itō Cabinet staggered and failed and the news of the new Kenseitō Cabinet was not yet out, the opposition papers thought the succession of a party cabinet unlikely in the near future, but an inevitable development in the indefinite future.[109] Thus the *Yorozu chōhō* hoped for a party cabinet after an indefinite time of protracted fighting and struggles:

> The *Kensei-to* which has appeared at such a time, is sure to win unparalleled popularity, and already a great party will become greater and greater as time goes on and the Clan Ministry heaps blunders upon blunders. A time will surely come, when the clannish statesmen find the opposition too strong for them to resist and are forced to hand over the reins of office to the champions of the people. But will that time come soon?[110]

For most, the time came too soon. As little as two days after the above article appeared, on 27 June 1898, the emperor ordered Ōkuma and Itagaki to form the new cabinet. Two weeks later, the *Japan Weekly Mail* observed about the general mood: 'It is a curious fact that the present Cabinet, though it rode into power on the crest of a wave of popular approval, is conspicuously without newspaper supporters. We can not recall any instance of a Ministry so lacking in defenders.'[111]

As was to be expected, the *Tōkyō nichinichi shinbun* bitterly opposed the Ōkuma Cabinet on grounds of principle. Its chief editor, Asahina Chisen, in a long essay in June 1898, laid out his arguments against party rule.[112] In general, parties bred the pursuit of self-interest, and self-interest ran counter to the interests of the state. Moreover, no party in Japan today yet possessed the qualifications to rule. Leaders of a ruling party needed trust (of the genrō, the administration and the leading intellectuals) and power (in the Diet, in the administration and in their own party). British parties may fulfill these conditions, and Prussian parties, too, to some extent, but these had a long history. The Japanese parties, even though they tried to wear the outer vestiges of British parties, failed utterly and merely put up 'an ape's imitation of humans, an amateur's village play' (*saru no hitomane, shiroto no mura-shibai*). Thus Asahina took recourse to the familiar argument that political progress in Japan (as in China) must be gradual in order to be substantial, and that the Japanese parties were not yet ready. As the *Tōkyō nichinichi shinbun* rejected the notion that the time for a 'responsible cabinet' had come, the paper also vehemently attacked the 'pernicious opinion' of more ardent Kenseitō-supporters that a 'Second Restoration' had come.[113]

The *Chūō shinbun* took a similar position, and asked his readers before the regular start of the Ōkuma Cabinet: 'Is the new cabinet an irresponsible cabinet?'[114] However, to the *Chūō* this was a rhetorical question. The *Chūō* saw early proof of irresponsibility in the fighting by party members for government office (the so-called 'office-hunting fever,' *ryokan-netsu*). The paper gleefully registered every new appointment in an 'Office-Hunting Chronicle' (*Ryokan-roku*), and dubbed the new cabinet a 'party-clan cabinet' (*tōbatsu naikaku*).[115]

The *Jiji shinpō* was one of the few newspapers that adapted swiftly to the new circumstances, very much in harmony with its credo to follow the power wherever it went. Thus, the newspaper soon withdrew its support of *hanbatsu* rule and accepted party rule as the new paradigm of the time. Fukuzawa typically argued that the founding of the state rested on real power. Rule was not possible without real power. The Tokugawa had demonstrated this principle, and now the *hanbatsu* politicians again. *Hanbatsu* rule had worked for some time to uphold political power and maintain public order. However, since the opening of the Diet, the political situation had gradually changed and now indicated that politics in future would be decided by popular vote.[116] Likewise, when the Ōkuma Cabinet fell, the *Jiji shinpō* shifted its allegiance back towards the *hanbatsu*-cabinet of Yamagata Aritomo as the new site of power, an act that, in the eyes of the more principled *Tōkyō nichinichi shinbun*, was like committing 'political suicide.'[117]

The *Nippon*, too, hailed the imminent demise of the Itō Cabinet as a time when the 'delusions' (*meimu*) of *hanbatsu* rule would be dispelled. To step up the pressure (or, as he had formulated it in the case of China, to increase the 'stimulus'), Kuga Katsunan called for a 'concert of powers' against the *hanbatsu* (much in the same way as he had called upon the civilized powers to 'stimulate' and pressure the recalcitrant government in China into reform).[118] However, once the Kenseitō had acceded to power, the *Nippon*, too, became skeptical about the 'Second Restoration.' Miyake Setsurei, for example, warned:

> Remember the First Restoration!
> You consider the overthrow of the *hanbatsu* as a Second Restoration, and you consider the formation of the Kenseitō Cabinet as the result of the overthrow of the *hanbatsu*? Fine, granted! But I want to warn our honorable ministers of this: Remember the first Restoration!
> History, in a sense, is something which repeats itself, and the origin of the name Second Restoration may lie in similarities with the first Restoration. Consequently, we cannot deny that one can draw analogies between the one process and the other. Mr. Ōkuma himself won an illustrious position in the first Restoration and will very well remember the real situation at the time. Now, if we give it a try and read the tales of the old times, there were probably two points which were considered as problematic in the Restoration, and those were: the demands for offices, and the conflict with colleagues.[119]

Miyake reflected on the personnel reshuffle that accompanied the cabinet change and the predictable jealousies and internal conflicts with anticipation (much in the same way as the personnel reshuffle in China was eyed with wariness).

The *Yorozu chōhō*, too, was skeptical. However, with its usual emphasis on individual morality and political rectitude, it saw the problem of the Ōkuma Cabinet more in the fact that its members were only of mediocre talent and, in times of danger and crisis, were not fit to save the country: 'Unless the men who come in power should be possessed of extraordinary talent, they would soon feel the burden too heavy for them to bear.' Ōkuma, Itagaki and the other leading members of the Kensei-to clearly did not possess those qualities.[120] Most of all, real, effective reforms needed 'exceptional decision' (*dai-eidan*), otherwise the law of gravity would pull the fledgling reformers into the same quagmire which they had set out to purge. However, the *Yorozu* feared that Ōkuma and his men lacked such decision.[121] Thus the same qualities that Shiga Sukegorō in the *Yorozu chōhō* professed to miss in China, the other writers of the *Yorozu chōhō* missed in Japan. In neither place there were 'unusual' (*hijō no hito*) or 'chivalrous' men (*ninkyō*) of 'exceptional talent' who, with great decision, would save the country.

The above should suffice to demonstrate that there existed considerable parallels in the Japanese perspective of simultaneous events in Japan and China, which in part may have (unconsciously) reinforced the Chinese perspective. After all, if everybody felt that the 'Second Restoration' in Japan was not a real one, how much less so could a 'first restoration' be in China? Yet it is revealing that, despite the parallels, such conscious comparisons were never drawn. This again stresses the unbridgeable gap which the late Meiji contemporaries must have felt (or wanted to see) between China and Japan. Even when it came to political stagnation and disintegration, the point of reference for Japan invariably would be Europe, not China. During the Ōkuma Cabinet, Japan's situation was readily compared with that of Spain or Italy. The military disaster of the Spanish-American war had greatly destabilized domestic politics in Spain, and Spanish domestic politics became a subject in Japan as well. Two weeks after the Ōkuma Cabinet came into power, the *Yorozu* published a letter by the historian and politician Takekoshi Yosaburō (1865–1950), who had just lost his position as a vice-minister in the previous Itō Cabinet.[122] In the letter, Takekoshi drew the attention of the readers to an article in the British monthly *The Contemporary Review*, in which the author attributed the cause for the ruin of Spain' to the 'office-hunting fever' of politicians (and 'idle talk,' *kūron*). Takekoshi observed that he was so struck with the similarities that he almost thought the author must have had known Japan's situation beforehand.[123] Two days after the letter appeared, the *Yorozu* announced to its readers that the Spanish Cabinet had resigned.[124] Takayama Chogyū in the *Taiyō* protested against 'absurd comparisons between Japan and Spain.'[125] However, even the cautious *Tōkyō nichinichi shinbun* declared in early September that Japan showed signs of 'ruin' (*bōkoku*) similar to those shown by Spain.[126]

The revolutionary situation in Italy, too, forebode (or promised) similar developments in Japan. The English section of the *Yorozu chōhō* observed that dissatisfaction in Italy was so widespread that revolution was threatening and riots were rampant:

> A still greater disaster would follow the heels of the riots and sweep over the whole country, unless a radical reform were not speedily introduced into her administrative system, which is in a most corrupted state.
>
> Fortunately, Japan's condition is not as yet so deplorable as Italy's, but it would be foolish to dream that she is quite free from any impending danger. To the far-seeing, there are manifest many a sign of an approaching revolution. It is a very significant fact that there are among the young and educated class many who are almost desperate as to the future prospect of this country and think and discuss quite freely that nothing but fire and blood would purify the country from her corrupted and dissolute state. In the government, in the society, in the commercial field, in the religious circle, in short, anywhere and everywhere, one is dismayed to find evils and vices rampant and spreading apace. Were this

state of things to go on, surely a revolution would come in no distant future.

[…] It will be seen on reading the above that there are many striking similarities between the condition of this our country and of the diseased European kingdom. We pray that Japan's statesmen would take warning from the sad example by [*sic*] Italy.[127]

Kawasaki Shizan had found similar revolutionary conditions in China. However, these were never adduced to reflect on Japan. Thus, if Japan would sink into chaos, it would do so in the European style.

The Ōkuma Cabinet, of course, did not lead to chaos or destruction, but soon gave way to the Yamagata Cabinet in November 1898. Of this, even the *Yorozu chōhō* was glad. Thus in November Kōtoku Shūsui welcomed the Yamagata Cabinet (Katsunan's 'saber cabinet') with the words:

It is being said that this cabinet is a so-called nonpartisan cabinet [*chōzen naikaku*] which ignores the parties. We fully agree with that, and in this point we must greatly welcome the Yamagata Cabinet.

Of course we fervently pray that the Japanese people will establish a true party cabinet, a truly responsible cabinet which will crown constitutional government. Unfortunately, the parties of today have absolutely not the qualification of a party and there is not a speck of responsibility in the party members of today. […][128]

Thus the radical *Yorozu chōhō* eventually came round to share the opinion of the ultra-conservative *Tōkyō nichinichi* – a rare sight – that Japan was not yet fit for party rule. In January 1898, the *Tōkyō Asahi* even called into question whether Japan was fit for constitutional government at all and thereby set the erstwhile record, as the *Japan Weekly Mail* observed.[129] Again, the parallels are unmistakable: for China, everybody hoped that the country would reform, but when the Hundred Days in late September 1898 faltered, nobody was surprised. For Japan, many wished for a 'responsible' party cabinet, but when the Ōkuma Cabinet faltered, most were elated and welcomed Yamagata. Thus in a sense the Hundred Days and the three months of party reign elicited a structurally common, if not conscious psychological reflex among the Japanese public. And just as the fall of the party cabinet did not lead to chaos and destruction, the end of the Hundred Days did not lead to the end of the Sino–Japanese rapprochement, but on the contrary, elicited even more accentuated professions of friendship on the Japanese side, as we shall see presently.

The government's stance: Itō Hirobumi's journey to Beijing

There has always been the romantic notion that the Kenseitō Cabinet during its short spell of power especially supported the Reform in China, as a sort of support between kindred spirits.[130] However, recent scholarship has observed, with some surprise, that there was no such support and that the Ōkuma Cabinet remained rather distant towards the Reform while it lasted.[131] In fact, as far as the short period allows for reasonable judgment, Ōkuma very much followed in the tracks of his predecessor and especially adhered to Itō's policy of neutrality in East Asian matters.[132] Thus, contrary to the lofty spirit which his party fellows professed while being in opposition, Ōkuma, for example, rejected any demands of assisting the Philippine revolutionary movement as 'idle fantasies' (*kūsō*).[133] However, this merely testifies to the fact that oppositional foreign politics in Meiji Japan was as much a matter of domestic politics, and that in office other rules and exigencies applied.

The continuities of Meiji official foreign politics in the matters of Chinese reform can be best observed in the famous instance of Itō Hirobumi's journey to Beijing and meeting of the Guangxu emperor on the very last of the Hundred Days.[134] Itō's resignation as prime minister and the subsequent Kenseitō intermezzo gave Itō a brief respite and enabled him to pursue plans of his own, one of which was an extended tour through Korea and China. We do not know for sure what the specific aims of the tour were, for several reasons, one of which was that the tour was cut short by the Kenseitō debacle, which made Itō hasten back to Tokyo at the beginning of November 1898 (albeit too late to participate in the domestic power struggle). Moreover, Itō would not tell, but simply declared the journey a pleasure tour (*man'yū*) which, considering the fact that he was an impassioned *kanshi* aficionado who wanted to see the poetic places for himself, may have been partly true.[135] On the other hand, since Itō planned to visit the newly opened ports in the Yangtze region and then travel southwards to Fujian, and since he delivered two speeches on the economic situation in China after having returned to Japan, the simple 'pleasure tour' may also have had the purpose of studying the situation in China and making a survey of Japan's possibilities of economic expansion in China, much in the same way as the British did at the time.[136]

Itō's understating the purposes of his tour may have had also different reasons. For one, as could be imagined, the visit of such an illustrious personage attracted the attention of the world and gave rise to all sorts of rumors, especially of secret negotiations for a military alliance between China and Japan. Such rumors could be heard in Japan and China as well, but characteristically seem to have come from a Western source picked up from among Reuters' flotsam of 'information.'[137]

Moreover, an important source which previous scholarship has failed to make use of enables us to understand better Itō's situation and demeanor in Beijing. Itō was accompanied by the politician and newspaper-owner Ōoka Ikuzō, who sent back minute accounts of the journey's progress to his newspaper *Chūō shinbun*. These accounts show Itō confronted with a deeply entrenched debate in Beijing on how to conduct reforms, the participants in which sought to exploit Itō's reputation as architect of the Meiji state for their own purposes. True to his policy, which at the same time was the official policy, Itō remained neutral and distant.

That Itō (and the Japanese government) did not positively seek contact with the Hundred Days reformers is not surprising, considering their reputation as seen above. More surprising is the bustle of activities to rescue the same reformers after Cixi's coup d'état, in which Itō cooperated with Ōkuma. However, again Ōoka's reports reveal that this was due less to sympathy with the reformers than to compliance with the international 'standard' to which Japan as the 'single civilized country' in the East felt itself to be bound.

The reluctant advisor: Itō's experience of the Hundred Days

Itō's little entourage met a seemingly enthusiastic welcome in China. The party arrived in Tianjin on 11 September 1898, and was welcomed by Ronglu (1836–1903), the newly appointed governor-general of Zhili and commander-in-chief of the three Beiyang armies. Ōoka described the spirit of the welcome thus:

> How eager China is in its reform one might guess even from the one detail of how Marquis Itō is being treated. The way everybody here, officials and the people, welcomes Marquis Itō, goes beyond the imagination of my countrymen. […] They view Marquis Itō as if he was the savior of East Asia [*Tōa no kyūseishu*], and it is being said that everybody, beginning with the Emperor and, of course, the reform party, but even the conservative faction [*shukyūha*] are impatiently awaiting Marquis Itō's coming to the capital, wanting to ask him whether in reforms, too, there should be some order [*kaikaku ni mo junjo aru beshi*].[138]

On the day following the arrival, Ronglu gave a banquet for his guests. Ōoka observed among the guests some former 'enemies,' namely Nie Shicheng, a famous army commander in the Sino–Japanese War, and also Yuan Shikai, former Korean Resident and now commander of the 'Newly Organized Army' at Tianjin. Little did the Japanese guests know that Ronglu and Yuan Shikai, barely more than a week after the banquet, would become the two key figures in ending the Hundred Days Reform abruptly by ousting the reformers. Instead, Ōoka described the banquet as bathed in the spirit of friendship and goodwill:

> Now, high and low are greatly excited and vent the opinion that a change of the political system and reforms is the best way to achieve wealth and power. As a result, there are many debaters who insist on learning from the precedents of our Restoration and the reforms and eagerly worship Japan. Among them, there are even some who petition that the Chinese emperor visit Japan. Thus, one never sees anyone who voices resentment about the past. They fervently praise the prescience of

Japan and applaud the sagacity of Marquis Itō. There are some who have already memorialized to the Commander-in-Chief [Ronglu], saying that one should ask Itō about political change and reform and then establish its method and order, or that one should memorialize to the Throne to invite Marquis Itō and make him advisor, etc.[139] However, Ronglu does not wait for such propositions and over and over again eagerly begs Marquis Itō to teach him. Yet, he does not adopt the proposition to make Marquis Itō an advisor, as this would be offensive to Marquis Itō.[140]

In contrast to this exuberant spirit, Itō's reactions seem rather cool. The frequent questions about the 'good order' (this question turns up on Ōoka's report in an almost formulaic manner[141]) obviously pointed at the entrenched domestic political debate about how to reform China, and Itō clearly did not want to meddle in this. When, on 14 September 1898, Itō met Prince Gong and three other ministers in Beijing,[142] Ōoka observed Itō's reaction to the standard question as to the 'order of priority' in reforms as follows:

> At this, Itō very much suppressed his usually boisterous ways [*tokui no chōshi o osaete*], assumed an extremely reserved manner and merely answered on the main points.[143]

The ministers kept questioning, but Itō did not venture any more detailed comments on the point.

The formal highlight of Itō's visit in Beijing was the audience with the Guangxu emperor on 20 September 1898. Ōoka left a minute report of this which, literally, went around the world.[144] However, considering the anticipation of the event, and the pomp and circumstance that accompanied it, the meeting itself was strangely anti-climactic. The audience lasted only 15 minutes,[145] and the recorded conversation between the emperor and Itō consisted of an exchange of pleasantries bordering on the meaningless. This may have been unexpected as, merely two weeks earlier, the emperor had sent two of his ministers to the acting Japanese minister Hayashi Gonsuke (who was present at Itō's audience) to solicit a close cooperation with Japan.[146] However, we know that a day before the audience took place, the Empress Dowager had returned to the Forbidden City, presumably, as Luke S. Kwong put it, 'to ensure that Kuang-hsu's meeting with Itō the next day would occasion nothing more than an exchange of kind wishes,'[147] and so it did. Ōoka, too, writes about a rumor that the Empress Dowager had been worried about the recent reforms and had secretly listened behind the curtains during Itō's audience.[148] It has been observed that the Guangxu emperor usually seemed fearful and inarticulate in Cixi's presence,[149] which matches with the impression Ōoka's record of the audience gives.

Just as Itō remained reserved towards the bureaucratic constituency of the reforms, he behaved neutrally towards the Kang-Liang group. Presumably on the afternoon following the audience (20 September), Itō also met Kang Youwei at the Japanese embassy.[150] The meeting must have been a brief one, too, as Kang Youwei was leaving Beijing that evening. Kang's 'Autobiography' thus devotes merely a fleeting reference to the meeting.[151] Itō himself, in his speeches and letters, never acknowledged having met Kang. Already on Itō's arrival, a member of the Japanese embassy had warned him about Kang, that he was 'frivolous' and a 'troublemaker,'[152] which was, as we have seen, the general opinion of the diplomatic corps in Beijing. Five days after Cixi's return to power, Itō reported the events back home, but conspicuously made no mention of Kang:

> However, on the twenty-first there was suddenly a political change [*seihen*]. It is being said that the present emperor was too reform-minded and that the preparations to copy everything from Japan even to the extent of changing the dress to Western style came to the ears of the Empress Dowager and greatly displeased her. Another explanation is that there had been a plot of ousting the Empress Dowager. However, which of these is true one really does not know in China.[153]

Ōoka did comment upon the reformers, but he, too, viewed them ambivalently as hot-headed radicals who pursued (too) drastic changes:

> Generally speaking, it is acknowledged by many people that the present political change was a reaction to the reforms. However, starting with Kang Youwei, who is publicly acknowledged in China and abroad as the leader of the reforms, as well as Tan Sitong, Yang Rui, Liu Guangdi, and Lin Xu, who were his disciples and were always close to the emperor, all of them are hot-headed men in their prime, full of a curious eagerness to push things forward. I have also met his most brilliant disciple Liang Qichao. Most of them are not conversant in any Western language. But because of the same writing they understand Japanese literature and read about history. Especially the proceedings of our Restoration they know by heart and eagerly strive to learn from it. That is, to cite only the essential points which provoked the present uproar, these were:
>
> - the cutting of the pigtails
> - the change of Manchu dress into Western dress
> - the moving of the capital to central China.
> - the abolishment of the Manchu White Banner rank
> - the ousting of the Empress Dowager.[154]

Thus, apart from a certain spiritual closeness to Japan, there was nothing – apart from their sympathies towards Japan rather than Russia – which commended the reformers into the special care of Itō and the Japanese government. And yet, Japan actively worked for their rescue.

The duty of a civilized country: Japan's rescue of the reformers

All the reformers who Ōoka mentioned above, except Kang and Liang, were summarily executed on 28 September 1898.[155] That Kang and Liang and other reformers could escape or were saved was, in no small measure, due to cooperation between the British and Japanese authorities.[156] Kang, with British assistance, arrived on 29 September in Hong Kong, where he stayed at the British police barracks until he moved on to Japan. Liang Qichao, on 21 September 1898, took refuge at the Japanese Legation and asked for protection (Ōoka presumably met him there). The acting minister in Beijing, Hayashi, cabled to Ōkuma that, fearing that Liang Qichao's presence might 'create suspicion on the part of China' and give offence to the Chinese government, he had advised Liang to leave Beijing the next day.[157] Liang cut off his tail, put on a European dress and, escorted by the Japanese consul Tei Nagamasa, left Beijing. Under the protection of Japanese warships, he and the reformer Wang Zhao were taken aboard a Japanese cruiser, just when he was about to be apprehended by Chinese troops.[158] Moreover, Prime Minister Ōkuma gave instructions to Hayashi that he, either singly or conjointly with other representatives of foreign powers, should advise the Chinese government to refrain from extreme measures and exercise moderation in all respects.[159] Unfortunately, the six reformers were executed on the very day Ōkuma sent off the telegram. Two more reformers escaped to Japan.[160] Itō Hirobumi himself, partly for personal reasons, actively participated in rescuing the politician Zhang Yinhuan (1837–1900) and Huang Zunxian from execution or imprisonment.[161]

The remarkable outburst of activity of the Japanese government after the failure of the Hundred Days has traditionally been attributed to two causes. The first was the influence that strong foreign policy advocates, especially members of the Tōa-kai and Dōbun-kai, exerted on Ōkuma.[162] However, this argument can be ruled out, as Itō in Beijing defended the rescue measures, and was certainly under no pressure. The second reason is seen in a fear that suppression of the reform movement by the Qing government would create another surge of anti-foreign sentiment in China and destabilize China even further.[163] There was a small anti-foreign riot on 30 September 1898 in Beijing (see below). Yet the rescue maneuvers seem unrelated to this event, and the above argument fails to explain how suppression of the reform movement specifically would create anti-foreign agitation.[164]

Thus the question remains why the Japanese government, despite its previous hands-off policy and the uncertain reputation of the reformers, nonetheless went to such trouble. In the light of the new sources, we would argue that Japan felt compelled to rescue the reformers less by the care for their personal safety or sympathy for China's reforms, but by concern for Japan's image as 'pioneer of civilization' in East Asia. After all, rescuing and taking up political refugees is simply what a civilized country (such as Britain, with which Japan cooperated) would do to meet the 'standard of civilization' as prescribed by international law.

On 24 September 1898, immediately after the end of the Hundred Days, Li Hongzhang invited Itō Hirobumi and Ōoka Ikuzō to a private dinner at his house.[165] Again, Ōoka's record of the conversation as published in the *Chūō shinbun* went around the world: the Shanghai-based *North-China Herald* republished it in translation, the *London Standard* took it from there, and was in turn quoted by the *New York Times*.[166] Ōoka describes part of the conversation as follows.

> The conversation at the table was unreserved throughout and most of it also touched upon politics. The subject was the issue of Kang Youwei, and Li Hongzhang first addressed Itō with the words: 'Kang maybe has fled and will go to your country. If he will really go to your country, I hope you will apprehend and extradite him at once?' Itō said: 'That is impossible. If the reason for his apprehension is non-political, in that case we might honor your wishes. However, in case it has a political meaning, you are well aware of the fact that according to international law, we cannot extradite him.' Li said: 'That is most unfortunate. In London, too, there has been an incident where we tricked a criminal of ours [*waga hannin o tabakarite*], called him to the Legation on false pretenses, apprehended him and shut him up, but the British Foreign Secretary filed a protest against it.'[167]

Readers in Japan, Britain and the United States at the time will have readily understood that the apprehension of the 'criminal' in London to which Li Hongzhang referred meant the famous 'kidnapping' of Sun Yat-Sen in November 1896. The authorities had planned to ship Sun back to China and execute him there, but, due to British intervention, had to release him after 12 days. Much to the chagrin of the Chinese authorities, soon afterwards Sun published an account of this incident under the title *Kidnapped in London* (1897), which made him instantly famous around the world, and greatly aided his funding activities for revolutionary causes (for example in Japan). Thus, as in Kang's case, it was the persecution that made Sun famous at first.

The duties of 'civilization', which Britain had performed for Sun, Japan was now to render to Kang and his group. All 'civilized' states since about 1840 refused to extradite persons whose offences were political, and especially Britain's definition of 'offences of a political character' was most liberal.[168] This was well known in China, and Kang's case was discussed in close parallel with that of Sun Yat-sen.[169] Nonetheless, the Chinese court and, even more important to Japanese interests in China, Governor-General Zhang Zhidong kept insisting that Japan should hand over or extradite Kang Youwei and his followers.[170] The foreign ministry under the new Yamagata Cabinet in December 1898 eventually yielded to the pressure and decided to persuade Kang to leave Japan for America. However, even then, this was not done directly, but through the good offices of Konoe Atsumaro and his Tōa dōbun-kai, which also funneled the travel expenses for Kang. Moreover, it was agreed that this concession to Chinese pressure would be limited to Kang. Thus Konoe voiced the concern that if Japan would lean too hard upon the reformers, Japan's international image as a law-abiding country might suffer.[171] Although Zhang Zhidong had asked for Liang Qichao's extradition as well, and repeatedly demanded that Liang's *Qingyibao* in Yokohama be shut down, the Japanese government granted neither, as befitted a 'truly civilized country.'

After the Hundred Days: the consolidation of public opinion

The Hundred Days Reform in itself had little significance in Japan while it lasted. However, on 21 September 1898, the Reform failed. Moreover, on 30 September 1898, a mob attacked foreigners in Beijing, among whom were two Japanese citizens, which prompted the Western powers to send troops into the Chinese capital.[172] Both events seem to have been unrelated, as there had been numerous riots in China throughout the year. However, in Japan the encroachment of the Western powers, the failure of the Reform and the continued riots finally added up to the general impression that China – contrary to the expectation of some observers – would not rise again, but was very much on the brink of chaos.

This led to a general consolidation of public opinion soon after the Hundred Days, the dogmatic core of which consisted of the following convictions: China was a 'friend' of Japan. Although willing to reform, it was quite helpless to do so on its own and needed the assistance and protection of Japan. However, the 'protection of China' (*Shina hozen*) was an endeavour to be pursued only in *cooperation* with the civilized powers and never by unilateral action; but if, in concert, with the Western powers, Japan could and should take action by direct intervention in Chinese domestic matters, if peace and stability could not be maintained otherwise.

On the one hand, reasons for the consolidation can be seen in elation that the radical reforms had failed and that China, possibly, would remain weak enough not to pose a threat to Japan any more (which, in turn, made it possible for China to become a 'friend'). On the other hand, concern that China might become too weak and thus potentially destabilize the region and Japan's relations with the powers, but also that China's weakness or eventual break-up may lead to increased labor immigration into Japan, made many observers wish for a weak but stable Chinese government.

Thus, after the Hundred Days we can observe a marked shift in Japanese discourse away from talk about pressuring the Chinese government into reforms towards 'managing' China in concert with the Western powers, signaling China's dramatic loss of political status and the beginning of its gradual effacement from discourse as a sovereign actor. The change is best illustrated in the *volte-face* of Japan's most conservative and pro-oligarchic newspaper, the *Nichinichi shinbun*. The high degree of consolidation of public opinion, in turn, is best seen in the comparison of the *Nichinichi*'s stance with a famous speech of its political enemy, Ōkuma Shigenobu, and with Konoe Atsumaro's statement as president of the Tōa dōbun-kai.

The position of the Tōkyō nichinichi shinbun: neutrality abandoned

The *Tōkyō nichinichi shinbun*, if we remember, throughout the Far Eastern Crisis supported the cautious non-intervention policy of the government towards China. As late as July 1898, we find that the *Nichinichi* considered China far from being a 'friend.' In fact, the newspaper described Sino–Japanese relations as highly problematic, even worse than with any Western power. Thus, on the occasion of Itō's visit to Beijing, the newspaper reflected on the state of the relations as follows:

> Just think for a moment: whether it be regions like America or Europe, despite the fact that they are distant, their races and writing are different, once we had opened the country and entered relations, traffic and contact instantly flourished, powerful men came to Japan or our powerful men went abroad, and although the ties are, historically speaking, still weak, does it not make one think of the world as a neighborhood, the world as one family? But between us and China, this is, on the contrary, not possible.[173]

Thus, far from talking about China as a friend, the *Nichinichi shinbun* saw Itō's visit to China as a good opportunity to *normalize* Sino–Japanese relations and possibly attract more Chinese to come to Japan and acquire a first-hand understanding about Japan.

Barely two months later, and only a few days after the failure of the Hundred Days, however, the *Nichinichi* suddenly changed course and, in a first reaction, offered Japan's sincere friendship and assistance:

> Under these circumstances, it goes without saying that our country, which welcomes students from abroad and receives offers of employment for military instructors, which is not only politically on friendly terms, but is also a useful friend [*ekiyū*] for the progress of civilization in China, must absolutely not neglect to pay attention to the unusual situation in the future.[174]

Moreover, in another statement three weeks later, Japan had advanced to China's 'closest neighbor, its oldest friend and ally, which knows its situation best [*saikyū no kōyū, mottomo jijō o shiru no ketsumei-koku*].'[175]

The conservative *Nichinichi* could barely hide its elation that the radical reform in China had failed. It acknowledged the enlightened measures of the emperor (such as sending Chinese students to Japan), which in a progressive country would have been a matter of course, but in China constituted a daring feat.[176] Too daring, as some would say, but then, in a country of such advanced decay and debilitation, maybe only drastic measures helped. However, the emperor had no assistance and the drastic measures had provoked a drastic reaction. Cixi's return to power was highly irregular. This, however, did not mean the end of the reforms. The *Nichinichi* described the empress dowager in unheard-of terms:

> In conclusion, if it is a government which shows goodwill towards us and seeks good-neighborly relations with us, considering the great interest of China, we should definitely not withhold direct and indirect help. As we have heard, the Empress Dowager is a modern and sagacious ruler. Among the projects that were planned during her regency, there were many progressive ones such as railway transportation, the postal service and others.[177]

Thus, in later reaction, the *Nichinichi* downplayed the Hundred Days as a simple power game which bore no relation to the question of reform, because *every* group in China served the public good, the 'project of civilization.'

> The idea of reform in China has started by taking advantage of the utter deterioration of the government in Beijing. But it would be not correct to say it was a controversy between Manchus and Han Chinese, or a controversy between a civilization faction and an anti-civilization faction. I would rather say it was a controversy between those who wanted to maintain the status quo [*genjō o iji sen to suru*] and those who wanted to break the status quo. After all, the inclination to develop civilization in China is not limited to the emperor and the reform faction alone. The Empress Dowager and those who have restored her position, have it, as well. Rather than a controversy about issues [*taibutsu-teki*], one should better say, it was a controversy about personalities [*taijin-teki*]. It was not a controversy about the project of civilization [*bunmei jigyō*], but a controversy about position and power [*ichi kenryoku*].[178]

This comment, of course, echoed the *Nichinichi*'s strong conviction of nonpartisanship in domestic politics (*chōzen-shugi*), but was not singular to the *Nichinichi*. For example, the Tōa dōbun-kai's official organ, the *Tōa jiron*, too, demonstrated a similar indifference towards personalities, possibly to facilitate further cooperation with China.[179] Moreover, the opinion that the failure of the Hundred Days was not the end of the reforms, but in fact was a necessary prelude for more moderate and therefore better reforms, was shared by many others as well, such as, for example, Naitō Konan or Konoe Atsumaro.[180] And as Douglas R. Reynolds has demonstrated, the Hundred Days Reform was indeed the prelude to another, more gradual reform movement in the last years of the Qing dynasty.[181]

The *Nichinichi*, however, also made it quite clear that China was too feeble to help itself, and that it urgently needed cooperation with its friends. Thus, on the occasion of the failure of the Hundred Days and the sending of troops into Beijing, it began to espouse the joint duty of the 'civilized countries' to protect China's integrity and stability (*hozen*) by financial assistance and direct intervention for the suppression of domestic uprisings. This laid the argumentative ground for Japan's participation in the Boxer expedition two years later. At the same time, it already signaled the shift of focus away from China itself and towards Japan's relations with the Western powers *concerning* China. Thus the *Nichinichi* argued:

> Now, if China wanted to reform everything fundamentally, its political system as well as its social organization, this will be absolutely hopeless, if the rich and the strong among its friends [*yūbō no fukyō naru mono*] do not unite and guarantee the support of China's finances and the prevention of inner disturbances. It is not difficult to foresee that China, sooner or later, will reach this point. However, as long as its friends, differing in interests and sentiments, do not unite in this, it will have to wait even longer for the time and opportunity.
>
> [...] If the friends in future unite and exert themselves for the development of China, avoid controversies on personalities and help its progress and civilization in substance, at the same time strive for the preservation of their own advantages [*jiko no rieki o hozen suru*], then China's future is absolutely not without hope. [...] If not all powers harmonize, one should pick out such countries as Britain, Germany, and America, with whom we have commercial relations, and confer with each other, and if we should achieve the unity, then let's push forward with all might and decision! I am sure, and there can be no doubt, that Russia and France will not oppose such a well meant proposition, and, as its closest neighbor, its oldest friend and ally which knows its situation best, it is Japan's mission to propose China's development and protection [*Shinkoku kaihatsu hozen*]. To hope this from our present incompetent [Ōkuma] cabinet would be almost like scolding a horse that it should get horns. However, if the present cabinet sees the urgency of the situation, the only thing left to do for it is to apologize for its incompetence and resign.[182]

Thus even the *Tōkyō nichinichi shinbun*, by the end of 1898, discarded its former hands-off policy and advocated domestic intervention for the sake of China's inner stability. In fact, the *Nichinichi* quite actively advocated sending foreign troops into China to restore order, and even attributed a special role to Japan:

> During the time of the disturbances in Korea [the Tonghak rebellion], we sent our troops into Korea for the reason that the power of the Korean government did not suffice to protect our legation, but also because one could not tell when the chaos of the neighboring country

would influence us. Thus, with the present disturbances in China, we cannot just stand aside and look on, for the sake of the protection of our legation as well as for the prevention of the fire spreading.

[...] Come to think of it, considering that the position of our empire makes it likely that the disaster might spread to our country and also harm trade and commerce, I think a self-defensive intervention is necessary. If there is a danger that the interests of all powers are equally injured, does not the power which has a powerful army close nearby, have the duty to restore order? This duty will certainly devolve on us rather than on Russia or Britain. Our empire must be prepared to send troops, for the sake of self-defense, but also as neighborly duty.[183]

This shows that when the question arose in 1900 whether to participate in an expedition to subdue the Boxers or not, the positive answer had already been given, at least in theory, by the end of 1898.

However, it should be noted that the *Tōkyō nichinichi* time and again stressed the necessity of acting in *coordination* with the Western powers, lest there be any misunderstanding of Japan's motives and China become the bone of contention among the powers, which would lead into another major conflict.

But if, after the partition, boundary issues cannot be settled diplomatically and become a matter of life and death, then the partition of that country, on the contrary, would bring disaster over the whole world. [...] this is the reason why I think it much better to preserve the integrity of the territory [*Shinkoku no kokudo o hozen suru*].[184]

Civilization and the tight web of international relations would not allow for unilateral, 'heroic' actions. And besides, territorial possessions were more a burden than a blessing, as the example of Taiwan showed:

To claim that one should destroy one of the biggest empires of the world and annex this huge territory and large population is a rather extravagant statement. The heroes in the past [like Toyotomi Hideyoshi] have frequently devised such grand schemes. However, at that time, the world was still uncivilized. Therefore it certainly cannot have been too difficult to plan such a thing. But they rarely succeeded. There might be times when they succeeded. But I have never heard that a way has been found to preserve it forever. But today, humanity has developed, and there is no room for the magic of heroes [*eiyū no majutsu*] any more. The web of international relations has grown ever tighter and does not allow one nation to wield its hand freely any more. Under such circumstances, who would devise again such a grand scheme against all common sense? But that aside, I understand that the goal of life is to enjoy the blessings of peace. One must realize that to acquire territory and to subjugate people is absolutely not to one's own advantage. This is the result of what in this century every

nation has experienced in its history of colonization. [...] It is certainly
not surprising that, after we acquired Taiwan, we are so much troubled
by the suppression of the local rebels [*dohi*] and by financial losses.[185]

Thus all arguments spoke for a joint protection of the integrity and stability
of China and, to some degree, for supporting the central power in Beijing,
irrespective of who was in power. After all, weak as it may be (and, from the
standpoint of the powers, should be), in the era of the 'new imperialism,'
Beijing, willy-nilly, fulfilled the crucial role of a regulator for the Western
powers.[186] A British observer, whose opinions on 'the future of China' the
Nichinichi introduced to its readers, explained this role as follows:

> However, if we look at it [the question of China's integrity] from another
> angle, presently the railway and telegraph business in China greatly
> prospers and shows a tendency of increasing centralization. Moreover,
> the powers want to have their own wishes gratified by the Beijing gov-
> ernment and also have already procured something. Rather than risk
> losing their relations with the Manchu court at one stroke, they think it
> more advantageous to preserve the dynasty as best as they can and thus
> procure advantages for themselves. That is, even if in one region of
> China one day suddenly a revolt occurs, the powers, as long as they
> consider it to their own advantage, will not spare the effort to help the
> Chinese government and suppress the revolts.[187]

The above arguments are quite telling when compared with the situation in
the Sino–Japanese War. The European powers in 1894–95 feared that the
war would destabilize China and eventually lead to conflict among the
Western powers about the 'realignment' of territories. Moreover, for commercial reasons as well, Britain would have very much wished for a con-
tinuance of the *status quo*. In 1895, *The Times* commented that if 'China
could have been guaranteed to remain in a torpid condition, if Japan had
not suddenly awakened to a consciousness of her naval and military strength
and begun to use it, we should, perhaps, have been better pleased to go on as
we have done for two or three generations.'[188] It tells much about the radically changed Japanese self-perception by the end of 1898 that the *Tōkyō
nichinichi shinbun* echoed the very same sentiments and that, by now, Japanese observers saw their own country safely positioned among the intervening powers, rather than being the target of an intervention.

Ōkuma Shigenobu's Tōhō kyōkai-speech, October 1898: the domestication of China

Nothing could illustrate the consolidation of China policy at the end of 1898
better than the fact that the *Tōkyō nichinichi* espoused the same doctrines as
its arch-enemy Ōkuma Shigenobu. The *hanbatsu*-friendly *Tōkyō nichinichi*

was notorious for hating Ōkuma, and during the Ōkuma Cabinet it did everything to bring it down.[189] Although the foreign policy of Ōkuma did not significantly differ from Itō's, now it was the *Nichinichi's* turn to defame it as 'vacillating and indecisive' (*injun kosoku*)[190] and to ridicule Ōkuma's foreign policy as 'the hobby of an amateur' (*heta no yokozuki*).[191] Yet nothing reveals the striking similarities of both positions better than the famous speech that Ōkuma Shigenobu delivered at the Imperial Hotel to the members of the Tōhō kyōkai (Oriental Association) in late October 1898.[192]

The fate of Ōkuma's Tōhō kyōkai speech in historiography is an interesting topic in itself. It has been variously cited as the *locus classicus* of a distinctive *Shina hozen-ron* of Ōkuma, although, as we have seen, the term *Shina hozen* was already a common notion at the time.[193] Western literature has the *Shina hozen-ron* also as 'Ōkuma Doctrine,' the content of which is popularly known as follows: 'Foreign minister Ōkuma Shigenobu contributed a rationale for government policy with this "Ōkuma Doctrine" under which Japan, long a recipient of China's culture and spirit in the past, would now repay its debt by holding the West at bay to provide the time necessary for China to reorganize under new leadership.'[194] However, this interpretation of Ōkuma's speech probably reflects unwillingly an interpretation of the *Shina hozen-ron* on the eve of the 'Greater East Asia Co-Prosperity Sphere.'[195] Ōkuma's speech of 1898 transported a different message, the main difference of which was that Ōkuma said nothing about 'holding the West at bay' but – on the contrary – even suggested the cooperation with the Western powers in intervening in China and thus was close to *Tōkyō nichinichi's* concept of *Shina hozen*.

The public speech of an acting foreign minister on foreign affairs was a rare event at a time of secret diplomacy and thus received wide attention accordingly. Many newspapers (such as the *Tōkyō nichinichi*) published full transcripts of the long speech and commented on it. Ōkuma was well aware of the fact and used the opportunity to defend himself; the self-deprecating reference to the *Nichinichi's* jibe of *heta no yokozuki* in the opening of the speech reflects this intention.[196] Unfortunately, the speech itself was a somewhat incoherent piece of work (a fact duly remarked on by the newspapers). The first half consisted of an overview of the history of Chinese relations with the 'barbarians' (starting from the Zhou), and only the latter half was devoted to the present Sino–Japanese relations and the recent motion of the Russian czar for global disarmament, a topic that very much occupied the minds of the people at the time.[197] Moreover, the logic of the speech even to contemporary listeners sometimes remained obscure.[198] However, the *Nippon* summarized Ōkuma's theses succinctly (and correctly) as follows:

- China throughout its history had troubles to defend itself against the barbarians;
- China's ups and downs in history were not caused by pressure from the outside [*gaibu no atsuryoku*];
- In general, the decline of a nation is self-induced [*jidō-teki naru*];

- Nations with a [long] history do not easily perish;
- Our empire has the duty to aid and protect China [*Shina no hozen fushoku*] (he did not say 'the right');
- The territory of China already today is pledged as a security to the powers;
- The powers view the Chinese people as colonial subjects;
- It is a delusion that the people of China do not have patriotism;
- If a hero appears and strives for the reforms of the political system, the Chinese people will likely become fervent patriots;
- The proposal of an international peace conference [*Bankoku heiwa kaigi*] has been put forward by the initiative of the merciful and compassionate Russian czar;
- The essence of diplomacy lies in peace;
- We will fight with all our might those who want to destroy peace.[199]

Ōkuma did not think that China would perish because of external factors (the pressure caused by the Western powers), but by internal factors only. Again, we can observe a significant shift of perspective from China's foreign problems to China's domestic problems after the Hundred Days and the riots. Consequently, Ōkuma's 'aid and protection' applied to China's domestic problems (such as financial difficulties or riots) only, and not to external problems with the foreign powers. Moreover, as a draft for this (or a similar) speech shows, Ōkuma intended to hint in his speech at cooperation with Britain in this matter.[200]

The above should suffice to indicate the similarities with the *Shina hozen-ron* of the *Tōkyō nichinichi shinbun*, which implicitly even acknowledged the harmony of opinions (if not of personal feelings). In its two commentaries on the speech, except for some very minor details, the *Nichinichi* could not find any fault with the Chinese part of the speech, and therefore concentrated its attacks on Ōkuma's observations concerning the Russian armament retrenchment proposal.[201]

At this point, it should be noted that there is an interpretation of Ōkuma's *Shina hozen* speech which argues that Ōkuma, contrary to his professed intentions of 'protecting China's integrity,' as a last resort even contemplated joining the powers and taking a piece of Chinese territory.[202] This opinion is based on a draft for a speech that Ōkuma wrote sometime in October 1898, in which he hinted at the possibility that – in the unlikely event that the Western powers would make China's division formal – Japan would adopt an 'appropriate measure of defense' (*seitō bōgyo*); Ōkuma scribbled in the margins of the draft that this was intended to hint at the possibility of Japan taking a share of China itself. And in fact, the *Tōhō kyōkai* speech, in its central passage on *Shina hozen*, also hinted at the dubious possibility that Japan would 'accept' Chinese territory if it was offered to Japan:

> Thus, with respect to the duty to lead one of the biggest nations of the world [...] it is most befitting that China is led by a neighboring

country, a country whose race is close, whose writing is the same, and whose feelings are the same. If such a country would lead, it could pretty much make China flourish. And supposed it would not flourish, then – like it or not – a responsibility for the Japanese would arise from this to rescue the Chinese from the present state of wretched misery. In this, there is no other country on the world, no matter how powerful it is, which possesses such advantages in China as Japan does. Moreover, it is close, and also speaking from the point of power, it is a strong country whose power in East Asia is absolutely not inferior to any in the world. It is a strong country, but it has no intention to attack and take somebody else's territory by means of this power (at this point, someone shouted 'Retrocession of Liaodong!'),[203] it has no such intention in the least. It has absolutely no intention of robbing. But, as I have said before, one cannot take away somebody else's country, but if somebody else offers it, in this case – a gift not accepted, on the contrary, brings evil (applause). Then one must accept it, like it or not.[204]

Such ambiguous remarks naturally inspire suspicions that Ōkuma really advocated the division of China, or at least Japan's appropriation of Chinese territory. However, it is doubtful whether Ōkuma's remarks should be taken at face value and not primarily as protestations of a strong intention to please and appease the audience (among whom, as the shouts indicate, were strong foreign policy advocates). As we have seen above, Ōkuma was criticized for his weak and dilatory policy. It is in this light that the gloss should be read which Ōkuma noted beside a similar passage of the draft speech mentioned above: 'This vaguely hints that if there was no other choice, Japan as an appropriate measure of defense would divide China, too. I thereby respond to the present public opinion which decries the foreign policy of the present cabinet as inactive [*mui*]. However, it is important that this point must be stated extremely carefully and also in vague terms.'[205] Indeed, the point had to be stated extremely carefully and in vague terms because Ōkuma – as well as any other statesman (and the *Tōkyō nichinichi*) – knew that the international situation in China allowed for neither taking nor 'accepting' any additional territory in China.

The founding of the Tōa dōbun-kai: the wane of China's polarizing power

In November 1898, the two societies Tōa-kai and Dōbun-kai merged to form the Tōa dōbunkai (with Konoe Atsumaro as its president). The initial reason for doing so was to pool government funding, as Ōkuma was unwilling to finance two independent societies of the same kind. The history of the Tōa dōbunkai, which eventually became the most important semi-official society operating on the continent until 1945, has been sufficiently well studied and does not need further explication here.[206] Let it suffice to say that the society, at its first meeting, decided on the following goals:

- to protect China's integrity and stability [*Shina o hozen su*];
- to aid China's improvement [*Shina no kaizen wo josei su*];
- to investigate current affairs in China and decide upon appropriate actions;
- to rouse public opinion [*kokuron o kanki su*].[207]

Again, Kuga Katsunan was a co-founding member of the society and played an important role in formulating its goals. Consequently, his newspaper *Nippon*, in accordance with the manifesto, redoubled its efforts to 'rouse public opinion' and began to advocate the new, domestically oriented *Shina hozen-ron*. In October, for example, Miyake Setsurei called upon his readers 'Pour your energies into China!'[208] However, this was gradually becoming mainstream public opinion, as we have seen, and there was actually no special need to rouse public opinion any further.

Although the new China policy soon became widely accepted, it is a telling characteristic of the strong foreign policy agitation that it would, nonetheless, keep on attacking an imaginary opponent and assume an air of elitist protest while it could. This is best illustrated by an article that Konoe Atsumaro wrote for the first edition of the society's organ *Tōa jiron* on 'The position of our empire and today's politicians.'[209] In this article, Konoe complained about the stupidity of the world, and glorified the martyrdom of like-minded chivalrous men who fought for China's integrity:

> With respect to the principle of protecting China [*Shina hozen-ron*] which I together with a few, but wise and truth-loving friends and fellows are espousing, I am certainly not someone who wants to chase the trends of the world with empty, abstract words and attract the attention of many people. I merely believe that, for the benefit and the glory of our empire, it is the only way to think where our empire stands today and see where it is headed in the future. I do not know for how much longer our demands will be suppressed by the vulgar opinion of the world. But if I can thereby stir up the so-called politicians of today with ever so little a sensation, it is enough. With this principle, I merely appeal to the pure and disinterested discourse [*seigi*] of the whole world and, with a small number of like-minded fellows, hope that it shows some effect in the realization of our goals.[210]

It should be obvious that by the time Konoe's article was published (December 1898), his defiant and elitist attitude was slightly anachronistic. If even the ultra-conservative *Tōkyō nichinichi shinbun*, the organ of Konoe's 'so-called politicians,' had adopted the *Shina hozen-ron*, it was ludicrous of Konoe to declare that this was the opinion of a small elite and speak of its 'suppression.' Especially so when the Tōa dōbun-kai, around the same time, busied itself in applying for government funding, and in April 1899 received a promise from Foreign Minister Aoki Shūzō for secret funding and hence became a semi-governmental organization.[211] However, the *shishi*-spirit of the strong foreign policy advocates was often elitist and rebellious on principle and demanded polarization, even if there was no real opposition.

Yet even the strong foreign policy advocates finally had to realize that China, in public opinion, had become uncontentious and had lost its polarizing power. The strong foreign policy movement gradually shifted its attention away from China and began to focus solely on Russia as political opponent. The Boxer Incident very clearly demonstrates the finality of China's effacement from the political landscape as an antagonizing power (although China remained of interest as an object of aid and intervention), and the rise of Russia instead.

5 The Boxer Incident and beyond, 1900–04

The Boxer Uprising of 1900, during which discontented Chinese, the so-called Boxers, besieged the diplomatic settlement in Beijing and finally fought and lost against an allied force from eight foreign countries (Japan among them), is another seminal event in modern Chinese history. In Chinese historiography, it is fraught with a symbolic power that has even increased over time.[1] For Japan, however, the Boxer Uprising marks the visible effacement of China as a sovereign actor from political discourse, and the rise of Russia instead as the new polarizing power.

The Boxer Incident brought Japanese soldiers back to China and, finally, to the gates of Beijing. However, the circumstances of the campaign radically differed from the war with China six years before, at least in the eyes of the Japanese public. Consequently, the public attitude also differed markedly from the exuberant jingoism of the war days. The Boxer Uprising at first was conceived as a primarily anti-Christian disturbance of passing significance and therefore no business of Japan. When the British government requested the Japanese government to send more troops than originally planned, this was understood as an invitation for Japan to join the 'club' of civilized powers, and the participation was viewed as an intervention for the sake of civilization. Due to the dogma of 'Sino–Japanese friendship,' it could not be viewed as a war anyway. However, the war reports of the Boxer expedition visibly demonstrate that calling China a 'friend' eventually meant the total loss of China as an independent power in the eyes of the Japanese public. Thus China was completely ignored in the event, and reports focused solely on Japan's competition with the Western powers, hinting at the rising tension with Russia. The Japanese public therefore soon lost interest in the Boxer expedition itself, and turned towards the 'real thing,' confrontation with Russia.

The Boxer Uprising and Japan's participation in the expedition

The origins of the 'Boxers,' as the insurgents were commonly called by foreigners, remain somewhat obscure.[2] The secret society known as Yihequan ('Righteous and Harmonious Fists') is generally believed to be an offshoot of an older sect or secret society with a potentially anti-dynastic background. Most famously, the Boxers practiced certain boxing and callisthenic rituals which they held made practitioners invulnerable even to bullets. However, the sectarian background of the movement is open to discussion, as it certainly drew on a high degree of pent-up social discontent among the peasantry in the North, who had been greatly impoverished by the general economic downslide and a series of floods and droughts since 1895. The movement, which first stirred in the province of Shandong in 1898, especially attacked missionaries and Christian Chinese, but soon turned against foreign things in general. Thus monuments of foreign civilization, such as churches, mines, railway stations and lines, were attacked and destroyed with a Luddite vengeance (some recruits had been Grand Canal boatmen and lost their work to Western-built railways).

The local authorities in Shandong and elsewhere did not stop the outbursts, and even encouraged them. The Chinese court long remained neutral to the developments. However, by late 1899 the movement started to solicit the support of the central government under the slogan 'support for the Qing and extermination of the foreigners' (*fu Qing mie yang*; note the similarity with the Japanese 'revere the emperor and expel all foreigners' fewer than 50 years ago). By May 1900, the disturbances had reached the outskirts of Beijing, and the Boxers freely burned churches and foreign residences, and killed Chinese who were suspected to be Christian. Around this time, the Empress Dowager changed her policy and began actively to support the Boxers as a way of ousting the foreign powers.

Meanwhile, the diplomatic corps in Beijing had requested protection from their countries; a first dispatch of marines (among them also Japanese) reached Beijing on 31 May 1900. A second dispatch started out from Tianjin soon after, but was repelled by the combined forces of Boxers and Qing soldiers. Russia, too, sent troops, and in the process stationed them in the key positions of Manchuria. In Beijing, the allied forces engaged with the Boxers first on 14 June 1900. A few days earlier, a first Japanese civilian had fallen victim to the disturbances: on 11 June the Japanese Legation secretary Sugiyama was killed outside the Yongding Gate. More famously, the German minister to Beijing, Clemens von Ketteler, was killed on 20 June 1900.[3]

Eventually, the Qing court came out into the open: on 19 June 1900 the Chinese Foreign Ministry issued the order that all foreigners should leave Beijing within 24 hours. On 20 June, the siege of Beijing began. On 21 June, the Chinese issued a 'declaration of war' in the form of an edict that blamed the foreign powers for initiating the hostilities, and voiced unmodified support for the 'righteous soldiers' who defended China against the aggressors. Another edict called on the provincial governors to act according to the conditions in the provinces and protect their territory 'so that foreigners cannot work their will.'[4] However, the three most influential governor-generals in the south, Zhang Zhidong, Liu Kunyi and Li Hongzhang, interpreted the edict in their own way and suppressed the Boxers and other uprisings within their jurisdiction. Thus the Boxer Uprising was effectively limited to Beijing and the surrounding province Zhili (one of the reasons why the affair in Japan is often called the 'North China Incident', *Hokushin jihen*).

The Japanese government at first took the affair rather lightly, probably because the attacks did not affect Japan immediately, but even more so because the information they received from their representative in Beijing did not sound too urgent. As late as 18 June 1900, the Japanese minister to Beijing, Nishi Tokujirō, wrote to Foreign Minister Aoki Shūzō that he had considered the tumult [*sōdō*] from the beginning as a regional affair without a revolutionary character, and that they were experiencing 'temporary difficulties' just now, but that this 'sooner or later will get better somehow [*nantoka naoru*].'[5] This statement is all the more remarkable as Nishi's secretary Sugiyama had been killed only a week ago.

The Japanese cabinet on 15 June decided to send a small contingent of troops to China, and informed the foreign ministers of its intention. However, soon after, the British government repeatedly and urgently pressed the Japanese government to send more than its proportional share to China, and quickly. Ever since the outbreak of the Boer War in October 1899, the British had amassed its forces wholly in South Africa and could spare none for other parts of the world. However, Russia was known to send massive troops too, and the British wanted Japanese soldiers to act as proxies and counterbalance the Russian soldiers on the mission.[6]

The Japanese cabinet decided on 6 July that it would comply with the British request, and informed the foreign ministers that it would send up to 22,000 men. The financial burden of this promise at first remained somewhat problematic: Japan's coffers had been already plundered for the previous armament expansion, and actually did not allow for such a massive military operation as promised. Nonetheless, the Japanese government entered the obligation without a guarantee of British financial assistance. However, after some initial hesitations, the British acting minister in Japan on 14 July 1900 finally informed Aoki that Britain *would* make a financial contribution of one million pounds. This remained unknown to the Japanese public until the beginning of August, and with good reason, as we shall see.

The news of the British request and Japan's compliance was received in Europe and the United States with mixed feelings. Apart from some very positive responses, especially in the American press,[7] there were reactions in Europe that viewed Japan's participation with less goodwill and again raised the 'yellow peril' banner high. In particular, a letter to the editor of the London *Times*, which spoke of Japan's thin 'veneer of civilization' and warned of the danger of entrusting Japan with the peace mission, received wide attention.[8] Again, Kurino Shin'ichirō, the Japanese minister in Paris who had already been active in the case of Konoe Atsumaro, rang alarm bells. In a hasty letter to Itō Hirobumi, he reported the deep impression the letter in *The Times* had made on the French public:

What I wanted to inform you next of is that in the *London Times* of the 12th instant there was a letter contributed by a British called 'Mitford' which by its extremely shallow discussion of our civilization produces effects in the European public opinion [*Ōshū genron shakai*] dis-advantageous to our country. Probably because this person has lived in Japan more than thirty years ago, he describes our feudal times and judges that its cruel and inhuman barbarism is no different from the present times in China, and that even today our people deep inside their heart are filled with the passions of barbarians.[9]

Such opinions were not taken lightly in Japan. As is well known, the Japanese Foreign Ministry thereupon launched a systematic campaign to influence the European and American press, and spent considerable sums to buy itself into the good opinion of the press, this time on a much grander scale than during the Sino–Japanese War.[10]

The Qing court, in the meantime, seemed to have second thoughts about its rash support of the Boxers. At the beginning of July 1900, the Chinese emperor sent telegrams to the heads of state of six powers, including Japan.[11] The imperial telegram addressed to the Japanese emperor was transmitted to foreign minister Aoki on 11 July 1900. Its intention was to persuade Japan to mediate between China and the powers. Typically, the telegram invoked China's and Japan's close historical and strategic ties ('lips and teeth'), and tried to suggest a common interest of action against the Western powers. The Qing court argued that there was a divide between East and West, with China and Japan as pillars of the East. The Western countries were already seeking prey, and it was not only China they were after. If China could not support itself any more, Japan, too, would have difficulties in supporting its independence. Therefore the Chinese emperor hoped that Japan would take the lead and 'restore the situation.'[12]

However, the Japanese government, despite similar professions of *dōbun dōshu* in informal talks, certainly had no intention of reciprocating such sentiments in front of the Western powers. Thus the Japanese government, in the name of the emperor, rather coolly replied that, so far, China had not been able to rescue the diplomats and subdue the rebels, although international law required it to do so. If the Chinese government would only do this, it could easily speak for itself in all other matters. Japan sent its troops only to rescue and subdue, and for no other reason. The telegram continued:

> Therefore, if you will swiftly rescue all foreign envoys from amidst the siege, this will suffice as proof that you do not wish to wage war. You must extinguish the causes of the disaster by yourself. The Japanese government, of course, feels deep sympathy and friendship for your government. If and when it thinks it really necessary, Japan will not dare to refuse to exert its powers. […][13]

Thus the Japanese government briskly ignored all rhetoric of solidarity and made it sufficiently clear that its position was with the allied powers. Not surprisingly, the Japanese response met with approval within and outside Japan.[14] Thus Japanese 'sympathy and friendship' extended itself towards China freely only when no other power was watching.

The progress of the military campaign is quickly told: on 14 July 1900, the allied forces – consisting mainly of Japanese and Russian soldiers – took the walled city of Tianjin and placed it under foreign control (until August 1902).[15] On 4 August the forces marched on to Beijing, and attacked the Chinese besiegers on 14 August. After the siege was broken, soldiers of the foreign troops burnt, looted and killed. Meanwhile, the Empress Dowager and the Emperor had fled the city; already on 7 August, Li Hongzhang had been appointed to sue for peace.

In October 1900, negotiations finally started with the allied powers and ended with the Boxer Protocol, signed on 7 September 1901. Japan was one of the 11 Protocol powers. The protocol provided for another huge indemnity, which was spread over 39 years; the Protocol powers, however, remitted their shares during the next decades, with the stipulation that they be used for cultural purposes (such as sending students abroad).[16] Moreover, the protocol stipulated the dismantling of the fort of Dagu and the right of the powers to station guards for their own defense in Beijing, both of which foreseeably rendered China's independence illusory, at least as far as the central government in Beijing was concerned.

The reactions of the Japanese public

The legal nature of the Boxer expedition

The Japanese public, although experiencing the Boxer conflict like a war, chose to declare it a friendly intervention or international police action on behalf of China and, more importantly, of civilization; this despite that fact that war itself held nothing negative, as we have seen, except for the fact that it needed an enemy. China, however, was a 'friend' according to the new dogma, albeit a powerless one, and therefore had no say in what was going on.

Declarations can be misleading as to the nature of their subject, but revealing in terms of intentions. Even today, the nature of the Boxer conflict seems to remain a matter of uncertainty, which is reflected in the variety of names for the incident: thus the movement of the Boxers is variously called a 'disturbance,' 'uprising' or 'rebellion.' In Japan, the usual term is 'North-China Incident' (*Hokushin jihen*). However, despite its pretences to neutrality, a certain confusion can be observed in the details: thus the Chinese court edict of 21 June 1900, which supported the Boxers, is referred to as a 'declaration of war' (*sensen*), and the Boxer conference starting in October 1900 is called 'peace conference' (*kōwa kaigi*), which implies the settlement of war issues. An authoritative study of the event straightforwardly includes the 'Boxer

War' (*Giwadan sensō*) in its title, although the reason why the author chose to do so is made less explicit.[17]

Of course, the uncertainty reaches back to the event itself. From the legal and diplomatic view at the time, there might have been ample reason not to call the conflict a war. Thus China and the eight allied powers never entered the formal state of war by issuing a proper declaration of war. The Chinese imperial edict of 21 June 1900, which is often somewhat carelessly called a 'declaration,' could never have the effect of invoking the formal state of war, as it was one of many edicts from the court not specially directed toward the enemy.[18] Moreover, news about the Chinese edicts sometimes contradicted itself and was met with great caution; if even the three insubordinate southern governor-generals called the edict an 'illegitimate order,' why should the Western powers heed it?[19] Yet, even more to the point, the Western powers did not *want* war with China, as it ran counter to their political interests. Especially, Britain did not want the conflict to spread to the south.[20] Yet technically the allied powers' forces were engaged in a military conflict not only with the Boxers, but with regular Qing troops under the command of the court as well, and thus were at war.[21] This the powers chose to ignore.

A similar treatment of the events can be observed among the Japanese public. Newspapers invariably referred to the developments in China as 'the China Incident' (*Shinkoku jiken*) or 'the North China Incident' (*Hokushin jihen*), thereby setting it apart from wars past and present. The *Tōkyō nichinichi*, for example, would refer in the same article to the 'Sino–Japanese War' (*Nisshin sensō*) in the past and to the present 'Chinese Incident,' clearly indicating that both were of a different character.[22] Moreover, ever since the Boer War had erupted in October 1899, the Japanese public had been informed daily and in detail about the war activities between Britain and the two Boer republics. This event, however, was squarely called the 'South African War' (*Nanfutsu sensō*), and there was no doubt about its nature.[23]

Yet, despite the clear distinction on a verbal level, in essence there was no great difference between the news coverage of the 'South African War' and the 'North China Incident.' In the latter, too, there was an 'enemy' or an 'enemy army' (*tekigun*), and there was fighting, even 'bitter fighting' (*gekisen*). The *Tōkyō nichinichi shinbun* on 19 June 1900 announced that war hostilities had finally begun.[24] Moreover, as in the Sino–Japanese War, and later, in the Russo–Japanese War, the newspapers sent special correspondents to accompany the Japanese forces and send home 'war reports' (*senpō*). Nor was death absent. On the contrary, the reports reveled in most gruesome details about the heroic deaths of brave Japanese soldiers, whose names then duly reappeared in the deaths lists on the same pages.

We should keep in mind that war, especially since the triumphs of the Sino–Japanese War, held a certain fascination for most of the people. It cannot be denied that, from the outset, there was the expectation that the expedition would be a similar triumph, which motivated some to join the expedition as war reporters. Thus the sinologist, literary critic and journalist Taoka Reiun remembered in his autobiography that the initial motive for joining the Boxer troops was because he had missed the Sino–Japanese War:

> The heroic determination which man displays when he has transcended the wish to survive, the wild bravery; I can observe in war the gigantic power of man. War is of all things existing the most heroic [*sōretsu*], the most sublime [*yūdai*], the greatest tragedy, and the most excellent tragic history. I, who did not have the chance to see the Sino–Japanese War, thought this incident a once-in-a-lifetime opportunity to experience what a war is.[25]

However, despite all this, the Japanese public refused to call the conflict a war, even when seeing it. The decision was motivated by several reasons, each of which implied that China's international status had by then reached a nadir.

The most extreme reason given at the time was that the conflict could not be measured by Western international law, as China was outside the pale of law. An editorial in the *Tōkyō nichinichi shinbun* argued that China had neither the will nor the power to accept and exact international law, hence was no 'regular subject' of international law. The allied powers should deal with China flexibly, under whatever heading, and not bound by legal precedence. After all, international law was a consensual affair among its practitioners, and the allied forces in their actions created new precedence, thus acting simultaneously in a legislative and executive function, as it were.[26]

Such a bold view could not go uncontested. The renowned international lawyer Ariga Nagao (1860–1921) responded to the *Nichinichi*'s sally on international law as follows:

> On 25 July, the leading article of the *Tōkyō nichinichi shinbun* emphatically discoursed on the subject of the China Incident and International Law; it ended with the verdict that the present incident in no way fell into the categories of international law, and it was the height of boorishness if one wanted to judge it at all costs by the principles of international law. [...] Firstly, the big problem is whether one should consider the occupation of Dagu and the rescue attack on Beijing by the allied forces eventually as a war or not. The governments of all countries officially declare that it is not a war. However, the decision on the basis of international law whether it is a war or not does not depend in the will of the combatant countries. Supposed it is not a war, should we then consider it as a case of domestic intervention [*kokunai kanshō*], i.e. an international police action [*kokusai keisatsu*], like the *Kokumin shinbun* once argued? If not, the only other thing which remains is that we must consider it as a case of reprisal [*hōfuku*] as the German emperor said in his speech.[27]

Ariga and his colleagues of the newly founded Japanese Society of International Law (Kokusai-hō gakkai) eventually agreed that, in essence, the incident must be qualified as a war.[28]

Although the majority of the Japanese public fully endorsed the view that international law should apply to the conflict, it chose the second option and declared the expedition to be an intervention, that is, an 'international police action.' This was mainly for ideological reasons. As we saw in Chapter 4, by the end of 1898 Japan, in the eyes of the public, had assumed the responsibility to help and assist its 'oldest friend', China. Such a thing was, of course, not to be done by war. Already Ōkuma, in his speech in October 1898, had made it quite clear that 'the project to advance the civilization of East Asia and to deliver this pitiful people [the Chinese] from its pains, [i.e.] lead it from hell to paradise' was a project of 'peace'.[29] And, again in January 1900, the former ambassador to China, Yano Fumio, during a semi-public address to the members of the Japan Club, assured his listeners that the Chinese were a peace-loving nation and avoided fighting as best as they could.[30]

Instead, it was agreed that Japan would aid and assist China's political stability by way of an international military intervention, if peace and stability could not be maintained otherwise, and this already on occasion of the anti-foreign riots in 1898. This is the reason why, at the beginning of June 1900, when Boxers showed a more generally xenophobic tendency, the overwhelming majority in Japan voiced its support for Japan's participation in an international intervention almost immediately.[31] It is also the reason why the public, while the expedition lasted, conscientiously tried to keep up the appearance of friendly intercourse with the Chinese, as the foreign correspondent of the *North-China Herald* observed:

> And indeed none of the Japanese who live in the large cities can long go about with the idea that all the Chinese are their enemies, for the Chinese Minister is still in Tokio, and the Chinese officers who left for home some time ago were seen off in the most friendly manner by great numbers of their Japanese fellow officers. And indeed any Japanese that you speak to on the subject will at once tell you that China is regarded by Japan as her best friend and that the Japanese have only gone to the Celestial Empire to put down rebels whose ill-advised action may lead to the partition of that Empire.[32]

However, it should be pointed out that qualifying the expedition as an intervention or 'police action' had significant implications for the relation of the involved parties. After all, in the light of traditional international law, this either made China a protectorate (and Japan one of its protective powers), or it negated China's status as sovereign, self-governing state altogether.[33] Thus, although the expedition was cloaked in terms of help between friends, calling China a 'friend,' in fact, already invoked its social death in international society.

It should be added that, since the expedition was declared an intervention, even those who became more and more critical of war at the turn of the century supported the expedition and did not object to it on moral grounds. This is especially true for the *Yorozu chōhō* writers, who are sometimes cited in this instance as an example of moral rectitude.[34] Anti-war editorials of the *Yorozu chōhō* during the time of the expedition were but a continuation of the Hague Peace Conference discussion, which had started in late 1898 and in which the *Yorozu* participated from early on,[35] and had nothing to do with the expedition. Kōtoku Shūsui, for example, like everybody else, supported the expedition unreservedly at the time, irrespective of his critique of the government's armament expansion and foreign policy in general.[36] And finally, the *Yorozu chōhō*'s series of 'investigative journalism,' which disclosed misdemeanors of Japanese personnel during the Boxer expedition, appeared between December 1901 and January 1902, long after the incident.[37] Thus, at the time of the expedition, there was virtually no-one who doubted that the expedition was justified in the name of civilization.

The Boxer expedition as a contest of civilization and an exercise for war

The Japanese 'war reports' from the Boxer expedition more or less subliminally conveyed the following messages to the reader: firstly, that China politically did not matter any more and merely constituted the background for a competition among the allied powers; and secondly, that Japan was a 'civilized country,' even more civilized than some other countries, especially Russia. The 'war reports' show the Boxer expedition not only as a contest in the disciplines of civilization, but also as a measure-taking of Japan's possible future enemy, Russia.

The request of the British government to send a much larger contingent to the continent than originally planned meant to the Japanese government and the public much more than just a geostrategic decision: it was seen as the formal acknowledgement that Japan was now 'civilized' enough to act as proxy of the world's superpower, and therefore eligible to join the ranks of the great and civilized powers.[38] The mission was designed accordingly. This began with the appointment of Major-General Fukushima Yasumasa (1852–1919) as the commander of the Japanese troops. Fukushima was not only well acquainted with Chinese military affairs (he had been on several 'information-gathering' tours in China, and since 1898 was in charge of superintending Chinese military education in Japan[39]), he also sported a distinctly 'cosmopolitan' personality. The *North-China Herald* applauded the choice: 'Major-General Fukushima, for instance, is well acquainted with English, French, Russian, German, and Chinese; and this, combined with his savoir faire, dash, and love of athletics, ought to make him a general favourite in the camp of the allies.'[40] And curry favor with the allies he must: Katsura Tarō, when appointing Fukushima, made it succinctly clear that Fukushima 'must show sufficient determination and pay sufficient attention about joining this alliance [*kono dōmei*],' even at the price of death.[41]

Fukushima faithfully related the message to his troops. When on board ship bound for China, Fukushima composed a war song to express his determination and instruct his soldiers on the occasion and purpose of their mission. The lyrics read awkwardly, but tell much about the spirit of the mission:

In the year of nineteen-hundred, in the nights of the first month of summer
> Black clouds appear in the west, in the troubled Chinese sky
> War reports are suddenly brought in, the Boxer bandits in the north of China
> First calling themselves 'righteous people' [*gimin*], put up the banner of *sonnō jōi* [revere the Emperor and expel all foreigners],
> They burn churches and kill foreigners,
> Running amok they have come near the gates of Beijing
> The bigoted party in the Chinese government, they are even delighted with this
> Because they do not take measures of pacification, the ravaging flames spread more and more
> The 'righteous people' turn into rebels [*zoku*], violence and chaos reach extremes
> At this point, the warships of the powers gathered in Dagu
> Marines rapidly stepped ashore, and they were not idle in protecting
> The guarded diplomatic settlements. Yet, the Chinese government does not do anything
> The connection between Beijing and Tianjin breaks off, the people in the diplomatic settlements
> are in danger growing day by day, how can there be any delay?
> The powers increase the soldiers ever more and make preparations, responding to the incident
> Our best soldiers, in fact, the Special Expedition Force
> bears the honor, and amidst shouts of joy the ships leave Ujina[42]
> Heading towards the Gulf of Zhili they go. If we now let our eyes wander over that place
> There Britain, France, Germany, Russia, Italy, Austria
> America, together seven countries, all fine fellows second to none,
> The elite vies among each other on that grand arena; even if their number be small,
> it is time now that we show the world the representatives of our army,
> the elite, native to our country; the responsibility to surpass in honor is grave
> when we are together on the battlefield, among the countries there might be differences of East and West
> but here we are brothers protecting the same countries; propriety is the flower of the warrior,
> Attentiveness, deference, endurance, and forbearance, in these things compete

Don't sneer or provoke, don't blunder in the important things,
When we are together on the battlefield, this is the place where you throw away your life
  solely and completely for your country, this is the place where you raise its glory
  Bravely charge forward, fight furiously, and break first the positions of the enemy
  Let the excellence of the men from the Country of the Gods shine forth among the Five Continents
  Let Our Emperor's Dignity and Virtue resound everywhere under the heaven.[43]

The peculiarly slanted perspective of this song is noteworthy: of 32 lines in total, only the first 14 are devoted to an introductory sequence that tells in a *naniwa-bushi*-like style of the occasion of the mission – the uncontrolled violence of the 'rebels' in the north. Incidentally, nothing could illustrate Japan's radically changed self-awareness better than comparing the Boxers with the Bakumatsu braves, who had likewise put up the 'banner of *sonnō jōi*' in their time. Thus, when Japan fought the Boxers, it was also fighting its own 'medieval' past, side by side with the Western powers.

However, the proportions of the song show that *this* conflict was not the important part of the mission. In fact, the remaining 18 lines of the song are devoted to a spectacle that seems wholly unrelated to the occasion. In Pindaresque style, the song praises the valor of the combatants and spurs the Japanese soldiers on to excel in the disciplines of the civilized soldier and gain the laurel of being first, if only the first to die. This creates the somewhat bizarre impression that the mission, in reality, was not about a 'peacekeeping operation,' but a sportive event to advertise one's country's prowess, albeit with equally fatal consequences. Yet this might have been exactly what Fukushima intended. Thus the real opponents of Japan in the Boxer incident were not the Boxers, but were in fact the Western powers.

The 'war reports' were an endless variation on this theme, and with the same proportions. One conspicuous feature of the 'war reports' is the almost complete effacement of the Chinese enemy from the scene, as if it figured only as the necessary extra for a far more important spectacle. The Boxers and Chinese soldiers usually manifested themselves only in a continuous shower of bullets and shells pouring down on the allied powers. They usually were invisible inside the fortress while the allied powers besieged it, and were suddenly (and mysteriously) gone when the fortress was finally taken.[44] And whereas the reports revel in details of the gory deaths of brave Japanese soldiers, the enemy was spared such honors. Thus, for all the reader knows, the scenes could have taken place anywhere around the world, say in South Africa during the Boer War (although in accounts of the latter we *do* see the face of the enemy).

On the other side, before the enemy's gates, the 'war reports' staged an almost Homeric spectacle of the allied forces' soldiers vying for recognition as the most brave, the most civilized. Thus, in the discipline of prowess, we see an endless succession of brave Japanese soldiers who charge first, advance first, fall and die first. A typical example (albeit without casualties) is the following news item, which was also brought to the attention of foreign observers:

> The Japanese *wild officer*
> In the dawn of the seventeenth instant, when the allied forces charged on the enemy and occupied the fort of Dagu, our soldiers and the British soldiers were rushing forward, each trying to get ahead. *They happen to fall into a deep hollow, and cannot go either way. At this, one Japanese officer jumps out with one leap, rightens himself up on the precipice and shouts the order 'Advance! Advance!'* The crowd recovers its impetus and bravely advances. *At this time, the first who takes the bastion and jumps onto the fort is a Japanese soldier.* You may have guessed that it was, again, *the Japanese officer* who shouted the advance order. As soon as this Japanese officer mounts the fort, *he wants to plant our flag there.* Just then, *a British officer* follows, *pulls out a British flag from his pocket and wants to hoist it.* They meet and argue who is first, without reaching a decision. At this, a British soldier under the command of the above officer xxxxxxxxxxxxxx[45] the heart of a military man is generous, and they quickly decide that Japan and Britain must simultaneously plant the flags. You may want to know who this officer is: It is no other than Company Commander of the army Lieutenant *Shiraishi Yoshie*. The British soldiers afterwards did not use his name when calling him, but instead called him the Japanese *wild officer* [*Nihon no wairudo ofisâ*], and it is said that the name *wild officer* is still much around the barracks.[46]

Thus the sportive contest as to who might hoist the flag first was solved amiably between Japan and Britain. After all, they were soon to be allies (the rather crude illustration of Fort Dagu, which accompanied the narrative, however, sets things right: *two* Japanese flags fly over the fort).

However, one should not be deceived by 'sportiveness' when it came to other nations. In a crooked, Churchillian sense of 'chivalry,' Japanese soldiers competed 'amiably' with other soldiers, who they would have to shoot four years later. The tension was not lost to onlookers. The *North-China Herald* observed:

> At the present moment Russia is certainly, however, on her best behavior; and one good feature in this most lamentable outbreak is the opportunity it is affording Russians and Japanese to meet one another in the field and to learn to respect one another's valour without having at the same time to butcher one another.[47]

The observation seems a trifle thoughtless, considering that Japanese und Russian soldiers were 'butchering' Chinese rebels in the meantime. Moreover, contrary to the above, the Japanese did *not* learn to respect the valor of the Russian soldiers. On the contrary, the 'war reports' abound in insinuations that the foreign soldiers were cowardly and lazy. This was insinuated even in rather trivial relations of war heroism such as the following:

> The bravery of Japanese soldiers (Zhifu, the ninth in the morning)
> According to what we have heard about the bitter fighting at the Tianjin Station on the third instant, our Japanese soldiers did not give in to a great number of enemies and bullets falling like rain, but fought furiously. Especially the soldiers from our Engineering Brigade built a pontoon bridge over the lower reaches of a stream near the station. Soldiers from some other country came, too, and helped them. At that moment, one of the enemy's artillery shells passed over the rooftop of the station and detonated only a few meters away. The danger was extreme and the soldiers of that other country all were alarmed and retreated. But our engineers alone stayed on and calmly completed the work. The foreign officers, who closely observe the conduct of our army, all did not fail to express their greatest respect. Therefore it is said that the relations between our army and the allied forces are extremely harmonious.[48]

Despite the harmony, foreign observers, too, eventually noticed the continuous slights in the Japanese press at their expense. The *North-China Herald* observed that the Europeans as a matter of course, but especially the Russians, were the target of the invective:

> The Japanese also believe that they have very much over-estimated the Russian soldier as a fighting machine. [...] It is not the Russian soldier alone that has fallen in the estimation of the Japanese, but the European soldier, be he Russian, English, French, or German. 'The European soldiers seem,' says the very able war-correspondent of the 'Nippon,' 'as compared with the Chinese even, to have undergone what I may call a species of literary effeminacy. The Chinese are certainly better fighters, in my opinion, than the much-dreaded Cossacks.'[49]

Apart from courage, proper conduct according to international law was another discipline in which the Japanese delegation sought to excel. The war reports abound with wondrous tales of the good behavior of the Japanese soldier, which won him not only the sympathy of his colleagues, but also the trust of the Chinese population. This was especially so after the capture of Tianjin, as we can gather from a typical token of news:

> After the Fall of Tianjin
> [...] After the fall of the city of Tianijn, the national soldiers run, and the Boxers disperse themselves. All is quiet and no longer does one

hear gunshots. Only in Yangcun it is said that there are still some Chinese soldiers.[50]

Our troops strictly observe military discipline and there is not a single case of violation. They work extremely hard for the protection of the native people. Therefore, the people consider our troops virtuous [*toku*] and fervently wish that they be put under our protection.

Tianjin is now without a government. Therefore it is considered that Japan, Britain, and Russia each send forth a representative, form a provisional government and execute the official business.[51]

More detailed news describes the 'moving' enthusiasm of the population who, old and young, men and women, leave their houses and offer the Japanese soldiers food, wine and tobacco, and wave little flags with the Hinomaru, 'as if it was a national holiday in Japan,' or little flags with the characters 'We follow Japan' (*Dai-Nippon junmin*).[52]

It should be noted that in reality, the victory at Tianjin was followed by several days of unrestrained killing, looting and raping.[53] Such atrocities were not reported in Japanese newspapers, but were implied by insinuations that the other powers (Germany and Russia) were less civilized, prone to unbridled violence and therefore less popular. The German Kaiser, for example, was berated for his verbal excesses when sending off his soldiers, and the *Nippon* exclaimed:

> 'Don't pardon anyone, don't take any prisoners, use your weapons!' This means 'Kill all, and every Chinese soldier!' and is a dictum which is placed outside of the norms of international law. To put it strongly, one could say that the German Emperor orders the expedition corps which he is sending off to China almost to commit a massacre. We don't have to lose a word about the barbaric behavior of the Chinese, but as the sovereign of a magnificent civilized nation [*dōdō taru bunmei-koku*] to order one's troops to commit a massacre, is not that an even more extreme occurrence directed against civilization [*hi-bunmei no dekigoto*] than the Chinese?![54]

However, the brunt of the censure was borne by Russia, as usual. The Tokyo correspondent of the *North-China Herald* observed:

> From several different sources, most of them trustworthy, Tokio has learned that their allies from the North are going in rather too largely for butchering innocent people and behaving generally like Vandals; and the Japanese are now asking the foreigners here, what about that 'awful massacre' of Port Arthur?[55]

Indeed, on 16 July 1900 in Blagoveshchensk, a city located at the confluence of the Amur and Zeya rivers, a Japanese intelligence officer reported to the headquarters the massacre of 3000 Chinese citizens by Russian Cossacks, immediately preceding the occupation of Manchuria. The 'Amur massacres' eventually became the symbol of 'Russian barbarism' in Japanese strong foreign policy folklore (and, incidentally, also a weapon in Chinese historiography to combat the negative image of the Boxers by pointing out the 'barbarity' of the Russian troops).[56]

We should add the cautionary remark that the 'war reports' were of a highly manipulative character and did not necessarily represent reality. Thus it is not surprising that the reports were an endless variation of Fukushima's war song, since the army authorities exerted a brutal censorship during the campaign and virtually dictated the reports to the special correspondents. This we learn from Taoka Reiun, who described the futility of their presence as follows:

> Life in the camps was idler than we had thought. Telling us that it was too dangerous, we were not allowed to observe the fighting. We were shut up in a separate room inside the headquarters, and there was nothing else to do but idling away the whole long day by reading, drinking, and having heated discussions. [...] The censorship of the authorities concerning our manuscripts was not strict, it was brutal. Except for what the person in charge told us, no other information was admitted. The little that was admitted was checked even for the words we used. Being someone who lives by language [*moji o motte tatsu*], I did not feel too pleased with fellows from the military meddling with my articles.[57]

Consequently, two days after Taoka had arrived in Tianjin, he and a large group of other reporters decided that their presence was dispensable and headed back to Japan.

Derision and disillusion

Whatever the truth of the war reports, they could not fail to incite some pride in the qualities of the Japanese troops among the public, and create the impression that they were as worthy as their allied fellows, if not even more so. Thus the politician and newspaper-owner Ōoka Ikuzō, for example, remembered in November 1900 that he was on his way back from a tour through Europe just when the Boxer expedition began. In the port of Penang, news of the bravery of the 'wild officer' Shiraishi, of which we have read above, reached the passengers and gave rise to lively discussions on the relative merit of 'yellow and white military men'.[58] In his discussion of the issue, Ōoka of course denied any connection between race and merit, and concluded with the reflection:

> Thus, if we try to compare the white and the yellow military man, there naturally may be some particular strong and weak points, but the Japanese

progress in the military field is absolutely not inferior to the white man. The eyes of the world will equally acknowledge this fact, too, especially since in the present North China Incident, we became the spearhead of the allied forces, and their main force, and put on a brilliant performance. The war achievements of the Japanese army in 1894/95 have been huge, and, in fact, its courage and valor have startled the world. However, since there was no witness present, it did not suffice to receive the public recognition of the experts of the world. The present China Incident, as it were, is like a regular Sumo tournament at the Ekōin [in Tokyo], and Japan is on top of the *banzuke* [the Sumo program, arranged in order of the competitors' hierarchy]. And Japan is not on one of those still lowly positions on the left, in fact, Japan is the Champion of the East [*Higashi no Ōzeki*].[59]

However, despite the gratifying feeling of seeing Japan in such exalted position, it must be said that the Boxer expedition was not popular for long, and by the end of July 1900 (before the allied troops reached Beijing), the foreign correspondent of the *North-China Herald* in Tokyo registered a significant drop in popularity:

> It must now be confessed that Japan never fought a more unpopular war than she is fighting at the present moment with China – or I suppose we should call it a 'military expedition.' The initial excitement has died away. The newspapers do their best to whip up the people a little, but without the slightest success, for the people refuse to be interested in the struggle.[60]

The foreign correspondent explained that the cause of this was the confusing situation of not fighting a war, but nonetheless being at arms. Moreover, the fighting proved to be far less glamorous than during the Sino–Japanese War, and took too long, so that the public soon became bored. Taoka Reiun's explanation (apart from the gruesome censorship) as to why he and many other special correspondents left Tianjin so soon points in this direction:

> Moreover, the bandits [*zoku*] fought with a vengeance and it did not look like Tianijn would be taken easily. And my knapsack was too poor to provide for many days or months. Our expectations had been that the allied army with irresistible force [*hachiku no ikioi*] would push towards Beijing in one go and would effect a treaty at the enemy's gates [*jōka no mei*].
> More than half of our group started out for home. I, too, joined them.[61]

Another reason why the Boxer expedition could hardly be seen as an unqualified success was the fact that the Japanese government and the military authorities might have tried too hard to impress the Western public and, involuntarily, exposed Japan to a mixture of sympathy, derision and outright racist condescension of the blandest sort. Thus the British-owned *North-China Herald* commented on Japan's motives in July 1900 as follows:

> As for gaining credit in the eyes of Europe, it is a powerful motive allied to vanity, self-distrust, and an intense yearning for sympathy, by which one can hardly help feeling touched. All these motives are laid bare in the official dispatches from the front, with that naiveté and unconsciousness of giving any offence [...] which is such a delightful trait in the Japanese character.[62]

The correspondent quoted some tokens of especially scurrilous news issued by the Japanese authorities such as: 'Lieutenant Shiraishi's bravery in entering the fort first [...] is said to have attracted the special notice of the allied forces many of whom afterwards asked his name.' or 'A portion of our detachment left for Tientsin by train early this morning [...] for Taku, and the rapidity with which they boarded the train elicited compliments from the forces of the other Powers'[63] (incidentally, Taoka Reiun described Japanese soldiers as rather 'awkward actors' [*donchō yakusha*], especially when mixing with the other troops[64]). The correspondent concluded:

> One would imagine from this that the Japanese are morbidly anxious for praise. At present they are, but it is not a normal occasion, and considering the overwhelming importance to the Japanese of their creating a good impression on the present occasion one can hardly blame them. It may be said, indeed, without exaggeration, that on the conduct of her officers and men in the present war depends the whole future of Japan. If the British Tommy takes to the Japanese Tommy as he takes to the Gurkha, all will be well; but there is just the possibility that he may conceive as rooted a dislike for him as the white labourer in British Columbia and Seattle does for the Japanese coolie, who is, after all, about the same status as the Japanese soldier. In that case Japan's energies would be for ever circumscribed within her five hundred isles.[65]

The Japanese public was, of course, not wholly ignorant of such condescending sentiments on the part of the Western powers. One incident in particular helped to cool its enthusiasm for the idealistic objectives of the Boxer expedition: this was the attitude of the British government towards Japanese participation. It should be remembered that the Japanese public was not informed of the initial offer of the British government that Britain would defray a part of the costs. However, at the beginning of August, the *Kokumin shinbun* printed a news item distributed by Reuters, that the British Chancellor of the Exchequer, Sir Michael Hicks Beach, had declared in the House of Commons that, with regard to Japan's dispatch of troops, Britain had no financial obligations toward Japan whatsoever, because Japan had not sent enough troops, and not soon enough anyway.[66]

To the Japanese public, this was insult heaped upon injury: firstly, that the British, who had begged Japan to help out, now declared the Japanese performance to be poor; but even more so, that the British government had even considered paying for Japan's services at all. This let Britain's request suddenly appear in a different light, turning the invitation to the club of civilized nations into Japan's employment as policemen in the service of Her Majesty. Thus a major German newspaper (which apparently thought that Britain still would meet its financial obligations) gleefully remarked at the *faux pas*:

> London could have known that the Japanese are a people much too proud to take cash money from the British for an enterprise which they want to be understood as being undertaken for the sake of civilization and humanity. London naturally believes that this offer was an act of generosity and magnanimity and is very surprised at the sensitivity of the Japanese. In Japan, people now will probably develop a better understanding of the expedition [the Boer War] which, under the mask of a higher civilization, has been undertaken to capture the goldmines in South Africa. Despite all the sweet words which the British press lavishes on the Japanese, the British still seem intent to treat the Japanese on the same level as the Chinese, otherwise they would not have taken the same liberty towards the Mikado as towards the Vice-Roy of Nanjing, who is said to be supported now by British money.[67]

The foreign correspondent of the *North-China Herald* in Tokyo, too, observed that 'they [the Japanese] are all of them convinced that England has an unpleasant habit of using other Powers as tools which she carelessly casts aside when done with. The Government did not therefore appear to be particularly anxious to let the public into its confidence about that guarantee.'[68]

Some Japanese observers felt, indeed, that Japan had been duped and abused as cheap labor for dirty work. This we can gauge, for example, from a commentary of Kuga Katsunan which appeared a few days after news of the (broken) British promise of payment became known.[69] According to Katsunan, the alleged lack of courage and propriety among the Western soldiers, which the Japanese press had been so diligent to point out, in fact was a sham and reflected rather badly on Japan's status in the eyes of the Western powers:

> If, with regards to the courage of the troops, the Western people are seen to be fearful and weak, this too, might not be an apt criticism. Because they consider it civilized to love their life and believe that their own life is so many times more valuable than the life of the Chinese. In this point, I must call on the recollection of the Japanese people, namely, that when Western people conquer an uncivilized population [*mikai jinmin*], they have as a principle the maxim 'In fighting the natives, make

natives the vanguard!' [*Dojin o utsu ni wa dojin o senpō seyo*] Like presently the French in their conquest of West Africa invariably use Algerian soldiers, and the Russians in their conquest of Central Asia use Cossacks, all follow the same principle. This time, if the Western powers eagerly encourage the Japanese soldiers and want to make them conquer North China, do they treat the Japanese soldiers not like the Cossack, the Algerian soldier, or the Indian soldier? It is just the same sort of using natives against natives. Is it after all such a case? The European and American troops in the area of Tianjin always leave the dangerous parts to the Japanese soldiers and would rather not advance fiercely, and this makes the Asian people [*Tōjin*], especially the Japanese reach the conclusion that they lack in courage. But one certainly cannot say that this is their characteristic nature. They all secretly say among themselves: 'Our life is not that cheap; fighting with the Chinese and trading their lives for it is the job of a people close to the Chinese.'[70]

Katsunan concluded that the Western powers sent Japan ahead, but would reap the benefits afterward. Thus the Japanese should not pride themselves vainly in their seemingly superior courage and discipline. Moreover, in two consecutive articles at around the same time, Katsunan began to re-emphasize the anti-Christian aspect of the conflict,[71] thus laying the argumentative ground for demanding Japan should pull out of the expedition.

However, it should be cautioned that there was also a much simpler reason for the drop in popularity and the shift of the public's attention away from the Boxer expedition, which was that it was soon enticed by the rising confrontation with Russia over Manchuria and Korea. Whereas anti-Russian sentiment had been latent in the war reports of the Boxer expedition, these broke out in August and September 1900 endemically, and continued (with varying intensity) until the beginning of war in 1904. It is no coincidence that Kuga Katsunan, who so vociferously voted for pulling out of the Boxer expedition, at the same time became one of the chief spokesmen of the anti-Russian strong foreign policy movement.

The Anglo–Japanese Alliance and the Russo–Japanese War

The Boxer Incident and the resulting Boxer Protocol of 1901 are usually seen as an unprecedented, or even all-time, nadir of China's international position in history.[72] Of course, this is subject to debate, as one could argue that China's position during and immediately after the Russo–Japanese War 1904–05 was even more helpless, albeit no less affected by its outcome.[73] Whatever the case may be, judged from the Japanese perspective it is hard to imagine that China's position at around 1900, as a powerless nonentity, subject to friendly intervention but with no subject of its own, could be surpassed. What followed in the aftermath of the Boxer Incident was consequently but a variation on this motif, albeit an important one, as it completed the psychological framework within which future Sino–Japanese relations worked. Thus the Russo–Japanese War exposed the reverse side of benevolent condescension towards China, which was hurt pride and irritation that China, like an ungrateful child, not only would reject Japan's help and guidance, but would even turn against its well meaning mentor. This became the standard reaction in the future whenever supposedly good intentions on the Japanese side were met with bouts of nationalism on the Chinese side.

The chain of events leading up to Japan's final confrontation with Russia has been the subject of many studies and needs no retelling here.[74] Let it suffice to say that already, since autumn 1899, war between Russia and Japan over the issue of Korea seemed not unlikely, at least among the public.[75] The Boxer Incident, with Russia occupying key positions, made this tension palpable to everyone, as we have seen, and extended it to Manchuria. Even Japan had made a clumsy – and abortive – attempt to extend its influence into South China on this occasion.[76] Moreover, in the wake of the expedition the Japanese public, as Itō Hirobumi observed with concern, was all for occupying Korea (and ousting Russia, by the by).[77]

Thus the Boxer Incident was accompanied by an evil foreboding that, after the object of the expedition was accomplished, the powers would start to act independently again, and pursue a partition of China beyond the *status quo*.[78] In July 1900, the United States issued a second Open Door note, which expanded the original note of 1899 by the preservation of Chinese territorial and administrative integrity.[79] More importantly, Britain and Germany in October 1900 agreed that this policy should apply to all Chinese territory within the limits of their influence, and signed a joint undertaking to observe certain principles, among which was the promise that both countries would 'direct their policy towards maintaining undiminished the territorial condition of the Chinese Empire.'[80] Japan declared its adherence to this agreement. Russia's reply however indicated that it would not adopt the Open Door policy for its own sphere of interest.

Despite the tensions, the Japanese government, especially under Itō, tried to solve the conflict by negotiations with Russia, largely based on the idea of exchanging the acknowledgment of Japanese interests in Korea with accepting Russia's domination in Manchuria (the so-called *Man-Kan kōkan-ron*). However, in June 1901, a fateful cabinet reshuffle occurred and, with Katsura Tarō, a younger generation came to share power with the *genrō* which was less cautious in foreign affairs and much more assertive than the previous one. Katsura was soon joined by Komura Jutarō as foreign minister, himself an advocate of a stronger Japanese foreign policy who also entertained ties with the non-governmental strong foreign policy movement.[81]

Katsura's accession to power was followed by swift rapprochement with Britain which finally, and especially against Itō Hirobumi's repeated warnings, ended in the first Anglo–Japanese Alliance, signed in January 1902.[82] Again, the preamble of the treaty declared that both countries were 'actuated solely by the desire to maintain the *status quo* and general peace in the extreme East, being moreover specially interested in maintaining the independence and territorial integrity of the Empire of China and the Empire of Corea, and in securing equal opportunities in those countries for the commerce and industry of all nations.'[83]

The Japanese public, when news of the alliance was broken in February 1902, was triumphant.[84] *The Japan Times* voiced the general sentiment as follows:

> We imagine that by this time every subject of His Most August Majesty the Emperor who can read and think is filled with the sensation of one who has suddenly awakened from dreams of youthful ambitions and vague aspirations to the consciousness of the fact that he has become a grown-up person of high position, of great reputation, and with a consequential burden of onerous responsibilities.[85]

Although *The Japan Times* expressed concern that the recent successes in the Sino–Japanese War and the Boxer expedition let some people harbor 'nebulous ambitions' which were undesirable, it allowed no doubt that this alliance with the foremost nation of the world signaled to all Japan's coming of age.

Not surprisingly, the same event was experienced in the opposite way in China.[86] The principal reaction among officials and intellectuals was shame that China was so utterly powerless to protect itself and had to rely itself on the powers of others, whose motives were dubious at best, and who placed China on the same level as Korea.[87] A Chinese newspaper, the *Jingzhong Ribao* (*The Alarm Bell*), illustrated China's situation quite poignantly. A caricature shows the towering figures of Britannia and Amaterasu both benevolently looking down on their two little protégés China and Korea, drawn as small children.[88] Whereas the Anglo–Japanese Alliance was felt to make Japan a 'grown-up person,' it degraded China to the stage of infancy.

The final stage of Russo–Japanese confrontation is quickly told: under pressure of the Anglo–Japanese alliance, Russia at first promised China a scaled withdrawal of its troops, but failed to continue as promised after the first partial withdrawal.[89] The Japanese government tried to reach a solution by negotiations with Russia, resuming the old idea of exchanging Manchuria for Korea. The Russian leadership, however, saw no necessity of a trade-off and insisted on maintaining its position in Korea as well. Finally, in December 1903, after a series of Imperial conferences and a fruitless exchange of diplomatic notes, the Japanese leadership decided to discontinue negotiations and prepare for war, Itō and Yamagata with more reluctance than the younger generation which had considered a final decisive confrontation with Russia as inevitable from early on. Japan initiated military action on 8 February 1904 and officially declared war on Russia two days later. During the preparations and throughout the war, Japan presented itself toward the national and global public as the disinterested champion of Chinese and Korean integrity and independence.

Although the parties fought about a part of Chinese sovereign territory; Japan fought ostensibly in order to retrieve Manchuria from Russian clasps only to return it to China; and the actual fighting would predictably take place on Chinese soil, the Qing court was not consulted on the issue, except for the recommendation that it should declare itself neutral.[90] This advice was pressed upon China not only by Japan, but also by Britain and the United States. The general fear was that China's participation would trigger a chain reaction, through which France would accede to the war due to the Franco-Russian alliance, which in turn would require Britain to join, and so on. On the Japanese side, the fear was that, apart from other complications, China's participation would unnecessarily nurture the rumors of a Yellow Peril, which the Russian side was anyway busy rekindling in the accompanying propaganda war.[91] Moreover, in an official statement, the Japanese government recommended China's neutrality because of its precarious financial and domestic situation, as China's participation not only might lead to unforeseeable consequences, but also would be to the detriment of China's commerce and finances, which in turn might trigger another domestic uprising.[92]

The Qing court formally declared neutrality on 12/13 February 1904. In its declaration, it made it clear that Manchuria was part of Chinese sovereign territory although, given the actual situation, it had to concede that enforcement of the rules of neutrality there would be impossible.[93] The Chinese leadership was under no illusion about the disinterestedness of the fighting parties, and was certain that, either way, China would lose something. However, although it was unwise to alienate Russia altogether, the majority seemed to be inclined to favor Japan, all the more so since the course of the war proved favorable for Japan. This was also the tendency of most Chinese observers, who, however, voiced their shame and (often politically motivated) fury that the Qing court was unable to, or too inept to, defend China on its own, and who gloomily predicted that Manchuria was but the writing on the wall.[94]

The strong foreign policy movement in Japan, which had rallied and lobbied with varying intensity for war with Russia since 1900, and the Japanese newspapers, which one by one had fallen in line with the pro-war advocates, rejoiced when Japan finally declared war.[95] They, too, hailed the war in terms of protecting China's (and Korea's) integrity and independence, which had been the war cry all along. However, when war began the Japanese attitude towards China and the Chinese government showed, among already familiar or predictable elements, an interesting variation on the theme of Sino–Japanese friendship.

Among the more familiar ingredients of war sentiments was mockery of China's weakness. Thus the *Tōkyō Asahi shinbun* derided the very thought that China should even consider joining the war. However, even if so, this would not activate the Franco-Russian alliance, as China was not a 'power' in the sense of the alliance any more.[96] During the war, China was mocked for not being able to enforce neutrality in its own country, let alone protect its citizens in Manchuria, submitting readily to the threats and extortion of Russia: the Qing court probably did not even understand the rules of neutrality, which would enable it to call in another neutral country for the protection of neutrality if China was unable to fulfill the duties of a neutral country in the first place.[97]

Moreover, it is conspicuous that the case of China now was often discussed alongside Korea without any distinctions, thus confirming the Chinese dread that China indeed had sunk to the level of its former vassal.[98] Finally, we can observe the usual attempts to dissociate Japan from China and Korea in the eyes of the West, lest there might be any misunderstandings as to Japan's place in the world. The *Nippon*, for example, argued against rumors of the 'yellow peril' in Europe that this narrative had lost all foundation considering Japan's many international successes in the past ten years. In fact, the 'yellow peril' theory had evolved, and today was no longer about the fundamental differences of race, religion or civilization, but was about national morality.[99] Finally, the yellow peril theory in its old form supposed that Japan would lead China and Korea against the West, and would be able to develop or 'Japanize' (*Nihon-ka/Nihon to konka*) those countries. However, considering the sorry state of China and Korea at the time, and their fundamental differences anyway, this was rather unlikely.[100] Such a statement was, of course, contrary to all that the *Nippon* (and the Japanese public since 1898) had previously said, but should be taken for what it was – a rather specious argument in wartime to bolster Japan's reputation in the West, not a fundamental statement on Sino–Japanese relations.

The new aspect of the Japanese attitude towards China was hurt pride and vindictive anger that the Chinese government would not show itself loyal to its friend Japan, but would even turn against its mentor and collude with Russia. The *Nippon*, for example, from early on in the war, observed that China had difficulties in enforcing strict neutrality, especially with respect to the prohibition of contraband items.[101] In fact China did have these problems, as it was too weak to enforce order, and Japan and Russia both took advantage of it. Thus the Qing court was under pressure, not only from the fighting parties, but also from European countries, which wanted to carry on trade in Chinese ports as usual.[102] However, the *Nippon* invariably saw Japan as the loser of these infringements, and attributed them not only to the weakness, but eventually to the malevolence of the Chinese leaders who wished Japan ill, despite the fact that Japan was sacrificing its money and blood to retrieve Manchuria for them. As we have seen, this was quite contrary to the real situation among the Chinese leadership, and indicates the level of mistrust and insecurity that still existed on the Japanese side, despite professions of friendship.

> The government and the people of our country since long have wished to see the Qing court as the protector of the Chinese people and to

conduct good-neighborly relations with it. And yet, the Qing court still
pursues its highhanded ways, looks down upon us as a small insignif-
icant country and in conspiring with the Russian court does not mind to
upset peace and stability in East Asia.[103]

In the following, the *Nippon* portrayed the Qing court (or alternatively, the
'Manchurian court') as a bunch of oriental despots who did not care about
the Chinese people and merely tried to preserve the power of the Manchurian rulers. In this, they were quite similar to the autocratic court of Russia,
the similarities to which the *Nippon* did not hesitate to support with a wild
theory on the common ethnic ancestry of both courts.[104] Thus the *Nippon*
reached the verdict: 'In the Qing court today there are truly no decent
people' (*Shin-tei konnichi jitsu ni hito nashi*).[105] However, at the same time,
the *Nippon* repeatedly stressed that this did not apply to the Chinese people,
as the Qing court did not represent its subjects (*Shina-jin no daihyō ni arazu*)
and even cited the Chinese press for pro-Japanese positions among the Chinese people.[106] Thus the idea of friendship on the people's level was kept up.

Another source of irritation was China's alleged bid for participation in
the Portsmouth negotiations. China did consider asking to be represented,
but eventually did not push the issue.[107] However, the Japanese press chafed
at the sheer ingratitude of even trying to participate, relating rumors that the
Qing court already had made secret agreements with Russia. The *Kokumin
shinbun*, for example, protested against China's participation, since it had
declared its neutrality and consequently should stick to it.[108] Moreover, if
China now entered the talks and the latter failed, China would become
involved in the *embroglio*, with the consequences described above. However,
more gravely than that weighed the sheer ingratitude of it:

> For the sake of China, we have given our best in the name of good-
> neighborly relations. The whole world knows it, and no Chinese person
> who feels so much as a spark of love for his own country will refuse to
> be moved by the supreme morality of our empire. From the start, there
> have been merely two ways for China to conduct herself: either rely on
> our empire and maintain her independence, or, if not, abandon herself to
> ruin and destruction, break-up and disintegration. There is no other
> choice.
>
> [...] And yet, at this juncture, this China now plans to participate in
> the Russo–Japanese peace talks, now notifies the powers that it will
> submit herself to the solution of the Manchurian question which the two
> powers Russia and Japan have agreed upon. What is the meaning of
> such untoward boldness? No doubt this is the height of not knowing
> one's proper station.[109]

Thus the increasingly self-assertive manner which Chinese diplomats began
to display in the wake of the Russo–Japanese War irritated Japanese observers.[110]

However, the storm blew over. As soon as the Portsmouth Treaty was signed, and Komura Jutarō in November 1905 hastened to Beijing to begin negotiations with China concerning the conferral of Russian rights to Japan as agreed in Portsmouth, Japanese commentaries became much more conciliatory and reverted to their former stance towards China.[111] Thus the *Nippon*, which clearly supported Komura's diplomacy, informed its readership of the pending Beijing talks and their progress in a much more sober and matter-of-fact manner, and completely dropped its abusive language against the Qing court.[112]

That things had finally gone back to 'business as usual' we can best observe in the *Nippon*'s commentary on the visit of a Chinese delegation to Tokyo in January 1906.[113] The *Nippon* guessed that the delegation, which was to stay for three weeks, after which it would travel on to the United States and Europe, had come to Japan to study the mechanics of constitutional government. The factual background for this assumption was the push for constitutional government in China, which had begun in 1904 within and outside Chinese government circles. This movement led to five official missions abroad to study constitutional government (two of them in 1905–06) and to the drafting of a 23-article Outline of a Constitution (*Xianfa dagang*), which was adopted in 1908 and was largely based on the Meiji model, albeit even more monarch-centered than its Japanese counterpart.[114]

The *Nippon* warmly welcomed the new tendency toward constitutionalism, and saw it as a sign that the Qing court had finally understood the urgency of reform, a lack of which would only invite danger from without and cause trouble within. This, in turn, led the *Nippon* to revise its former verdict and conclude that the Qing court, in fact, consisted of decent people (*chōtei mata hito ari to sezu ya*).[115] Moreover, the *Nippon* explained that the reforms would be much easier to carry out than, say, in Russia, as in China there existed at least a certain tradition of reform and a minimum degree of rule of law. Moreover, as in the case of Japan's Meiji Restoration, knowledge about political participation was widespread among the Chinese population so that elections might produce surprisingly many successful candidates.

The parallel with the Meiji Restoration indicates that China was restored into the graces of the *Nippon*. Thus the article ended on a positive note and wished the delegation success:

> If the [Qing] court does not rashly provoke a confrontation, tries to live in harmony with the other countries as much as possible and devotes itself to the improvement of its domestic affairs, then things on the whole will work out, and it will surely not meet the misfortune of a revolution.[116]

Conclusion

In the decade between 1895 and 1904, relations between China and Japan and the international status of the two countries underwent a fundamental change with lasting consequences especially for the mutual perspective of those countries, repercussions of which can be traced through the history of modern Sino–Japanese relations up to the present. This book examines the shifting attitude of the Japanese public toward China in the years between 1895 and 1904 through comments in major periodicals on important China-related events. The results of this study can be summarized as follows:

China's role in the Japanese discourse on politics in the decade between 1895 and 1904 underwent a fundamental transformation. The complex process reflected not only a pivotal shift in the underlying power relations between the two nations, but also Japan's steady rise as a 'civilized' nation among the Western powers and the domestic turmoil which adaptation to this new role entailed.

During the early Meiji period, Japan challenged China as the direct political competitor in East Asia. Despite the fact that Chinese culture maintained a high status as classical education in Meiji society, the political China assumed the role of Japan's ideological adversary, echoing Western clichés of 'oriental' stagnancy and degeneration. At the same time, Japanese attitudes betrayed a profound sense of insecurity and loathing of condescension from both sides, China and the West. The Sino–Japanese War 1894–95 led to the most fateful and lasting power shift in the history of modern Sino–Japanese relations. However, for all the satisfaction and triumph that this afforded, a feeling of unease remained that China, at some point in time, might regain its strength. Moreover, the war inadvertently brought on the full globalization of East Asia. The Tripartite Intervention, although a bitter shock to the Japanese public, was understood in these terms and prompted the Japanese government to initiate an ambitious armament-expansion program, which enforced a withdrawal from international politics and wrought havoc on domestic politics, finances and the economy. The expansion of the Western powers during the Far Eastern Crisis 1897–98 into China led to a gradual Sino–Japanese rapprochement, albeit on a merely informal level, as the Japanese government tried to calm Western racialist fears or rumors of a

Sino–Japanese alliance. The Japanese public rejected the idea of a racially or culturally motivated solidarity with China, but by the end of 1898 generally advocated Japan's responsibility for the 'protection of China' (*Shina hozen*). Advocates of a strong foreign policy attacked the 'weak-kneed' stance of the government and demanded that Japan protest against Germany's and Russia's actions in China. Moreover, commentators across political divisions routinely called for reforms in China, and argued that Japan had a special responsibility to help China reform, even if that meant pressuring the Chinese government by threats of force. However, the cool reactions to the Hundred Days Reform in China in 1898 show that too drastic (and too independent) a reform was not welcome in Japan, either. The general opinion was that China could not, and should not, progress too fast, which may have been motivated partly by fear that China might become a competitor again. It is telling that the most marked professions of friendship for China, even among the formerly neutral press, came forth only after the Hundred Days Reform had failed. However, the unwillingness to acknowledge real progress in China may have had its cause also in the leaden Meiji interwar years, which were pervaded by a sense of political and social stagnation. By late 1898, continued domestic unrest in China led to the general acceptance across political boundaries of Japan's joint responsibility with the Western powers to 'protect China's integrity and stability' by financial aid and even domestic intervention. Consequently, the Japanese public readily supported the Boxer expedition in 1900 as a mission of 'civilization.' For the same reason, it rejected viewing the conflict as a war, although it very much looked like one. Moreover, despite general insistence that the expedition was on China's behalf, the incident visibly demonstrates China's gradual effacement from political discourse. The 'war reports' from the Boxer expedition barely acknowledge China's role, and focus instead on Japan's competition with the Western powers for distinction as a courageous and law-abiding nation, even more civilized than some European powers, although this sense of competition was hardly reciprocated. Moreover, the war reports hint at intensifying tensions with Russia, and the Japanese public, which gradually lost interest in the rather unglamorous Boxer expedition, soon turned its attention toward the more exciting conflict with Russia over Korea and Manchuria instead. Thus Russia eventually replaced China as the new polarizing power in Meiji political discourse. In the Russo–Japanese War, Japanese accusations of Chinese ingratitude despite Japan's sacrifices, especially the allegation that the Qing court took Russia's side in the war and would even dare to consider joining the Portsmouth peace talks, show the reverse side of Japan's 'friendship' towards China and completed the psychological framework within which Sino–Japanese relations eventually worked.

Considering the problem that initially motivated this study – the contentious nature of Sino–Japanese relations after the Sino–Japanese War – how does the above development reflect on the issue? To begin with the more transparent aspect, it is true that one could describe Sino–Japanese relations as exceptionally 'harmonious' (see the introduction) in the sense that, apart from Japan's participation in the Boxer expedition and war in Manchuria, the Japanese government refrained from the use of force against China and, considering what came after the fall of the Qing dynasty, maintained a rather moderate policy towards its former enemy. The Japanese government did not join the powers in the scramble for concessions in 1898, and even though Japan did acquire the Russian positions in Port Arthur, Dalian and South Manchuria, the details were at least negotiated with some moderation during the Beijing talks, a concession which, if Komura had acted fully in the spirit of the Western powers, he would probably not have bothered to make.[1] Thus, if William Langer criticizes Europe's treatment of China in the whole period from 1895 to 1900 as being 'devoid of all consideration and of all understanding', the dominant note being always 'that force is the father of peace and that the only method of treating successfully with China is the method of the mailed fist,'[2] this does not hold true for Japan's China policy in the same period. On the contrary, the foreign policy of the late Meiji period has been often commended for its relative moderation and realism, both of which, however, got lost somewhere in the following generations.[3] Thus there may have been powerful figures, especially in the army, who, like so many European leaders in the late 1890s, believed that China's break-up was imminent and that Japan should have a share in the following distribution.[4] However, most civilian leaders, such as Itō Hirobumi, were, as Peter Duus calls them, 'cautious imperialists,' who were confident that China could (and should) remain intact and who acted accordingly.[5]

Of course, one could argue, as the opposition always did at the time, that Japan's cautiousness was merely a sign of weakness. Marius B. Jansen, too, observed that 'Meiji leaders [...] were often moderate not by choice, but because of Japan's international handicaps,' the biggest of which certainly was that, until 1904, Japan simply lacked real capacity for formal imperialism.[6] However, this only states the obvious, and does not detract from the merit of those leaders who did realistically assess Japan's strength and did not overreach themselves, as did Japanese leaders of the following generations, who thereby laid the foundation for the future destabilization of the continent.

Japan's informal cooperation with China in the years following the Sino–Japanese War gives ample proof of this policy. The cooperation might have laid the groundwork for Japan's 'informal empire' in China and might nonetheless have been, for all its informality, imperialism, but in the period under discussion this at least was done with the collaboration of those Chinese politicians, students and revolutionaries who hoped to profit from Japan, each in their own way.

The Japanese public had an attitude to match this policy, despite often vehement protests to the contrary. Thus, to begin with another observation of the more obvious, the Sino–Japanese War did not have the effect of turning respect into contempt and undermining 'a millennium of harmonious

Sino–Japanese relations.'[7] Apart from the fact that such a millennium probably never existed and that Chinese classical culture enjoyed undiminished respect with those who were still conversant in it, the war alone would not have changed the Japanese public attitude for good, if it were not for the subsequent contribution of the Western powers and the failure of the Hundred Days Reform to expose China's weakness and helplessness for all to see. Moreover, these events paradoxically did not encourage the Japanese public to continue its prewar harangue against China as the 'common enemy' of civilization, but led to a rapprochement between China and Japan which, in the Japanese public view, was rationalized as the revival of the Sino–Japanese friendship.

This friendship was, of course, of a rather special kind. Firstly, the fact that these professions of friendship generally came forth only after China's defeat and additional proof of the irreversibility of the power shift indicates that the friendship was built on China's subordination and would last only as long as China remained in this position. Thus the relationship was never meant to be a bond of equals. This is also apparent in the quite different treatment which Chinese labor immigrants received in Japan, as they remained possibly dangerous to the Japanese labor society, whereas the Chinese officials and students, who were wooed and lured to Japan, were deemed potentially useful.

Moreover, if one part of the Sino–Japanese friendship was bolstered on a feeling of superior strength, the slogan of 'protecting China's integrity and stability' (*Shina hozen*), which became the generally accepted view by the end of 1898, was rather predicated on the awareness of Japan's weak position among the other powers. Thus the slogan, which essentially called for the protection of the territorial *status quo* in China, was a direct reaction to the scramble for concessions that, if it had continued, would have led to a closing off of spheres and excluded Japan from the 'Great Game.' In that sense, the Japanese intention of keeping the Door open very much resembled the China policy of the Western powers before the 1890s, and anticipated the new consent among the powers as a consequence of the Boxer expedition and the Russo–Japanese War.[8] The fact that the Japanese public arrived at this conclusion already in 1898, earlier than others, might be owed to Japan's relative weak position at the time.

In this situation, the Japanese professions of friendship towards China were, of course, calculated to facilitate Japan's informal expansion in China through creating a bond of mutual exploitation with their Chinese partners.[9] The invocation of a common bond of race and culture (*dōbun dōshu*) and of the strategic significance of their cooperation (the 'lips and teeth'), incidentally, fall into the same category, as such assurances were quickly discarded when they threatened to hurt Japan's interests, especially its reputation among the Western powers.

The admixture of overbearing friendliness, cautiousness and calculation is well demonstrated in a statement by the 'China expert' Shiga Sukegorō, although few of his contemporaries would have dared to put it so bluntly:

For the sake of China and the whole of Asia it is natural to hope that our government, our ministers abroad and the people will offer help and advice as much as they can, and that this will yield good results. However, we should also be careful to stay within certain limits, lest our help and advice attracts too much attention or is too intrusive. This is absolutely not weakness or indecision. To avoid the form while grasping the substance, isn't that the best way to achieve the ultimate goal? Especially now that the hunting for concessions is so in vogue it is perfectly clear that our policy must not be too rash or too obvious. For now, we should keep our eyes fixed on the future and devise a plan of how to ultimately secure victory. Otherwise, we will come upon many obstacles or even fail with our long-term policy altogether.

An individual, when dealing with the world, needs both boldness and circumspection. The same applies for a country perched between the great powers. [...][10]

The mixture of condescending benevolence and cunning ambition, of course, throws a somewhat darker light on the 'Golden Decade' of Sino–Japanese cooperation between 1898 and 1912.[11] However, it must be conceded that, for the above reasons, the Japanese public, too, eventually accommodated itself to the more cautious China policy of the civilian leaders at the time, despite protests to the contrary. There were, of course, numerous instances when strong foreign policy advocates demanded 'the method of the mailed fist' in dealing with China, even to the point of joining the powers in the race for concessions. However, such demands were frequently motivated by quite extraneous reasons, such as the wish to excite public opinion and incite it against the domestic political enemy, the 'weak-kneed' Meiji oligarchs. When in power, strong foreign policy advocates close to the parties did not act differently from their enemies. Thus commentators in general demonstrated a remarkable flexibility, if not opportunism, in adjusting their previously held position to the more expedient China policy at the time. Such flexibility may have not existed in the case of Korea, as the latter was a relatively less contested terrain among the powers, but in the case of the vast, 'globalized' empire China, things were different.[12]

Yet it would be wrong to attribute the public attitude toward China policy to pure pragmatism and the pursuit of national self-interest only. Of irrational motives, there was prejudice enough against China's backwardness, as we have seen, but there was even more pride about Japan's accomplishments as a 'civilized' nation – the only civilized nation in East Asia, according to the self-esteem of late Meiji citizens, and also to the sympathetic assurances of Westerners visiting the Far East. As frequent outbursts against Chinese 'arrogance' indicate, the intensity of this pride stood in direct proportion to the humiliation that the Japanese believed to have suffered from Sino-centrist condescension previously. However, this attitude could not fail to show a similar arrogance towards China, including the self-assurance that Japan would know better how to help China than the Chinese themselves. It is no great surprise that Chinese overseas students in Japan, while acknowledging the sorry state of their nation, would not take kindly to the overbearing attitude of their surroundings, assume a vindictive attitude to Japan similar to the Japanese attitude to China, and leave with a generally anti-Japanese bias.[13]

This is not to say that, in internal debates, Japanese intellectuals were unreflective of Japan's course of modernization and fully satisfied with how it went. On the contrary, the time after the Sino–Japanese War teemed with dissatisfaction, as if, with Japan's rapid rise to power, many people suddenly became sick of 'civilization' and had enough of it. However, even though such intellectuals as Kōtoku Shūsui, Taoka Reiun or Okakura Tenshin may have rallied against the ills of civilization, such a critique was grounded in a global discourse of *Zivilisationsmüdigkeit* and certainly had no intention of questioning Japan's relative superiority over China.[14]

It is in this context that we have to situate the endeavors of the Tokyo school of 'oriental history' (*Tōyō-shi*) to create a historical narrative for Japan which would place the nation on the same level as, if not above, the Occident and explain Japan's special status in the East, especially towards contemporary *Shina*, 'a disorderly place – not a nation – from which Japan could both separate itself and express its paternal compassion and guidance.'[15] Such a project certainly coincided with the mainstream of the Japanese public opinion. In this respect, Naitō Konan's view on politics and Sinology was certainly more original, if also more ambivalent. On the one hand, Naitō routinely held forth the Meiji Restoration as a model and the necessity of Japan's help and assistance to China's reform, which was completely in tune with the late Meiji common sense, as we have seen. On the other hand, he argued against the facile adoption of Western civilization and in favor of a thorough understanding of the historical circumstances of China's needed reforms, so as to be able to protect China's traditions and maintain East Asia's cultural integrity.[16] Most late Meiji contemporaries would not have given much for the latter in real politics.

This finally leads us to the other side of the equation, Japan's changing relations with the Western powers in the years 1895–1904. Generally speaking, the Meiji period can be seen as a remarkable example of cultural transference, as the same deference to an exterior standard of civilization and the (one-sided) ambition to compete with its originator applied to China and the Western powers before and after the Meiji Restoration, respectively.[17] For the time being, China remained the political competitor in the early Meiji period. However, as the Sino–Japanese War and subsequent events led to the rapid decline of China's star in political discourse and the rise of the Western powers as the new antagonists (first Russia, later the USA), China disappeared, but the psychological baggage remained and shaped future relations with the remaining powers. This included the one-sided sense of competition and the resentment that unfailingly surfaced whenever Japan's efforts were considered to be not sufficiently acknowledged. Thus, having finally attained great power status, but retaining the old baggage of former conflict, Japan entered a new stage of international politics in the twentieth century.

If China 'disappeared' between 1894 and 1904, this merely applied to its status as a relevant antagonist in political discourse, not to Japanese foreign politics in general. On the contrary, China remained, and even dominated Japan's Foreign Ministry activities and thinking until 1945, to the extent that Japanese foreign policy is seen as having been 'constantly hostage to events in China.'[18] However, it is outside the scope of this study to give a more detailed account of this complex story.[19] Instead, this last section will highlight some of the central events in Sino–Japanese relations after 1905, which conspicuously reflected the structural patterns of Sino–Japanese interaction as developed above.

The Russo–Japanese War and the Beijing Conference marked the inception of a new era in the history of East Asia and re-established relative stability in the area.[20] For China, Japan's emergence as great power had the effect that it 'did remove the fear of territorial partition which had threatened the moribund Ch'ing empire since 1895.'[21] However, the Qing empire soon collapsed, and in 1912 the tumultuous years of Republican China began. Ironically, the Chinese students who Japanese agencies had intended to train for (Japanese-guided) reform contributed through their revolutionary activities to the downfall of the Qing.[22] The Japanese government, true to the rationale that a stable and compliant empire best suited Japan's China policy, would have preferred to continue with the Qing court, and had not supported the downfall (although it had not suppressed the revolutionary elements in Japan, either). Thus it was only after some hesitation and vacillation that it followed Britain, which supported the new Republican government.[23] Otherwise, it continued to oppose the partition of China and in 1912, and again in 1915, overruled plans of the military to provoke a military clash and establish 'independent' regimes in Manchuria and Mongolia.[24] As during the Far Eastern Crisis, the public, too, discussed the fall of the Qing in terms of partition or protection of China, with the same conclusion that it was Japan's responsibility to guarantee the latter.[25]

However, within the limits of the international framework, the Japanese government did not fail to realize its potential, either. In 1910, Japan annexed Korea. Moreover, with the outbreak of the European war in 1914, Japan, too, declared war on Germany and demanded the unconditional transfer of all of German's leased territory in Jiaozhou Bay, supposedly for the purpose of returning this area to China. Emboldened by the success of having obtained the base, the Japanese government proceeded in 1915 to present China's new president Yuan Shikai with the ill-famed Twenty-One Demands, which in part concerned the transfer and extension of the German concessions for Shandong and, by its fifth group of 'desirable items,' would have turned China into a Japanese protectorate.

The story is well known and therefore does not need to be retold.[26] Let it suffice to say that Japan's actions (which, to be sure, were not uncontentious among the Japanese leadership) greatly affected Japan's reputation, especially in the USA, and antagonized even further the rampant anti-Japanese feelings among young Chinese to the point of the so-called May Fourth Movement in 1919. Yet the typical reaction of the Japanese public to these attacks very much resembled the situation during the Russo–Japanese War 1904–05, in that many Japanese commented on the sheer ingratitude of the Chinese, who had done nothing during the war but now expected to swiftly reap the benefits of Japan's actions and, moreover, slandered Japan for not returning Shandong immediately without some compensation for its gallant action on behalf of China.[27]

The end of the First World War led to a gradual territorial rollback and military containment of Japan in East Asia. Thus, on the occasion of the Washington Conference of 1921–22, the agreements resulting from which replaced the Anglo–Japanese Alliance and provided for a general arms limitation, Japan also returned Shandong to China. However, for all the spirit of integration, cooperation and relative restraint which recommended Japan's foreign policy in the 1920s, Japan's interest in north-eastern China remained a problem. Japan, as a result of the Russo–Japanese War, had acquired the Russian concessions in South Manchuria, most importantly the so-called 'Kwantung Leased Territory' of Port Arthur and Dalian. Already in 1895, the Belgian minister to Japan, Albert d'Anethan, had mixed feelings about the relative merits of a Japanese foothold in China:

> One can criticize, and perhaps with reason, that in annexing a part of Chinese territory, Japan loses the advantages of her insular position. As a result of the conquest, we shall see Japan obliged to strengthen her means of defense considerably more and to keep part of the Army on war footing for a long time. On the other hand, she assures thereby the independence [of Korea] or rather her 'protectorate' over Korea, making a land attack against the peninsula extremely difficult.[28]

As a consequence of the Russo–Japanese War, Manchuria came to be included in this strategic rationale, and Japan's 'special rights and interests' in Manchuria became a dogma which even the most liberal foreign minister dared not dispute in the following decades, nor saw a necessity to do so.[29] However, Manchuria was the millstone that dragged Japan into another war with China.[30] Thus, when Ian Nish observes that the Beijing Conference of 1905 'has its echoes throughout the first half of the twentieth century,' this is especially true for Port Arthur and Manchuria.[31]

The order of stability that had been reached in 1905 was predicated on China remaining as weak as it was then. However, with the Kuomintang under Chiang Kai-shek getting stronger and moving northwards, Japanese military circles saw Japan's security cordon in Manchuria threatened and reacted with increasing aggression. Finally, in 1931, the Manchurian Incident occurred, which, after a period of small-scale warfare, sent Japan 1937 into full-fledged war with China. Again, the war was not declared officially for several reasons, one of which was to avoid the USA declaring neutrality, as both parties were dependent on American supplies, but also because it contradicted the professed nature of the action, as during the Boxer expedition.[32]

The conflict with China was, as usual, clad in ideological terms, the fiction being that Japan was not fighting against, but on behalf of, the Chinese people to free it from the 'traitorous' Nationalist Government.[33] Thus the pretences of the Sino–Japanese friendship could be kept up. On the occasion, Japanese China scholars most fondly remembered the Japanese 'Golden Age of China diplomacy', the Sino–Japanese friendship at the turn of the century.[34] However, Japanese observers at the same time registered with increasing dismay that the Chinese failed to see the campaign in the same way.[35]

In more general terms, the fiction was that Japan fought for China to 'stimulate' its energies (thus echoing interpretations after the first Sino–Japanese War) and bring the two countries closer together in their mission of reviving the whole of Asia.[36] These sentiments found their most prominent expression in the declaration of the Konoe cabinet of 1938 that Japan intended to create a New Order in East Asia where the 'Asian peoples must turn their backs on the self-centered individualistic materialism in Europe, accept the common ideals of Asia and devote themselves to lives rooted in Asia.'[37] However, as it was 40 years before, it is doubtful whether the intended co-prosperity sphere of Asians was ever meant to become a community of equals, and whether those pan-Asianist sentiments had increased in substance over time.

This New Order was, of course, directed as an autonomous block against the USA rather than Europe. For a long time, but especially after 'factual war' with China had begun, the Japanese military and the public had accused the USA of supporting anti-Japanese elements in China, and especially of protecting the Nationalist government in Chongqing. This was also the official reason for attacking and declaring war on the USA in late 1941. However, for all those accusations against the USA, the proclamations of an autonomous Asian bloc and the ideological attempts to 'overcome modernity,' it is questionable whether this ever transcended the pattern of competition that had been in place for a long time. Thus it has been argued that, within the course of Japan's consistent attempts to be integrated into fully fledged membership of the international community, even the period of aberration during the early 1930s and 1945 was in part motivated as a reaction against the perceived rejection from the circle in which it wanted to find its place.[38]

Defeat in war in 1945 relieved Japan from political competition and tied it into a new order closer than many Japanese would have wished for. In proportion to its reduced political status, Japan turned inward and focused on economic reconstruction. This also shaped Sino–Japanese relations for the following decades. Thus, although economic exchange soon took up again between the countries, diplomatic contact with Beijing lay dormant.[39] This changed only in 1972, after the United States' sudden acknowledgement of the People's Republic, followed by China and Japan signing the Chinese-Japanese Treaty of Peace and Friendship of 1978. Since then, political relations have gradually intensified, although they still do not justice to the intensity and productivity of Sino–Japanese economic relations.

Having arrived in the present, how would a late Meiji citizen, a little more than 100 years later, view the current state of Sino–Japanese relations? At first sight, he or she would probably not feel too disoriented, and would recognize parallels with Japan's situation at the turn of the nineteenth century.[40] They would feel dismayed that China has regained its strength in the fields of politics, economics and security and is catching up with Japan again. They would probably register anti-Japanese protest in China, especially among the youth, with equal bafflement and attribute it to the misguided politics of its government. They would bemusedly observe the issues that are at stake in public discourse, but would eventually attribute history issues and human rights to those questions of 'national morality' which, according to Kuga Katsunan in 1905, would dominate international disputes henceforth. And finally, they would probably rejoice at the degree of productivity of Sino–Japanese economic relations and praise it as an exceptional example of the traditional Sino–Japanese friendship.

However, the same Meiji citizen would also fail to comprehend the fundamentally altered situation of both countries today. Globalization has progressed infinitely more than 100 years before, and has taken a decided turn from geostrategics to economics. China has considerably more influence in world politics than ever, not to speak of economic power. Japan has returned to a cautious foreign policy and cooperates within a closely knit international framework. And despite increasing elements of competition, for the first time in history there is now the chance for both nations to strike up a partnership on a more equal basis. In the process, the lessons of the late nineteenth century will lead us to distrust the verbal and symbolic excesses that so frequently disrupt public discourse, to view Sino–Japanese relations with more soberness and detachment than in the past, and hopefully both countries will find a balanced mutual understanding in the future. This is the practical significance of the dynamics of Sino–Japanese relations in the late Meiji period for us today.

Notes

Introduction

1 Immanuel Hsu, 'Late Ch'ing foreign relations, 1866–1905,' in John K. Fairbank and Kwang-Ching Liu (eds), *The Cambridge History of China, Vol. 2: Late Ch'ing, 1800–1911, Part 2*, Cambridge: Cambridge University Press, 1978, p. 129; Jürgen Osterhammel, *China und die Weltgesellschaft: vom 18 Jahrhundert bis in unsere Zeit* (China and the international society: from the eighteenth century to the present), Munich: C. H. Beck, 1989, p. 202.

2 A. Iriye, 'Japan's drive to great power status' in: Jansen, Marius B. (ed.) *Cambridge History of Japan, Vol. 5: The Nineteenth Century*, Cambridge, New York: Cambridge University Press, 1989, p. 777.

3 Gerrit W. Gong, *The Standard of 'Civilization' in International Society*, Oxford: Clarendon Press, 1984, p. 30.

4 William L. Langer, *The Diplomacy of Imperialism*, 2nd edn, New York: Alfred A. Knopf, 1965, pp. 167, 677.

5 Archibald Rosebery as quoted by Valentine Chirol, 'The Far Eastern Question,' part 1, *The Times*, 24 September 1895, p. 3.

6 Donald Keene, 'The Sino–Japanese War of 1894–95 and its Cultural Effects in Japan,' in Donald Shively (ed.), *Tradition and Modernization in Japanese Culture*. Princeton, NJ: Princeton University Press, p. 126; S. C. M. Paine, *The Sino–Japanese War of 1894–1895: Perceptions, Power and Primacy*, Cambridge: Cambridge University Press, 2003, pp. 4, 298–99.

7 See Douglas R. Reynolds, *China, 1898–1912: The Xinzheng Revolution and Japan*, Cambridge, MA: Harvard University Press, 1993, pp. xvi–xviii, 5–6; for other positive assessments (albeit with many more reservations) see Marius B. Jansen, *The Japanese and Sun Yat-Sen*, Cambridge, MA: Harvard University Press, 1967, pp. 218–20; Sanetō Keishū, *Nitchū hi-yūkō no rekishi* (The history of Sino–Japanese unfriendly relations), Tokyo: Asahi shinbunsha, 1973, p. 19.

8 On the various aspects of Sino–Japanese interactions see Jansen, *Japanese and Sun Yat-Sen*; Peter Duus et al. (eds), *The Japanese Informal Empire in China, 1895–1937*, Princeton, NJ: Princeton University Press, 1989; Paula Harrell, *Sowing the Seeds of Change: Chinese Students, Japanese Teachers, 1895–1905*, Stanford, CA: Stanford University Press, 1992; Douglas R. Reynolds, *China, 1898–1912*; Zhai Xin, *Tōa dōbunkai to Chūgoku: kindai Nihon ni okeru taigai rinen to sono jissen* (*The Tōa dōbun-kai and China: the ideology and practice of foreign relations in modern Japan*), Tokyo: Keiō gijuku daigaku shuppan-kai, 2001; Li Tingjiang, *Nihon zaikai to kindai Chūgoku: Shingai kakumei o chūshin ni* (The Japanese business world and modern China around the time of the Chinese Revolution 1911), 2nd edn, Tokyo: Ochanomizu shobō, 2003; Joshua A. Fogel (ed.), *Late Qing China and Meiji Japan: Political and Cultural Aspects*, Norwalk, CT: Eastbridge, 2004.

9 On Japanese Sinology and 'Oriental history,' see Joshua A. Fogel, *Politics and Sinology: The Case of Naitō Konan (1866–1934)*, Cambridge, MA: Council on East Asian Studies, Harvard University, 1984; Stefan Tanaka, *Japan's Orient: Rendering Pasts into History*. Berkeley and Los Angeles: University of California Press, 1993.

10 On Chinese overseas students in Japan, see Harrell, *Sowing the Seeds;* F. Huang, *Chinese Students in Japan in the Late Ch'ing Period*, translated by Katherine P. K. Whitaker, Tokyo: Tokyo Press, 1982; Sanetō Keishū, *Chūgoku-jin Nihon ryūgaku-shi zōho* (A history of Chinese students in Japan, enlarged edn), Tokyo: Kuroshio shuppan, 1970.

11 Akira Iriye, *China and Japan in the Global Setting*, Cambridge, MA: Harvard University Press, 1992, p. 139.

12 On patriotism and the use of foreigners as 'ideological mirror' see Carol Gluck, *Japan's Modern Myths: Ideology in the Late Meiji Period*, Princeton, NJ: Princeton University Press, 1985, pp. 127–38.

13 See Masuda Tomoko, 'Nisshin sengo keiei' (The post-1895 management program), in Inoue Matsusada *et al.* (eds), *Nihon rekishi taikei* (An outline of Japanese history), Tokyo: Yamakawa shuppan-sha, 1987, Vol. 4, p. 732.

14 On the 'social problems,' see Gluck, *Japan's Modern Myths*, pp. 26–35.

15 Gong, *Standard of 'Civilization'*, pp. 10, 30.

16 Gong, *Standard of 'Civilization'*, pp. 48–51; R.J. Vincent, 'Race in International Relations,' *International Affairs*, Vol. 58, No. 4 (Autumn 1982), pp. 661–66.

17 For the Korean case see Alexis Dudden, *Japan's Colonization of Korea: Discourse and Power*, Honolulu: University of Hawaii Press, 2005.

18 Gong, *Standard of 'Civilization'*, p. 39.

19 For a discussion of this problem in intellectual history in general, see Kano Masanao, *Shihon-shugi keisei-ki no chitsujo ishiki* (System consciousness in the formation period of capitalism), Tokyo: Chikuma shobō, 1969, pp. 16–23.

20 For more information on the (metropolitan) newspaper world and newspaper readership in the 1890s, see Nishida Taketoshi, *Meiji jidai no shinbun to zasshi* (Newspapers and magazines in the Meiji era), Tokyo: Shibundō, 1961, pp. 237–45; James L. Huffman, *Creating a Public: People and Press in Meiji Japan*, Honolulu: University of Hawaii Press, 1997, pp. 224–70; Yamamoto Taketoshi, *Kindai Nihon no shinbun no dokusha-sō* (Newspaper readership in modern Japan), Tokyo: Hōsei daigaku shuppan-kyoku, 1981, pp. 91–182; see also Sasaki Takashi, *Media to kenryoku* (The media and power), Tokyo: Chūō kōron shinsha, 1999.

21 F.G. Notehelfer, *Kōtoku Shūsui: Portrait of a Japanese Radical*, Cambridge: Cambridge University Press, 1971, p. 44.

22 See '*Jiji shinpō* no jisatsu' (The suicide of the *Jiji shinpō*), *Tōkyō nichinichi shinbun*, Nov. 16, 1898.

23 Thus it is claimed that Hayashi 'was practically responsible during many years for the attitude of the *Jiji shinpō* on foreign affairs,' see Hayashi Tadasu, *The Secret Memoirs of Count Tadasu Hayashi*. A. M. Pooley (ed.), London: Eveleigh Nash, 1915, p. 27 (introduction).

24 In 1895, a letter to the editor of the *Kokumin shinbun* complained about 'the dislike of the *Jiji shinpō* for China' (*Jiji shinpō no Shina-kirai*), see 'San-shinbun no monokirai' (The dislikes of three newspapers), *Kokumin shinbun*, July 25, 1895, p. 2. For example, the *Jiji shinpō* in the same year quoted an article in the Shanghai-based newspaper *Shenbao*, which criticized the demeaning caricatures of Chinese in the *Jiji shinpō*, see 'Shina shinbun, Jiji shinpō no manga o tsūba su' (A Chinese newspaper condemns the caricatures of the Jiji shinpō), *Jiji shinpō*, 8 March 1895, p. 2 [the short *Shenbao* article, dated 26 February 1898 (solar calendar) is reprinted as *kanbun* text]. To illustrate the Chinese reaction graphically, the recalcitrant *Jiji shinpō* added to the same text a no less demeaning caricature of

an enraged Chinese in a reading-room, tearing and stamping on the pages of the *Jiji shinpō* which, in turn, showed demeaning caricatures of (pig-tailed) Chinese.

25 The newspaper *Nippon* sometimes gave its title in Roman letters as '*NIPPON*', thus, it was not read *Nihon*, as western literature often has it.

26 Tokutomi Sohō, *Sohō jiden* (The Autobiography of Tokutomi Sohō), Tokyo: Heibonsha, 1982, p. 179.

27 For a more detailed study of Kuga Katsunan's positions, see Marutani Yoshinori, *Kuga Katsunan kenkyū* (Studies on Kuga Katsunan), Tokyo: Keisō shobō, 1990; Koyama Fumio, *Kuga Katsunan: 'Kokumin' no sōshutsu* (Kuga Katsunan: creating 'the nation'), Tokyo: Misuzu shobō, 1990.

28 In May 1898 the *Japan Weekly Mail* welcomed the sentencing of the editor and printer of the newspaper in a libel suit; it was about time, it wrote, 'to send to their proper place, the convict's cell, men so indifferent to every moral principle as the conductors of the vile sheet' ('The Yorozu choho,' *Japan Weekly Mail*, 14 May 1898, p. 497).

1 China in the Tokugawa and early Meiji period

1 The above description of the Tokugawa international order is based on: Ronald P. Toby, 'Reopening the Question of Sakoku: Diplomacy in the Legitimation of the Tokugawa Bakufu', *Journal of Japanese Studies*, Vol. 3, No. 2 (Summer 1977), pp. 323–63; K. Tashiro, 'Foreign Relations during the Edo Period: Sakoku Reexamined', *Journal of Japanese Studies*, Vol. 8, No. 2 (Summer 1982), pp. 283–306; Ronald P. Toby, *State and Diplomacy in Early Modern Japan: Asia in the Development of the Tokugawa Bakufu*, Stanford, CA: Stanford University Press, 1984; Arano Yasunori, 'Kaikin to sakoku' (Maritime bans and national isolation), in Arano Yasunori *et al.* (eds), *Gaikō to sensō* (Diplomacy and war), Tokyo: Tōkyō daigaku shuppan-kai, 1992, pp. 191–222; Tsuruta Kei, 'Kinsei Nihon no yotsu no 'kuchi' (The four 'portals' of Tokugawa Japan), in *ibid.*, pp. 297–316.

2 Tashiro, 'Foreign Relations', p. 287.

3 See Toby, 'Reopening the Question', pp. 331–36, for the attempts at reconciliation with China between 1610 and 1625.

4 On the Chinese world order and tributary system, see John K. Fairbank and S. Y. Teng, 'On the Ch'ing Tributary System', *Harvard Journal of Asiatic Studies*, Vol. 6, No. 2 (June 1941), pp. 135–246; John K. Fairbank (ed.), *The Chinese World Order: Traditional China's Foreign Relations*, Cambridge, MA: Harvard University Press, 1968.

5 T. F. Tsiang, lecture delivered at the London School of Economics as cited by Fairbank/Teng, 'On the Ch'ing Tributary System', p. 140.

6 For more information on this symbolic exclusion of China in diplomatic protocol, see Toby, *State and Diplomacy*, especially pp. 168–230.

7 Bob T. Wakabayashi, 'Opium, Expulsion, Sovereignty, China's Lessons for Bakumatsu Japan', *Monumenta Nipponica*, Vol. 47, No. 1 (Spring 1992), p. 2.

8 On the central position of Chinese civilization in the Tokugawa world, see Marius B. Jansen, *China in the Tokugawa World*, Cambridge, MA: Harvard University Press, 1992, pp. 53–91; for literature especially, see Donald Keene, 'Characteristic Responses to Confucianism in Tokugawa Literature', in Peter Nosco (ed.), *Confucianism and Tokugawa Culture*, Princeton, NJ: Princeton University Press, 1984, pp. 120–37; for a view of the 'pattern' of Tokugawa aesthetics against its Chinese 'ground', see David Pollack, *The Fracture of Meaning: Japan's Synthesis of China from the Eighth through the Eighteenth Centuries*, Princeton, NJ: Princeton University Press, 1986, pp. 185–226.

9 See Ōba Osamu, *Edo jidai ni okeru Chūgoku bunka juyō no kenkyū* (Studies on the reception of Chinese culture in the Edo period), Tokyo: Dōhōsha, 1984; on the interrelatedness of Chinese and Japanese culture at the textual level in the Tokugawa Period, see Masuda Wataru, *Japan and China: Mutual Representations in the Modern Era*, translated by Joshua A. Fogel, Richmond, Surrey: Curzon, 2000.

10 Jansen, *China in the Tokugawa World*, p. 76.

11 On the problem of Sinocentrism in Tokugawa Japan, see Harootunian, Harry D., 'The Functions of China in Tokugawa Thought', in Akira Iriye (ed.), *The Chinese and the Japanese*, Princeton, NJ: Princeton University Press, 1980, pp. 9–36; Kate Wildman Nakai, 'The Naturalization of Confucianism in Tokugawa Japan: the Problem of Sinocentrism', *Harvard Journal of Asiatic Studies*, Vol. 40, No. 1 (June 1980), pp. 157–90; Toby, *State and Diplomacy*, pp. 211–30; Sakayori Masashi, 'Ka'i shisō no shosō' (Aspects of Sino-centric thinking), in Arano Yasunori *et al.* (eds), *Ji-ishiki to sōgo rikai* (Self-consciousness and mutual understanding), Tokyo: Tōkyō daigaku shuppankai, 1993, pp. 27–58.

12 Nakai, 'Naturalization', pp. 159–63, 187.

13 Harootunian, 'Function of China', p. 16, quoting Yamazaki Ansai.

14 *Ibid.*, pp. 14–15; Nakai, 'Naturalization', pp. 173–81.

15 Nakai argues that the hyperbole of the Japanese Confucianists was consciously ironic and shows their insight into the absurdity of the assertion of 'absolute truths' ('Naturalization', pp. 197–99).

16 On Chinese attitudes towards Japan, see Ishihara Michihiro, 'Mindai Chūgoku-jin no Nihon-kan' (Chinese views of Japan in the Ming Dynasty), *Rekishi kyōiku* 8.1 (January 1960), pp. 44–51; for Chinese knowledge about Japan in the mid-nineteenth century, see D. R. Howland, *Borders of Chinese Civilization: Geography and History at Empire's End*, Durham, NC and London: Duke University Press, 1996, 18–26.

17 Howland, *Borders*, p. 24.

18 For this assertion, see Nakai, 'Naturalization', p. 173; Harootunian, 'The Functions of China', p. 14.

19 Jonathan Spence, *The Search for Modern China*, New York, London: W.W. Norton, 1990, pp. 58–64.

20 *Ibid.*, p. 63.

21 Jansen, *China in the Tokugawa World*, pp. 56–59; Nakai, 'Naturalization', pp. 170–72.

22 On the attitude of the Kokugaku-sha towards China, see Harootunian, 'Functions', pp. 17–29.

23 Harootunian, 'Functions', p. 18; Jansen, *China in the Tokugawa World*, p. 83.

24 See Uete Michiari, 'Taigai-kan no tenkai' (Shifting paradigms in Japanese views of the world), in Hashikawa Bunzō and Matsumoto Sannosuke (eds), *Kindai Nihon seiji shisō-shi* (A history of modern Japanese political thought), Tokyo: Yūhikaku, 1971, Vol. 1, pp. 33–74; Watanabe, Hiroshi, 'Shisō mondai toshite no 'kaikoku': Nihon no baai' (The 'opening of the country' as an intellectual problem: Japan's case), Park Choong Seok and Watanabe Hiroshi (eds), *Kokka rinen to taigai ninshiki: jūshichi jūkyū-seiki* (The concept of the State and the perception of foreign countries: seventeenth to nineteenth century), Tokyo: Keiō gijuku daigaku shuppan-kai, 2001, pp. 281–329.

25 Shinobu Seizaburō (ed.), *Nihon gaikō-shi 1853–1972* (A history of Japanese foreign policy, 1853–1972), Tokyo: Mainichi shinbunsha, 1974, Vol. 1, p. 80; see also Harald Kleinschmidt, *Das europäische Völkerrecht und die ungleichen Verträge um die Mitte des 19. Jahrhunderts* (European international law and the unequal treaties in the mid-nineteenth century), Tokyo: OAG Gesellschaft für Natur-und Völkerkunde Ostasiens Tokyo, 2007.

26 For popular protest against the treaty revision process in Japan in the late 1880s and early 1890s, see Kenneth B. Pyle, *The New Generation in Meiji Japan: Problems of Cultural Identity 1885–1895*, Cambridge, MA: Harvard University Press, 1969, pp. 99–117; see also Kazuo Komiya, *Jōyaku kaisei to kokunai seiji* (Treaty revisions and domestic politics), Tokyo: Yoshikawa kōbunkan, 2001.

27 A. von Bulmerincq, *Das Völkerrecht oder das internationale Recht* (International law). Freiburg i.B.: J. C. B. Mohr, 1889. p. 206 (translated from the German).

28 For Japan's role in the emergence of the standard, see Gong, *Standard of Cvilization*, pp. 29–30; for a discussion of a definition of this standard, see *ibid.*, pp. 14–23.

29 Bulmerincq, *Völkerrecht*, p. 207: 'As much as nations which do not belong to the international community of law cannot demand relations, likewise states belonging to the community cannot force relations on nations not belonging to the community [...], on the contrary, the non-community state can refuse relations completely, or limit them to certain places.'

30 T. F. Tsiang, 'Sino–Japanese Diplomatic Relations, 1870–94', *The Chinese Social and Political Science Review*, Vol. 17, No. 1 (April 1933), p. 8; Bulmerincq, *Völkerrecht*, p. 207: foreign consuls in China have the right to issue passports to the citizens of their state for the non-treaty ports and the Chinese hinterland; the Chinese authorities were obligated to accept these. In Japan, consuls had no such right, *ibid.* pp. 340–41. On the presence of foreigners in Japan 1858–99, see J. E. Hoare, *Japan's Treaty Ports and Foreign Settlements: the Uninvited Guests*, Sandgate, Folkestone: Japan Library, 1994.

31 On the conclusion of the Sino–Japanese treaty, see Tsiang, 'Sino–Japanese Diplomatic Relations', pp. 4–16; Li Qizhang, 'Nisshin shūkō jōki seiritsu katei no sai-kentō' (A re-examination of the negotiation and ratification process of the Sino–Japanese Treaty of Amity), *Shigaku zasshi*, Vol. 115, No. 7 (2007), pp. 65–82; on Soejima Taneomi's mission to Beijing to exchange the instruments of ratification, see Wayne C. McWilliams, 'East Meets East: the Soejima Mission to China, 1873', *Monumenta Nipponica*, Vol. 30, No. 3 (Autumn 1975), pp. 237–75.

32 Tsiang, 'Sino–Japanese Diplomatic Relations', p. 10.

33 *Ibid.*; see also Shinobu, *Nihon gaikō-shi*, Vol. 1, p. 83.

34 Marlene Mayo, 'A Catechism of Western Diplomacy: the Japanese and Hamilton Fish, 1873', *Journal of Asian Studies*, Vol. 26, No. 3 (May 1967), p. 404.

35 Li, 'Nisshin shūkō jōki', p. 76.

36 See also Jansen, *China in the Tokugawa World*, p. 97.

37 For more details on the Taiwan-expedition see Tsiang, 'Sino–Japanese Diplomatic Relations', pp. 15–34; Shinobu, *Nihon gaikō-shi*, Vol. 1, pp. 93–96; Robert Eskildsen, 'Of Civilization and Savages: the Mimetic Imperialism of Japan's 1874 Expedition to Taiwan', *American Historical Review*, Vol. 107, No. 2 (February 2002), pp. 388–418.

38 Eskildsen, 'Of Civilization and Savages', p. 395.

39 Shinobu, *Nihon gaikō-shi*, Vol. 1, p. 94; on the Ryūkyū controversy, see *ibid.*, pp. 114–16; Tsiang, 'Sino–Japanese Diplomatic Relations, pp. 34–53; Wieland Wagner, *Japans Aussenpolitik in der frühen Meiji-Zeit (1868–1894)* (Japan's foreign policy in the early Meiji period, 1869–94), Stuttgart: Franz Steiner Verlag, 1990, pp. 145–54.

40 For a list of tributary embassies during the Qing period see Fairbank/Teng, 'Ch'ing Tributary System', pp. 193–97; until 1871, the missions from the Ryūkyūs were quite regular, the last ones were in 1875 and 1877, after which Japan stopped the sending of missions.

41 Shinobu, *Nihon gaikō-shi*, Vol. 1, p. 115.

42 *Ibid.*

43 Tsiang, 'Sino–Japanese Diplomatic Relations', p. 52; Shinobu, *Nihon gaikō-shi*, Vol. 1, p. 118.

44 Marius B. Jansen, 'Japanese Views of China During the Meiji Period', in Albert Feuerwerker *et al.* (eds), *Approaches to Modern Chinese History*, Berkeley, CA: University of California Press, 1967, pp. 167–68.

45 See Peter Duus, *The Abacus and the Sword: the Japanese Penetration of Korea, 1895–1910*, Berkeley, CA: University of California Press, 1995, p. 64; Akira Iriye, 'Japan's drive to great power status' in: Marius B. Jansen (ed.), *Cambridge History of Japan*, Vol. 5: *The Nineteenth Century*, Cambridge, New York: Cambridge University Press, 1989, p. 763; Peattie, 'The Japanese Colonial Empire', p. 219; the second quote is from Inoue Kowashi, 'Chōsen seiryaku iken-an' (Opinion paper concerning our Korean strategy, 1882) in Shibahara *et al.* (eds), *Taigaikan* (Views of foreign affairs), Tokyo: Iwanami shoten, 1991, pp. 52–54. For a more detailed discussion of Kowashi's strategy paper, see presently.

46 Bonnie B. Oh, 'Sino–Japanese Rivalry in Korea, 1876–85', in Akira Iriye (ed.), *The Chinese and the Japanese: Essays in Political and Cultural Interaction*, Princeton, NJ: Princeton University Press, 1980, p. 45.

47 Tsiang, 'Sino–Japanese Diplomatic Relations', pp. 60. On the conclusion of the Treaty and China's role, see K. Kim, *The Last Phase of the East Asian World Order: Korea, Japan, and the Chinese Empire, 1860–1882*, Berkeley, CA: University of California Press, 1980, pp. 204–55; Wagner, *Japans Aussenpolitik*, pp. 129–34; Dudden, *Japan's Colonization of Korea*, pp. 52–55.

48 See Duus, *Abacus and Sword*, p. 54. On China's Korea policy after 1875, see Kim, *Last Phase of the East Asian World Order*, pp. 256–300.

49 Tsiang, 'Sino–Japanese Diplomatic Relations', p. 78.

50 *Ibid.*, p. 87; Wagner, *Japans Aussenpolitik*, p. 186.

51 Tsiang, 'Sino–Japanese Diplomatic Relations', p. 106.

52 Shinobu, *Nihon gaikō-shi*, Vol. 1, p. 121; Huang at the time was working as a secretary of the Chinese mission in Tokyo. On Huang Zunxian, see N. Kamachi, *Reform in China: Huang Tsun-hsien and the Japanese Model*, Cambridge, MA: Council on East Asian Studies, Harvard University, 1981.

53 Tsiang, 'Sino–Japanese Diplomatic Relations', p. 64.

54 'Chōsen seiryaku iken-an' (Opinion paper concerning our Korea strategy), in Shibahara, *Taigaikan*, pp. 52–54; it is interesting to note that in 1882 Special Envoy to China Enomoto Takeaki proposed the same idea to the American minister to China J. R. Young, however omitting China as a co-guarantor. The omission was duly noted (Tsiang, 'Sino–Japanese Diplomatic Relations', p. 90).

55 'Kōshin jihen shori ni tsuki iken-an' (Opinion on measures to be taken in the Kōshin Incident), in: Shibahara, *Taigaikan*, pp. 57–60.

56 *Ibid.*, p. 59.

57 See Duus, *Abacus and the Sword*, p. 64.

58 *Ibid.*, p. 62.

59 Tsiang, 'Sino–Japanese', p. 52.

60 Hara Takeshi, 'Gunji-teki shiten kara mita Nisshin sensō' (The Sino–Japanese war from a military viewpoint), in Higashi-Ajia kindai-shi gakkai (ed.), *Nisshin sensō to Higashi-Ajia sekai no hen'yō* (The first Sino–Japanese war and the transformation of East-Asia), Tokyo: Yumani shobō, 1997, Vol. 2, pp. 94–95; for a detailed study of Japan's Korea policy and its armament expansion plans, see Takahashi Hidenao, *Nisshin sensō e no michi* (The road to the Sino–Japanese war), Tokyo: Tōkyō sōgensha, 1995.

61 For a close discussion of the relation between 'civilization' (*bunmei kaika*) and cultural centrality, formerly occupied by Chinese culture, see Watanabe, Hiroshi, *Higashi Ajia no ōken to shisō* (Confucianism and After: Political Thought in Early Modern East Asia), Tokyo: Tokyo daigaku shuppansha, 1997, pp. 244–57.

62 Benedict Anderson, *Imagined Communities: Reflections on the Origins and Spread of Nationalism*, revised edn, London: Verso, 1991, pp. 4, 67, 81, 110.

63 For another case of universalizing Western civilization in a non-European coun-
   try, the Ottoman empire, see Cemil Aydin, *The Politics of Anti-Westernism in
   Asia: Visions of World Order in Pan-Islamic and Pan-Asian Thought*, New York:
   Columbia University Press, 2007, pp. 16–24.

64 For an English translation, see Fukuzawa Yukichi, *An Outline of a Theory of
   Civilization*, translated by David A. Dilworth and G. Cameron Hurst, Tokyo:
   Sophia University, 1973.

65 Hinohara Shōzō, 'Nihon wa Tōyō-koku taru bekarazu', *Jiji shinpō*, 11/13/14
   November 1884. The article is also discussed by Maruyama Masao, 'Fukuzawa
   Yukichi no "Datsua ron" to sono shūhen' (Fukuzawa Yukichi's Datsua ron and
   its context), *Maruyama Masao techō*, No. 20 (January 2002), pp. 5–9; for a short
   biography of Hinohara see Okabe Yasuko, 'Shōden Hinohara Shōzō' (A short
   biography of Hinohara Shōzō), *Fukuzawa techō*, No. 110 (2001), pp. 12–30.

66 Hinohara, 'Nihon wa Tōyō-koku taru bekarazu', 11 November 1884.

67 On reform in late Qing China, see Onogawa Hidemi, *Shin-matsu seiji shisō
   kenkyū* (Studies in Late Qing political thought), Tokyo: Misuzu shobō, 1969,
   pp. 8–85.

68 'Shina kesshite keibu su-bekarazu' ('We must never look down upon China'),
   Tōkyō nichinichi shinbun, 28 November 1875, in Shibahara, *Taigaikan*, pp. 257–
   60; 'Shinkoku keishi su-bekarazaru ron' ('Why we must not look down upon
   China'), *Yūbin hōchi shinbun*, 12 January 1878, in Shibahara, *Taigai-kan*, pp.
   260–62.

69 The caricature appeared in the 21 June 1879 issue of the *Marumaru*; see Obinata
   Sumio, 'Jiyūminken-ki no higashi-Ajia jōsei ninshiki: 'Marumaru chinbun' manga
   no sekai o yomu' (The perception of East Asian conditions during the Jiyū
   minken era: reading the world of *Marumaru chinbun*'s caricatures), *Bunka kokusai
   kenkyū* (Tōkyō toritsu tanki daigaku), Vol. 1 (February 1997), pp. 32, 34.

70 The comment of the spectators for the part of Japan reads: 'He is only small, but
   does he not progress with quick steps, steadfast on its course like a dragonfly?
   But he is so much in a hurry to get ahead, his feet are still a little insecure.
   Whoa, how fast is he' (the dragonfly is one of the traditional symbols for Japan).

71 On this subject, see Donald Keene, 'The Survival of Chinese Literary Traditions
   in the Meiji Era', in Yue-him Tam (ed.), *Sino–Japanese Cultural Interchange:
   Aspects of Literature and Language Learning*, Hong Kong: Institute of Chinese
   Studies, University of Hong Kong, 1985, Vol. 2, pp. 75–90.

72 *Ibid.*, p. 75. Marius B. Jansen calls the 'Tokugawa-era Sinophile' which survived
   in Meiji times an 'aristocratic affectation' ('Some Continuities in Meiji Views of
   China', in Yue-him Tam (ed.), *Sino–Japanese Cultural Interchange: Aspects of
   Literature and Language Learning*, Hong Kong: Institute of Chinese Studies,
   University of Hong Kong, 1985, Vol. 3, p. 247); although one might concede,
   that it was a 'high culture' affair, it was certainly not restricted to 'high society',
   as the examples above show.

73 Keene, 'Survival of Chinese Literary Traditions', p. 83.

74 Katsunan's *kanshi* are collected and translated by Takematsu Kōmei in *Kuga Katsunan shi tsūyaku* (A translation of Kuga Katsunan's Chinese poems), Hirosaki-shi:
   Tsugaru shobō, 1981.

75 Keene, 'Survival of Chinese Literary Traditions', pp. 85–88.

76 *Ibid.*, pp. 82–83; Jansen, 'Some Continuities', pp. 246–47; Samuel C. Chu,
   'China's Attitudes toward Japan at the Time of the Sino–Japanese War', in
   Akira Iriye (ed.), *The Chinese and the Japanese: Essays in Political and Cultural
   Interaction*, Princeton, NJ: Princeton University Press, 1980, p. 85; on the social
   interaction of Japanese Sinophiles with Chinese embassy members see Zhang
   Weixiong, *Bunjin gaikō-kan no Meiji Nihon: Chūgoku shodai chūnichi kōshi-dan
   no ibunka taiken* (The Meiji Japan of literati diplomats: the foreign culture

experience of the first Chinese diplomatic mission to Japan), Tokyo: Kashiwa shobō, 1999, pp. 45–91.

77 Margaret Mehl, 'Private Academies for Chinese Learning (*Kangaku juku*) in the Meiji Period', in Joshua A. Fogel (ed.), *Late Qing China and Meiji Japan: Political and Cultural Aspects*, Norwalk, Ct.: Eastbridge, 2004, p. 102.

78 Hirakawa Sukehiro, 'Japan's turn to the West', in Marius B. Jansen, ed., *The Cambridge History of Japan, Vol. 5: The Nineteenth Century*, Cambridge: Cambridge University Press, 1989, p. 494, quoting Inoue Kowashi's proposal of 1881 'Kangaku o susumu' (Promoting Chinese studies). For the controversy over *kanbun* in national education, see also K. Sato, '"Same Language, Same Race": the Dilemma of Kanbun in Modern Japan', in Frank Dikötter (ed.), *The Construction of Racial Identities in China and Japan: Historical and Contemporary Perspectives*. London: Hurst & Co., 1997, pp. 126–30.

79 See Kenneth B. Pyle, 'Early Meiji Conservatism' in Marius B. Jansen (ed.), *The Cambridge History of Japan, Vol. 5: The Nineteenth Century*, Cambridge, New York: Cambridge University Press, 1989, p. 684.

80 Pyle, *The New Generation*, pp. 67–71, 193–94; Pyle, 'Early Meiji Conservatism', p. 692.

81 Thus Carol Gluck observes: 'It is a trivialization of their task to regard the ideologists [in general] as anti-Western, which the majority emphatically were not, or as apostles of a return to the past, which had little hold on most of them' (*Japan's Modern Myths: Ideology in the Late Meiji Period*, Princeton, NJ: Princeton University Press, 1985, p. 20). Oguma Eiji argues that Inoue Tetsujirō (1855–1944), Kimura Takatarō (1870–1931) and Takayama Chogyū's theories of pure 'Japaneseness' ran against the tendency of early Meiji 'Japanese' self-images, which were generally more open and receptive (*A Genealogy of 'Japanese' Self-Images*, translated by David Askew, Melbourne: Trans Pacific Press, 2002, pp. 39–45).

82 For a third way of direct confrontation with China, i.e. through travels on the continent, see Joshua A. Fogel, *The Literature of Travel in the Japanese Rediscovery of China*, 1862–1945, Stanford, CA: Stanford University Press, 1996.

83 Iwakabe Yoshimitsu, 'Nisshin senjihō-ka no zainichi Chūgoku-jin mondai' (The legal problem of Chinese residing in Japan during the first Sino–Japanese War), in Higashi-Ajia kindai-shi gakkai (ed.), *Nisshin sensō to Higashi-Ajia sekai no hen'yō* (The first Sino–Japanese war and the transformation of East-Asia), Tokyo: Yumani shobō, 1997, Vol. 2, p. 209; for specific numbers of Chinese residing in the various treaty ports, see N. Kamachi, 'The Chinese in Meiji Japan: Their Interactions with the Japanese before the Sino–Japanese War', in Akira Iriye (ed.), *The Chinese and the Japanese: Essays in Political and Cultural Interaction*, Princeton, NJ: Princeton University Press, 1980, pp. 60–61.

84 Kamachi, 'Chinese in Japan', pp. 64–65.

85 Matsuoka Bunpei, 'Reimei-ki rōdō kumiai undō no tokushitsu: 'Rōdō sekai' to Chūgoku zakkyo mondai' (The characteristics of the early labor movement: the magazine *Rōdō sekai* and the Chinese mixed residence problem', *Shisen* 48 (1974), p. 18.

86 Thus *tōjin* – a person from China – in the seventeenth century was simply a word for foreigner, and also applied to Westerners such as Engelbert Kaempfer, see Jansen, *China in the Tokugawa World,* pp. 86–87.

87 See Kamachi, 'Chinese in Meiji Japan', pp. 66–69; Sato, 'Same Language, Same Race', p. 122.

88 Hara Takashi, *Shin-jōyaku jisshi junbi* (Preparing for the implementation of the New Treaties), 2nd edn, Osaka: Osaka Mainichi shinbun-sha, 1899, pp. 57–61.

89 'Shina-jin no naichi zakkyo' ('Mixed residence with the Chinese'), *Jiji shinpō*, 27 February, 1894, p. 2.

90 On early Meiji views of international politics, see Banno Junji, *Meiji – shisō no jitsuzō* (Meiji – the true nature of thought), Tokyo: Sōbunsha, 1977, pp. 23–83; Sakeda Masatoshi, *Kindai Nihon ni okeru taigai-kō undō no kenkyū* (Studies on the strong foreign-policy movement in modern Japan), Tokyo: Tōkyō daigaku shuppan-kai, 1979, pp. 1–73; Banno Junji, *Kindai Nihon no gaikō* (Modern Japanese foreign policy), Tokyo: Kenbun shuppan, 1985, pp. 3–74; Wagner, *Japans Aussenpolitik*, pp. 189–251; Shibahara Takuji, 'Taigai-kan to nashonarizumu (Views of foreign affairs and nationalism), in Shibahara *et al.* (eds), *Taigai-kan* (Views of foreign affairs), Tokyo: Iwanami, 1991, pp. 458–534.

91 KKZ 1:145. Incidentally, Katsunan's *Kokusai-ron* was also translated into the Chinese, see Paula Harrell, *Sowing the Seeds of Change: Chinese Students, Japanese Teachers, 1895–1905*, Stanford, CA: Stanford University Press, 1992, p. 93.

92 On Herbert Spencer's eminence in late nineteenth-century European political discourse, see John Bowle, *Politics and Opinion in the Nineteenth Century: An Historical Introduction*, London: Jonathan Cape, 1954, pp. 224–36.

93 M. Nagai, 'Herbert Spencer in Early Meiji Japan', *Far Eastern Quarterly*, Vol. 14, No. 1 (November 1954), p. 55.

94 For such a usage, see for example Kuga Katsunan, 'Waga teikoku no tai-Kan seisaku o bōgai suru kuni wa kore bunmei-koku ni arazu' (A country which obstructs our Korea policy is not a civilized country), *Nippon* 29 July 1894 (KKZ 4:564), or 'Kyōfū-ron' (On the spirit of chivalry), *Yorozu chōhō*, 16 July 1898.

95 See F. G. Notehelfer, *Kōtoku Shūsui: Portrait of a Japanese Radical*, Cambridge: Cambridge University Press, 1971, p. 91.

96 'Kyōfū-ron', *Yorozu chōhō*, 16 July 1898. The article discusses primarily social issues, not international politics; however, the definition works for both.

97 For the translation of *taigai kō(ha)* and *taigai-kō undō*, I borrow from the *Japan Weekly Mail* the phrases 'strong foreign-policy advocates' and 'strong foreign policy agitation', respectively (see, for example, 'The strong foreign policy agitation', *Japan Weekly Mail*, 16 April 1898, p. 390, 'Meeting of strong foreign-policy politicians', *Japan Weekly Mail*, 23 April 1898, p. 415).

98 See K. Miwa, 'Fukuzawa Yukichi's 'Departure from Asia': a Prelude to the Sino–Japanese War', in Edmund Skrzypczak (ed.), *Japan's Modern Century*, Tokyo: Sophia University and Charles E. Tuttle, 1968, pp. 1–26.

99 See, for example, Marius B. Jansen, 'Ōi Kentarō: Radicalism and Chauvinism', *Far Eastern Quarterly*, Vol. 11, No. 3 (1952), p. 305; on Japanese Pan-Asianism, see Takeuchi Yoshimi's classical essay 'Ajia-shugi no tenbō' (A survey of Asianism), in Takeuchi Yoshimi (ed.), *Ajia-shugi* (Asianism), Tokyo: Chikuma shobō, pp. 7–63, and Sven Saaler and Viktor Koschmann (eds), *Pan-Asianism in Modern Japanese History*. London, New York: Routledge, 2007.

100 The Ryūkyū question in the Japanese public was – strictly speaking – discussed more as a matter of 'national unification', rather than as an international issue (Shibahara, *Taigaikan*, p. 416). However, most *jiyū minken* writers welcomed the Ryūkyū policy of the government, i.e. the assertive stance against China; see Itō Teruo (ed.), *Ajia to Kindai Nihon: Han-shinryaku no shisō to undō* (Asia and modern Japan: anti-invasionist thought and action, Tokyo: Shakai hyōron-sha, 1990, p. 17; Obinata, 'Jiyū minken-ki', pp. 32–33.

101 Jansen, 'Ōi Kentarō', pp. 309–10. The party of adventurers was rounded up in Ōsaka and elsewhere in November 1885, shortly before it could set off.

102 Takeuchi, 'Ajia-shugi', p. 27.

103 For example, see Asano Takeshi, 'Shinmin no furutte kyō-Ro ni kō suru wo kikite kan ari' (I am deeply moved when hearing that the Chinese people stand up and resist strong Russia'), *Chōya shinbun*, 31 January 1879, in Shibahara, *Taigai-kan*, pp. 262–64; 'Tōyō renkō ron' (On an East Asian alliance), *Yūbin hōchi shinbun*, 19 November 1879, *ibid.*, pp. 265–68.

104 Cited in Jansen, 'Japanese Views', pp. 171–72; see also Jansen, *China in the Tokugawa World*, p. 104.
105 Jansen, 'Japanese Views', p. 166; Miwa, 'Fukuzawa Yukichi's 'Departure from Asia',' p. 25.
106 Takeuchi, 'Ajia-shugi', pp. 32–37; Jansen, 'Japanese Views', pp. 169–71.
107 On the Japanese perspective in general, see Tanaka Masatoshi, 'Shinfutsu sensō to Nihon-jin no Chūgoku-kan' (The Sino-French War and Japanese views of China), *Shisō*, No. 512 (February 1967), pp. 14–34.
108 See, for example, 'Nansurezo sore Furansu o togamuru ya' (Why blame France?), *Jiyū shinbun*, 28/29/30 August 1884, in Shibahara, *Taigai-kan*, pp. 285–93; 'Gaikan ni taisuru seitai no tokushitsu' (The relative success of political systems coping with foreign troubles), *Chōya shinbun*, 19/20 September 1884, *ibid.*, pp. 298–304.
109 'Nansurezo sore Furansu o togamuru ya', *ibid.*, p. 289.
110 'Shina no haiboku wa Nippon no saiwai nari' (China's defeat is Japan's luck), *Tōkyō Yokohama mainichi shinbun*, 29/30 August 1884, *ibid.*, pp. 293–98.
111 *The North-China Herald*, 2 May 1884 (GSN 2:293), commenting on Fukuzawa, 'Furansu wa Shina no onjin nari' (France is the benefactor of China), *Jiji shinpō*, 4 March 1884 (FYZ 9:409–12).
112 Carl Schmitt, *Der Begriff des Politischen: Text von 1932 mit einem Vorwort und drei Corollarien* (The concept of the political: the text of 1932 with a preface and three corollaries), 7th edn, Berlin: Duncker & Humblot, 2002, p. 27 (my translation).
113 See, for example, 'Kōa no mondai oyobi Tōyō no gensei' (The problem of reviving Asia and the present state of East Asia), *Yūbin hōchi shinbun*, 6/18 June 1884, in Shibahara, *Taigai-kan*, pp. 280–85; 'Kaika to kaika no sensō' (A war between [real] and [imagined] civilization), *Chōya shinbun*, 18 September 1884, repr. *ibid.*, pp. 304–7; 'Yonjūnen-rai no Nippon oyobi Shina' (Japan and China during the last forty years), *Yūbin hōchi shinbun*, 2/3 October 1884, *ibid.*, pp. 307–12.
114 FYZ 10:239–40.
115 See, for example, the famous caricature 'Pekin yumemakura' (The Beijing dream-pillow) by Imaizumi Ippyō (1865–1904), drawn after an idea of Fukuzawa Yukichi and distributed as a supplement of the *Jiji shinpō* on 5 September 1884, which shows a Mandarin lost in his opium reveries while he is being attacked by the Western powers; see Nyūsupąku (ed.), *Shinbun manga no me – hito seiji shakai* (People, politics and society as seen through the eyes of newspaper caricatures), Yokohama: Nyūsupâku (Nihon shinbun hakubutsukan), 2003, pp. 14, 133; Sakai Tadayasu and Shimizu Isao (eds), *Nisshin sensō-ki no manga* (Caricatures of the Sino–Japanese war period), Tokyo: Chikuma shobō, 1985, pp. 8–9; or, again, the illustration by Imaizumi, in *Jiji shinpō*, 8 August, 1894, which shows a Japanese soldier putting a bullet with the inscription 'civilization' through the head of an opium-smoking Chinese (Nyūsupâku, *Shinbun manga no me*, pp. 50, 141).
116 Uchimura, 'Justification for the Korean War', *The Japan Weekly Mail*, 11 August 1894, in *Uchimura Kanzō zenshū* (The collected works of Uchimura Kanzō), Suzuki, Toshirō *et al.* (eds), Tokyo: Iwanami shoten, 1980–84, Vol. 3, p. 43: for a further discussion of this article, see Chapter 2.
117 Cited by Edward Said, *Orientalism: Western Conceptions of the Orient*. London: Penguin Books, 1995, pp. 38–39; Sir Evelyn Baring (Lord Cromer) was British Consul-General in Egypt, 1883–1907. – For an overview of the European perspective of Asia since the sixteenth century, see Jürgen Osterhammel, 'Vielfalt und Einheit im neuzeitlichen Asien' (Unity and Diversity in Early Modern and Modern Asia), in Jürgen Osterhammel (ed.), *Asien in der Neuzeit, 1500–1950: sieben historische Stationen* (Asia in Early Modern and Modern Times, 1550–1950: seven historical chapters), Frankfurt a.M.: Fischer Taschenbuch Verlag, 1994, pp. 9–25; especially for China, see Raymond Dawson, *The Chinese Chameleon: An Analysis of European Conceptions of Chinese Civilization*. Oxford: Oxford

University Press, 1967; for American perceptions, see Philip P. Choy, Lorraine Dong and Marion K. Horn, *The Coming Man: 19th Century American Perceptions of the Chinese*, Seattle, WA: University of Washington Press, 1995.

118 Maruyama, 'Fukuzawa Yukichi no 'Datsua ron' to sono shūhen', pp. 5–9.

119 For negative images of China during the late Tokugawa period, see R. H. van Gulik, 'Kakkaron: a Japanese Echo of the Opium War', *Monumenta Serica* 4 (1939/40), pp. 478–545; Wakabayashi, 'Opium, Expulsion, Sovereignty', pp. 1–25.

120 Fukuzawa, 'Datsua-ron', FYZ 10:240.

121 The Kōakai was founded 1880 in Tōkyō; see M. Kuroki, 'The Asianism of the Kōakai and the Ajia Kyōkai', in Sven Saaler and Viktor Koschmann (eds), *Pan-Asianism in Modern Japanese History*, London, New York: Routledge, 2007, pp. 34–51.

122 Hinohara, 'Nihon wa Tōyō-koku taru bekarazu', 13 November 1884. This is probably the first mention of the word 'leave Asia' (*datsua*), which today is often used to sum up Japan's course in modern history (often in combination with *nyūō*, 'join Europe'). It is usually attributed to Fukuzawa, but in all probability was Hinohara's creation.

123 See Miwa, 'Fukuzawa Yukichi's 'Departure from Asia',' p. 15; S. C. M. Paine, *The Sino–Japanese War of 1894–1895: Perceptions, Power and Primacy*, Cambridge: Cambridge University Press, 2003, pp. 111, 119; Urs Matthias Zachmann, 'Blowing Up a Double Portrait in Black and White: The Concept of Asia in the Writings of Fukuzawa Yukichi and Okakura Tenshin', *positions: east asia cultures critique*, Vol. 15, No. 2 (2007), pp. 353–55.

124 Chu, 'China's attitudes toward Japan', p. 77; on Chinese perspectives of Japan in the early Meiji period, see also Harrell, *Sowing the Seeds of Change*, pp. 14–19.

125 See Howland, *Borders of Chinese Civilization*, pp. 18–26.

126 Chu, 'China's attitudes toward Japan', pp. 88.

127 Howland, *Borders of Chinese Civilization*, pp. 7, 23; Harrell, *Sowing the Seeds*, p. 16.

128 Chu, 'China's attitudes', p. 80; see also Jansen, *China in the Tokugawa World*, pp. 113–14: 'Contemporary elites in both China and Korea, whatever the realities of their institutional makeup, considered Japan's young samurai government more nuisance than neighbor, until it was too late.'

129 M. Mutsu, *Kenkenroku: A Diplomatic Record of the Sino–Japanese War, 1894–95*, ed. and translated by Gordon Mark Berger, Princeton, NJ: Princeton University Press, 1982, pp. 27–28.

130 Cited by Donald Keene, 'The Sino–Japanese War of 1894–95 and its Cultural Effects in Japan', in Donald Shively (ed.) *Tradition and Modernization in Japanese Culture*, Princeton, NJ: Princeton University Press, p. 143. The song was originally composed by Yokoi Tadanao (1857–1928) and bore the title 'Pekin made' (To Beijing).

131 D. Tao, 'Nishimura Tenshū's Journey to the Yangtze Basin in 1897–98', *Sino–Japanese Studies*, Vol. 4, No. 1 (October 1991), pp. 33, 35.

132 See Paine, *Sino–Japanese War*, p. 15, with further references.

133 See Mutsu, *Kenkenroku: a Diplomatic Record*, p. 111; Pyle, *New Generation*, 86, on Japanese reactions, to a speech of Edwin Arnold in Japan in 1891.

134 Ōuchi Chōzō, 'Kazan-kō no bunka hatsuyō' (Prince Konoe's promotion of culture), *Shina*, Vol. 25, No. 2/3 (February 1934), p. 185; the manuscript of Konoe's speech is recorded in the *Konoe Atsumaro nikki* (The diary of Konoe Atsumaro), Konoe Atsumaro nikki kankō-kai (ed.), Tokyo: Kajima kenkyūjo shuppan-kai, 1968–69, Vol. 2, pp. 322–24, however without the above comment as remembered by Konoe's former private secretary.

2 The Sino–Japanese War, the Tripartite Intervention, and Japan's 'postwar management'

1 William L. Langer, *The Diplomacy of Imperialism*, 2nd edn, New York: Alfred A. Knopf, 1965, p. 167.

2 For a more detailed study of developments up to the Japanese decision of war, see Takahashi Hidenao, *Nisshin sensō e no michi* (The road to the Sino–Japanese War), Tokyo: Tōkyō sōgensha, 1995. On the war and its impact on Western perceptions, see S. C. M. Paine, *The Sino–Japanese War of 1894–1895: Perceptions, Power and Primacy*, Cambridge: Cambridge University Press, 2003. On the immediate war experience of Japanese abroad and at home, see Stewart Lone, *Japan's First Modern War: Army and Society in the Conflict with China, 1894–95*, Basingstoke: Macmillan, 1994. On the Tripartite Intervention, see Frank W. Ikle, 'The Triple Intervention: Japan's Lesson in the Diplomacy of Imperialism', *Monumenta Nipponica*, Vol. 22, No. 1–2 (1967), pp. 122–30; Ian Nish, *The Anglo–Japanese Alliance: The Diplomacy of Two Island Empires, 1894–1907*, 2nd edn, London: Athlone Press, 1985, pp. 16–30; Urs Matthias Zachmann, 'Imperialism in a Nutshell: Conflict and the 'Concert of Powers' in the Tripartite Intervention, 1895', *Japanstudien*, Vol. 17 (2005), pp. 57–82.

3 Paine, *Sino–Japanese War*, p. 114.

4 Mutsu Munemitsu, as cited by Samuel C. Chu, 'China's Attitudes toward Japan at the Time of the Sino–Japanese War', in Akira Iriye (ed.), *The Chinese and the Japanese: Essays in Political and Cultural Interaction*, Princeton, NJ: Princeton University Press, 1980, p. 83; see also Paine, *Sino–Japanese War*, p. 118.

5 'Sakunen no dekigoto' (Last year's events), *Jiji shinpō*, 1 January 1894, p. 2.

6 In contrast, the Sino–Japanese War in the New Year's issue of 1895 was, of course, *the* event. Thus, whereas the 1894 New Year's cartoon had shown the rapid drop of stocks by depicting a falling bunch of turnips (*kabu*), the 1895 New Year's issue showed the rapid decline in China's luck by depicting a huge balloon falling from the sky with desperate Chinese inside; see Huffman, James L., *Creating a Public: People and Press in Meiji Japan*, Honolulu: University of Hawaii Press, 1997, p. 213.

7 The *Jiji shinpō* announced the government's decision on 9 June 1898 (p. 7: 'Seifu guntai o haken su' – The government dispatches troops).

8 The series started on 16 June 1894, p. 2 ('Meiji 17-nen Keijō no ran' – the Seoul riots of 1884).

9 Paine, *Sino–Japanese War*, p. 116.

10 See Shinobu Seizaburō (ed.), *Nihon gaikō-shi 1853–1972* (A history of Japanese foreign policy, 1853–1972), Tokyo: Mainichi shinbunsha, 1974, Vol. 1, pp. 161–62; Takahashi, *Nisshin sensō*, p. 313. – For the immediate effects of the war on domestic politics and the role of the emperor, see Lone, *Japan's First Modern War*, pp. 78–65.

11 See for example Kuga, 'Tenshin jōyaku o ikan' (What about the Tianjin Treaty), *Nippon*, 7 July 1894 (KKZ 4:542–43); on the suzerainty question as the central issue, see also M. Mutsu, *Kenkenroku: A Diplomatic Record of the Sino–Japanese War, 1894–95*, edited and translated by Gordon Mark Berger, Princeton, NJ: Princeton University Press, 1982, p. 77.

12 See Kuga, 'Tenshin jōyaku o ikan', KKZ 4:542; Paine, *Sino–Japanese War*, p. 115.

13 Kuga, 'Sensen no mikotonori wo yomu' (On reading the Imperial Declation of War), *Nippon*, 4 August 1894 (KKZ 4:568).

14 Kuga, 'Sensen no mikotonori wo yomu', KKZ 4:568.

15 *The Japan Weekly Mail*, 11 August 1894, in Uchimura, Kanzō, *Uchimura Kanzō zenshū* (The collected works of Uchimura Kanzō), Suzuki, Toshirō et al. (eds), Tokyo: Iwanami shoten, 1980–84, Vol. 3, pp. 38–48. The text was written originally for the English-speaking readership, since the British opinion at the beginning of the war was very critical of Japan (see Mutsu, *Kenkenroku: A Diplomatic Record*, p. 106). On the construction of the 'just war' argument, see also Ōhama Tetsuya, *Shomin no mita Nisshin-Nichiro sensō* (The people's view of the Sino–Japanese and Russo–Japanese War), Tokyo: Tōsui shobō, 2003, pp. 19–46.

16 Most famous for this argument is Fukuzawa Yukichi's 'Nisshin sensō wa bun'ya no sensō nari' (The war between Japan and China is a war between civilization and barbarism), *Jiji shinpō*, 29 July 1894 (FYZ 14:491–92); see also Mutsu, *Kenkenroku: A Diplomatic Record*, pp. 27–28.

17 Kuga Katsunan, 'Waga teikoku no tai-Kan seisaku o bōgai suru kuni wa kore bunmei-koku ni arazu' (A country which obstructs our Korea policy is not a civilized country'), *Nippon*, 29 July 1894 (KKZ 4:563).

18 Kano Masanao claims that this argument was applied already during the war (*Fukuzawa Yukichi*, Tokyo: Century Books, 1967, p. 175). The argument is some-times attributed to Uchimura's 'Justification,' but Uchimura does not use it there.

19 Takahashi, *Nisshin sensō*, p. 517.

20 Hara Takeshi, 'Gunji-teki shiten kara mita Nisshin sensō' (The Sino–Japanese War from a military viewpoint), in Higashi-Ajia kindai-shi gakkai (ed.), *Nisshin sensō to Higashi-Ajia sekai no hen'yō* (The first Sino–Japanese War and the transformation of East-Asia), Tokyo: Yumani shobō, 1997, Vol. 2, pp. 93–95; these and the following numbers are largely based on Vol. 1 of the *Meiji nijūshichi hachi-nen Nisshin sen-shi* (A history of the Sino–Japanese War of 1894/5), Tokyo: Tokyo insatsu, 1904; repr. Yumani shobō, 1998.

21 Mutsu, *Kenkenroku: A Diplomatic Record*, pp. 83, 106–12; see also Ōhama, *Shomin no mita Nisshin-Nichiro sensō*, pp. 47–48, on the mood of the first days of the war.

22 Hara, 'Gunji-teki shiten kara mita Nisshin sensō', pp. 95, 97.

23 *Ibid.*, p. 92.

24 *Ibid.*, p. 97, citing also the numbers for the other battles. For allegations of Japanese violations of the international law in the battle of Tianzhuangtai, see Paine, *Sino–Japanese War*, p. 176.

25 See Fujimura, *Nisshin sensō*, pp. 183–84.

26 Miyake Setsurei, *Jiden* (Autobiography), Tokyo: Heibonsha, 1982, p. 380. This is a statement made in retrospect, but the phrase turns up frequently in contemporary comments on the war as well. For a documentation of the war frenzy in popular culture, see Donald Keene, 'The Sino–Japanese War of 1894–95 and Its Cultural Effects in Japan', in Donald Shively (ed.), *Tradition and Modernization in Japanese Culture*. Princeton, NJ: Princeton University Press, pp. 121–75.

27 On the newspaper business during wartimes, see James L. Huffman, *Creating a Public: People and Press in Meiji Japan*, Honolulu: University of Hawaii Press, 1997, pp. 199–223.

28 See Keene, 'The Sino–Japanese War', pp. 135–36.

29 For illustrations from Kobayashi Kiyochika's notorious *Nippon banzai! Hyaku-sen hyakushō* ('Hurray Japan! Every page/war a laughter', 1895) depicting such scenes, see Gunter Diesinger (ed.), *Japanische Farbholzschnitte II: Kriegsbilder aus der Meiji-Zeit* (Japanese colored woodblock prints II: war illustrations of the Meiji period), Hamburg: Museum für Kunst und Gewerbe Hamburg, 1986, pp. 26, 43.

30 Mutsu, *Kenkenroku: A Diplomatic Record*, p. 110.

31 Such was the title of a famous war ditty by Yokoi Tadanao, see Keene, 'Sino–Japanese War', pp. 142–43.

32 See 'Hi-kōwa' (Against peace), *Kokumin shinbun*, 17 March 1895, p. 2; 'Kōwa-shi ni kan suru yoron' (The public opinion on the peace mission), *Kokumin shinbun*, 17 March 1895, p. 4; Fukuzawa Yukichi, 'Heiwa no kikai imada juku sezu' (The time for peace has not come, yet), *Jiji shinpō*, 29 March 1895 (FYZ 15:112–15).

33 Albert d'Anethan, *The d'Anethan Dispatches from Japan, 1894–1910*, Georg Alexander Lensen (ed.), Tallahassee, FL: Diplomatic Press, 1967, p. 45.

34 See, for example, Kuga, 'Taishin-saku' ('Our China policy'), *Nippon*, 24/25/26 September 1894 (KKZ 4:619–23); Fukuzawa, 'Gaisen shimatsu ron' (How to

deal with war'), *Jiji shinpô*, 1–7 February 1895 (KKZ 15:40–60), especially part 1, 'Kano fukushū-ryoku o gensai subeshi' (We must reduce their powers to take revenge).

35 Uchimura, 'A Retrospect', *Yorozu chōhō*, 14/15/16 December 1897, in *Uchimura Kanzō zenshū*, Vol. 5, pp. 191–96, the quote on 193; see also Naitō Konan, 'Hisen ron' ('Against war'), *Yorozu chōhō*, 23–24 December 1898, in *Naitō Konan zenshū* (*The Collected works of Naitō Konan*), Naitō Kenkichi and Kanda Kiichirō (eds), Tokyo: Chikuma shobō, 1969–76, Vol. 2, pp. 213–15. On this article in the context of Naitō's position, see Joshua A. Fogel, *Politics and Sinology: the Case of Naitō Konan (1866–1934)*, Cambridge, MA: Council on East Asian Studies, Harvard University, 1984, pp. 70–71.

36 Kuga, 'Taishin-saku', KKZ 4:622–23.

37 *The Times*, 23 April 1895 (GSN 2:621).

38 The imperial edict concerning the Intervention bears the date 10 May and was published in the *Official Gazette* (*Kanpō*) on 11 May 1895. The *Jiji shinpō* published it in an extra edition on 13 May and the Peace Treaty on 14 May (p. 3). The *Tōkyō nichinichi shinbun* published the edict on 14 May; the *Kokumin shinbun* also on 14 May alongside the Peace Treaty (p. 3). However, since the Japanese newspapers were connected to the international news pool, their editors had known of the Intervention all along but had been forced to keep silent (see Paine, *Sino–Japanese War*, p. 289).

39 See Paine, *Sino–Japanese War*, pp. 289–91; Huffman, *Creating a Public*, pp. 218–19.

40 See, for example, Ikle, 'Triple Intervention', pp. 122, 129–30.

41 Tokutomi Sohō, *Sohō jiden* (The Autobiography of Tokutomi Sohō), Tokyo: Heibonsha, 1982, p. 195.

42 The exchange began with Asahina Chisen's 'Iwayuru sekinin mondai' (The so-called responsibility question), *Tōkyō nichinichi shinbun*, 30 July 1895, to which Katsunan replied with 'Kinō no Tōkyō nichinichi shinbun' (Yesterday's *Tōkyō nichinichi shinbun*), 31 July 1895 (KKZ 4:159–61). The exchange lasted well into August 1895. On questioning the responsibility of the government and the 'postwar management,' see Sakeda Masatoshi, *Kindai Nihon ni okeru taigai-kō undō no kenkyū* (Studies on the strong foreign-policy movement in modern Japan), Tokyo: Tōkyō daigaku shuppan-kai, 1979, pp. 77–84.

43 See, for example, Ōhama, who places the whole interwar chapter (*Shomin no mita Nisshin nichiro sensō*, pp. 65–100) under the heading of this motto.

44 Miyake, 'Shōtan gashin', *Nippon*, 15 May 1895, p. 1 (part 1 of planned three parts), 27 May 1895, p. 2 (part 2); between 16 and 26 May publication of the *Nippon* was suspended. Ōhama, for example, claims that Miyake had *made* the slogan the 'voice of the time' (*Shomin no mita Nisshin nichiro sensō*, pp. 79–80).

45 'Takigi ni ga shi, tan o namu', *Kokumin shinbun*, 10 May 1895, p. 2.

46 Miyake, 'Shōtan gashin', 27 May 1895.

47 Ōkuma Shigenobu, 'Ōkuma haku no enzetsu' (Count Ōkuma's speech), *Tōkyō nichinichi shinbun*, 23 October 1898, p. 5.

48 'Sensō no junbi' (War preparations), *Kokumin shinbun*, 19 July 1895, p. 2.

49 The Ottoman empire was named 'Sick Man of the East' first by the Russian czar Nicholas I in 1844. For the analogy, see also Paine, *Sino–Japanese War*, p. 18, with further references.

50 'Shina to Toruko' (China and Turkey), *Kokumin shinbun*, 14 February 1895, p. 2.

51 Ozaki Yukio, 'Taishin seisaku' (Our China policy), *Taiyō*, Vol. 1, No. 1 (1 January 1895), pp. 42–44. In contrast, see Ozaki's attitude towards China in 1884 as described (albeit in retrospect) in *The Autobiography of Ozaki Yukio: the Struggle for Constitutional Government in Japan*, translated by Hara Fujiko, Princeton, NJ: Princeton University Press, 2001, pp. 76–83. In 1884 Ozaki went to Shanghai as a correspondent of the *Yūbin Hōchi shinbun* and came to advocate

war against China. This was in line with the generally aggressive attitude towards China at the time (see Chapter 1).

52 'Shinkoku no kyū ni omomuku beshi', *Nippon*, 23 June 1895, p. 1.

53 See 'Zen-sekai no shippai (kinji no gaikō shakai)' (A failure of the whole world – the diplomatic community in recent times), *Kokumin shinbun*, 18 June 1895, p. 5; the article enumerates the specific blunders of the various countries involved or not involved in the Tripartite Intervention (Japan, China, the Tripartite powers and Britain).

54 Miyake Setsurei, 'Gaikō-jutsu o Shina ni manabe' (Learn the skills of diplomacy from China), *Nippon*, 11 May 1895, p. 1. The rhetoric flourish is Miyake at his best.

55 Mahan, 'A Twentieth-Century Outlook', *Harper's Monthly Magazine*, Vol. 5, No. 568 (September 1897), pp. 521–33. Mahan's article is also discussed in the context of other American opinions on the 'competition of races' by Akira Iriye, *Pacific Estrangement: Japanese and American Expansion, 1897–1911*, Cambridge, MA: Harvard University Press, 1971, pp. 31–32.

56 Mahan, 'Twentieth-Century Outlook', pp. 523, 525.

57 Fukuzawa Yukichi, 'Kūron no toki ni arazu' (It is not the time for idle talk), *Jiji shinpō*, 14 April 1898 (FYZ 16:299). Fukuzawa reconfirmed his conviction in 'Shina-hei ōi ni mochiu beshi' (Chinese soldiers are exceedingly usable), *Jiji shinpō*, 15 April 1898 (FYZ 16:301–3).

58 For details see Matsuoka Bunpei, 'Reimei-ki rōdō kumiai undō no tokushitsu: 'Rōdō sekai' to Chūgoku zakkyo mondai' (The characteristics of the early labor movement: the magazine *Rōdō sekai* and the Chinese mixed residence problem'), *Shisen* 48 (1974), p. 18; Hara Takashi, *Shin-jōyaku jisshi junbi* (Preparing for the implementation of the New Treaties), 2nd edn, Osaka: Osaka Mainichi shinbun-sha, 1899, pp. 52–55.

59 Hara, *Shin-jōyaku jisshi junbi*, p. 56.

60 Tokutomi Sohō, *Shakai to jinbutsu* (Society and People), Tokyo: Min'yūsha, 1899, p. 85. Tokutomi identified as those qualities: absolute reliability in commercial transactions, resilience and perseverance in the face of adverse circumstances and hostile environments, strong bonding power that allows them to draw on existing networks wherever they go and, finally, the ability to make a cool-headed and well calculated decision even in critical situations. – For other explicit comparisons of Chinese with Jewish people at the time, see e.g. the chapter 'Yūdaijin' (Jews) in the essay collection *Sanshi suimei* (The Glory of Nature), ed. Kuga Katsunan, Tokyo: Rikugun juken kōgi-roku henshū-jo, 1897, pp. 186–93, especially p. 192 (judging from the style, Miyake Setsurei is a likely author); see also Yamagata Aritomo's opinion paper quoted in Chapter 3.

61 Matsuoka, 'Reimei-ki rōdō kumiai', p. 26; N. Kamachi, 'The Chinese in Meiji Japan: Their Interactions with the Japanese before the Sino–Japanese War', in Akira Iriye (ed.), *The Chinese and the Japanese: Essays in Political and Cultural Interaction*, Princeton, NJ: Princeton University Press, 1980, p. 73.

62 Nakanishi Ushirō, 'Nippon teikoku no ninmu' (The mission of the Japanese Empire), *Taiyō*, Vol. 1, No. 1 (1 January 1895), p. 48; according to the editor's note Nakanishi was born 1861 in Kumamoto, entered the Dōshisha in 1884 to study English, later made a tour to the USA, and on his return became the dean of the 'bungaku-ryō' of the Honpa-honganji in Kyōto, on the side editing the monthly *Keisei hakugi*.

63 'Kokuun no dai-tenkai', *Kokumin shinbun*, 31 March 1895, p. 2; for Tokutomi Sohō's interpretation of the war in this spirit see Pyle, *New Generation*, pp. 175, 177; Huffman, *Creating a Public*, p. 212.

64 Taoka Reiun, 'Heisenchū no Tenshin' (Tianjin under fire), *Kyūshū nippō*, 29 July 1900, in *Taoka Reiun zenshū* (Collected Works of Taoka Reiun), Nishida Masaru (ed.), Tokyo: Hōsei daigaku shuppan-kyoku, 1969–87, Vol. 5, pp. 68–69.

65 The USA originally planned to construct a transisthmian canal through Nicaragua, but was blocked by the Nicaraguan president José Santos Zelaya (in office 1893–1909). When rumors became known that Zelaya would grant building rights to Japanese entrepreneurs, the USA in 1909 supported a (successful) revolt against the Zelaya government. Nevertheless, the canal was eventually built in Panama.

66 Konoe Asumaro, 'Kaikoku no bokkō ni kan suru yōmu' (Urgent tasks cocerning Japan's rise as a maritime nation), *Shinsei* No. 47 (5 January 1895), p. 13.

67 When Kuga Katsunan speaks of 'intervention into domestic politics,' this regularly refers to the Western powers' stance during the treaty revision process, see his 'Kokunai kanshō-ron' (On domestic intervention), *Nippon*, 24 August – 5 September 1889 (KKZ 2:197–221).

68 'Kokusai kanshō' (International intervention), *Nippon*, 4 June 1895 (KKZ 5:104–5).

69 'Dōmei' (Alliances), *Kokumin shinbun*, 29 May 1895, p. 2.

70 'Dōmei-ron' (On Alliances), part 1, *Tokyō Asahi shinbun*, 5 August 1896, p. 1.

71 See e.g. 'Nichiei dōmei no setsu ni tsuite' (About the Anglo–Japanese alliance theory), *Jiji shinpō*, 1 August 1897 (FYZ 16:63–65); this was one of Fukuzawa's 'pet opinions.'

72 'Nichei dōmei okonawaru beki ka' (Is an Anglo–Japanese alliance feasible?), *Kokumin shinbun*, 12 July 1895, p. 2. The name of the British is given as Frederick Greenwood.

73 On the Anglo–Japanese rapprochement after the Tripartite Intervention in general, see Nish, *Anglo–Japanese Alliance*, pp. 35–41.

74 Paine, *Sino–Japanese War*, p. 297.

75 Mutsu Munemitsu wryly comments on this sudden change of sentiments in *Kenkekroku: A Diplomatic Record*, pp. 106–7; for a rather curious example of pro-Japanese war enthusiasm in Europe, see Rolf Harald Wippich (ed.), *'Haut sie, dass die Lappen fliegen!': Briefe von Deutschen an das japanische Kriegsministerium während des chinesisch-japanischen Krieges 1894/95* ('Beat them to pulp!': German letters to the Japanese War Ministry during the Sino–Japanese War, 1894/95), Tokyo: OAG Gesellschaft für Natur-und Völkerkunde Ostasiens Tokyo, 1997.

76 'The Other Side of the Question', *The North-China Herald*, 7 December 1894 (GSN 2:568).

77 Mahan, 'A Twentieth-Century Outlook', p. 525.

78 The phrase became (and stayed) fashionable since the discussion of Britain's accession or non-accession to the Tripartite Intervention in the European public. On the political career of this phrase, see Heinz Gollwitzer, *Die Gelbe Gefahr: Geschichte eines Schlagwortes. Studien zum imperialistischen Denken* (The Yellow Danger: the history of a catchphrase. Studies on imperial thought), Göttingen: Vandenhoeck und Ruprecht, 1961; Ute Mehnert, *Deutschland, Amerika und die 'Gelbe Gefahr': zur Karriere eines Schlagwortes in der Großen Politik, 1905–1917* (Germany, America and the 'Yellow Peril': the career of a catchphrase in international politics, 1905–17), Stuttgart: Frany Steiner Verlag, 1995.

79 This Hungarian general of uncertain name is quoted in the previous news item on the same page with a calculation on the costs of a future great war in Europe ('Sensō no daika'): in the past 25 years, the European countries because of Bismarck's politics had spent 125 billion francs on armament expansion; one month of intensive fighting would cost five billion francs; since six months would produce one million dead, ergo killing one person would cost 155,000 francs.

80 'Kōshoku jinshu no bokkō' (The rise of the yellow race), *Kokumin shinbun*, 18 July 1895, p. 3.

81 Gollwitzer, *Gelbe Gefahr*, pp. 211–13.

82 'Tōyō, Seiyō o osou no zu' (A picture of the East attacking the West), *Kokumin shinbun*, 8 January 1896, p. 3.

83 Gollwitzer, *Gelbe Gefahr*, p. 207.

84 'Senshō no kyoei ni hokoru bekarazu' (We must not pride ourselves in the vain glory of victory), *Jiji shinpō*, 30 June 1897 (FYZ 16:30–33).

85 Masuda Tomoko, 'Nisshin sengo keiei' (The postwar management after the Sino–Japanese War), in Inoue Matsusada *et al.* (eds), *Nihon rekishi taikei* (An outline of Japanese history), Tokyo: Yamakawa shuppan-sha, 1987, Vol. 4, p. 732.

86 See, for example, Itō Hirobumi's speech in the House of Peers, on 11 January 1896, on the subject of the 'Administration after the Sino–Japanese War' ('Nisshin sengo no keiei') in Itō Hirobumi, *Itō kō enzetsu-shū* (A collection of Marquis Itō's speeches), Tokyo: Nippō-sha, 1899; *Itō-kō zenshū*, Vol. 2, pp. 46–50. Critics such as Kuga Katsunan would use the term only with considerable irony.

87 See Yamagata Aritomo's opinion paper on armament expansion, 15 April 1895 in *Yamagata Aritomo iken-sho*, Ōyama Azusa (ed.), Tokyo: Hara shobō, 1966, pp. 228–40.

88 Masuda, 'Nisshin sengo keiei', p. 738.

89 See 'The British and Russian Naval Squadrons in the Far East', *The North-China Herald*, 20 May 1896 (GSN 3:29–30); the numbers slightly varied, as another chart in the *North-China Herald* dated 22 May 1896 (*ibid.*) shows.

90 Hara, 'Gunji-teki shiten kara mita Nisshin sensō', pp. 94–95

91 Masuda, 'Nisshin sengo keiei', p. 738.

92 Iguchi Kazuki, 'Nichiro sensō' (The Russo–Japanese War), in Iguchi Kazuki (ed.), *Nisshin Nichiro sensō* (The Sino–Japanese and the Russo–Japanese War), Tokyo: Yoshikawa Kōbunkan, 1994, p. 76. See also Paine, *Sino–Japanese War*, p. 327.

93 For Japan's military long-term strategy, see I. Hata, 'Continental Expansion, 1905–41', in Peter Duus (ed.), *The Cambridge History of Japan, Vol. 6: The Twentieth Century*, Cambridge, New York: Cambridge University Press, 1988, pp. 271–76.

94 Masuda, 'Nisshin sengo keiei', p. 738 fn. 4, with further references; Iguchi, 'Nichiro sensō', p. 75.

95 Masuda, ' Nisshin sengo keiei', pp. 738–39, fn. 4, 7.

96 Iguchi, 'Nichiro sensō', p. 78.

97 For the original distribution as planned by Matsukata, see Masuda, 'Nisshin sengo keiei', 739, fn. 8, with further references.

98 *Ibid.*, ' Nisshin sengo keiei', p. 750, fn. 12; however, Iguchi, 'Nichiro sensō', p. 78, gives an average of 40–50% of the annual expenditure.

99 See Eric Hobsbawm, *The Age of Empire*, New York: Vintage Books, 1989, p. 307; Gregor Schöllgen, *Das Zeitalter des Imperialismus* (The age of Imperialism), 4th revised edn, München: R. Oldenbourg Verlag, 2000, p. 82.

100 See Niall Ferguson, 'Public Finance and National Security: the Domestic Origins of the First World War Revisited', *Past and Present*, No. 142 (February 1994), p. 154, Table 2: Britain 42.9 per cent; France 30 per cent; Germany 29.4 per cent.

101 On this phase of Korean abstention, see Duus, *Abacus and the Sword*, pp. 103–33.

102 *Ibid.*, pp. 108–12.

103 'Corea', *The North-China Herald*, 21 February 1896 (GSN 3:10).

104 Shinobu, *Nihon gaikō-shi 1853–1972*, Vol. 1, pp. 188–91.

105 On the occupation of Taiwan between May and November 1895 and the anti-Japanese guerilla war, see Fujimura, *Nisshin sensō*, pp. 194–202.

106 Uchimura, 'A Retrospect', *Yorozu chōhō*, 14–16 December 1897, in *Uchimura Kanzō zenshū*, Vol. 5, p. 194.

107 'Japan: Japan and the Chinese Crisis', *North-China Herald*, 4 July 1900 (GSN 3:232). For another example, see 'Giwadan-hi to Taiwan seiban' (The Boxer-bandits and the Taiwan aborigines), *Tōkyō Asahi shinbun*, 15 June 1900, p. 2.

108 Mark R. Peattie, 'The Japanese Colonial Empire, 1895–1945', in Peter Duus (ed.): *The Cambridge History of Japan, Vol. 6: The Twentieth Century*, Cambridge, New York: Cambridge University Press, 1988, pp. 229–30, with further references.

109 Hobsbawm, *Age of Empire*, p. 307.

110 See the *Kanpō [Official Gazette]*, 28 March 1896 and 30 December 1898, in Nakayama Yasumasa *et al.* (eds), *Shinbun shūsei Meiji hennen-shi* (A Meiji chronicle through newspaper sources), Tokyo: Zaisei keizai gakkai, 1934–36, Vol. 9, pp. 389–90; Vol. 10, p. 330.

111 Iguchi, 'Nichiro sensō', p. 79; Mark Metzler, *Lever of Empire: The International Gold Standard and the Crisis of Liberalism in Prewar Japan*, Berkeley, CA: University of California Press, 2006, p. 31.

112 *Ibid.*, p. 32; Hugh T. Patrick, 'External Equilibrium and Internal Convertibility: Financial Policy in Meiji Japan', *Journal of Economic History*, Vol. 25, No. 2 (June 1965), p. 206.

113 *Ibid.*, p. 207; Metzler, *Lever of Empire*, 30–32.

114 Takamura Naosuke, 'Nisshin senji, sengo no zaisei to kinyū' (Financial policy and the money market during and after the Sino–Japanese War), in Inoue Matsusada *et al.* (eds), *Nihon rekishi taikei* (An outline of Japanese history), Tokyo: Yamakawa shuppan-sha, 1987, Vol. 4, p. 815.

115 *Ibid.*, p. 821; Patrick, 'External Equilibrium', p. 209.

116 See, for example, Fukuzawa, 'Ōi ni gaishi o iru beshi' (We must import large amounts of foreign capital), *Jiji shinpō*, 1 January 1898 (FYZ 16:202–3); 'Gaishi yu'nyū no michi' (How to import foreign capital), *ibid.*, 29 May 1898 (FYZ 16:354–56).

117 'Gaishi yu'nyū no kiseikai', *Chūō shinbun*, 5 May 1898, p. 2.

118 'I-kō I-haku no Yokohama-yuki' (Count Itō's and Viscount Inoue's visit to Yokohama), *Chūō shinbun*, 12 June 1898, p. 2.

119 'Gaishi yu'nyū ni tsuite' (On the import of foreign capital), *Chūō shinbun*, 17 June 1898, p. 2.

120 So, for example in late 1897, see Fukuzawa, 'Jitsugyō-ka no gunbi shukushō undō ni tsuite' (On the armament retrenchment agitation among entrepreneurs), *Jiji shinpō*, 14 November 1897 (FYZ 16:151–53); 'Spirit of the Vernacular Press', *Japan Weekly Mail*, 27 November 1897, pp. 558–59.

121 On Japan's 'Continental Strategy' during the 'postwar management' years, see Li Tingjiang, *Nihon zaikai to kindai Chūgoku: Shingai kakumei o chūshin ni* (The Japanese business world and modern China around the time of the Chinese Revolution 1911), 2nd edn, Tokyo: Ochanomizu shobō, 2003, pp. 83–95; Takamura, 'Nisshin senji', pp. 813–14. See also Duus, *Abacus and Sword*, pp. 135–6.

122 'Shinkoku no bunkatsu' (The partition of China), *Tōkyō nichinichi shinbun*, 25 October 1898, p. 2.

123 Thus, in the United States in the years 1890–1914, there was the myth of China as unlimited market for American goods, despite obvious appearances to the contrary, see Paul A. Varg, 'The Myth of the China Market, 1890–1914', *The American Historical Review*, Vol. 73, No. 3 (February 1968), pp. 742–43; see also Jürgen Osterhammel, *China und die Weltgesellschaft: vom 18. Jahrhundert bis in unsere Zeit* (China and the international society: from the eighteenth century to the present), Munich: C. H. Beck, 1989, p. 171–72.

124 See Ōkuma Shigenobu's Tōhō kyōkai speech in October 1898, *Ōkuma-haku enzetsu-shū* (A collection of Count Ōkuma's speeches), Waseda daigaku henshū-bu (ed.), Tokyo: Waseda daigaku, 1907, p. 29. For a more detailed discussion of this speech see Chapter 4.

125 'Jinmin no taigai jigyō' (Private enterprises abroad), *Chūō shinbun*, 20 April 1898, p. 1.

126 Akira Iriye, *China and Japan in the Global Setting*, Cambridge, MA: Harvard University Press, 1992, p. 8; Peattie, 'Japanese Colonial Empire', p. 222; Hilary Conroy, 'Lessons from Japanese Imperialism', *Monumenta Nipponica*, Vol. 21, No. 3/4 (1966), p. 336; Marius B. Jansen, 'Japanese Views of China During the Meiji Period', in Albert Feuerwerker, Rhoads Murphey, and Mary C. Wright (eds), *Approaches to Modern Chinese History*, Berkeley, CA: University of California Press, 1967, p. 187. With regard to social problems in domestic politics, Carol Gluck has observed a similar reluctance among Meiji observers to talk about economic factors, although they were not denied, either; see *Japan's Modern Myths: Ideology in the Late Meiji Period*, Princeton, NJ: Princeton University Press, 1985, pp. 29–30.

127 For an overview see George Akita, *Foundations of Constitutional Government in Modern Japan, 1868–1900*, Cambridge, MA: Harvard University Press, 1967, pp. 106–54.

128 Masuda, 'Nisshin sengo keiei', pp. 743–44.

129 Ibid., p. 746; Kuga Katsunan discusses the sudden change of the Jiyūtō (and of Itō Hirobumi as well) in 'Seikai kongo no kikan' (The marvelous spectacle of the political world), *Nippon*, 27 July 1895 (KKZ 5:155–56).

130 On the beginning of this movement see 'Atago-kan yūshikai' (The Atago-kan group of activists), *Kokumin shinbun*, 18 June 1895, p. 2.

131 See *Tōkyō nichinichi shinbun* and *Jiji shinpō*, 16 February 1896, in Nakayama, *Shinbun shūsei Meiji hennen-shi*, Vol. 9, p. 374. The Diet was immediately suspended by imperial order from 15–24 February 1896. In the meantime, Yamagata Aritomo put pressure on the leaders of the Kokumintō, so that the party finally voted against its own motion on 25 February 1896.

132 'Gunbi kakuchō to gaisei' (Armament expansion and foreign policy), *Nippon*, 23 December 1898 (KKZ 6:183).

133 On the very real exhaustion which the people experienced after several rounds of donations and funding through war bonds, see Lone, *Japan's First Modern War*, pp. 87–92.

134 See Gluck, *Japan's Modern Myths*, pp. 26–35 for social critique; for civilization critique in the late Meiji period, see Kano, *Shihon-shugi keiseiki*, pp. 481–88, 515–30.

135 Gluck, *Japan's Modern Myths*, p. 20.

136 'Kokumin no mahi' (The paralysis of the nation), *Chūō shinbun*, 17 May 1897, in *Kōtoku Shūsui zenshū* (The collected works of Kōtoku Shūsui), Kōtoku Shūsui zenshū henshū iinkai (ed.), Tokyo: Meiji bunken, 1968–73, Vol. 1, pp. 230–32.

137 *Ibid.*, pp. 231–32. The emphasis follows the original.

138 See 'Senshō no kyoei ni hokoru bekarazu' (We must not pride ourselves in the vain glory of victory), FYZ 16:30–32.

139 According to the weekly digest of the *Japan Weekly Mail*, 4 December 1897, pp. 586–87.

140 See Komatsu Midori, 'Seisui no kiun' (The rise and decline of nations), *Taiyō*, Vol. 4, No. 18 (5 September 1898), pp. 7–11.

3 The Far Ear Eastern Crisis of 1987–98

1 William L. Langer, *The Diplomacy of Imperialism*, 2nd edn, New York: Alfred A. Knopf, 1965, p. 411.

2 For the developments in foreign politics that led to the Far Eastern Crisis and the Crisis itself, see *ibid.*, pp. 385–414 and 445–83; Shinobu Seizaburō (ed.), *Nihon gaikō-shi 1853–1972* (A history of Japanese foreign policy, 1853–1972), Tokyo: Mainichi shinbunsha, 1974, Vol. 1, pp. 198–201; Ian Nish, *The Anglo-*

Japanese Alliance: the Diplomacy of Two Island Empires, 1894–1907, 2nd edn,
London: Athlone Press, 1985, pp. 46–62; Rolf Harald Wippich, *Japan und die
deutsche Fernostpolitik 1984–1898: Vom Ausbruch des Chinesisch-Japanischen
Krieges bis zur Besetzung der Kiautschou-Bucht: ein Beitrag zur Wilhelminischen
Weltpolitik* (Japan and German Far East policies: from the outbreak of the
Sino–Japanese War to the occupation of Kiao-chow: a study on Wilhelminian
Weltpolitik), Stuttgart: Steiner Verlag, 1987, pp. 325–401.

3 For an assessment of the Far Eastern Crisis, see Langer, *Diplomacy*, pp. 415,
   476–80.

4 See Banno Junji, *Meiji – shisō no jitsuzō* (Meiji – the true nature of thought),
   Tokyo: Sōbunsha, 1977, pp. 98–109; Sakeda Masatoshi, *Kindai Nihon ni okeru
   taigai-kō undō no kenkyū* (Studies on the strong foreign-policy movement in
   modern Japan), Tokyo: Tōkyō daigaku shuppan-kai, 1979, pp. 92–108.

5 This refutes Marius B. Jansen's claim that, in the late Meiji period, there existed,
   across all political positions, the 'gloomy view of a racial struggle,' see Jansen,
   'Japan and the Revolution of 1911', in John K. Fairbank and Kwang-Ching Liu
   (eds), *The Cambridge History of China, Vol. 2: Late Ch'ing, 1800–1911*, Part 2,
   Cambridge: Cambridge University Press, 1980, p, 363.

6 Langer, *Diplomacy*, pp. 448–54.

7 *Ibid.*, p. 454.

8 *Ibid.*, pp. 464–65, quoting an address of Sir Michael Hicks Beach on 17 January
   1898 in Swansea.

9 *Ibid.*, p. 467.

10 *Ibid.*, pp. 461, 681

11 The 'showy' date of the event gives another proof of the fact that the occupation
    of the commercially useless Weihaiwei was a concession to the public which
    cried for a 'sensational action' (Chamberlain, with some cynicism), *ibid.*, p. 462.

12 Akira Iriye, *Pacific Estrangement: Japanese and American Expansion, 1897–1911*,
    Cambridge, MA: Harvard University Press, 1971, pp. 63–65.

13 Shunpo-kō tsuishō-kai, *Itō Hirobumi den* (The life of Itō Hirobumi), three
    volumes, Tokyo, Hara shobō, 1970, Vol. 3, pp. 328–31.

14 *Ibid.*, Vol. 3, pp. 328–29.

15 Langer, *Diplomacy*, pp. 472–73.

16 *Ibid.*, pp. 460, 471.

17 The amendment to the official note promising the non-alienation merely secured
    Japan a privileged position *if and when* China decided to take in foreign inves-
    tors, see Shinobu Seizaburō (ed.), *Nihon gaikō-shi*, pp. 200–201; see also *Tokyo
    Asahi shinbun* and *Tokyo nichinichi shinbun*, 28 April 1898, in Nakayama Yasu-
    masa *et al.* (eds), *Shinbun shūsei Meiji hennen-shi* (A Meiji chronicle through
    newspaper sources), Tokyo: Zaisei keizai gakkai, 1934–36, Vol. 10, pp. 225.

18 See Douglas R. Reynolds, *China, 1898–1912: The Xinzheng Revolution and
    Japan*, Cambridge, MA: Harvard University Press, 1993, pp. 20–22.

19 See D. Tao, 'Nishimura Tenshū's Journey to the Yangtze Basin in 1897–98', in:
    Sino–Japanese Studies, Vol. 4, No. 1 (October 1991), pp. 28–43; for Zhang Zhi-
    dong's position in Japan's China policy, see Li Tingjiang, 'Zhang Zhidong and
    his Military Advisors: a Preliminary Analysis of Modern Japan's China Policy',
    translated by Douglas Howland, in Joshua Fogel (ed.), *Late Qing China and Meiji
    Japan: Political and Cultural Aspects*, Norwalk, CT: Eastbridge, 2004, pp. 39–61.

20 Reynolds, *China*, p. 29; on Chinese overseas students in Japan, see Paula Harrell,
    Sowing the Seeds of Change: Chinese Students, Japanese Teachers, 1895–1905,
    Stanford, CA: Stanford University Press, 1992; F. Huang, *Chinese Students in Japan
    in the late Ch'ing Period*, translated by Katherine P. K. Whitaker, Tokyo: Tokyo
    Press, 1982; Sanetō F., Keishū, *Chūgoku-jin Nihon ryūgaku-shi zōho* (A history of
    Chinese students in Japan, enlarged edn), Tokyo: Kuroshio shuppan, 1970.

21 Shinobu, *Nihon gaikō-shi*, Vol. 1, pp. 200–201; Li Tingjiang, *Nihon zaikai to kindai Chūgoku: Shingai kakumei o chūshin ni* (The Japanese business world and modern China around the time of the Chinese Revolution 1911), 2nd edn, Tokyo: Ochanomizu shobō, 2003, pp. 83–95.

22 Reynolds, *China*, pp. xvi–xviii, 5–6.

23 On the invocation of *dōbun dōshu* on this occasion, see Reynolds, *China*, p. 22; Tao, 'Nishimura Tenshū's Journey', p. 33; Richard C. Howard, 'Japan's Role in the Reform Program of K'ang Yu-wei', in Jung-Pang Lo (ed.), *Kang Yu-wei: A Biography and a Symposium*, Tucson, AZ: University of Arizona Press, 1967, p. 284.

24 See Kong Xiangji and Murata Yūjirō, *Han wei ren zhi de Zhong-Ri jiemeng ji qita: Wan-Qing Zhong-Ri guanxi-shi xintan* (A little-known Sino–Japanese alliance and other matters: new studies on the history of Late Qing Sino–Japanese relations), Chengdu: Boshu shushe, 2004, pp. 68–73.

25 *Yamagata Aritomo iken-sho*, Ōyama Azusa (ed.), Tokyo: Hara shobō, 1966, pp. 252–53.

26 See Nakayama, *Shinbun shūsei Meiji hennen-shi*, Vol. 10, p. 148.

27 *Ibid.*, Vol. 10, p. 151.

28 'Tôyô kinsei to gunbi' (The recent situation in East Asia and armaments), *Nippon*, 5 December 1897 (KKZ 5:638); Katsunan cautioned the reader that these rumours of a second Tripartite assault might be the fabrications of British agency. After all, it was suspicious how often such alarming rumours came from British subjects, and how very well they served the aims to incite East Asian people against Britain's enemies, the continental powers.

29 A 'golden jar, without blemish' is a simile from the dynastic history *Nanshi* (ed. Li Yanshou), according to which emperor Wu compared his strong and independent empire with a perfect golden vessel; see Morohashi Tetsuji, *Dai-Kanwa jiten* (Chinese-Japanese character dictionary), Tokyo: Taishūkan shoten, 1955–59, No. 40152, p. 56.

30 'Taigai no shintai' (Deciding our course of action abroad), *Jiji shinpō*, 28 November 1897 (FYZ 16:164).

31 On the 'pathology' of imperialism and Japan's foreign policy, see Hilary Conroy, 'Lessons from Japanese Imperialism', *Monumenta Nipponica*, Vol. 21, No. 3/4 (1966), p. 337.

32 *Tōkyō nichinichi shinbun*, 21 December 1897 (Nakayama, *Shinbun shūsei*, 10: 155). Vladivostok was inaccessible from December to mid-April every year; thus the Russian fleet had to winter elsewhere, as it had done sometimes in the Jiaozhou Bay.

33 'Shinkoku no gaisai' (China's foreign loans), *Tōkyō nichinichi shinbun*, 5 February 1898, p. 2.

34 'Shinkoku no shōkin' (The Chinese Indemnity), *Tōkyō nichinichi shinbun*, 16 February 1898, p. 2.

35 'Jinmin no taigai jigyō' (Private enterprises abroad), *Chūō shinbun*, 20 April 1898, p. 1.

36 'Taigai no shintai', FYZ 16:163. However, Fukuzawa very much questioned the true value of international law itself and thus was, eventually, positively impressed by Germany's resolute actions.

37 'Dokutei no gūi-ga' (An allegorical picture by the German emperor), 2 March 1898, p. 4.

38 'Kyōga' (Comic illustrations), *Tōkyō nichinichi shinbun*, 6 March 1898, p. 10.

39 Kuga Katsunan, 'Taigai shisō no kakushin' (A reform in foreign policy thinking), *Nippon*, 5 May 1898 (KKZ 6:70–71); the *Chūō shinbun*, too, ridicules the theatrical, but eventually ineffectual foreign policy of Germany, according to *Japan Weekly Mail*, 19 March 1898, p. 278. In the speech with which the

brother was sent off to the Far East, the German emperor used the same pompous imagery as in the so-called Knackfuss painting; see Langer, *Diplomacy*, p. 459.

40 For a short account of Nakamura's career as one of the founders of Japanese studies of international law, see Ichimata Masao, *Nihon no kokusaihō-gaku o kizuita hitobito* (The people who built Japanese international legal studies), Tokyo: Nihon kokusai mondai kenkyū-jo, 1973, pp. 91–105.

41 Strauch was 'extraordinary professor' in Heidelberg in the years 1865–1904, see Dagmar Drüll, *Heidelberger Gelehrtenlexikon, 1803–1932* (A compendium of scholars in Heidelberg, 1803–1932), Berlin: Springer, 1986, p. 264.

42 Nakamura sent minute records of his stay in Heidelberg, the manuscript of the presentation in German along with the comments of his audience in Japanese to Konoe; for this episode, see the *Konoe Atsumaro nikki* (The diary of Konoe Atsumaro), Konoe Atsumaro nikki kankō-kai (ed.), Tokyo: Kajima kenkyūjo shuppan-kai, 1968–69, Vol. 2, pp. 34–41 (sub. 1 April 1898, the letter dated 20 February 1898).

43 Konoe, *Konoe Atsumaro nikki*, Vol. 2, p. 37 (originally in German).

44 *Ibid.* (originally in Japanese).

45 *Ibid.*, Vol. 2, p. 41.

46 'Minkan yūshi no undo' (An agitation of private activists), *Chūō shinbun*, 6 April 1898, p. 2.

47 For these continuities, see Urs Matthias Zachmann, 'Guarding the Gates of Our East Asia: Japanese Reactions to the Far Eastern Crisis (1897–98) as a Prelude to the War', in Rotem Kowner, *Rethinking the Russo–Japanese War, 1904–5, Vol. 1: Centennial Perspectives.* Folkestone, Kent: Global Oriental, 2007, pp. 13–30.

48 *Japan Weekly Mail*, 16 April 1898, p. 386.

49 'Chanben-gumi no naijō' ('The internal situation of the Chanben-group'), *Chūō shinbun*, 18 April 1898, p. 2.

50 An account of the outrage is given by the *Tōkyō Asahi shinbun*, 12 May 1898, in Nakayama, *Shinbun shūsei Meiji hennen-shi*, Vol. 10, p. 234.

51 This was duly observed by the *Japan Weekly Mail* (14 May 1898, p. 500) in its customary sardonic way.

52 Interview with Ōkuma Shigenobu in the *Hōchi shinbun*, according to *Japan Weekly Mail*, 21 May 1898, p. 530.

53 'Shina to Nihon' (China and Japan), *Kokumin shinbun*, 3 December 1897, p. 2.

54 See also, for example, 'Nisshin dōmei no shin-igi' (The true meaning of a Sino-Japanese alliance), *Taiyō*, Vol. 4, No. 11, pp. 53–54. Incidentally, the most popular analogy in 1894–95 was the Franco-Prussian War of 1870–71. The Franco-German relations, however, did not work so well as a model for post-war rapprochement.

55 Taoka Reiun, 'Tōa no dai-dōmei', *Yorozu chōhō*, 25/28/30 November 1897, in *Taoka Reiun zenshū* (Collected Works of Taoka Reiun), Nishida Masaru (ed.), Tokyo: Hōsei daigaku shuppan-kyoku, 1969–87, Vol. 2, pp. 430–35.

56 The text is reprinted in the *Konoe Atsumaro nikki*, supplement, pp. 62–63. As to the reading of the character *fu/tsuketari*: a similar title in the *Yorozu chōhō* (13 June 1895, p. 2) has the reading (in *furigana*) as *Seiyūkai, tsuketari Gotō-haku* ('The Seiyūkai and Count Gotō'); the *tsuketari* serves to combine two not directly related subjects in one title.

57 For example, Banno Junji, *Meiji – shisō no jitsuzō*, p. 86; Reynolds, *China, 1898–1912*, pp. 10–11; Sushila Narsimhan, *Japanese Perceptions of China in the Nineteenth Century: Influence of Fukuzawa Yukichi.* New Delhi: Phoenix Publishing House, 1999. p. 182; Cemil Aydin, *The Politics of Anti-Westernism in Asia: Visions of World Order in Pan-Islamic and Pan-Asian Thought*, New York: Columbia University Press, 2007, pp. 54–55.

58 For short accounts of Konoe's political life and thought, see Marius B. Jansen, 'Konoe Atsumaro', in Akira Iriye (ed.), *The Chinese and the Japanese: Essays in*

Political and Cultural Interaction, Princeton, NJ: Princeton University Press, 1980, pp. 107–23; Aibara Shigeki, 'Konoe Atsumaro to Shina hozen-ron' (Konoe Atsumaro and the Preservation of China-argument), in Okamoto Kōji (ed.), *Kindai Nihon no Ajia-kan* (Modern Japan's views of Asia), Kyōto: Minerva shobō, 1998, pp. 51–77. See also Yamamoto Shigeki, *Konoe Atsumaro: sono Meiji kokka-kan to Ajia-kan* (Konoe Atsumaro: his views on the Meiji state and Asia), Kyōto: Minerva shobō, 2001.

59 Jansen, 'Konoe Atsumaro', pp. 111–13; Aibara, 'Konoe Atsumaro to Shina hozen ron', p. 55.

60 On the founding of the Dōbun-kai and Tōa dōbun-kai, see Zhai Xin, *Tōa dōbunkai to Chūgoku: kindai Nihon ni okeru taigai rinen to sono jissen* (*The Tōa dōbun-kai and China: the ideology and practice of foreign relations in modern Japan*), Tokyo: Keiō gijuku daigaku shuppan-kai, 2001, pp. 72–73; Sakeda Masatoshi, *Kindai Nihon ni okeru taigai-kō undō*, pp. 114–28; Douglas R. Reynolds, 'Training Young China Hands: Tōa Dōbun shoin and its Precursors, 1886–1945', in Peter Duus, Ramon H. Myers and Mark R. Peattie (eds), *The Japanese Informal Empire in China, 1895–1937* Princeton, NJ: Princeton University Press, 1989, pp. 224–26.

61 See the entry in Konoe's diary, *Konoe Atsumaro nikki*, Vol. 1, p. 331.

62 Konoe, *Konoe Atsumaro nikki*, supplement, p. 62.

63 A large part of this passage consists of a quote from 'somebody who lately came back from China' and describes the desperate political situation there. This person was most likely Shiraiwa Ryūhei (1867–1942), a former student and *(p 68)* devoted follower of Arao Sei and a shipping entrepreneur in China; on Shiraiwa, see Nakamura Tadashi's introduction to the *Shiraiwa Ryūhei nikki: Ajia-shugi jitsugyōka no shōgai* (The diary of Shiraiwa Ryūhei: the life of an Asianist *source* entrepreneur), Nakamura Tadashi (ed.), Tokyo: Kenbun shuppan, 1998. Shiraiwa, who had only recently come back from China, visited Konoe on 26 November 1897, two weeks before Konoe dictated the article, and they talked about the situation in China (see Konoe, *Konoe Atsumaro nikki*, Vol. 1, p. 326). The founding of the Dōbun-kai in June 1898 was largely owing to Shiraiwa's initiative (Zhai, *Tōa dōbun-kai*, pp. 72–73; Reynolds, 'Training China Hands', p. 224).

64 Ōuchi Chōzō, 'Konoe Kazan-kō to Tōa dōbun shoin' (Prince Konoe and the Tōa dōbun shoin), *Shina*, Vol. 25, No. 2/3 (February 1934), pp. 143–47; Ōuchi, 'Kazan-kō no bunka hatsuyō' (Prince Konoe's promotion of culture), *Shina*, Vol. 25, No. 2/3 (February 1934), pp. 179–80. Konoe mentions the interview in his diary, see *Konoe Atsumaro nikki*, Vol. 1, p. 260 (9 August 1897). See also Aibara, 'Konoe Atsumaro to Shina hozen-ron', pp. 57–58.

65 It should be noted that *bunmei* in the 1920s became a pejorative concept, and was supplanted by the concept of 'culture,' *bunka*, see T. Najita and H.D. Harootunian, 'Japanese revolt against the West: political and cultural criticism in the Twentieth Century', in Peter Duus, *The Cambridge History of Japan*, Vol. 6: *The Twentieth Century*, Cambridge, New York: Cambridge University Press, 1988, p. 735; *note* thus if Ōuchi in the 1930s speaks of *bunka*, he means the Meiji concept of *bunmei*.

66 Ōuchi, 'Konoe Kazan-kō', p. 146.

67 'Kō-jinshu dōmei no zehi tokushitsu' (The relative merits of a Yellow Race alliance), *Tenchijin*, Vol. 2 (February 1898), pp. 7–11; this article is also briefly mentioned by Aibara, 'Konoe Atsumaro to Shina hozen-ron', p. 71; Yamamoto, *Konoe Atsumaro*, pp. 92–93.

68 'Kō-jinshu dōmei no zehi tokushitsu', p. 9.

69 *Ibid.*, pp. 9–10.

70 *Ibid.*, 10.

71 The first passage could be identified as a passage from 'Shina bunkatsu tōtei manukaru bekarazu' (The partition of China is absolutely inevitable), *Jiji shinpō*,

14 January, 1898 (FYZ 16:213–16); the second from 'Shina bunkatsu-go no udemae wa ikan' (How about the skills [to rule] after the partition of China?), *Jiji shinpō*, 15 January 1898 (FYZ 16:216–20).

72 'Ōkuma-haku no Tōhō-ron' (Count Ōkuma's views on East Asia), *Tenchijin*, Vol.2 (February 1898), politics section, pp. 1–7, for the portion devoted to the question of a 'racial alliance' see pp. 5–6.

73 'Nisshin dōmei no shin-igi', *Taiyō*, Vol. 4, No. 11, p. 54.

74 'Russia, China, and Japan', *Japan Weekly Mail*, 30 April 1898, p. 463.

75 *Ibid.*

76 For another example of such specious Russian argumentation, see Kuga Katsunan, 'Shina bunkatsu no mondai: Ōshū ni okeru shikisha no kansatsu' (The problem of China's partition: the view of experts in Europe), in: *Nippon*, 26 February 1898 (KKZ 6:31–33), where Katsunan extensively cites a Russian expert who claims that Russians were being half Asiatic and therefore best suited to civilize China.

77 Konoe, *Konoe Atsumaro nikki*, Vol. 2, pp. 47–52 (sub 12 April 1898; the letter is dated 3/4 March 1898).

78 Nakamura sent Konoe a clipping of the article, see *ibid.*, Vol. 2, pp. 51–52. The article gives a fairly accurate abstract of Konoe's essay. The *Heidelberger Tageblatt* ended with the comment that the *Kokumin shinbun* agreed with Konoe and that it suggested the same policy towards China as Prussia pursued towards Austria in 1866.

79 *Ibid.*, Vol. 2, pp. 49–50; Nakamura copied the article in the original language, German, and inserted two short remarks of his own, which are left out in the translation as indicated.

80 It is unclear what the italics represent in the *Konoe Atsumaro nikki*, whether Nakamura's emphasis or those of the *Frankfurter Zeitung*.

81 Konoe, 'Teikoku no ichi to gendai no seijika' (The position of our empire and today's politicians), *Tōa jiron*, No. 1 (10 December 1898), p. 6.

82 See Sugano Tadashi, *Shinmatsu Nitchū kankei-shi no kenkyū* (Studies on Late Qing Sino–Japanese relations), Tokyo: Kyūko shoin, 2002, p. 348.

83 Kunaichō (ed.), *Meiji Tennō-ki* (Record of the Meiji Emperor), Tokyo: Yoshikawa Kōbunkan, 1968–77. Vol. 9, pp. 472–73.

84 On Takayama's position within the discussion of the racial homogeneity or diversity of the Japanese nation, see E. Oguma, *A Genealogy of 'Japanese' Self-Images*, translated by David Askew, Melbourne: Trans Pacific Press, 2002, pp. 41–44.

85 Takayama, 'Jinshu kyōsō toshite mitaru Kyōkutō mondai' (The Far Eastern Question seen as a racial competition), *Taiyō*, Vol. 4, No. 2 (20 January 1898), pp. 30–39.

86 Takayama, 'I-jinshu dōmei' (An alliance between different races), *Taiyō*, Vol. 4, No. 5 (5 March 1898), p. 31.

87 See, for example, his article 'Jūkyū seiki – sōron' (The nineteenth century – Introduction), *Taiyō*, Vol. 6, No. 8 (15 June 1900), p. 26, where Takayama basically repeated his earlier conviction of the Far Eastern Question as a racial competition.

88 Takayama Chogyū, 'Sensen-roku' (Verbose Notes), *Taiyō* Vol. 4, No. 15 (20 July 1898), 32; the *Yadong shibao* quote has not been identified yet.

89 On the Chinese reformist press after the Sino–Japanese War, see H. Chang, 'Intellectual Change and the Reform Movement, 1890–98', in John K. Fairbank and Kwang-Ching Liu (eds), *The Cambridge History of China, Vol. 2: Late Ch'ing, 1800–1911, Part 2*, Cambridge, London, New York: Cambridge University Press, 1980, pp. 333–36.

90 Luke S. Kwong, *A Mosaic of the Hundred Days: Personalities, Politics, and Ideas of 1898*, Cambridge, MA: Harvard University Press, 1984, pp. 139, 141; see also

Wang Shuhuai, *Wairen yu wuxu bianfa* (Foreigners and the Hundred Days Reform), Taibei: Jinghua yinshuguan, 1965, pp. 162–76.

91 Benjamin Schwartz, *In Search of Wealth and Power: Yen Fu and the West*, Cambridge, MA: Belknap Press, 1964, p. 131. On the Japanese side, the newspaper was handled by the Japanese consul Tei Nagamasa (1826–1916) and the newspaperman Nishimura Hiroshi, see Nakashita Masaharu, *Shinbun ni miru Nitchū kankei-shi: Chūgoku no Nihon-jin keieishi* (Sino–Japanese relations as seen through newspapers: China's Japanese-run newspapers), Tokyo: Kenbun shuppan, 1996, pp. 7, 31–61). In 1899 the Tōa dōbun-kai, too, decided to fund the *Guowenbao*, see Zhai Xin, *Tōa dōbun-kai to Chūgoku*, p. 86.

92 Nakashita, *Shinbun ni miru Nitchū kankei-shi*, pp. 1–8. For a detailed discussion of the activities of the Tōa dōbun-kai to influence Chinese public opinion through the Shanghai-based Chinese-language newspaper *Tongwen hubao*, see Zhai, *Tōa dōbun-kai to Chūgoku*, pp. 133–82.

93 On the *Yadong shibao*, the Itsubi-kai and the Dōbun-kai, see Zhai, *Tōa dōbun-kai to Chūgoku*, p. 25 (fn. 22), pp. 73–75.

94 For an overview of Japanese Pan-Asianism, see Sven Saaler, 'Pan-Asianism in modern Japanese history', in Sven Saaler and Viktor Koschmann (eds), *Pan-Asianism in Modern Japanese History*, London, New York: Routledge, 2007, pp. 1–18; see also Aydin, *Politics of Anti-Westernism in Asia*, pp. 54–59, 89–91.

95 For Miyazaki's early pan-Asian dreams, see *My Thirty-Three Years' Dream: the Autobiography of Miyazaki Tōten*, translated by Etō Shinkichi and Marius B. Jansen, Princeton, NJ: Princeton University Press, 1982, pp. 47, 62f.

96 See Marius B. Jansen, *The Japanese and Sun Yat-Sen*, Cambridge, MA: Harvard University Press, 1967, p. 33.

97 See, for example, 'Taigai no shintai' (Deciding our course of action abroad), *Jiji shinpō*, 28 November 1897 (FYZ 16:163); 'Kaigun kakuchō no hoka aru bekarazu' (Expanding the navy is the only option), *Jiji shinpō* 20 January 1898 (FYZ 16:221).

98 'Shina bunkatsu imasara odoroku ni tarazu' (The partition of China shouldn't surprise us anymore), *Jiji shinpô*, 13 January 1898 (FYZ 16:208–9). The text is clearly written by a person other than Fukuzawa, as Fukuzawa is being referred to in the third person.

99 Fukuzawa, at the same time as he attributed the imminent fall of China to Confucianism, started a new campaign against 're-feudalistic' tendencies in Japan: 'Haigai shisō to jukyō-shugi' (Anti-foreign thought and Confucianism), *Jiji shinpō*, 13 March 1898 (FYZ 16:273); 'Jukyō-shugi no gai wa sono fuhai ni ari' (The evil of Confucianism lies in its degeneracy), *Jiji shinpō*, 15 March 1898 (FYZ 16:276); 'Jukyō no fukkatsu no seki wa ima no tōkyoku-sha ni ari' (The responsibility for the resurgence of Confucianism lies with those in power now), *Jiji shinpō*, 16 March 1898 (FYZ 16:278).

100 This term of traditional medicine describes the body in varying parts: muscles, veins, flesh, bones, and hair; head, neck, arms and legs, etc.

101 'Taigai no shintai', FYZ 16:164.

102 'Jûyonen mae no Shina bunkatsu ron' (My prediction of China's partition fourteen years ago), *Jiji shinpô*, 12 January 1898 (FYZ 16:204).

103 'Tôyô no Pôrando' (The Poland of the East), *Jiji shinpô*, 15/16 October 1884 (FYZ 10:72–80)

104 'Faguo zhaohui guafen Zhongguo shi' (France's memorandum concerning the partition of China), *Zhixinbao* No. 45 (1898, Guangxu 24/2/11), pp. 18–20.

105 'Taigai no shintai', 163–64.

106 'Shina bunkatsu-go no udemae wa ikan' (How about the skills [to rule] after the partition of China?), *Jiji shinpō*, 15 January 1898 (FYZ 16:216).

107 *Ibid.*, p. 220.

108 'Shina-jin shitashimu beshi' (We must make friends with the Chinese), *Jiji shinpō*, 22 March 1898 (FYZ 16:284–87).

109 *Ibid.*, 286.

110 *Ibid.*, pp. 285–86.

111 'Shina-jin shitsubō su bekarazu', *Jiji shinpō*, 16 April 1898 (FYZ 16:303–6).

112 *Ibid.*, p. 305.

113 *Ibid.*, pp. 305–6.

114 'Ka o henjite fuku to nasu beshi', *Jiji shinpō*, 17 May 1898, p. 2; this article is not included in the *Fukuzawa Yukichi zenshū*.

115 *Ibid.*

116 'Hosha shinshi no kogen ni tanomu ni tarazu', *Jiji shinpo*, 4 September 1884 (FYZ 10:31–33).

117 'Ka o henjite fuku to nasu beshi', *Jiji shinpō*, 17 May 1898, p. 2.

118 *Jiji shinpō*, 3 February 1898, p. 5.

119 See e.g. Yasukawa Junosuke, *Fukuzawa Yukichi no Ajia ninshiki: Nihon kindaishi-zō o toraekaesu* (Fukuzawa Yukichi's perception of Asia: re-understanding the image of modern Japanese history), Tokyo: Kōbunken, 2000, p. 21; Hatsuse, Ryūhei, '"Datsua ron" saikō' (Reconsidering the "Datsua ron"), in Hirano Ken'ichirō (ed.), *Kindai Nihon to Ajia: bunka no kōryū to masatsu* (Modern Japan and Asia: cultural exchange and conflict), Tokyo: Tōkyō daigaku shuppan-kai, 1984, p. 21.

120 'Jiji shinpō no jisatsu' (The suicide of the *Jiji shinpō*), *Tōkyō nichinichi shinbun*, 16 November 1898, p. 4.

121 For Yano's initiative, see Reynolds, *China*, p. 29.

122 'Shinajin shitashimu beshi', FYZ 16:285–86.

123 If we browse, for example, just the issues of the reformist newspaper *Zhixinbao* in 1898, we find regular translations, excerpts and paraphrases of articles from Japanese newspapers. For *Jiji shinpō* articles, see for example, 'Faguo zhaohui guafen Zhongguo shi' ('France's memorandum concerning the partition of China'), *Zhixinbao* 45 (Guangxu 24/2/11), pp. 18–20; 'Chaoxian weixindang-ren you cheng' ('Korea's reform party successful'), *Zhixinbao* 75 (Guangxu 24/11/11), p. 10–11. – The *Jiji shinpō*-editors from early on were well aware of being watched by the Chinese press (see Introduction).

124 For a detailed study of Kuga Katsunan's positions, see Marutani Yoshinori, *Kuga Katsunan kenkyū* (Studies on Kuga Katsunan), Tokyo: Keisō shobō, 1990; Koyama Fumio, *Kuga Katsunan: 'Kokumin' no sōshutsu* (Kuga Katsunan: creating 'the nation'), Tokyo: Misuzu shobō, 1990; for a prospect of Katsunan's political thought in the years 1898–1900, see Yamaguchi Kazuyuki, 'Kuga Katsunan no gaiseiron: Meiji 31 – 33-nen' (Kuga Katsunan's opinions on foreign policy, 1898–1900), *Komazawa shigaku*, No. 27 (March 1980), pp. 1–26, No. 28 (March 1981), pp. 1–30; see also Sakeda, *Kindai Nihon*, pp. 92–98.

125 'Minkan yūshi no undo', *Chūō shinbun*, 6 April 1898, p. 2; one of the early names for the group was also the 'Kairakuen-gumi,' the Kairakuen group.

126 On the founding of the Tōa-kai, see Zhai, *Tōa dōbun-kai*, pp. 68–72; Sakeda, *Kindai Nihon*, pp. 110–14; Reynolds, 'Training China Hands', p. 225.

127 Katsunan uses the term 'blackmail' (*kyōhaku*), for example, in 'Shinsei no bunmei-koku' ('Really civilized countries'), KKZ 6:61.

128 'Juryoku shinpo no jidai' (The age of the progress of brute force), *Nippon*, 5 February 1898 (KKZ 6:19–20).

129 See 'Rekkoku no tai-Shin kyodō' (The actions of the powers in China), *Nippon*, 25 December 1898 (KKZ 5:645–46); 'Taigai shisō no kakushin' (A reform in foreign policy thinking), *Nippon*, 8 May 1898 (KKZ 6:70–71). Incidentally, in September 1898 Ōishi Masami, who was Katsunan's associate in the Taigai dōshikai and Shinpotō minister in the Ōkuma cabinet, restated the opinion that

the Western powers had transferred the conflict from the Near Eastern Question (Turkey) to the Far Eastern question to keep it away from home, and thus brought danger into East Asia, see 'Ōishi-shi no gaikōron' (Mr. Ōishi's opinions on foreign policy), *Tōkyō nichinichi shinbun*, 11 September 1898, p. 2.

130 'Shina bunkatsu no mondai: Ōshū ni okeru shikisha no kansatsu' (The problem of China's partition: the view of experts in Europe), KKZ 6:31–32.

131 'Shinsei no bunmei-koku', KKZ 6:61.

132 'Taigai shisō no kakushin', KKZ 6:71.

133 'Tōyō kinsei to gunbi' (The recent developments in East Asia and armament expansion), *Nippon*, 5 December 1897 (KKZ 5:638–39); 'Gaikō to kokuryoku' (Diplomacy and national power), *Nippon*, 9 April 1898 (KKZ 6:56–58).

134 'Gunbi kakuchō to gaisei' (Armament expansion and foreign policy), *Nippon*, 23 December 1898 (KKZ 6:183).

135 'Shinsei no bunmei-koku', KKZ 6:62.

136 For an overview of opinions in the Japanese public about the Spanish-American War, see Iriye, *Pacific Estrangement*, pp. 57–62.

137 'Kinsei-ron' (Balance of power), *Nippon*, 7 April 1898 (KKZ 6:55–56).

138 'Taigai shisō no kakushin', KKZ 6:71.

139 'Taigai shisō no kakushin', KKZ 6:70–71.

140 *Ibid.*, p. 71.

141 'Sekai bunmei no shōgai', *Nippon*, 11 February 1898 (KKZ 6:23–24).

142 Konoe famously developed the idea of an 'Asian Monroe Doctrine' (*Ajia no Monrō-shugi*) in his interview with Kang Youwei in November 1898 (see Konoe, *Konoe Atsumaro nikki*, Vol. 2, p. 195). Considering his other statements and the usual strategy in Sino–Japanese interactions, this, however, has to be taken *cum grano salis*; see also Yamamoto, *Konoe Atsumaro*, p. 108; Aibara, 'Konoe Atsumaro to Shina hozen', p. 60; Jansen, 'Konoe Atsumaro', pp. 117–18.

143 'Shina naichi no kakushin o unagasu beki gi – Shashi no henran o kikai toshite', *Nippon*, 13 May 1898 (KKZ 6:74–75).

144 *Ibid.*, p. 74.

145 'Tai-Shin mondai wa ikan' (How to deal with the Chinese problem), part 2, *Nippon*, 26 June 1898 (KKZ 6:88).

146 This is an allusion to a story in the Chinese classic *Zuozhuan* (Xi gong, year 30) in which the state Zheng persuades Qin to discontinue its attacks by promising Qin its assistance: 'If you leave off Zheng and acknowledge it as master in the East [*dongdao zhu*], it will supply your passing envoys with all they need, and so it shall be not to your detriment, either' (Chinese University of Hongkong, Institute of Chinese Studies (ed.), *Chunqiu zuozhuan zhuzi suoyin / A Concordance to the Chunqiu Zuozhuan*, Hong Kong: Commercial Press, 1995, Vol. 1, p. 116). The story seemed to be well known among Katsunan's contemporaries. Fukuzawa Yukichi, for example, quoted the same story in his 'Plan for the Division of China' to justify Japan's share of Taiwan and Fujian province ('Jūyo-nen mae no Shina bunkatsu-ron', FYZ 16:207). In Katsunan's case, too, the story serves to reinforce Japan's claims over East Asia, and especially China.

147 'Shina naichi no kakushin o unagasu beki gi', KKZ 6:74.

148 'Tai-Shin-saku no yōdō' (The essential method of dealing with China). *Nippon*, 16 May 1898 (KKZ 6:75–76).

149 *Ibid.*, p. 76.

150 *Ibid.*, p. 76.

151 Jansen, 'Japanese Views of China During the Meiji Period', in Albert Feuerwerker, Rhoads Murphey and Mary C. Wright (eds), *Approaches to Modern Chinese History*, Berkeley, CA: University of California Press, 1967, p. 164.

152 Banno Junji, *Meiji: shisō no jitsuzō*, pp. 3–6.

153 Tōyama Shigeki, 'Fukuzawa Yukichi no keimō-shugi to Kuga Katsunan no rekishi-shugi' (Fukuzawa's enlightenment thinking and Kuga Katsunan's historicism), in Uete Michiari (ed.), *Kuga Katsunan shū*, Tokyo: Chikuma shobō, 1987, pp. 493–94.

154 For the idea of the imperialist 'civilizing mission,' see Boris Barth and Jürgen Osterhammel (eds), *Zivilisierungsmissionen: imperiale Weltverbesserung seit dem 18. Jahrhundert* (Civilizing missions: imperialist reformism since the eigtheenth century), Konstanz: UVK Verlagsgesellschaft, 2005.

4 The Hundred Days Reform, 1898

1 On the problems of interpretation, see Luke S. Kwong, *A Mosaic of the Hundred Days: Personalities, Politics, and Ideas of 1898*, Cambridge, MA: Harvard University Press, 1984, pp. 3–13; Y. Wong, 'Revisionism Reconsidered: Kang Youwei and the Reform Movement of 1898,' *Journal of Asian Studies*, Vol. 51, No. 3 (August 1992), pp. 513–15; Rebecca E. Karl and Peter Zarrow (eds), *Rethinking the 1898 Reform Period: Political and Cultural Change in Late Qing China*, Cambridge, MA: Harvard University Asia Center, 2002, pp. 2–10.

2 Karl and Zarrow, *Rethinking the 1898 Reform Period*, pp. 4–5.

3 *Ibid.*, pp. 6–7.

4 See for example Richard C. Howard, 'Japan's Role in the Reform Program of K'ang Yu-wei,' in Jung-Pang Lo (ed.), *Kang Yu-wei: A Biography and a Symposium*, Tucson, AZ: University of Arizona Press, 1967, pp. 281–312; Peng Zezhou, 'Kō Yūi no henpō undō to Meiji ishin' (Kang Youwei's reform movement and the Meiji Restoration), *Jinbun gakuhō*, Vol. 30 (March 1970), pp. 149–93; Yamane Yukio, 'Bojutsu henpō to Nihon: Kō Yūi no 'Meiji ishin' haaku o chūshin ni shite' (The Hundred Days Reform and Japan: Kang Youwei's grasp of the 'Meiji Restoration'), in: *Kindai Nihon to Chūgoku* (Modern Japan and China), Tokyo: Yamakawa shuppansha, 1976, pp. 1–36; John E. Schrecker, 'The Reform Movement of 1898 and the Meiji Restoration as Ch'ing-I Movement,' in Akira Iriye, *The Chinese and the Japanese: Essays in Political and Cultural Interactions*, Princeton, NJ: Princeton University Press, 1980, pp. 96–106; Li Shaojun, 'Bojutsu henpō: Nihon o mohan to shita Chūgokujin' (The Hundred Days Reform – the Chinese modeling themselves on Japan), *China 21*, Vol. 9 (May 2000), pp. 225–40; Peter Zarrow, 'Late Qing Reformism and the Meiji Model: Kang Youwei, Liang Qichao, and the Japanese Emperor,' in Joshua A. Fogel, *The Role of Japan in Liang Qichao's Introduction of Modern Western Civilization to China*. Berkeley, CA: Institute of East Asian Studies, University of California, 2004, pp. 40–67.

5 Marius B. Jansen, *Japan and China: from War to Peace, 1894–1972*, Chicago, IL: Rand Mc.Nally College Publishing Co., 1975, p. 136.

6 Shimura Toshiko, 'Bojutsu henpō to Nihon: Nisshin sensō-go no shinbun o chūshin to shite' (The Hundred Days Reform and Japan in Japanese newspapers after the Sino–Japanese War), *Tōkyō toritsu daigaku hōgaku zasshi*, Vol. 6, No. 2 (March 1966), p. 273.

7 See for example Jansen, *Japan and China*, p. 136; Ian Nish, 'An Overview of Relations between China and Japan, 1895–1945,' in Christopher Howe (ed.), *China and Japan: History, Trends, and Prospects*, Oxford: Clarendon Press, 1996, p. 24.

8 On the emerging power structure, see Kwong, *Mosaic*, pp. 34–40.

9 Kwong, *Mosaic*, p. 154.

10 Ssu-yü Teng and John K. Fairbank (eds), *China's Response to the West: A Documentary Survey*, Cambridge, MA: Harvard University Press, 1979, p. 210.

11 Kwong, *Mosaic*, p. 157, with further references.

12 Kang's version of the audience appeared on 17 October 1898, in the *North-China Herald*, reprinted from the *Chinese Mail*; see Teng and Fairbank, *China's Response*, pp. 177–79.

13 Kwong, *Mosaic*, p. 180.

14 On Huang Zunxian's involvement in the Chinese post-war reform movement, see N. Kamachi, *Reform in China: Huang Tsun-hsien and the Japanese Model*, Cambridge, MA: Council on East Asian Studies, Harvard University, 1981, pp. 191–236.

15 Kwong, *Mosaic*, pp. 175–76. For translated selections of Feng Guifen's (1809–74) *Jiaobin-lu kangyi*, see Teng and Fairbank, *China's Reponse*, pp. 51–54; for Zhang's *Quanxue pian*, see *ibid.*, pp. 166–74.

16 For an overview, see Peng, 'Kō Yūi no henpō undō,' pp. 163–70.

17 Kang Youwei observed that this caused considerable excitement in the capital; see Kang Youwei, 'Chronological Autobiography of K'ang Yu-wei,' translated by Jung-Pang Lo, in Jung-Pang Lo (ed.), *K'ang Yu-Wei: A Biography and a Symposium*, Tucson, AZ: University of Arizona Press, 1967, p. 100. However, as we shall see, Japanese newspaper sources reveal that the abolishment elicited mixed reactions in the capital.

18 Kwong, *Mosaic*, p. 15.

19 See for example 'Shina no kaikaku ni tsuite' (On the reforms in China), *Jiji shinpō*, 22 September 1898, p. 2; 'Shinkoku no kansei no kaikaku' (On the reform of the bureaucracy in China), *Nippon*, 22 September 1898, p. 1.

20 For Naitō Konan's opinions on Chinese reform at the time, see Joshua A. Fogel, 'To Reform China: Naitō Konan's Formative Years in the Meiji Press,' *Modern Asian Studies*, Vol. 16, No. 3 (1982), pp. 353–95; Fogel, *Politics and Sinology: the Case of Naitō Konan (1866–1934)*, Cambridge, MA: Council on East Asian Studies, Harvard University, 1984, pp. 84–91.

21 See for example 'Shinkoku no seihen' (The political change in China), *Tōkyō nichinichi shinbun*, 25 September 1898, p. 2; 'Shinkoku kaikaku-ha no ichi-tonza' (A major setback for the reformers in China), *Chūō shinbun*, 25 September 1898, p. 2; 'Rinkoku no seihen' (The political change in our neighbor country), *Kokumin shinbun*, 25 September 1898, p. 1..

22 In the 1890s Japan had no news agency for foreign news, and relied on Reuters and their own special correspondents. For Japan's access to foreign news in Meiji times and later, see Sasaki Takashi, *Media to kenryoku* (The media and power), Tokyo: Chūō kōron shinsha, 1999, pp. 298–309; Uchikawa Yoshimi, 'Jūkyū seiki kōhan-ki no sekai to Nihon no kokusai hōdō' (The world in the late nineteenth century and international news coverage in Japan), in Kokusai nyūsu jiten shuppan iinkai, Mainichi komyunikêshonzu (eds), *Gaikoku shinbun ni miru Nihon* (Japan as seen through foreign newspapers), Tokyo: Mainichi komyuni-kêshonzu, Vol. 2 (1990), pp. vi–xi.

23 Shimura, 'Bojutsu henpō,' p. 273. The problem is that most of Shimura's sources with *specific* information about the Hundred Days are dated September 1898 and after, that is, *post factum*.

24 'Shinkoku no genron jiyū' (Freedom of Speech in China), *Chūō shinbun*, 5 June 1898, p. 1.

25 *Chūō shinbun*, 3 June 1898, p. 2, with a portrait of Prince Gong.

26 'Shanghai tsūshin' (Shanghai news), *Tōkyō nichinichi shinbun*, 24 June 1898, p. 1. The edict is given in full Japanese translation.

27 See for example 'Shinkoku ni-daijin no shintai' (Personnel matters concerning two Chinese ministers), *Chūō shinbun*, 18 June 1898, p. 2; 'Shinkoku katsudō no ki' (An opportunity for action in China), *Nippon*, 24 June 1898, p. 2; 'Shanghai tsūshin,' *Tōkyō nichinichi shinbun*, 24 June 1898, p. 1; 'Pekin tokuhō,' *Yorozu chōhō*, 2 July 1898, p. 1.

28 'Pekin tokuhō,' *Yorozu chōhō*, 3 July 1898; the dispatch is dated 16 June 1898, the day of the audience; the dispatch also mentions Huang Zunxian and Liang Qichao being granted imperial attention (see Kwong, *Mosaic,* p. 181; Teng and Fairbank, *China's response,* p. 149).

29 *Kokumin shinbun*, 29 July 1898, in Nakayama Yasumasa *et al.* (eds), *Shinbun shūsei Meiji hennen-shi* (A Meiji chronicle through newspaper sources), Tokyo: Zaisei keizai gakkai, 1934–36, Vol. 10, p. 269; also Meiji nyūsu jiten hensan iinkai, Mainichi komyunikêshonzu (eds), *Meiji nyūsu jiten* (Meiji news encyclopaedia), nine vols, Tokyo: Mainichi komyunikêshonzu, 1983–86, Vol. 6, p. 330.

30 'Shina ikan' (How is the situation in China?), part 1, *Tōkyō nichinichi shinbun*, 27 July 1898, p. 1; contrary to Kang Youwei, who claimed that the abolition of the eight-legged essay was 'greeted with joy' among the people ' (Chronological Autobiography,' p. 100), the correspondent of the *Nichinichi* rather observed a great 'panic.' For candidates, who had spent decades to master the style, this is rather understandable.

31 'Shinkoku no kinji' (Recent China affairs), *Tōkyō nichinichi shinbun*, 20/24 August 1898, p. 1.

32 See for example *Tōkyō nichinichi shinbun*, 11 September 1898, p. 3.

33 Kwong, *Mosaic,* p. 13; on the controversy about the authenticity of Kang's memorials, see Wong, 'Revisionism Reconsidered,' pp. 513–15.

34 In February 1898, Kawasaki reported to the *Taiyō* about the 'Occupation of Kiaochow by Germany and the situation of the East,' see *Taiyō*, Vol. 4, No. 4 (February 1898), p. 19.

35 See Kawasaki, 'Man-Shin teikoku to sono jinzai' (the *Taiyō's* English list of contents reads 'Chinese Empire and her Men of Ability'). The *Taiyō* series is basically an elaboration of parts 4–9 of the *Chūō* series.

36 'Shinkoku no keisei masa ni ippen sen to su,' *Chūō shinbun*, 22–24 September 1898.

37 Kawasaki, 'Sengo no Shina,' 17 April 1898.

38 Kawasaki, 'Sengo no Shina,' 16 April 1898.

39 See Fogel, 'To Reform China,' pp. 374–75.

40 H. Chang, 'Intellectual Change and the Reform Movement, 1890–98,' in John K. Fairbank and Kwang-Ching Liu (eds), *The Cambridge History of China, Vol. 2: Late Ch'ing, 1800–1911, Part 2*, Cambridge, London, New York: Cambridge University Press, 1980, p. 306; see also Fogel, 'To Reform China,' p. 377.

41 Kawasaki, 'Sengo no Shina,' 18 March 1898.

42 *Ibid.*

43 Kawasaki, 'Sengo no Shina,' 20–22 March, 24–28 March, 2 May 1898; this part of Kawasaki's analysis was republished in the *Taiyō* in late August and September under the title 'Man-Shin teikoku to sono jinzai,' as well as in late September in the *Chūō shinbun* under the title 'Shinkoku no keisei masa ni ippen sen to su.' In each case adjustments to the analysis were marginal.

44 'Sengo no Shina,' *Chūō shinbun*, 20 April 1898; Shizan discusses the *kakumei-ha* in 'Sengo no Shina,' 24 April, 2 May 1898.

45 The Tongzhi era lasted from 1862 to 1874, the Guangxu era started in 1875; Cixi's regency nominally ended in 1889.

46 The phrase *kanka manbu* – 'soft song and slow dance' – is taken from Bo Juyis (772–846) 'Song of unending sorrow' (*Chang hen ge*), see Morohashi Tetsuji, *Dai-Kanwa jiten* (Chinese–Japanese character dictionary), Tokyo: Taishūkan shoten, 1955–59, No. 11110:56. The passage describes how the infatuated emperor whiles away his time with his concubine until revolt ends the happiness. For a translation see Witter Bynner, *Three-hundred poems of the T'ang Dynasty 618–906*, Taipei: Book World Co., pp. 120–25.

47 'Sengo no Shina,' *Chūō shinbun*, 25 April 1898.

48 Kwong, *Mosaic*, pp. 153–54; Douglas R. Reynolds, *China, 1898–1912: The Xinzheng Revolution and Japan*, Cambridge, MA: Harvard University Press, 1993, p. 35; and even more positive, Sue Fawn Chung, 'The Image of the ✓ Empress Dowager Tz'u-Hsi,' in Paul A. Cohen and John E. Schrecker (eds), *Reform in Nineteenth-Century China*, Cambridge, MA: Harvard University Press, 1976, p. 102.

49 P. Ho, 'Weng T'ung-Ho and the "One Hundred Days of Reform",' *Far Eastern Quarterly*, Vol. 10, No. 2 (February 1951), p. 134.

50 'Sengo no Shina,' *Chūō shinbun*, 26 April 1898.

51 Ho, 'Weng T'ung-Ho,' p. 134; Kwong, *Mosaic*, pp. 160–65.

52 Kwong, *Mosaic*, p. 41; Chung, 'The Image of the Empress Dowager,' p. 102; Sue Fawn Chung, 'The Much-Maligned Empress Dowager: A Revisionist Study of the Empress Dowager Tz'u-His (1835–1908),' *Modern Asian Studies*, Vol. 13, No. 2 (1979), pp. 177–96.

53 'Sengo no Shina,' *Chūō shinbun*, 20 April 1898.

54 'Ri Kōshō dangai seraru' (Li Honghzhang accused), *Chūō shinbun*, 23 March 1898, p. 1.

55 'Sengo no Shina,' *Chūō shinbun*, 26 April 1898.

56 'Sengo no Shina,' *Chūō shinbun*, 24 April 1898. For some reasons, Shizan listed Zhang as 'quasi Hunan-ha' (*jun-Konan-ha*). For Zhang as Kang's patron, see Kwong, *Mosaic*, pp. 147–51.

57 Daniel H. Bays, 'Chang Chih-Tung after the '100 Days': 1898–1900 as a transitional period for reform constituencies,' in Paul A. Cohen and John E. Schrecker (eds), *Reform in Nineteenth-Century China*, Cambridge, MA: Harvard University Press, 1976, pp. 321–22.

58 For news items on Zhang's career, see for example *Chūō shinbun*, 7 May 1898, p. 1 (Zhang's appointment as *gunki daijin*); 8 May 1898, p. 2 (same); 29 May 1898, p. 1 (Zhang on the issue of Weihaiwei).

59 For two of the earliest articles on Kang, see 'Shinkoku kaikaku-ha no shin-dantai,' *Chūō shinbun*, 19 May 1898, p. 2; 'Shinkoku no kinjō' (The recent situation in China), *Chūō shinbun*, 24 June 1898, p. 1. The latter has a portrait of Kang Youwei, but reckons Kang still among Zhang Zhidong's faction, which is a gross misrepresentation.

60 Kawasaki, 'Sengo no Shina,' 18 March 1898.

61 'Shinkoku no keisei masa ni ippen to su,' *Chūō shinbun*, 22–24 September 1898.

62 Shiga in 1888 published a political novel entitled *Kokotsu no yakuwan* (Ōsaka-fu: Obuchitō); in 1894, Shiga also published a three-volume history of the Satake clan of Akita-han, entitled *Satake sankan-shi* (Akita: Shūsui-dō). Shiga signs the preface with 'a former vassal of the Satake, Shabaku manshi, Shiga Sukegorō.'

63 See Shiga's short explanation in 'Shina mondai' (The Chinese question), *Yorozu chōhō*, 23 September 1898.

64 In the *Tōkyō nichinichi*, Shiga uses the pseudonym 'Shabaku manshi,' in the *Yorozu* the pseudonym 'Ryūko.' Only the article 'Shina mondai,' *Yorozu chōhō*, 23 September 1898, reveals the identity of 'Ryūko' as 'Shiga Shabaku.'

65 'Enkei tokuhō' (Special report from Yangjing/Beijing), *Yorozu chōhō*, 14 June 1898, p. 1.

66 The quoted passage is taken from the reform edict of 11 June 1898; the second quote is from a different edict with a similar intent, but cannot yet be identified.

67 As the *Chūō shinbun* reports ('Shinkoku no genron jiyū,' 5 June 1898, p. 1), a public censor had memorialized to the throne to close down newspapers which openly criticized officials for their ineptitude and corruption; however, the emperor turned this down, declaring that he welcomed criticism and suggestion which contributed to the wellbeing of the state.

68 'Pekin tokuhō' (dated 16 June 1898), *Yorozu chōhō*, 3 July 1898.

69 'Kyōfū-ron,' *Yorozu chōhō*, 16–17 July 1898.
70 'Kaikaku wa eidan o yō su,' *Yorozu chōhō*, 10 July 1898, p. 1.
71 Shiga, 'Shina ikan,' 27 July 1898.
72 Shiga, 'Shina ikan,' 28 July 1898.
73 Shiga, 'Shina ikan,' 28 July 1898.
74 *Ibid.*
75 Shiga, 'Shina mondai,' September 1898.
76 Shiga, 'Shina ikan,' 28 July 1898.
77 Shiga, 'Shina mondai,' 23 September 1898.
78 Shiga, 'Shina mondai,' *Yorozu chōhō*, 23 September 1898.
79 The phrase *dai-yūi no shi* is, of course, a pun on Kang Youwei's name (in Japanese Kō Yūi).
80 Kang Youwei, in fact, was ordered to go to Shanghai and manage the publication of the *Shiwubao* as the 'official' reform organ.
81 Yang Shenxiu was one of the censors with whom Kang Youwei cooperated most closely in 1898, see Kwong, *Mosaic*, p. 158. Yang submitted some of Kang's memorials under his own name, as Kang had no privilege to submit memorials.
82 Shiga, 'Shina mondai,' *Yorozu chōhō*, 25 September 1898.
83 See Kwong, *Mosaic*, pp. 184–87. For Kang Youwei's reputation in the Shanghai press, with translations of *Shenbao* articles on Kang, see Andrea Janku, *Nur leere Reden: Politischer Diskurs und die Shanghaier Presse im China des späten 19. Jahrhunderts* (Just idle talk: political discourse and the Shanghai press in China in the late nineteenth century), Wiesbaden: Harrassowitz, 2003, pp. 268–303.
84 See Fogel, 'To Reform China,' pp. 373–76; Fogel, *Sinology and Politics*, pp. 85–91, 100.
85 See Shimura, 'Bojutsu henpō,' p. 274.
86 On the *Nippon-jin* articles in June and July 1898, see Zhai Xin, *Tōa dōbunkai to Chūgoku: kindai Nihon ni okeru taigai rinen to sono jissen* (The Tōa dōbun-kai and China: the ideology and practice of foreign relations in modern Japan), Tokyo: Keiō gijuku daigaku shuppan-kai, 2001, pp. 70–71; on the Tōa dōbun-kai's attitude toward Kang and Liang, *ibid.*, pp. 81–87; the Tōa-kai's members such as Kuga Katsunan or Inukai Tsuyoshi initially were much more idealistic and supportive about the Hundred Days (*ibid.*, pp. 68–72). However, they too eventually acquiesced in the *realpolitik* course of the new Tōa dōbun-kai and distanced themselves from Kang and Liang (on Kuga Katsunan's harsh critique of the reformers in the *Tōa jiron* of January 1899, for example (*ibid.*, p. 82).
87 'Shinkoku kaikaku-ha no senpō,' *Yorozu chōhō*, 25 September 1898, p. 1.
88 Kwong, *Mosaic*, pp. 5–10; see also Reynolds, *China*, p. 34.
89 Bays, 'Chang Chih-tung,' p. 319.
90 This *chengyu* is based on a story in the *Sanguozhi*. Lu Meng from Wu is the typical person who will not make progress, come what may; see Morohashi, *Dai-Kanwa jiten*, No. 3386: 145.
91 'Nani o motte Shinjin ni oshien ka' (How are we going to teach the Chinese?), *Nippon*, 1 September 1898, p. 1.
92 'The other side of the question,' *The North-China Herald*, 7 December 1894 (GSN 2:568).
93 See for example 'Kōshoku jinshu no bokkō' (The rise of the Yellow Race), *Kokumin shinbun*, 18 July 1895, ch. 2.
94 See for example the celebratory special issue of the *Taiyō* in April 1898 (Vol. 4, No. 9).
95 'Gendai Nihon no kaika' (The civilization of present-day Japan), speech delivered in August 1911 in Wakayama, in Natsume, *Sōseki bunmeiron-shū* (A reader of Natsume Sōseki's civilization critique), Miyoshi Yukio (ed.), Tokyo: Iwanami shoten, 1986, p. 38.

96 For a similar discussion of 'Chinese slowness' in Japan during the second Sino–Japanese War, see Ben-Ami Shillony, 'Friend or foe: the ambivalent images of the U.S. and China in wartime Japan,' in James W. White, Michio Umegaki and Thomas R. H. Havens (eds), *The Ambivalence of Nationalism: Modern Japan between East and West*, Lanham, MD: University Press of America, 1990, pp. 202–3.

97 The words *butabuta* and *okashina* are written with the characters 'pig' (*buta*) and China (*Shina*), respectively. 'Walking Match of Civilization,' *Marumaru chinbun*, 21 June 1879; see Obinata Sumio, 'Jiyūminken-ki no higashi-Ajia jōsei ninshiki: 'Marumaru chinbun' manga no sekai o yomu' (The perception of East Asian conditions during the Jiyū minken era: reading the world of *Marumaru chinbun*'s caricatures), *Bunka kokusai kenkyū*, Vol. 1 (February 1997), pp. 32, 34.

98 'Shinajin shitashimu beshi' (We must make friends with the Chinese), *Jiji shinpō*, 22 March 1898 (FYZ 16:286).

99 'Taishin-saku no yōdō' (The essential method of dealing with China), *Nippon*, 16 May 1898 (KKZ 6: 75–76).

100 Howard, 'Japan's Role,' p. 296; Peng Zezhou, 'Kō Yūi no henpō undō,' pp. 163–64; Paula Harrell, *Sowing the Seeds of Change: Chinese Students, Japanese Teachers, 1895–1905*, Stanford, CA: Stanford University Press, 1992, p. 27.

101 As Paula Harrell observes, the belief that China 'possessed of superior human and material resources, could surely outstrip this small island neighbor' was the presumption of most Chinese at the time, not only Kang Youwei, but also Chinese overseas students and officials visiting Japan (*Sowing the Seeds of Change*, pp. 58, 212).

102 Konoe Atsumaro, *Konoe Atsumaro nikki* (The diary of Konoe Atsumaro), Konoe Atsumaro nikki kankō-kai (ed.), Tokyo: Kajima kenkyūjo shuppan-kai, 1968–69, Vol. 2, pp. 195–96 (12 November 1898).

103 On Konoe's attitude toward the Hundred Days and the reformers, see Zhai Xin, *Tōa dōbun-kai to Chūgoku*, 76–81; Banno, *Meiji – shisō no jitsuzō* (Meiji – the true nature of thought), Tokyo: Sōbunsha, 1977, pp. 104–7.

104 Zhai Xin, *Tōa dōbun-kai to Chūgoku*, p. 74.

105 'Some Thoughts on the Situation,' *North-China Herald*, 24 October 1898, quoting the *Japan Mail*, 10 October 1898 ('Responsibility and Responsibility'), GSN 3:167; on the Shanghai-based *Shenbao*'s attacks on Kang, see Janku, *Nur leere Reden*, pp. 268–303.

106 See for example the *Frankfurter Zeitung*, 23 September 1898 (GSN 3:162–63): 'Nun hat der junge Mann [the emperor] seinen Fürwitz mit seinem Throne, wenn nicht gar mit seinem Leben bezahlen müssen' ('Now, the young man has had to pay for his brazenness by losing the throne, or maybe even his life'). *The Times*, 24 September 1898 (*ibid.*, pp. 163–64) was more sympathetic, but could not help quoting examples from Gibbon's *History of the Decline and Fall of the Roman Empire*.

107 David Duncan, *The Life and Letters of Herbert Spencer*, London: Methuen & Co., 1908, p. 319, letter dated 21 August 1892.

108 For fairness' sake, it should be mentioned that the London *Times* in January 1904 criticized Spencer's advice in another instance (on mixed residence in Japan) as being 'as narrow, as much imbued with antipathy to real progress, as ever came from a self-sufficient, short-sighted Mandarin, bred in contempt and hatred of barbarians' (*ibid.*, p. 323), but by 1904 the attitude towards Japan had already changed significantly.

109 The *Japan Weekly Mail* summarized the commentaries in the vernacular press as 'long arguments marshalled by our contemporaries for the purpose of proving that 'clan cabinets' are out of date, that the progress of the country must be interrupted unless the party system of government is introduced, and that the nation can no longer brook the fruitless friction now taking place between the

administration and the political associations' ('Spirit of the Vernacular Press,' *Japan Weekly Mail*, 2 July 1898, p. 2).

110 'Political Notes,' *Yorozu chōhō*, 25 June 1898, p. 2.

111 'Spirit of the Vernacular Press,' *Japanese Weekly Mail*, 16 July 1898, p. 50.

112 'Waga kuni no seitō no shōrai' (The future of the parties in our country), *Tokyo nichinichi shinbun*, 15 June 1898, p. 26 (the article appeared in the celebratory 8000th issue of the newspaper).

113 'Jasetsu o hai su' (In rejection of a dangerous opinion), *Tōkyō nichinichi shinbun*, 30 September 1898, p. 2; see also 'Ishin kōshin wa mu-seiji' (Restorations and reforms are non-partisan), *Chūō shinbun*, 17 July 1898, p. 1.

114 'Shin-naikaku wa mu-sekinin naikaku ka' (Is the new cabinet is an irresponsible cabinet?), *Chūō shinbun*, 29 June 1898, p. 1.

115 'Ryokan-roku' (The office-hunting chronicle), starting on 8 July 1898, p. 2; 'Shin naikaku wa tōbatsu naikaku nari' (The new cabinet is a party-clan cabinet), *Chūō shinbun*, 2 July 1898, p. 1.

116 'Seiken no iji wa seitō ni yoru no hoka nashi' (Maintaining political power is possible only through the means of parties), *Jiji shinpō*, 12 June 1898 (FYZ 16:380). Fukuzawa initially favored Itō's plans to rule through the means of a 'government party' (see FYZ 16:382). However, when these plans failed, Fukuzawa began to support the rule of popular parties (see FYZ 16:408).

117 'Jiji shinpō no jisatsu,' *Tōkyō nichinichi shinbun*, 16 October 1898, p. 4.

118 'Hi-hanbatsu renmei' (An anti-*hanbatsu* alliance'), *Nippon*, 19/20/22 June 1898 (KKZ 6: 82–86).

119 'Daiichi ishin ni kangamiyo' (Remember the first Restoration!), *Nippon*, 11 July 1898, p. 1.

120 'Political Notes,' *Yorozu chōhō*, 29 June 1898, p. 2.

121 'Kaikaku wa eidan o yō su' (Reforms need bold decision), *Yorozu chōhō*, 10 July 1898, p. 1.

122 Politically speaking, Takekoshi Yosaburō was a follower of Saionji Kinmochi (1849–1940). Saionji had been Minister of Education in Itō's cabinet from 12 January–30 April 1898, and Takekoshi had been his Vice Minister.

123 Takekoshi, 'Yorozu chōhō kisha sokka' (Letter to the editor), *Yorozu chōhō*, 13 July 1898, p. 1. The title of the article was translated into the Japanese as 'Supein no reiraku' (The ruin of Spain), the name of the author given as 'Jiron.' According to the *Tōkyō nichinichi shinbun*, 4 September 1898, p. 5, the article appeared in the June 1898 issue of *The Contemporary Review*.

124 'Supein naikaku no jishoku' (The resignation of the Spanish cabinet), *Yorozu chōhō*, 15 July 1898, p. 2.

125 'Dare ka waga kuni o Supein ni hi suru mono zo' (Absurd comparison between Japan and Spain), *Taiyō*, Vol. 4, No. 16, 20–25. Takayama observed that two or three magazines lately sported the following absurd theory: the Spanish were arrogant and vainglorious, they rejected people of a different religion or race. Towards other countries, they were not seeking harmony, but greatly hurt the feelings of the powers. In their country, they vainly propagated 'making the country rich and strengthening the army' (*fukoku kyōhei*) and knew nothing but 'loyalism and patriotism' (*chūkun aikoku*). This was exactly like Japan, and Spain is a memento for what may happen to Japan. Takayama, however, protested against this theory.

126 'Bōkoku no kizashi' (Symptoms of national decay), *Tōkyō nichinichi shinbun*, 4 September 1898, p. 5. The *Nichinichi* also discusses the theses of the *Contemporary Review* article.

127 'Lessons from Italy,' *Yorozu chōhō*, 10 August 1898, p. 2.

128 'Yamagata naikaku o kangei su' (We welcome the Yamagata Cabinet), *Yorozu chōhō*, 8 November 1898, in *Kōtoku Shūsui zenshū* (The collected works of

Kōtoku Shūsui), Kōtoku Shūsui zenshū henshū iinkai (ed.), Tokyo: Meiji bunken, 1968–73, Vol. 2, p. 147.

129 'A Record,' *Japan Weekly Mail*, 14 January 1898, p. 31.

130 See for example Jansen, *Japan and China*, p. 136; Marius B. Jansen, *The Japanese and Sun Yat-Sen*, Cambridge, MA: Harvard University Press, 1967, p. 53.

131 See Liao Longgan, 'Bojutsu henpō-ki ni okeru Nihon no taishin gaikō' (Japan's China policy during the Hundred Days Reform), *Nihon rekishi*, No. 471 (August 1987), pp. 74–76; Shimura, 'Bojutsu henpō,' pp. 285–89.

132 Yamaguchi Kazuyuki, 'Kenseitō naikaku no seiritsu to kyokutō jōsei (The emergence of the Kensei-tō cabinet and the political situation in the Far East), Nihon kokusai seiji gakkai (ed.), *Nihon gaikō-shi kenkyū (Nisshin/Nichiro sensō)* (Studies on the diplomatic history of Japan: the Sino–Japanese and the Russo–Japanese War), Tokyo: Yūhikaku, 1962, pp. 95–99.

133 Yamaguchi, 'Kenseitō naikaku,' p. 97; Ian Nish, *The Anglo–Japanese Alliance: The Diplomacy of Two Island Empires, 1894–1907*, 2nd edn, London: Athlone Press, 1985, pp. 67–69.

134 For a discussion of Itō's journey, see Peng Zezhou, 'Itō Hirobumi to Bojutsu henpō' (Itō Hirobumi and the Hundred Days Reform), *Rekishi-gaku kenkyū*, No. 406 (March 1974), pp. 17–29; Liao, 'Bojutsu henpō-ki,' pp. 68–72. However, both studies overlook Ōoka Ikuzō's reports of his journey with Itō and thus miss an important source.

135 See the announcements of Itō's tour: 'Marquis Ito to visit China,' *New York Times*, 15 July 1898, p. 4; 'Itō kō toshin no junbi' (Marquis Itō's preparations for traveling to China), *Nippon*, 16 July 1898, p. 2; 'Itō kō no Shinkoku-yuki' (Marquis Itō's journey to China'), *Chūō shinbun*, 18 July 1898, p. 2.

136 In Shanghai, Itō briefly met the British Rear Admiral Charles Beresford (1846–1919) who, after having returned from China, published *The Break-Up of China with an Account of Its Present Commerce, Currency, Waterways, Armies, Railways, Politics and Future Prospects* (London, New York: Harper & Brothers, 1899). On the meeting, see 'China's Commercial Policy,' *New York Times*, 10 October 1898, p. 7. For a record of the speeches, see Itō Hirobumi, *Itō kō zenshū* (Collected works of Itō Hirobumi), Komatsu Midori (ed.), Tokyo: Shōwa shuppansha, 1928, Vol. 2, section 'Scholarly speeches,' pp. 1–20, and *Itō kō enzetsu-shū* (A collection of Marquis Itō's speeches), Tokyo: Nippō-sha, 1899, Vol. 1, pp. 1–48; the *Zhixinbao* gave a summary of a *Nippon* article on Itōs speech in 'Yiteng lun Zhongguo caizheng' (Itō discusses Chinese finances), *Zhixinbao* 78 (Guangxu 24/12/11), pp. 10–12.

137 See the identical news in 'Itō kō toshin no shin'i' (The real reason of Marquis Itō's journey to China), *Yorozu chōhō*, 17 July 1899, p. 2 and in 'Yiteng laihua mingyi' (The purpose of Itō's visit to China), *Guowenbao*, 31 August 1898 (Guangxu 24/7/14), in Zhongguo shixue-hui (ed.), *Wuxu bianfa* (The Hundred Days Reform), four vols, Shanghai: Shenzhouguo guangshe, 1953, Vol. 3, p. 397. The *Guowenbao* explicitly cites a Western newspaper as the source of this news.

138 Ōoka Ikuzō, 'Itō kō nyūshin no kōkei' (The spectacle of Itō's arrival in China), *Chūō shinbun*, 24 September 1898, p. 2; see also *Guowenbao* 12–14 September 1898 (Guangxu 24/7/27–29), in Zhongguo shixue-hui, *Wuxu bianfa*, Vol. 3, pp. 400–405. On the public reaction in China to Itō's visit in general, see Kwong, *A Mosaic*, pp. 203–10; Howard, 'Japan's Role,' pp. 301–02.

139 For some of these memorials, see Kwong, *A Mosaic*, p. 209; Howard, 'Japan's Role', p. 301.

140 Ōoka, 'Tenshin ni okeru Itō kō' (Marquis Itō in Tianjin), *Chūō shinbun*, 29 September 1898, p. 2.

141 See the quotations above, and also 'Pekin ni okeru Itō kō' ('Marquis Itō in Beijing'), *Chūō shinbun*, 29 September 1898, p. 2.

142 The three other ministers were: Liao Shouheng (1839–1903), President of the Board of Punishment in 1898; Chongli (d. 1907), General Commandant of the Gendarmerie and President of the Board of Punishment; Zhang Yinhuan (1837–1900), Vice-President of the Board of Revenues and Zongli yamen Minister.

143 Ōoka, 'Pekin ni okeru Itō kō,' *Chūō shinbun*, 29 September 1898.

144 For Ōoka's report, see 'Itō kō ikkō ekken' (The audience of Marquis Itō's group with the emperor), *Chūō shinbun*, 9 October 1898; a translation of Ōoka's record was printed by the *North-China Herald*, 24 October 1898 ('Marquis Itō and the Emperor of China,' in GSN 3:168–69). The *New York Times*, in turn, reprinted the translation of the *North-China Herald* in its own columns on 18 December 1898 (p. 8) under the quaint title: 'A Tripartite Interview: Three Famous Men Talk Together the Day Before One of Them Loses the Throne.' The translation in Teng and Fairbank, *China's Response*, pp. 179–80, is indirectly (via the *Zoku Itō Hirobumi hiroku*) based on Ōoka's report.

145 'Itō kō Shintei ni essu' (Marquis Itō is received by the Chinese emperor), *Chūō shinbun*, 27 September 1898, p. 2.

146 Kong Xiangji and Murata Yūjirō, *Han wei ren zhi de Zhong-Ri jiemeng ji qita: Wan-Qing Zhong-Ri guanxi-shi xintan* (A little-known Sino–Japanese alliance and other matters: new studies on the history of Late Qing Sino–Japanese relations), Chengdu: Boshu shushe, 2004, pp. 69–71.

147 Kwong, *Mosaic*, p. 211; Kwong claims that the action had been prompted by Cixi's perusal of the Zongli yamen's record of the interview with Itō. Given Itō's reticence, this is rather unlikely.

148 'Itō kō Shintei ni essu,' *Chūō shinbun*, 27 September 1898, p. 2; for a discussion of this incident, see also the chapter 'Itō Hirobumi to Chūgoku' (Itō Hirobumi and China) in Hashikawa Bunzō, *Jungyaku no shisō: Datsua ron igo*. Tokyo: Keisō shobō, 1973, pp. 78–153, p. 147.

149 Kwong, *Mosaic*, p. 211.

150 The *Nippon* published a record of the interview of dubious authenticity, see 'Itō Hirobumi Kō Yūi no kaiken' (The interview between Itō Hirobumi and Kang Youwei), *Nippon*, 1–2 November 1898, p. 2; the meeting must have been much shorter as recorded.

151 Kang, 'Autobiography,' p. 127.

152 Liao, 'Bojutsu henpō-ki,' p. 69.

153 Itō, *Itō-kō zenshū*, Vol. 1, letters, p. 179; Shunpo-kō tsuishō-kai, *Itō Hirobumi den* (The life of Itō Hirobumi), Tokyo, Hara shobō, 1970, Vol. 3, p. 399.

154 Ōoka, 'Shinkoku seihen no gen'in' (The causes of the political change in China), *Chūō shinbun*, 9 October 1898.

155 Two others were Kang Guangren (1867–98), Kang Youwei's younger brother, and the censor Yang Shenxiu (1849–98), a close associate of Kang.

156 On the rescue of Kang and Liang by Britain and Japan, respectively, see Wang Shuhuai, *Wairen yu wuxu bianfa* (Foreigners and the Hundred Days Reform), Taibei: Jinghua yinshuguan, 1965, pp. 188–91.

157 Gaimushō (ed.), *Nihon gaikō monjo* (Japanese documents on foreign affairs), Tokyo: Nihon kokusai rengō kyōkai, 1949-, Vol. 31, book 1, No. 555.

158 *Ibid.*, Vol. 31, book. 1, No. 560, Hayashi to Ōkuma, 22 September 1898; No. 565 Tei to Hatoyama, 30 September 1898; Kang, 'Chronological Autobiography', pp. 133–34.

159 Gaimushō, *Nihon gaikō monjō*, Vol. 31, book. 1, No. 561, dated 28 September 1898.

160 These were Wen Tingshi and Zhang Binglin, see Liao, 'Bojutsu henpō-ki,' pp. 77–78.

161 Kwong, *A Mosaic*, pp. 220–21, 225; Liao, 'Bojutsu henpō-ki,' p. 77.

162 *Ibid.*, p. 78. The Tōa-kai did present Ōkuma Shigenobu with a petition to support the reforms and rescue the reformers, see Zhai Xin, *Tōa dōbun-kai to Chūgoku*, p. 70. The Dōbun-kai, for the reasons mentioned above, certainly did not.

163 Liao, 'Bojutsu henpō-ki,' p. 79.

164 The political change that ended the Hundred Days took place without any public commotion; foreigners were attacked in Beijing on 30 September 1898 (see below). But already on 28 September 1898, Ōkuma had ordered Hayashi to advise the Chinese government to refrain from extreme measures.

165 According to Ōoka, one more guest appeared, Sun Jianai (1827–1909), head of the new Imperial College and an opponent of Kang Youwei. The way Ōoka phrases this seems to indicate that society shunned Li Hongzhang at the time, and only Sun had answered the invitation. See Ōoka, 'Ri Kōshō to no taiwa' (A conversation with Li Hongzhang), *Chūō shinbun*, 11 October 1898.

166 'A Triparite Interview: Three Famous Men Talk Together the Day Before One of Them Loses His Throne,' *New York Times*, 12 December 1898, p. 8.

167 Ōoka, 'Ri Kōshō to no taiwa,' *Chūō shinbun*, 11 October 1898.

168 A. von Bulmerincq, *Das Völkerrecht oder das internationale Recht* (International law). Freiburg i. B.: J. C. B. Mohr, 1889, pp. 243, 246; it seems that this in principle even pertained to such 'offences' as *meurtre, assassinat* or *empoisonnement* of political figures.

169 For a discussion of Kang's case with reference to Sun Yat-sen and precedence in international law, see 'Lun Kang Youwei dani budao shi' ('On Kang Youwei's high treason'), *Shenbao*, 24 October 1898 as translated in Janku, *Nur leere Reden*, pp. 269–76; the author points out that, although 'political criminals' may enjoy the protection of international law in general, China's treaties with the European powers and Japan required the treaty powers to hand over Chinese criminals to the Chinese authorities, making no explicit exception for political criminals (*ibid.*, p. 275).

170 See Bays, 'Chang Chih-tung,' pp. 320–21, 324; Liao, 'Bojutsu henpō-ki,' pp. 80–82; Zhai, *Tōa dōbun-kai*, pp. 80–86.

171 Konoe, *Konoe Atsumaro nikki*, Vol. 2, p. 238; Zhai, *Tōa dōbun-kai*, p. 83.

172 See 'Pekin no funjō to rekkoku no undō' (The unrest in Beijing and the movements of the powers), *Chūō shinbun*, 7 October 1898, p. 2; 'Pekin no keisei' (The situation in Beijing), *Tōkyō nichinichi shinbun*, 13 October 1898 (p. 3), 15 October 1898 (p. 2).

173 'Itō-kō o okuru' (Sending off Marquis Itō), *Tōkyō nichinichi shinbun*, 27 July 1898, p. 2.

174 'Shinkoku no seihen,' *Tōkyō nichinichi shinbun*, 25 September 1898.

175 'Shinkoku oyobi sono yūbō' (China and its friends), *Tōkyō nichinichi shinbun*, 16 October 1898.

176 'Shinkoku no seihen,' *Tōkyō nichinichi shinbun*, 25 September 1898.

177 *Ibid.*

178 'Shinkoku oyobi sono yūbō,' *Tōkyō nichinichi shinbun*, 16 October 1898.

179 See Zhai, *Tōa dōbun-kai*, p. 75, quoting *Tōa jiron*-articles from November 1898.

180 Fogel, *Politics and Sinology,* p. 88; Fogel, 'To Reform China,' p. 375. For Konoe, see above.

181 Reynolds, *China*, pp. 1, 34–38.

182 'Shinkoku oyobi sono yūbō,' *Tōkyō nichinichi shinbun*, 16 October 1898.

183 'Shinkoku no henran ni tai suru junbi' (Preparations against further disturbances in China), *Tōkyō nichinichi shinbun*, 8 October 1898, p. 2.

184 'Shinkoku no bunkatsu' (The partition of China), *Tōkyō nichinichi shinbun*, 25 October 1898, p. 2.

185 'Shinkoku no bunkatsu,' *Tōkyō nichinichi shinbun*, 25 October 1898.

186 See Jürgen Osterhammel, *China und die Weltgesellschaft: vom 18. Jahrhundert bis in unsere Zeit* (China and the international society: from the eighteenth century to the present), Munich: C. H. Beck, 1989, p. 211.

187 'Shinkoku no shōrai' (The future of China), part 2, *Tōkyō nichinichi shinbun*, 18 September 1898, p. 1.

188 *The Times*, 23 April 1895 (GSN 2:621–22).
189 In fact, the 'Republican Speech Affair' – *Kyōwa enzetsu jiken* – starting in August 1898, which involved the minister Ozaki Yukio and led to the final downfall of the Cabinet, was largely due to the misrepresentation of Ozaki's speech in the *Tōkyō nichinichi* and the following witch-hunt; see Satō Yoshimaru, 'Ozaki Yukio bunshō no 'Kyōwa enzetsu jiken' no nazo' (The mystery of the 'Republican Speech Affair' involving Education Minister Ozaki Yukio), *Nihon rekishi*, no, 682 (March 2005), p. 37.
190 See 'Gen-naikaku no injun kosoku' (The indecision and vacillation of the present cabinet), *Tōkyō nichinichi shinbun*, 5 October 1898, p. 2.
191 See 'Ōkuma haku no enzetsu' (Count Ōkuma's speech), 22 October 1898, p. 2.
192 For a short description of the Asianist society Tōhō kyōkai, see Harrell, *Sowing the Seeds of Change*, p. 21. Ōkuma was a member of the society. Other prominent members were, for example, Konoe Atsumaro, Kuga Katsunan and Komura Jutarō.
193 Ōkuma himself published a revised version of the speech in 1907 under the heading 1907, see *Ōkuma-haku enzetsu-shū* (A collection of Count Ōkuma's speeches), Waseda daigaku henshū-bu (ed.). Tokyo: Waseda daigaku, 1907, pp. 20–38.
194 Marius B. Jansen, 'Japan and the Revolution of 1911,' in John K. Fairbank and Kwang-Ching Liu (eds), *The Cambridge History of China, Vol. 2: Late Ch'ing, 1800–1911, Part 2*, Cambridge: Cambridge University Press, 1980, p. 346; see also Jansen, *The Japanese and Sun Yat-Sen*, p. 53; Jansen, *Japan and China*, p. 136.
195 Jansen cites for this 'Doctrine' Watanabe Ikujirō's work of 1938 on modern Japanese diplomacy (*Kinsei Nihon gaikō-shi*), see *The Japanese and Sun Yat-Sen*, p. 53.
196 Ōkuma, *Ōkuma enzetsu-shū*, p. 20.
197 See Ōkuma, *Ōkuma enzetsu-shū*, pp. 20–29 for the historical part; pp. 29–34 on China's present relations; pp. 34–38 on the Russian proposal of disarmament.
198 See 'Tōhō kyōkai ni okeru Ōkuma gaimu daijin no enzetsu' (The speech of Foreign Minister Ōkuma at the Tōhō kyōkai), *Nippon*, 21 October 1898, p. 1.
199 *Ibid.*
200 Yamaguchi, 'Kenseitō,' p. 97, referring to No. A 894 of the Ōkuma papers. Yamaguchi attributes the draft to an intended speech on foreign policy in the next Diet.
201 'Ōkuma-haku no enzetsu' (The speech of Count Ōkuma), *Tōkyō nichinichi shinbun*, 22 October 1898, p. 2; 'Ōkuma-haku no mujun' (Count Ōkuma's contradictions), *Tōkyō nichinichi shinbun*, 23 October 1898, p. 2.
202 Uno Shun'ichi, 'Itō Hirobumi to Ōkuma Shigenobu' (Itō Hirobumi and Ōkuma Shigenobu), in Takeuchi Yoshimi and Hashikawa Bunzō (eds), *Kindai Nihon to Chūgoku* (Modern Japan and China), Tokyo: Asahi shinbunsha, 1974, Vol. 1, p. 48; Yamaguchi, 'Kenseitō naikaku,' p. 97, both referring to No. A 894 of the Ōkuma papers but attributing the draft to different purposes.
203 The interjection is not recorded in the *Ōkuma enzetsu-shū*, p. 34, but in 'Ōkuma haku no enzetsu,' *Tōkyō nichinichi shinbun*, 23 October 1898.
204 'Ōkuma haku no enzetsu,' *Tōkyō nichinichi shinbun*, 23 October 1898.
205 Yamaguchi, 'Kenseitō naikaku,' p. 97, quoting No. A 894 of the Ōkuma papers.
206 See Zhai, *Tōa dōbunkai to Chūgoku*; Reynolds, 'Training Young China Hands'; Sakeda, *Kindai Nihon ni okeru taigai-kō undō*, pp. 109–31.
207 Tōa dōbun-kai, 'Tōa dōbunkai shuisho' (Foundation Manifesto of the Tōa dōbunkai), *Tōa jiron* 1 (December 1898), p. 1.
208 Miyake Setsurei, 'Shina n chikara o sosoge,' *Nippon*, 10 October 1898, p. 1.
209 Konoe, 'Teikoku no ichi to gendai no seiji-ka,' *Tōa jiron*, No. 1 (10 December 1898), pp. 5–7.
210 *Ibid*, p. 6. – The term *seigi* (Chinese *qingyi*) is difficult to translate in this context; for the Chinese reform context see Schrecker, 'The Reform Movement of 1898 and the Meiji Restoration as Ch'ing-I Movement' (1980).
211 Zhai, *Tōa dōbun-kai*, pp. 82, 85; Reynolds, 'Training China Hands,' pp. 225–26.

5 The Boxer Incident and beyond

1 On the various stages of the 'Boxer myth' see Paul A. Cohen, 'The Contested Past: The Boxers as History and Myth,' *Journal of Asian Studies*, Vol. 51, No. 1 (February 1992), pp. 82–113 and *History in Three Keys: The Boxers as Event, Experience, and Myth*, New York: Columbia University Press, 1997. pp. 211–88.

2 The origins of the Boxer Uprising are discussed in detail by Joseph W. Esherick, *The Origins of the Boxer Uprising*, Berkeley, CA: University of California Press, 1987; see also Kobayashi Kazumi, *Giwadan sensō to Meiji kokka* (*The Boxer War and the Meiji State*), Tokyo: Kyūko shoin, 1986, pp. 2–61; however, it should be noted that Kobayashi's simple equation of the Boxer movement as anti-imperialist is problematic. For a historical overview of the Boxer Uprising in its successive stages, see Cohen, *History in Three Keys*, pp. 14–56.

3 After the war, the German government insisted that a monument (the Ketteler monument) was erected on the spot where the diplomat had been killed; the monument was demolished in the fall of 1918 amidst a jeering crowd celebrating Germany's defeat in the war (see Cohen, 'Contested Past,' p. 85 for some less enthusiastic reactions to the 'vandalism').

4 Esherick, *Origins*, p. 303; the edict was issued on 20 June 1900. It was reprinted in Japanese translation in the *Jiji shinpō*, 2 July 1900, in Nakayama Yasumasa *et al.* (eds), *Shinbun shūsei Meiji hennen-shi* (A Meiji chronicle through newspaper sources), Tokyo: Zaisei keizai gakkai, 1934–36, Vol. 11, p. 91; *Kokumin shinbun*, 2 July 1900, p. 1 ('Haigai no jōyu' – A xenophobic edict); and probably *Tōkyō nichinichi shinbun*, 11 July 1900, p. 2 ('Shinkoku seifu no ketsui' – The Decision of the Chinese government).

5 Cited by Sugano Tadashi, *Shinmatsu Nitchū kankei-shi no kenkyū* (Studies on Late Qing Sino–Japanese relations), Tokyo: Kyūko shoin, 2002, p. 342; for an earlier publication of Sugano's study see 'Giwadan jihen to Nihon no yoron' (The Boxer Incident and Japanese public opinion), *Hisutoria* No. 44/45 (June 1966), pp. 26–50.

6 For the Boxer Uprising in the international context, see William L. Langer, *The Diplomacy of Imperialism*, 2nd edn, New York: Alfred A. Knopf, 1965, pp. 677–710; for China's position, see Immanuel C. Y. Hsu [Hsü], 'Late Ch'ing foreign relations, 1866–1905,' in John K. Fairbank and Kwang-Ching Liu (eds), *The Cambridge History of China, Vol. 2: Late Ch'ing, 1800–1911, Part 2*, Cambridge: Cambridge University Press, 1978, pp. 115–30; for Britain and Japan, see Ian Nish, *The Anglo–Japanese Alliance: The Diplomacy of Two Island Empires, 1894–1907*, 2nd edn, London: Athlone Press, 1985, pp. 80–95, Nish, 'Japan's Indecision During the Boxer Disturbances,' *Journal of Japanese Studies* Vol. 20, No. 4 (1961), pp. 449–61; Paul A. Varg, 'The Foreign Policy of Japan and the Boxer Revolt,' *Pacific Historical Review*, Vol. 15, No. 3 (1946), pp. 279–85.

7 For example see 'A Good Example,' *The New York Times*, 8 July 1900 (GSN 3:235); 'The Powers and Japan,' *The New York Times*, 8 July 1900 (GSN 3:235).

8 'Japan and the Crisis: to the Editor of The Times,' *The Times*, 12 July 1900 (GSN 3:239); the letter was signed 'A. B. Freeman Mitford, Travellers' Club' and, for example, reprinted in excerpts by the *London & China Express* on 13 July 1900 ('Mr. Freeman Mitford's Views'), see Itō Hirobumi kankei monjo kenkyū-kai (ed.), *Itō Hirobumi kankei monjo* (Documents relating to Itō Hirobumi), Tokyo: Hanawa shobō, 1973–80, Vol. 4, p. 378.

9 Itō Hirobumi kankei monjo kenkyūkai, *Itō Hirobumi*, Vol. 4, p. 375–79; the letter is dated 17 July 1900. Later Kurino also telegraphed to Foreign Minister Aoki Shūzō to the same effect, see Robert B. Valliant, 'The Selling of Japan: Japanese Manipulation of Western Opinion, 1900–905,' *Monumenta Nipponica*, Vol. 29, No. 4 (1974), pp. 416–17. It is telling that Kurino would inform Itō on

the subject earlier than his superior Aoki; both Kurino and Itō had a rather strained relationship with Aoki.

10 For the Boxer Incident, cf. Valliant, 'The Selling of Japan,' pp. 416–21.

11 A Japanese translation of the Chinese telegram as well as of the Japanese response is printed in *Kokumin shinbun*, 21 July 1900, p. 1 ('Shinkoku jihen to Nisshin ryōkoku kōtei no go-shinden', The Chinese incident and the imperial telegrams of the Chinese and the Japanese emperors). For the background of the telegrams, see Gaimushō gaikō shiryō-kan Nihon gaikō-shi jiten hensan iinkai, *Nihon gaikō-shi jiten* (A Lexicon of Japanese Diplomatic History), Tokyo: Yamakawa shuppansha, 1992, pp. 240–41.

12 'Shinkoku jihen to Nisshin ryōkoku kōtei no go-shinden,' *Kokumin shinbun*, 21 July 1900.

13 *Ibid.*

14 Gaimushō gaikō shiryō-kan, *Nihon gaikōshi jiten*, p. 241.

15 On the Battle of Tianjin, see Cohen, *History in Three Keys*, pp. 53–54. See also below.

16 For Japan, see Sophia Lee, 'The Foreign Ministry's Cultural Agenda for China: the Boxer Indemnity,' in Peter Duus *et al.* (eds), *The Japanese Informal Empire in China*, Princeton, NJ: Princeton University Press, 1989, pp. 272–306. Incidentally, the Boxer indemnity, together with other funds, secured the financial basis of the Tōa dōbun-kai since 1923, see Douglas R. Reynolds, 'Training Young China Hands: Tōa Dōbun shoin and its Precursors, 1886–1945,' in Peter Duus, Ramon H. Myers and Mark R. Peattie (eds), *The Japanese Informal Empire in China, 1895–1937* Princeton, NJ: Princeton University Press, 1989, pp. 255–56.

17 Kobayashi, *Giwadan sensō to Meiji kokka*.

18 Esherick, *Origins*, p. 303.

19 See 'Shintei chokuyu no mujun' (The inconsisteny of the edicts of the Chinese emperor), *Tōkyō nichinichi shinbun*, 12 July 1900, p. 2; 'Shōchoku mata chikara nashi' (The edicts are void), *Kokumin shinbun*, 2 July 1900, p. 1; 'Ayashiki jōyu' (A dubious edict), *Kokumin shinbun*, 11 July 1900, p. 2. – See also Hsu, 'Late Ch'ing foreign relations,' p. 123.

20 Langer, *Diplomacy of Imperialism*, p. 691.

21 *Ibid.*, p. 694.

22 See 'Shōjutsu' (A reward), *Tōkyō nichinichi shinbun*, 8 July 1900.

23 For a long description of the Boer War, see 'Nanfutsu sensō' (The South African war), *Tōkyō nichinichi shinbun*, 1/7 January 1900, which contains 'the discourse of a [Japanese] officer of the army.' For more information on Japanese reactions to the Boer War, see Hiratsuka Kentarō, 'Kuga Katsunan to Minami-Afurika sensō' (Kuga Katsunan and the South African war), *Gendai-shi kenkyū*, No. 48, (February 2002), pp. 1–19.

24 'Sentan tsui ni hiraku' (War hostilities have finally begun), *Tōkyō nichinichi shinbun*, June 19, 1900, p. 2.

25 Taoka Reiun, *Sakkiden* (A checkered life), in *Taoka Reiun zenshū* (Collected Works of Taoka Reiun), Nishida Masaru (ed.), Tokyo: Hōsei daigaku shuppan-kyoku, 1969–87, Vol. 5, p. 611.

26 'Shinkoku jiken to kokusai kōhō' (The China incident and international public law), *Tōkyō nichinichi shinbun*, 25 July 1900, p. 2.

27 Ariga Nagao, 'Shinkoku jiken to kokusai-hō' (The China incident and international law), *Gaikō jihō*, Vol. 3, No. 32 (1900), p. 73.

28 Ariga Nagao, 'Kokusai-hō gakkai to Shinkoku jiken' (The Japanese Society of International Law and the China Incident), *Gaikō jihō*, Vol. 3, No. 33 (1900), p. 87; Ariga's colleague Terao Tōru (1858–1925), too, in the issue of 1 August 1900 of the *Hōgakkai zasshi*, argued that the Incident was a war.

29 'Ōkuma-haku no enzetsu' (Count Ōkuma's speech), *Tōkyō nichinichi shinbun*, 23 October 1898.

30 'Nippon kurabu no bansan-kai' (The dinner banquet of the Japan Club), *Tōkyō nichinichi shinbun*, 19 January 1900. The Japan Club was a network founded in 1897 by influential members of the Japanese society such as Konoe Atsumaro and Komura Jutarō; see, for example, Konoe's diary, *Konoe Atsumaro nikki*, Konoe Atsumaro nikki kankō-kai (ed.), Tokyo: Kajima kenkyūjo shuppan-kai, 1968–69, Vol. 1, pp. 323, 330.

31 Sugano, *Shinmatsu Nitchū kankei-shi*, pp. 338–41.

32 'Japan (From our own correspondent),' *The North-China Herald*, 22 August 1900 (GSN 3:255).

33 A leading German authority on international law at the time observed on the legitimacy of interventions: 'No sovereign, self-governing state needs to suffer any interference in its domestic affairs, if it has not suggested an intervention by itself or is obliged to suffer it on the basis of a treaty. Nonetheless, there have often occurred interventions in the past, even forcible ones, and also upon the decision of several states on conferences [...]. A state has the right to conduct a forcible intervention against another state only, if it is granted by the latter the right to do so, or if it is authorized by treaty as a guaranteeing alliance – or protective power'; A. von Bulmerincq, *Das Völkerrecht oder das internationale Recht* (International law), Freiburg i.B.: J. C. B. Mohr, 1889, p. 379.

34 See for example Kobayashi, *Giwadan sensō*, pp. 371–509, devoting the whole section on *genron-jin* exclusively to *Yorozu chōhō* contributors.

35 For example, 'Hisen-ron' (Against war), *Yorozu chōhō*, 23/24 December 1898.

36 See especially 'Taishin undō,' *Yorozu chōhō*, 22 June 1900, in *Kōtoku Shūsui zenshū* (The collected works of Kōtoku Shūsui), Kōtoku Shūsui zenshū henshū iinkai (ed.), Tokyo: Meiji bunken, 1968–73, Vol. 2, pp. 353–55. Kobayashi tries to adduce Kōtoku's more general critique of the Japanese government, military expansion, Western imperialism, etc. as a 'proof' that Kōtoku (should have) opposed the Boxer expedition as well (*Giwadan sensō*, pp. 463–74).

37 See Kobayashi, *Giwadan sensō*, pp. 372–428.

38 Kobayashi, *Giwadan sensō*, p. 210.

39 *Ibid.*, p. 219; Douglas R. Reynolds, *China, 1898–1912: The Xinzheng Revolution and Japan*, Cambridge, MA: Harvard University Press, 1993, p. 26.

40 'Japan: From our own correspondent,' *The North-China Herald*, 25 July 1900 (GSN 3:243).

41 *Katsura Tarō jiden* (The Autobiography of Katsura Tarō), cited by Kobayashi, *Giwadan sensō*, p. 220.

42 The port of Ujina, south of Hiroshima, was the shipping base for the army since the Sino–Japanese War.

43 *Fūzoku gahō*, suppl. no. 215 (5 Sept. 1900), pp. 4–5; also cited by Kobayashi, *Giwadan sensō*, pp. 221–23.

44 See the reports of Hamada in the *Kokumin shinbun*: 'Tenshin rōjō' (The Siege of Tianjin), *Kokumin shinbun*, 14 July (p. 2), 15 July (p. 2), 20 July (p. 2) 1900; 'Tenshin no sakkon' (Tianjin these days), *Kokumin shinbun*, 22 July 1900, pp. 1–2; 'Tenshin-jō no kanraku' (The surrender of Tianjin), *Kokumin shinbun*, 24 July 1900, p. 2.

45 This passage has been censored in the original.

46 Baba Teijirō, 'Baba tokuhain senpō dai-kyū' (War report of special correspondent Baba, No. 9), *Tōkyō nichinichi shinbun*, 5 July 1900 (passages in italics indicate triple size-characters in the original); the incident was also brought to foreign attention, see for example *The North-China Herald*, 25 July 1900 ('Japan'): 'Lieutenant Shiraishi's bravery in entering the fort first,' says Captain Nagamine, 'is said to have attracted the special notice of the allied forces, many of whom afterwards asked his name' (GSN 3:234).

47 'Japan,' *The North-China Herald*, 4 July 1900, in GSN 3:231.
48 'Nihon-hei no yūkan' (The bravery of Japanese soldiers), *Tōkyō nichinichi shinbun*, 12 July 1900, p. 2.
49 'Japan,' *The North-China Herald*, 15 August 1900, in GSN 3:253–54.
50 On the occupation of Yangcun, see *Kokumin shinbun*, 14 August 1900, p. 1 ('Yōson no senryō'); the place was occupied on 6 August 1900, which means that it took considerable time to subdue the 'few Chinese soldiers' there.
51 'Tenshin no kanraku-go' (Tianjin after the surrender), *Kokumin shinbun*, 23 July 1900, p. 1.
52 'Kanraku-go no Tenshin to waga gunki no gensei' (Tianjin after the surrender and the strictness of our military discipline), *Kokumin shinbun*, 28 July 1900, p. 1; Hamada, 'Tenshin jōnai no sakkon' (The situation in Tianjin these days), *Kokumin shinbun*, 29 July 1900, p. 1. The *Anhui suhuabao* in 1905 published so-called 'National Humiliation Pictures,' one of which shows a 'shameless' Chinese waving a *shunmin/junmin*-flag (for a reprint see Cohen, *History in Three Keys*, p. 242).
53 Cohen, *History in Three Keys*, p. 53.
54 *Nippon*, 27 August 1900, in Nakayama, *Shinbun shūsei Meiji hennen-shi*, vol 11, p. 114.
55 'Japan,' *The North-China Herald*, 1 August 1900 (GSN 3:248).
56 For the Japanese coverage of the massacre, see Kobayashi, *Giwadan*, pp. 226–27; for a discussion of the Amur River massacres in Chinese historiography see Cohen, *History in three Keys*, pp. 277–80; see also Gotelind Müller, 'Chinesische Perspektiven auf den Russisch-japanischen Krieg' ('Chinese perspectives of the Russo–Japanese War'), in Maik Hendrik Sprotte *et al.* (eds), *Der Russisch-Japanische Krieg 1904/5: Anbruch einer neuen Zeit?* (*The Russo–Japanese War 1904/5: The Dawn of a New Era?*), Wiesbaden: Harrassowitz, 2007, p. 207, with further references.
57 Taoka, *Sakkiden*, in *Taoka Reiun zenshū*, Vol. 5, pp. 617–20.
58 Ōoka Ikuzō, 'Kōhaku no gunjin' (Yellow and white military men), *Taiyō*, Vol. 6, No. 14 (November 1900), p. 14.
59 *Ibid.*, p. 17.
60 'Japan: from our correspondent,' *North-China Herald*, 26 July 1900 (GSN 3:255).
61 Taoka, *Sakkiden*, in *Taoka Reiun zenshū*, Vol. 5, p. 620.
62 'Japan (From our Correspondent),' *The North-China Herald*, 25 July 1900 (GSN 3:243).
63 *Ibid.*
64 See Taoka, *Sakkiden*, in *Taoka Reiun zenshū*, Vol. 5, pp. 614–18.
65 'Japan (From our Correspondent),' *The North-China Herald*, 25 July 1900 (GSN 3:243).
66 'Shinkoku jihen to Nichiei' (The China Incident and Anglo–Japanese relations), *Kokumin shinbun*, 3 August 1900, p. 2.
67 *Frankfurter Zeitung*, 6 August 1900 (GSN 3:249), translated from the German.
68 'Japan: from our own correspondent,' *North-China Herald*, 22 August 1900 (GSN 3:256).
69 For a general discussion of Katsunan's position, see Yamaguchi Kazuyuki, 'Kuga Katsunan no gaiseiron: Giwadan jihen to zengosaku' (Kuga Katsunan's views on foreign policy: the China Incident and its settlement), *Komazawa shigaku*, No. 35 (May 1986), pp. 3–50.
70 'Ōshū-gun no kiritsu oyobi yūki' (The discipline and courage of the Western forces), *Nippon*, 15 August 1900 (KKZ 6:543).
71 'Shintei no kō-jihei' (A good excuse for the Chinese government), *Nippon*, 11 August 1900 (KKZ 6:539–40); 'Kyōhi mondai to Shina' (The Christian rogues problem and China), *Nippon*, 13 August 1900 (KKZ 6:541–42).

72 See for example Hsu, 'Late Ch'ing foreign relations,' p. 129; Jeffrey N. Wasserstrom (ed.), *Twentieth Century China: New Approaches*, London: Routledge, 2003, pp. 9–15.

73 Jürgen Osterhammel, *China und die Weltgesellschaft: vom 18. Jahrhundert bis in unsere Zeit* (China and the international society: from the eighteenth century until the present), Munich: C. H. Beck, 1989, p. 202; Müller, 'Chinesische Perspektiven,' pp. 204, 229.

74 For studies on the Russo–Japanese War and its origins, see John Albert White, *The Diplomacy of the Russo–Japanese War*. Princeton, NJ: Princeton University Press, 1964; S. Okamoto, *The Japanese Oligarchy and the Russo–Japanese War*, New York: Columbia University Press, 1970; Ian Nish, *The Origins of the Russo–Japanese War*, London: Longman, 1985; Josef Kreiner (ed.), *Der Russisch-Japanische Krieg (1904/05)* (*The Russo–Japanese War, 1904/05*), Göttingen: V& R unipress, 2005; John W. Steinberg *et al.* (eds.), *The Russo–Japanese War in Global Perspective: World War Zero*, two volumes, Leiden: Brill, 2005/7; Maik Hendrik Sprotte *et al.* (eds.), *Der Russisch-Japanische Krieg 1904/5*; Rotem Kowner (ed.), *The Impact of the Russo–Japanese War*, London: Routledge, 2007; Rotem Kowner (ed.), *Rethinking the Russo–Japanese War, 1904–5, Vol. 1: Centennial Perspectives*, Folkestone: Global Oriental, 2007.

75 Langer, *Diplomacy of Imperialism*, p. 690.

76 For this incident, see Nish, 'Japan's Indecision,' pp. 450–56.

77 See Shunpo-kō tsuishō-kai, *Itō Hirobumi den* (The life of Itō Hirobumi), Tokyo, Hara shobō, Vol. 3, 1970, pp. 465–66; Nish, 'Japan's Indecision,' p. 457.

78 *Ibid.*, 451.

79 On the Open Door policy, see Hsu, 'Late Ch'ing foreign relations,' pp. 113–15; Langer, *Diplomacy of Imperialism*, pp. 684–87.

80 See Nish, *Anglo–Japanese Alliance*, p. 105, with the full wording of the agreement.

81 Ian Nish, *Japanese Foreign Policy, 1869–1942: Kasumigaseki to Miyakezaka*, London: Routledge & Kegan Paul, 1977, pp. 60–61.

82 For Itō's resistance and the conclusion of the First Anglo–Japanese Alliance, see Nish, *Anglo–Japanese Alliance*, pp. 185–228.

83 For the full text of the treaty see *ibid.*, pp. 216–17.

84 Y. Oka, 'The first Anglo–Japanese Alliance in Japanese public opinion,' in Sue Henny and Jean-Pierre Lehmann (eds), *Themes and Theories in Modern Japanese History: Essays in Memory of Richard Storry*, London: The Athlone Press, 1988, pp. 185–93; there were, of course, also a few critics, such as Uchimura Kanzō of the *Yorozu chōhō*, and Natsume Sōseki, who was at the time in London, see Ōhama Tetsuya, *Shomin no mita Nisshin-Nichiro sensō* (The people's view of the Sino–Japanese and Russo–Japanese War), Tokyo: Tōsui shobō, 2003, pp. 99–100.

85 'The Anglo–Japanese Alliance,' *The Japan Times*, 13 February 1902, p. 1.

86 On the impact of the Anglo–Japanese Alliance on China, see Hsu, 'Late Ch'ing foreign relations,' pp. 134–38.

87 See Hsu, 'Late Ch'ing foreign relations,' pp. 135–36, citing Zhang Zhidong and Yuan Shikai to this effect.

88 See Müller, 'Chinesische Perspektiven,' pp. 215, 237, with a reproduction of the caricature. The caricature appeared in March 1904 and alludes graphically to the famous illustration of Kitazawa Rakuten (1876–1955) of the Anglo–Japanese Alliance in the *Jiji shinpō*, 18 February 1902, which in turn alludes to the so-called Knackfuss painting of 1895.

89 Nish, *Japanese Foreign Policy*, pp. 69–71.

90 See Ian Nish, 'China and the Russo–Japanese War,' *International Studies* (STICERD, London School of Economics), 2004, pp. 1–4; Hsu, 'Late Ch'ing foreign relations,' pp. 158–59; Müller, 'Chinesische Perspektiven,' pp. 208–9.

91 Nish, 'China and the Russo–Japanese War,' p. 3; on Japan's propaganda campaign, see Valliant, 'Selling of Japan,' pp. 421–38.

92 See the *Kanpō* (*Official Gazette*), 19 February 1904, as cited by Nakayama, *Shinbun shūsei*, Vol. 12, pp. 192–93.

93 Nish, 'China and the Russo–Japanese War,' pp. 4–5.

94 For case studies of the Chinese public opinion during the Russo–Japanese War, see Müller, 'Chinesische Perspektiven,' pp. 209–29.

95 For anti-Russian agitation since 1900, see Okamoto, *Japanese Oligarchy*, pp. 62–69, 81–96; Sakeda Masatoshi, *Kindai Nihon ni okeru taigai-kō undō no kenkyū* (Studies on the strong foreign-policy movement in modern Japan), Tokyo: Tōkyō daigaku shuppan-kai, 1979, pp. 133–315; Banno Junji, *Meiji – shisō no jitsuzō* (Meiji – the true nature of thought), Tokyo: Sōbunsha, 1977, pp. 110–22; especially on the press between 1903 and 1905 see James L. Huffman, *Creating a Public: People and Press in Meiji Japan*, Honolulu: University of Hawaii Press, 1997, pp. 271–309.

96 *Tōkyō Asahi shinbun*, 4 February 1904, as cited by Nakayama, *Shinbun shūsei*, Vol. 12, p. 179.

97 See for example 'Manshū no Shina-jin' (The Chinese in Manchuria), *Nippon*, 12 April 1904 (KKZ 8:324–25). This article and the following may have been written by Kuga Katsunan; however, as Katsunan at the time was already ill and busy arranging the future of the *Nippon*, the last part of the *Kuga Katsunan zenshū* also contains articles that are clearly not written by Katsunan.

98 For example 'Shin-Kan no jinshin' (The public sentiment in China and Korea), *Nippon*, 12/13 March 1904 (KKZ 8:282–85); 'Shin-Kan-jin to Rojin' (The relation of the Chinese and Koreans with the Russians), *Nippon*, 28 June 1904 (KKZ 8:426–27); 'Shina Chōsen no seifu' (The governments of China and Korea), *Nippon*, 2 July 1904 (KKZ 8:429–30).

99 'Kōka-ron no shinka' (The progress of the yellow peril-theory), *Nippon*, 24/25 June 1905 (KKZ 9:140–43).

100 'Shin-Kan-jin to Rojin' (The relation of the Chinese and Koreans with the Russians), *Nippon*, 28 June 1904 (KKZ 8:426–27, esp. p. 427); 'Kōka-ron no shinka,' *Nippon*, 24/25 June 1905 (KKZ 9:141).

101 See for example 'Shinkoku chūritsu mondai' (The problem of China's neutrality'), *Nippon*, 13 May 1904 (KKZ 8:368–69); however China's infringement of its duty as a neutral country was a steady complaint in all articles dealing with China during the war.

102 Nish, 'China and the Russo–Japanese War,' pp. 5–6.

103 'Ro Shin dōrui-ron' (On China and Russia belonging to the same kind), *Nippon*, 17/18 July 1905 (KKZ 9:158).

104 'Manjin-chō to Roshia (chūritsu no ayashiki yuen)' (The Manchurian court and Russia: why neutrality is dubious), *Nippon*, 15 April 1904 (KKZ 8:328–29).

105 'Ro Shin dōrui-ron,' *Nippon*, 17/18 July 1905 (KKZ 9:156).

106 'Shina-jin no sengo-saku' (The postwar strategy of the Chinese), *Nippon*, 12 July 1904 (KKZ 8:435–36); in this article, the *Nippon* discusses an issue of the Chinese newspaper *Shuntian shibao*.

107 Nish, 'China and the Russo–Japanese War, p. 9; Müller, 'Chinesische Perspektiven,' p. 229.

108 'Shinkoku no kyōgū' (China's circumstances), *Kokumin shinbun*, 11 July 1905, p. 1.

109 'Shinkoku no taido' (China's attitude), *Kokumin shinbun*, 15 July 1905, p. 1.

110 On the new self-confidence which Chinese diplomats displayed in the Manchurian negotiations, see Nish, 'China and the Russo–Japanese War,' pp. 10–11; White, *Diplomacy of the Russo–Japanese War*, p. 330.

111 On the Beijing negotiations 17 November–22 December 1905, see Nish, 'China and the Russo–Japanese War,' pp. 10–13; White, *Diplomacy of the Russo–Japanese War*, pp. 330–46.

112 See 'Shinkoku seifu no shōdaku: keishiki ni tomaru ya ina ya' (The consent of the Chinese government: will it remain a matter of formalities?), *Nippon*, 21 October 1905 (KKZ 9:231–33); 'Shintei to no danpan' (The negotiations with the Qing court), *Nippon*, 22 November 1905 (KKZ 9:256–57).

113 'Shinkoku daijin no chakkyō' (The visit of a Chinese minister to Tokyo), *Nippon*, 22 January 1906 (KKZ 9:300–301). The *Nippon* assumes that one minister, whose name is given as Chuyang or Chu Yang, visits Tokyo; in fact, two Chinese delegations of specially appointed ministers visited Japan around that time, the one in question probably the mission led by the ministers Zaize, Shang Qiheng and Li Shengduo; see Norbert Meienberger, *The Emergence of Constitutional Government in China (1905–1908): The Concept Sanctioned by the Empress Dowager Tz'u-Hsi*, Bern: Peter Lang, 1980, p. 29. – For study tours especially in the field of education, see Paula Harrell, *Sowing the Seeds of Change: Chinese Students, Japanese Teachers, 1895–1905*, Stanford, CA: Stanford University Press, 1992, pp. 40–60.

114 For the movement toward constitutional government in China and Japanese influences, see Meienberger, *The Emergence of Constitutional Government*; Reynolds, *China*, pp. 186–92; Lin Mingde, 'Qing-mo Min-chu Riben zhengzhi dui Zhongguo de yingxiang (The influence of the Japanese political system on China in the Late Qing period and early Republican era), in Yue-him Tam (ed.), *Sino–Japanese Cultural Interchange: Aspects of Literature and Language Learning*, Hong Kong: Institute of Chinese Studies, Chinese University of Hong Kong, 1985, Vol. 3, pp. 187–99.

115 'Shinkoku daijin no chakkyō,' *Nippon*, 22 January 1906 (KKZ 9:301).

116 *Ibid.*

Conclusion

1 See Ian Nish, 'China and the Russo–Japanese War,' *International Studies* (STICERD, London School of Economics), 2004, p. 13.

2 William L. Langer, *The Diplomacy of Imperialism*, 2nd edn, New York: Alfred A. Knopf, 1965, p. 704.

3 See for example I. Hata, 'Continental Expansion, 1905–41,' in Peter Duus (ed.), *The Cambridge History of Japan, Vol. 6: The Twentieth Century*, Cambridge, New York: Cambridge University Press, 1988, p. 275; Marius B. Jansen, 'Japanese Views of China During the Meiji Period,' in Albert Feuerwerker, Rhoads Murphey and Mary C. Wright (eds), *Approaches to Modern Chinese History*, Berkeley, CA: University of California Press, 1967,' p. 188; Hilary Conroy, 'Lessons from Japanese Imperialism,' *Monumenta Nipponica*, Vol. 21, No. 3/4 (1966), p. 337.

4 Duus, 'Japan's Informal Empire in China, 1895–1937: An Overview,' in Duus, Peter *et al.* (eds), *The Japanese Informal Empire in China, 1895–1937*, Princeton, NJ: Princeton University Press, 1989, pp. xxii–xxiii; for the European view see Langer, *Diplomacy*, pp. 681, 684.

5 Duus, 'Japan's Informal Empire,' pp. xxii–xxiii.

6 Jansen, 'Japanese Views,' p. 188; Douglas R. Reynolds, 'Training Young China Hands: Tōa Dōbun shoin and its Precursors, 1886–1945,' in Peter Duus, Ramon H. Myers and Mark R. Peattie (eds), *The Japanese Informal Empire in China, 1895–1937* Princeton, NJ: Princeton University Press, 1989, p. 211.

7 See, however, S.C.M. Paine, *The Sino–Japanese War of 1894–1895: Perceptions, Power and Primacy*, Cambridge: Cambridge University Press, 2003, pp. 4, 298–99.

8 On this consequence, see Immanuel Hsu, 'Late Ch'ing foreign relations, 1866–1905,' in John K. Fairbank and Kwang-Ching Liu (eds), *The Cambridge History of China, Vol. 2: Late Ch'ing, 1800–1911, Part 2*. Cambridge: Cambridge University Press, 1978, pp. 115, 129.

9 See Hirano Ken'ichirō's assessment of late Meiji Sino–Japanese relations as quoted in Douglas R. Reynolds, *China, 1898–1912: the Xinzheng Revolution and Japan*, Cambridge, MA: Harvard University Press, 1993, p. xviii.

10 Shiga Sukegorō, 'Shina ikan' (How is the situation in China?), part 2, *Tōkyō nichinichi shinbun*, 28 July 1898.

11 For a similar conclusion, see Li Tingjiang, 'Zhang Zhidong and his Military Advisors: a Preliminary Analysis of Modern Japan's China Policy,' translated by Douglas Howland, in Joshua Fogel (ed.), *Late Qing China and Meiji Japan: Political and Cultural Aspects*, Norwalk, CT: Eastbridge, 2004, pp. 54–55.

12 For Korea's gradual effacement as an autonomous entity from political discourse, see Alexis Dudden, *Japan's Colonization of Korea: Discourse and Power*, Honolulu: University of Hawai'i Press, 2005; Wolfgang Seifert, 'Japan Großmacht, Korea Kolonie – völkerrechtliche Entwicklungen vor und nach dem Vertrag von Portsmouth 1905' (Great power Japan, Korea the colony – developments in international law before and after the Portsmouth Treaty 1905), in Maik Hendrik Sprotte, Wolfgang Seifert and Heinz-Dietrich Löwe (eds), *Der Russisch-Japanische Krieg 1904/5: Anbruch einer neuen Zeit? (The Russo–Japanese War 1904/5: the dawn of a new era?)*, Wiesbaden: Harrassowitz, 2007, pp. 55-82.

13 See Paula Harrell, *Sowing the Seeds of Change: Chinese Students, Japanese Teachers, 1895–1905*, Stanford, CA: Stanford University Press, 1992, p. 211.

14 See F. G. Notehelfer, *Kōtoku Shūsui: Portrait of a Japanese Radical*, Cambridge: Cambridge University Press, 1971, pp. 55–87; R. Loftus, 'The Inversion of Progress: Taoka Reiun's *Hibunmei-ron*,' *Monumenta Nipponica*, Vol. 40, No. 2 (Summer 1985), pp. 191–208; Zachmann, 'Blowing Up a Double Portrait in Black and White: The Concept of Asia in the Writings of Fukuzawa Yukichi and Okakura Tenshin,' *positions: east asia cultures critique*, Vol. 15, No. 2 (Fall, 2007), pp. 355–62.

15 Stefan Tanaka, *Japan's Orient: Rendering Pasts into History*. Berkeley and Los Angeles: University of California Press, 1993, p. 108.

16 See for example Naitō Konan's conversations with Chinese intellectuals during a trip to China in 1899 as described by Joshua A. Fogel, *Politics and Sinology: The Case of Naitō Konan (1866–1934)*, Cambridge, MA: Council on East Asian Studies, Harvard University, 1984, pp. 91–110.

17 See Watanabe Hiroshi, *Higashi Ajia no ōken to shisō* (Confucianism and After: Political Thought in Early Modern East Asia), Tokyo: Tokyo daigaku shuppansha, 1997, pp. 248–57.

18 Duus, 'Japan's Informal Empire,' pp. xi–xii; Ian Nish, *Japanese Foreign Policy, 1869–1942: Kasumigaseki to Miyakezaka*, London: Routledge & Kegan Paul, 1977, p. 88.

19 For a more detailed overview of Sino–Japanese relations until 1945, see Marius B. Jansen, *Japan and China: from War to Peace, 1894–1972*, Chicago, IL: Rand McNally College Publishing Co., 1975; Akira Iriye, *China and Japan in the Global Setting*, Cambridge, MA: Harvard University Press, 1992, pp. 41–88; Ian Nish, 'An Overview of Relations between China and Japan, 1895–1945,' in Christopher Howe (ed.), *China and Japan: History, Trends, and Prospects*, Oxford: Clarendon Press, 1996, pp. 23–45. For case studies of Chinese attitudes toward Japan, see Y. Lu, *Re-understanding Japan: Chinese Perspectives, 1895–1945*, Honolulu: Association for Asian Studies and University of Hawaii Press, 2004.

20 John A. White, *The Diplomacy of the Russo–Japanese War*, Princeton, NJ: Princeton University Press, 1964, p. 342; Nish, 'China and the Russo–Japanese War,' p. 16;

21 Hsu, 'Late Ch'ing foreign relations,' p. 141.

22 Harrell, *Sowing the Seeds*, pp. 216–17; for Japan's contribution, see also Marius B. Jansen, 'Japan and the Revolution of 1911,' in John K. Fairbank and Kwang-Ching

Liu (eds), *The Cambridge History of China, Vol. 2: Late Ch'ing, 1800–1911, Part 2*, Cambridge: Cambridge University Press, 1980, pp. 339–74.

23 See M. Ikei, 'Japan's Response to the Chinese Revolution of 1911,' *Journal of Asian Studies* Vol. 25, No. 2 (February 1966), pp. 213–27.

24 Hata, 'Continental Expansion,' p. 279.

25 For example, in February 1913 the *Taiyō* devoted a series of interviews to the question: 'Division or Protection? The problem of a fundamental policy for the Chinese continent' ('Bunkatsu ka hozen ka: Tai-Shina tairiku no konpon seisaku mondai,' *Taiyō*, Vol. 19, No. 11, pp. 99–131); among the interviews is one with Shiraiwa Ryūhei (pp. 108–13); on Japanese reactions to the Chinese Revolution see Nozawa Yutaka, 'Chūgoku kakumei, Roshia kakumei e no shisō-teki taiō' (The intellectual response to the Chinese and the Russian Revolution), in Furuta Hikaru *et al.* (eds), *Kindai Nihon shakai shisō-shi*, Tokyo: Yūhikaku, 1971, Vol. 2, pp. 39–69.

26 See Hata, 'Continental expansion,' pp. 277–82; Nish, *Japanese Foreign Policy*, pp. 93–103.

27 See comments of the *Tōkyō nichinichi shinbun* and *Taiyō* as quoted by Sanetō Keishū, *Nitchū hi-yūkō no rekishi* (The history of Sino–Japanese unfriendly relations), Tokyo: Asahi shinbunsha, 1973, pp. 54, 60; see also Y. Katō, 'Japanese Perceptions of China and the United States, 1914–19,' translated by Roger Brown, in Sven Saaler and Viktor Koschmann (eds), *Pan-Asianism in Modern Japanese History*, London, New York: Routledge, 2007, pp. 67–81.

28 Albert d'Anethan, *The d'Anethan Dispatches from Japan, 1894–1910*, Georg Alexander Lensen (ed.), Tallahassee, FL: The Diplomatic Press, 1967, p. 45.

29 See Nish, *Japanese Diplomacy*, p. 156 on Foreign Minister Shidehara Kikujirō's East Asia policy in the 1920s.

30 Duus, 'Japan's Informal Empire,' pp. xxiii, xxviii.

31 Nish, 'China and the Russo–Japanese War,' p. 13.

32 See Kita Hiroaki, *Nitchū kaisen: Gun-hōmukyoku bunsho kara mita kyokoku itchi taisei e no michi* (The beginning of the Sino–Japanese War: the road to the national unity system as seen from documents of the Army Legal Affairs Bureau), Tokyo: Chūô shinsho, 1994, pp. 8–10.

33 See Ben-Ami Shillony, 'Friend or foe: the ambivalent images of the U.S. and China in wartime Japan,' in James W. White, Michio Umegaki and Thomas R. H. Havens (eds), *The Ambivalence of Nationalism: Modern Japan between East and West*, Lanham, MD: University Press of America, 1990, pp. 197–207.

34 See, for example, the Sinologue Kanzaki Kiyoshi 1936 as quoted by Reynolds, *China, 1898–1912*, p. 7.

35 Shillony, 'Friend or foe,' pp. 200–204.

36 See Iriye, *China and Japan*, p. 78.

37 Kawai Tatsuo, *Hatten Nihon no mokuhyō* (1938) as translated by Nish, *Japanese Foreign Policy*, p. 304.

38 Hisashi Owada, 'Japan, International Law, and the International Community,' in Andō Nisuke (ed.), *Japan and International Law: Past, Present and Future. International Symposium to Mark the Centennial of the Japanese Association of International Law*, The Hague: Kluwer, 1999, p. 370.

39 For a brief overview of Sino–Japanese relations after the war, see Jansen, *Japan and China*, pp. 447–509; Iriye, *China and Japan*, 91–135, Iriye, 'Chinese-Japanese Relations, 1895–1990,' in Christopher Howe (ed.), *China and Japan: History, Trends, and Prospects*, Oxford: Clarendon Press, 1996, pp. 46–59.

40 Harrell, *Sowing the Seeds*, pp. 221–22: 'The present scene and its players bear an uncanny likeness to turn-of-the-century-counterparts.' For overviews and analyses of current Sino–Japanese relations, see Glenn D. Hook *et al.* (eds), *Japan's International Relations: Politics, Economics and Security*, 2nd edn, London: Routledge,

2005, pp. 190–202; M. Söderberg (ed.), *Chinese–Japanese relations in the Twenty-first Century: Complementarity and Conflict*, London: 2002; Caroline Rose, *Interpreting History in Sino–Japanese Relations: A Case Study in Political Decision-Making*, London: Routledge, 1998; Caroline Rose, *Sino–Japanese Relations: Facing the Past, Looking to the Future?* London: Routledge, 2005; for Chinese perspectives of Japan after 1982, see Allen S. Whiting, *China Eyes Japan*, Berkeley, CA: University of California Press, 1989.

Bibliography

Primary sources

(Note: the following bibliography lists only those newspaper editorials and articles that are not already included in the collected works of individual authors.)

Anonymous or unidentified author in *Chūō shinbun* 中央新聞, 'Minkan yūshi no undō' 民間有志の運動 (An agitation of private activists), 6 April 1898, p. 2.

——, 'Chanben-gumi no naijō' チャン弁組の内情 ('The internal situation of the Chanben-group'), 18 April 1898, p. 2.

——, (Hakken 柏軒), 'Jinmin no taigai jigyō' 人民の対外事業 (Private enterprises abroad), 20 April 1898, p. 1.

——, 'Shinkoku no kinjō (Pekin yori no tokuhō)' 清国の近状（北京よりの特報? (The recent situation in China: special report from Beijing), 24 June 1898, p. 1.

——, 'Kō Yūi-shi' 康有為氏 (Mr Kang Youwei), 24 June 1898, p. 1.

——, 'Shin-naikaku wa mu-sekinin naikaku ka' 新内閣は無責任内閣か (Is the new cabinet an irresponsible cabinet?), 29 June 1898, p. 1.

——, 'Shin naikaku wa tōbatsu naikaku nari' 新内閣は党閥の内閣なり (The new cabinet is a party-clan cabinet), 2 July 1898, p. 1.

——, 'Ishin kōshin wa mu-seiji' 維新更新は無政治 (Restorations and reforms are nonpolitical), 17 July 1898, p. 1.

——, 'Shinkoku kaikaku-ha no ichi-tonza' 清国改革派の一頓挫 (A major setback for the reformers in China), 25 September 1898, p. 2.

——, 'Shinkoku no seihen' 清国の政変 (The political change in China), 25 September 1898, p. 2.

Anonymous or unidentified author in *The Japan Times*, 'The Anglo–Japanese Alliance', 13 February 1902, p. 1.

Anonymous or unidentified author in *Jiji shinpō* 時事新報, 'Shina-jin no naichi zakkyo' 支那人の内地雑居 ('Mixed residence with Chinese'), 27 February 1894, p. 2.

——, 'Shina shinbun, *Jiji shinpō* no manga o tsūba su' 支那新聞、時事新報の漫画を痛罵す (A Chinese newspaper condemns the caricatures of the *Jiji shinpō*), 8 March 1895, p. 2.

——, 'Ka o henjite fuku o nasu beshi' 禍を変じて福を為す可し (One must turn misfortune into one's blessings), 17 May 1898, p. 2.

——, 'Shina no kaikaku ni tsuite' 支那の改革に就いて (On the reforms in China), 22 September 1898, p. 2.

Anonymous or unidentified author in *Kokumin shinbun* 国民新聞, 'Shina to Toruko' 支那と土耳古 (China and Turkey), 14 February 1895, p. 2.

——, 'Hi-kōwa' 非講和 (Against peace), 17 March 1895, p. 2.

——, 'Kōwa-shi ni kan suru yoron' 講和使に関する輿論 (The public opinion on the peace mission), 17 March 1895, p. 4.

——, 'Kokuun no dai-tenkai' 国運の大転廻 (A vital turn in our country's fate), 31 March 1895, p. 2.

——, 'Takigi ni ga shi tan o namu' 薪に臥し胆を嘗む (Sleeping on firewood and licking bile), 10 May 1895, p. 2.

——, 'Dōmei' 同盟 (Alliances), 29 May 1895, p. 2.

——, 'Zen-sekai no shippai (kinji no gaikō shakai)' 全世界の失敗（近時の外交社会） (A failure of the whole world – the diplomatic community in recent times), 18 June 1895, p. 5.

——, 'Nichiei dōmei okonawaru beki ka' 日英同盟行はる可き乎 (Is an Anglo–Japanese alliance feasible?), 12 July 1895, p. 1.

——, 'Sensō no junbi' 戦争の準備 (War preparations), 17 July 1895, p. 2.

——, 'Kōshoku jinshu no bokkō' 黄色人種の勃興 (The rise of the yellow race), *Kokumin shinbun*, 18 July 1895, p. 3.

——, 'Tōyō, Seiyō o osou no zu' 東洋、西洋を襲うの図 (A picture of the East attacking the West), 8 January 1896, p. 3.

——, 'Shina to Nippon' 支那と日本 (China and Japan), 3 December 1897, p. 2.

——, 'Rinkoku no seihen' 隣国の政変 (The political change in our neighbor country), 25 September 1898, p. 1.

——, 'Shinkoku jihen to Nisshin ryōkoku kōtei no go-shinden' 清国事変と日清両国皇帝の御親電 (The Chinese incident and the imperial telegrams of the Chinese and the Japanese emperors), 21 July 1900, p. 1.

——, 'Tenshin no kanraku-go' 天津の陥落後 (Tianjin after the surrender), 23 July 1900, p. 1.

——, 'Kanraku-go no Tenshin to waga gunki no gensei' 陥落後の天津と我軍規の厳正 (Tianjin after the surrender and the strictness of our military discipline), 28 July 1900, p. 1.

——, 'Shinkoku no kyōgū' 清国の境遇 (China's circumstances), 11 July 1905, p. 1.

——, 'Shinkoku no taido' 清国の態度 (China's attitude), 15 July 1905, p. 1.

Anonymous or unidentified author in *The New York Times*, 'A tripartite interview: three famous men talk together the day before one of them loses the throne', 18 December 1898, p. 8.

Anonymous or unidentified author in *Nippon* 日本 (Dangori 曇五里), 'Shinkoku no kyū ni omomuku beshi' (We must hasten to China's rescue) 清国の急に赴く可し, *Nippon*, 23 June 1895, p. 1.

——, (Suiken 随軒), 'Nani o motte Shinjin ni oshien ka' 何を以て清人に教へん乎 (How are we going to teach the Chinese?), 1 September 1898, p. 1.

——, (Gyokuzan 玉山), 'Shinkoku no kansei no kaikaku' 清国の官制の改革 (On the reform of the bureaucracy in China), 22 September 1898, p. 1.

——, 'Tōhō kyōkai ni okeru Ōkuma gaimu daijin no enzetsu' 東方協会に於ける大隈外務大臣の演説 (The speech of Foreign Minister Ōkuma at the Tōhō kyōkai), 21 October 1898, p. 1.

——, 'Itō Hirobumi Kō Yūi no kaiken' 伊藤博文康有為の会見 (The interview between Itō Hirobumi and Kang Youwei), 1 November 1898, p. 5.

Anonymous or unidentified author in *Taiyō* 太陽, 'Nisshin dōmei no shin-igi' 日清同盟の真意義 (The true meaning of a Sino–Japanese alliance), Vol. 4, No. 11 (20 May 1898), pp. 52–55.

Anonymous or unidentified author in *Tenchijin* 天地人, 'Kō-jinshu dōmei no zehi tokushitsu' 黄人種同盟の是非得失 (The relative merits of a Yellow Race alliance), Vol. 2 (February 1898), pp. 7–11.

——, 'Ōkuma-haku no Tōhō-ron' 大隈伯の東方論 (Count Ōkuma's views on East Asia), Vol. 2 (February 1898), politics section, pp. 1–7.

Anonymous or unidentified author in *Tōkyō Asahi shinbun* 東京朝日新聞, 'Dōmei-ron' 同盟論 (On Alliances), 5 August (p. 1), 6 August 1896 (p. 2).

——, 'Giwadan-hi to Taiwan seiban' 義和団匪と台湾生蕃 (The Boxer-bandits and the Taiwan aborigines), 15 June 1900, p. 2.

Anonymous or unidentified author in *Tōkyō nichinichi shinbun* 東京日日新聞, 'Shinkoku no gaisai' 清国の外債 (China's foreign loans), 5 February 1898, p. 2.

——, 'Shinkoku no shōkin' 清国の償金 (The Chinese Indemnity), 16 February 1898, p. 2.

——, 'Dokutei no gūi-ga' 独帝の寓意画 (An allegorical picture by the German emperor), 2 March 1898, p. 4.

——, 'Kyōga' 狂画 (Comic illustrations), 6 March 1898, p. 10.

——, 'Itō kō o okuru' 伊藤侯を送る (Sending off Marquis Itō), 27 July 1898, p. 2.

——, 'Shin-kokumin no kaihatsu' 清国民の開発 (Developing the Chinese people), 31 August 1898, p. 2.

——, 'Bōkoku no kizashi' 亡国の徴 (Symptoms of national decay), 4 September 1898, p. 5.

——, 'Ōishi-shi no gaikō-ron' 大石氏の外交論 (Mr Ōishi's opinions on foreign policy), 11 September 1898, p. 2.

——, 'Shinkoku no shōrai' 清国の将来 (The future of China), part 2, 18 September 1898, p. 1.

——, 'Shinkoku no seihen' 清国の政変 (The political change in China), 25 September 1898, p. 2.

——, 'Jasetsu o hai su' 邪説を排す (In rejection of a dangerous theory), 30 September 1898, p. 2.

——, 'Gen-naikaku no injun kosoku' 現内閣の因循姑息 (The indecision and vacillation of the present cabinet), 5 October 1898, p. 2.

——, 'Shinkoku no henran ni taisuru junbi' 清国の変乱に対する準備 (Preparations against further disturbances in China), 8 October 1898, p. 2.

——, 'Shinkoku oyobi sono yūbō' 清国及其友邦 (China and its friends), 16 October 1898, p. 2.

——, 'Ōkuma haku no enzetsu' 大隈伯の演説 (Count Ōkuma's speech), 21 October (p. 3), 22 October (p. 4), 23 October 1898 (p. 5).

——, 'Ōkuma-haku no enzetsu' 大隈伯の演説 (Count Ōkuma's speech), 22 October 1898, p. 2.

——, 'Ōkuma haku no mujun' 大隈伯の矛盾 (Count Ōkuma's contradictions), 23 October 1898, p. 2.

——, 'Shinkoku no bunkatsu' 清国の分割 (The partition of China), 25 October 1898, p. 2.

——, '*Jiji shinpō* no jisatsu' 時事新報の自殺 (The suicide of the *Jiji shinpō*), 16 November 1898, p. 4.

——, 'Nanfutsu sensō' 南弗戦争 (The South African war), 1 January 1900 (p. 45), 7 January (pp. 5–6).

——, 'Nippon kurabu bansan-kai' 日本倶楽部晩餐会 (The dinner banquet of the Japan Club), 19 January 1900, p. 1.

——, 'Sentan tsui ni hiraku' 戦端遂に開く (War hostilities have finally begun), 19 June 1900, p. 2.

——, 'Shōjutsu' 賞恤 (A reward), 8 July 1900, p. 1.

——, 'Nippon-hei no yūkan' 日本兵の勇悍 (The bravery of Japanese soldiers), 12 July 1900, p. 2.

——, 'Shinkoku jiken to kokusai kōhō' 清国事件と国際公法 (The China incident and international law), 25 July 1900, p. 2.

Anonymous or unidentified author in *Yorozu chōhō* 萬朝報 (Kashū 蝦洲), 'Kaikaku wa eidan o yō su' 改革は英断を要す (Reforms need bold decision), 10 July 1898, p. 1.

——, (Kashū 蝦洲), 'Kyōfū-ron' 俠風論 (On the spirit of chivalry), 16/17 July 1898, p. 1.

——, 'Lessons from Italy', *Yorozu chōhō*, 10 August 1898, p. 2.

——, 'Shinkoku no seihen ni tsuite' 清国の政変に就いて (On the political change in China), 26 September 1898, p. 1.

Anonymous or unidentified author in *Zhixinbao* 知新報, 'Faguo zhaohui guafen Zhongguo shi' 法国瓜分中国事 (France's memorandum concerning the partition of China), No. 45 (1898, Guangxu 24/2/11), pp. 18–20.

——, 'Yiteng lun Zhongguo caizheng' 伊藤論中国財政 (Itō discusses Chinese finances), No. 78 (1898, Guangxu 24/12/11), pp. 10–12.

Ariga, Nagao 有賀長雄, 'Shinkoku jiken to kokusai-hō' 清国事件と国際法 (The China Incident and international law), *Gaikō jihō*, Vol. 3, No. 32 (1900), pp. 73–74.

——, 'Kokusai-hō gakkai to Shinkoku jiken' 国際法学会と清国事件 (The Japanese Society of International Law and the China Incident), *Gaikō jihō*, Vol. 3, No. 33 (1900), pp. 87–88.

Asahina, Chisen 朝比奈知泉, 'Iwayuru sekinin mondai' 所謂責任問題 (The so-called responsibility question), *Tōkyō nichinichi shinbun*, 30 July 1895, p. 2.

——, 'Waga kuni no seitō no shōrai' 我邦政党の将来 (The future of the parties in our country), in: *Tōkyō nichinichi shinbun*, 15 June 1898, p. 26.

Baba, Teijirō 馬場定次郎, 'Baba tokuhain senpō dai-ichi' 馬場特派員戦報第一 (War report of special correspondent Baba, No. 1), *Tōkyō nichinichi shinbun*, 26 June 1900, p. 1.

——, 'Baba tokuhain senpō dai-kyū' 馬場特派員戦報第九 (War report of special correspondent Baba, No. 9), *Tōkyō nichinichi shinbun*, 5 July 1900, p. 3.

von Bulmerincq, A., *Das Völkerrecht oder das internationale Recht* (International law). Freiburg i.B.: J. C. B. Mohr, 1889.

Chinese University of Hongkong, Institute of Chinese Studies (ed.), *Chunqiu zuozhuan zhuzi suoyin* 春秋左伝逐字索引 / *A Concordance to the Chunqiu Zuozhuan*, two vols, Hongkong: The Commercial Press, 1995.

Chirol, Valentine, 'The Far Eastern Question', part 1, *The Times*, 24 September 1895, p. 3.

d'Anethan, Albert, *The d'Anethan Dispatches from Japan, 1894–1910*, Georg Alexander Lensen (ed.), Tallahassee, FL: The Diplomatic Press, 1967.

Fukuzawa, Yukichi 福沢諭吉, *Fukuzawa Yukichi zenshū* 福沢諭吉全集 (The collected works of Fukuzawa Yukichi). Keiō gijuku 慶応義塾 (ed.). 22 vols, Tokyo: Iwanami shoten, 1969–71.

——, *An Outline of a Theory of Civilization*, translated by David A. Dilworth and G. Cameron Hurst. Tokyo: Sophia University, 1973.

Gaimushō 外務省 (ed.), *Nihon gaikō monjo* 日本外交文書 (Japanese documents on foreign affairs), Tokyo: Nihon kokusai rengō kyōkai, 1949.

Hamada, Yoshizumi 濱田佳澄, 'Tenshin no rōjō' 天津の籠城 (The Siege of Tianjin), *Kokumin shinbun*, 14 July 1900 (p. 2), 15 July (p. 2), 20 July (p. 2).

——, 'Tenshin no sakkon' 天津の昨今 (Tianjin these days), *Kokumin shinbun*, 22 July 1900, pp. 1–2.

——, 'Tenshin-jō no kanraku' 天津城の陥落 (The surrender of Tianjin), *Kokumin shinbun*, 24 July 1900, p. 2.

——, 'Tenshin jōnai no sakkon' 天津城内の昨今 (The situation in Tianjin these days) *Kokumin shinbun*, 29 July 1900, p. 1.

Hara, Takashi 原敬, *Shin-jōyaku jisshi junbi* 新条約実施準備 (Preparing for the implementation of the New Treaties), 2nd edn, Osaka: Osaka Mainichi shinbun-sha, 1899.

Hayashi, Tadasu, *The Secret Memoirs of Count Tadasu Hayashi*. A. M. Pooley (ed.), London: Eveleigh Nash, 1915.

Hinohara, Shōzō 日原昌造 (Toyoura-sei 豊浦生), 'Nihon wa Tōyō-koku taru bekarazu' 日本ハ東洋国タルベカラズ (Japan must not be an Oriental country), *Jiji shinpō* 時事新報, 11/13/14 November 1884.

Itō, Hirobumi 伊藤博文, *Itō kō enzetsu-shū* 伊藤侯演説集 (A collection of Marquis Itō's speeches), three vols, Tokyo: Nippō-sha, 1899.

——, *Itō kō zenshū* 伊藤公全集 (Collected works of Itō Hirobumi), Komatsu Midori 小松緑 (ed.), three vols, Tokyo: Shōwa shuppansha, 1928.

Itō Hirobumi kankei monjo kenkyū-kai 伊藤博文関係文書研究会 (ed.), *Itō Hirobumi kankei monjo* 伊藤博文関係文書 (Documents relating to Itō Hirobumi), eight vols, Tokyo: Hanawa shobō, 1973–80.

Kang Youwei 康有為, 'Chronological Autobiography of K'ang Yu-wei' [*Nanhai xiansheng zibian nianpu* 南海先生自編年譜], translated by Jung-Pang Lo, in Jung-Pang Lo (ed.), *K'ang Yu-Wei: A Biography and a Symposium*, Tucson, AZ: University of Arizona Press, 1967, pp. 17–174.

Katsunan, Kuga 陸羯南 (ed.), *Sanshi suimei* 山紫水明 (The Glory of Nature), Tokyo: Rikugun juken kōgi-roku henshū-jo, 1897.

——, *Kuga Katsunan zenshū* 陸羯南全集 (The collected works of Kuga Katsunan), Nishida, Taketoshi 西田長寿, Uete Michiari 植手通有 and Sakai Yūkichi 坂井雄吉 (eds), 10 vols, Tokyo: Misuzu shobō, 1968–85.

Kawasaki, Shizan 川崎紫山, 'Sengo no Shina' 戦後の支那 (China after the war), *Chūō shinbun*, 16–18/20–22/24–28 April, 2 May 1898.

——, 'Man-Shin teikoku to sono jinzai' 満清帝国と其人材, (The Chinese Empire and her Men of Ability'), *Taiyō*, Vol. 4, No. 17 (20 August 1898), pp. 15–21; Vol. 4, No. 18 (5 September 1898), pp. 16–25.

——, 'Shinkoku no keisei masa ni ippen to su' 清国の形勢将に一変とす (The situation in China is about to change), *Chūō shinbun*, 22–24 September 1898.

Kokusai nyūsu jiten shuppan iinkai, Mainichi komyunikêshonzu 国際ニュース事典出版委員会, 毎日コミュニケーションズ (eds), *Gaikoku shinbun ni miru Nihon* 外国新聞に見る日本 (Japan as seen through foreign newspapers), 10 vols, Tokyo: Mainichi komyunikêshonzu, 1989–93.

Komatsu, Midori 小松緑, 'Seisui no kiun' 盛衰の機運 (The rise and decline of nations), *Taiyō*, Vol. 4, No. 18 (5 September 1898), 7–11.

Konoe, Atsumaro 近衛篤麿, 'Kaikoku no bokkō ni kan suru yōmu' 開国の勃興に関する要務 (Urgent tasks concerning Japan's rise as a maritime nation), *Seishin* 精神 No. 47 (5 January 1895), pp. 10–19.

——, 'Teikoku no ichi to gendai no seijika' 帝国の位地と現代の政治家 (The position of our empire and today's politicians), *Tōa jiron* 東亜時論, No. 1 (10 December 1898), pp. 5–7.

——, *Konoe Atsumaro nikki* 近衛篤麿日記 (The diary of Konoe Atsumaro), Konoe Atsumaro nikki kankō-kai 近衛篤麿日記刊行会 (ed.), six vols, Tokyo: Kajima kenkyūjo shuppan-kai, 1968–69.

Kōtoku, Shūsui 幸徳秋水, *Kōtoku Shūsui zenshū* 幸徳秋水全集 (The collected works of Kōtoku Shūsui), Kōtoku Shūsui zenshū henshū iinkai 幸徳秋水全集編集委員会 (ed.), 12 vols, Tokyo: Meiji bunken, 1968–73.

Mahan, Alfred Thayer, 'A Twentieth-Century Outlook', *Harper's Monthly Magazine*, Vol. 5, No. 568 (September 1897), pp. 521–33.

Meiji nyūsu jiten hensan iinkai, Mainichi komyunikêshonzu 明治ニュース事典編纂委員会, 毎日コミュニケーションズ出版部 (eds), *Meiji nyūsu jiten* 明治ニュース事典 (A Meiji news encyclopaedia), nine vols, Tokyo: Mainichi komyunikêshonzu, 1983–86.

Miyake, Setsurei 三宅雪嶺, 'Gaikō-jutsu o Shina ni manabe' 外交術を支那に学べ (Learn the skills of diplomacy from China), *Nippon*, 11 May 1895, p. 1.

——, 'Shōtan gashin 嘗胆臥薪' (Licking bile and sleeping on firewood), *Nippon*, 15 May 1895 (p. 1), 27 May 1895 (p. 2).

——, 'Daiichi ishin ni kangamiyo' 第一維新に鑑みよ (Remember the first Restoration!), *Nippon*, 11 July 1898, p. 1.

——, 'Shina ni chikara o sosoge' 支那に力を注げ (Pour your energies into China!), *Nippon*, 10 October 1898, p. 1.

——, *Jiden* 自伝 (Autobiography). Tokyo: Heibonsha, 1982.

Miyazaki, Tōten 宮崎滔天, *My Thirty-Three Years' Dream: the Autobiography of Miyazaki Tōten*, translated by Etō Shinkichi and Marius B. Jansen, Princeton, NJ: Princeton University Press, 1982.

Mutsu, Munemitsu 陸奥宗光, *Kenkenroku: A Diplomatic Record of the Sino–Japanese War, 1894–95*, edited and translated by Gordon Mark Berger, Princeton, NJ: Princeton University Press, 1982.

Naitō, Konan 内藤湖南, *Naitō Konan zenshū* 内藤湖南全集 (*Collected works of Naitō Konan*), Naitō Kenkichi 内藤乾吉 and Kanda Kiichirō 神田喜一郎 (eds), 14 vols, Tokyo: Chikuma shobō, 1969–76.

Nakanishi, Ushirō 中西牛郎, 'Nippon teikoku no ninmu' 日本帝国の任務 (The mission of the Japanese Empire), *Taiyō*, Vol. 1, No. 1 (1 January 1895), pp. 47–50.

Nakayama, Yasumasa 中山泰昌 *et al.* (eds), *Shinbun shūsei Meiji hennen-shi* 新聞集成明治編年史 (A Meiji chronicle through newspaper sources), 15 vols, Tokyo: Zaisei keizai gakkai, 1934–36.

Natsume, Sōseki 夏目漱石, *Sōseki bunmeiron-shū* 漱石文明論集 (A reader of Natsume Sōseki's civilization critique), Miyoshi Yukio 三好行雄 (ed.), Tokyo: Iwanami shoten, 1986.

Ōkuma, Shigenobu 大隈重信, *Ōkuma-haku enzetsu-shū* 大隈伯演説集 (A collection of Count Ōkuma's speeches), Waseda daigaku henshū-bu (ed.), Tokyo: Waseda daigaku, 1907.

Ōoka, Ikuzō 大岡育造, 'Itō kō nyūshin no kōkei' 伊藤侯入清の光景 (The spectacle of Marquis Itō's arrival in China), *Chūō shinbun*, 24 September 1898, p. 2.

——, 'Tenshin ni okeru Itō kō' 天津に於ける伊藤侯 (Marquis Itō in Tianjin), *Chūō shinbun*, 29 September 1898, p. 2.

——, 'Pekin ni okeru Itō kō' 北京に於ける伊藤侯 (Marquis Itō in Beijing), *Chūō shinbun*, 29 September 1898, p. 2.

——, 'Itō kō ikkō no ekken' 伊藤侯一行の謁見 (The audience of Marquis Itō's group with the emperor), *Chūō shinbun*, 9 October 1898, p. 1.

——, 'Shinkoku seihen no gen'in' 清国政変の原因 (The causes of the political change in China), *Chūō shinbun*, 9 October 1898, p. 2.

——, 'Ri Kōshō to no taiwa' 李鴻章との対話 (A conversation with Li Hongzhang), *Chūō shinbun*, 11 October 1898, p. 2.

——, 'Kōhaku no gunjin' 黄白の軍人 (Yellow and white military men), *Taiyō* 太陽, Vol. 6, No. 14 (November 1900), pp. 14–17.

Ozaki Yukio 尾崎行雄, 'Taishin seisaku' 対清政策 (Our China policy), *Taiyō*, Vol. 1, No. 1 (1 January 1895), pp. 40–47.

——, *The Autobiography of Ozaki Yukio: The Struggle for Constitutional Government in Japan*, translated by Hara Fujiko, Princeton, NJ: Princeton University Press, 2001.

Shibahara, Takuji 芝原拓自, Ikai Takaaki 猪飼隆明 and Ikeda Masahiro 池田正博 (eds), *Taigaikan* 対外観 (Views of foreign affairs), Tokyo: Iwanami shoten, 1991.

Shiga, Sukegorō 志賀祐五郎 (Ryūko 龍湖), 'Enkei tokuhō' 燕京特報 (Special report from Beijing), *Yorozu chōhō*, 14 June 1898, p. 1.

——, (Ryūko 龍湖), 'Pekin tokuhō' 北京特報 (Special report from Beijing), *Yorozu chōhō*, 3 July 1898, p. 1.

——, (Shabaku manshi 遮莫漫士), 'Shina ikan' 支那如何 (How is the situation in China?), *Tōkyō nichinichi shinbun*, 27 July 1898, p.1, 28 July, p.1.

——, (Shiga Shabaku 志賀遮莫), 'Shina mondai' 支那問題 (The China question), *Yorozu chōhō*, 23/25 September 1898, p. 1.

Shiraiwa, Ryūhei 白岩龍平, *Shiraiwa Ryūhei nikki: Ajia-shugi jitsugyōka no shōgai* 白岩龍平日記ーアジア主義実業家の生涯 (The diary of Shiraiwa Ryūhei: the life of an Asianist entrepreneur), Nakamura, Tadashi 中村義 (ed.), Tokyo: Kenbun shuppan, 1998.

Takayama, Rinjirō 高山林次郎 (Chogyū 樗牛), 'Jinshu kyōsō toshite mitaru kyokutō mondai 人種競争として見たる極東問題' (The Far Eastern Question seen as a racial competition), *Taiyō*, Vol. 4, No. 2 (20 January 1898), pp. 30–39.

——, 'I-jinshu dōmei' 異人種同盟 (An alliance between different races), *Taiyō*, Vol. 4, No. 5 (5 March 1898), p. 31.

——, 'Sensen-roku' 詹詹録 (Verbose Notes), *Taiyō* Vol. 4, No. 15 (20 July 1898), 32–41.

——, 'Dare ka waga kuni o Supein ni hi suru mono zo' 誰か我邦を西班牙に比するものぞ (Absurd comparison between Japan and Spain), *Taiyō*, Vol. 4, No. 16 (5 August 1898), 20–25.

——, 'Jūkyū seiki – sōron' 十九世紀 ー 総論 (The nineteenth century – Introduction), *Taiyō*, Vol. 6, No. 8 (15 June 1900), 19–32.

Takekoshi, Yosaburō 竹越与三郎, 'Yorozu chōhō kisha sokka 萬朝報記者足下' (Letter to the editor), *Yorozu chōhō*, 13 July 1898, p. 1.

Taoka Reiun田岡嶺雲, *Taoka Reiun zenshū* 田岡嶺雲全集 (Collected Works of Taoka Reiun), Nishida, Masaru 西田勝 (ed.), three vols, Tokyo: Hōsei daigaku shuppan-kyoku, 1969–87.

Tōa dōbun-kai 東亜同文会, 'Tōa dōbun-kai shui-sho' 東亜同文会主意書 (Foundation Manifesto of the Tōa dōbun-kai), *Tōa jiron* 東亜時論, No. 1 (10 December 1898), p. 1.

Tokutomi Sohō 徳富蘇峰, *Shakai to jinbutsu* 社会と人物 (Society and People), Tokyo: Min'yūsha, 1899.

——, *Sohō jiden* 蘇峰自伝 (The Autobiography of Tokutomi Sohō), Tokyo: Heibonsha, 1982.

Uchimura, Kanzō 内村鑑三, *Uchimura Kanzō zenshū* 内村鑑三全集 (The collected works of Uchimura Kanzō), Suzuki Toshirō 鈴木俊郎 *et al.* (eds), 42 vols, Tokyo: Iwanami shoten, 1980–84.

Yamagata, Aritomo 山縣有朋, *Yamagata Aritomo iken-sho* 山縣有朋意見書 (The opinion papers of Yamagata Aritomo), Ōyama Azusa 大山梓 (ed.), Tokyo: Hara shobō, 1966.

Zhongguo shixue-hui 中国史学会 (ed.), *Wuxu bianfa* 戊戌变法 (The Hundred Days Reform), four vols, Shanghai: Shenzhouguo guangshe, 1953.

Secondary sources

Aibara, Shigeki 相原茂樹, 'Konoe Atsumaro to Shina hozen-ron' 近衛篤麿と支那保全論 (Konoe Atsumaro and the preservation of China-argument), in Okamoto Kōji 岡本幸治 (ed.), *Kindai Nihon no Ajia-kan* 近代日本のアジア観 (Modern Japan's views of Asia), Kyōto: Minerva shobō, 1998, pp. 51–77.

Akita, George, *Foundations of Constitutional Government in Modern Japan, 1868–1900*, Cambridge, MA: Harvard University Press, 1967.

Anderson, Benedict, *Imagined Communities: Reflections on the Origins and Spread of Nationalism*, revised edn, London: Verso, 1991.

Arano, Yasunori 荒野泰典, 'Kaikin to sakoku' 海禁と鎖国 (Maritime prohibitions and national isolation), in Arano Yasunori *et al.* (eds), *Gaikō to sensō* 外交と戦争 (Diplomacy and war), Tokyo: Tōkyō daigaku shuppan-kai, 1992, pp. 191–222.

Aydin, Cemil, *The Politics of Anti-Westernism in Asia: Visions of World Order in Pan-Islamic and Pan-Asian Thought*, New York: Columbia University Press, 2007.

Banno Junji 坂野潤治, *Meiji – shisō no jitsuzō* 明治 思想の実像 (Meiji – the true nature of thought), Tokyo: Sōbunsha, 1977.

——, *Kindai Nihon no gaikō* 近代日本の外交 (Modern Japanese foreign policy), Tokyo: Kenbun shuppan, 1985.

Barth, Boris and Jürgen Osterhammel (eds), *Zivilisierungsmissionen: imperiale Weltverbesserung seit dem 18. Jahrhundert* (Civilizing missions: imperialist reformism since the eighteenth century), Konstanz: UVK Verlagsgesellschaft, 2005.

Bays, Daniel H., 'Chang Chih-Tung after the '100 Days': 1898–1900 as a transitional period for reform constituencies', in Paul A. Cohen and John E. Schrecker (eds), *Reform in Nineteenth-Century China*, Cambridge, MA: Harvard University Press, 1976, pp. 317–25.

Bowle, John, *Politics and Opinion in the Nineteenth Century: An Historical Introduction*, London: Jonathan Cape, 1954.

Chang, Hao, 'Intellectual Change and the Reform Movement, 1890–98', in John K. Fairbank and Kwang-Ching Liu (eds), *The Cambridge History of China*, Vol. 2: *Late Ch'ing, 1800–1911*, Part 2, Cambridge, London, New York: Cambridge University Press, 1980, pp. 274–338.

Choy, Philip P., Lorraine Dong and Marion K. Horn, *The Coming Man: 19th Century American Perceptions of the Chinese*, Seattle, WA: University of Washington Press, 1995.

Chu, Samuel C., 'China's Attitudes toward Japan at the Time of the Sino–Japanese War', in Akira Iriye (ed.), *The Chinese and the Japanese: Essays in Political and Cultural Interaction*, Princeton, NJ: Princeton University Press, 1980, pp. 74–95.

Chung, Sue Fawn, 'The Image of the Empress Dowager Tz'u-Hsi', in Paul A. Cohen and John E. Schrecker (eds), *Reform in Nineteenth-Century China*, Cambridge, MA: Harvard University Press, 1976, pp. 101–10.

——, 'The Much-Maligned Empress Dowager: A Revisionist Study of the Empress Dowager Tz'u-Hsi (1835–1908)', *Modern Asian Studies*, Vol. 13, No. 2 (1979), pp. 177–96.

Cohen, Paul A., 'The Contested Past: The Boxers as History and Myth', *Journal of Asian Studies*, Vol. 51, No. 1 (February 1992), pp. 82–113.

——, *History in Three Keys: The Boxers as Event, Experience, and Myth*. New York: Columbia University Press, 1997.

Conroy, Hilary, 'Lessons from Japanese Imperialism', *Monumenta Nipponica*, Vol. 21, No. 3/4 (1966), pp. 334–45.

Dawson, Raymond, *The Chinese Chameleon: An Analysis of European Conceptions of Chinese Civilization*. Oxford: Oxford University Press, 1967.

Diesinger, Gunter (ed.), *Japanische Farbholzschnitte II: Kriegsbilder aus der Meiji-Zeit* (Japanese colored woodblock prints II: war illustrations from the Meiji period), Hamburg: Museum für Kunst und Gewerbe Hamburg, 1986.

Drüll, Dagmar, *Heidelberger Gelehrtenlexikon, 1803–1932* (A compendium of Heidelberg scholars, 1803–1932), Berlin: Springer, 1986.

Dudden, Alexis, *Japan's Colonization of Korea: Discourse and Power*. Honolulu: University of Hawai'i Press, 2005.

Duncan, David, *The Life and Letters of Herbert Spencer*, London: Methuen & Co., 1908.

Duus, Peter, Ramon H. Myers and Mark R. Peattie (eds), *The Japanese Informal Empire in China, 1895–1937*, Princeton, NJ: Princeton University Press, 1989.

Duus, Peter, *The Abacus and the Sword: the Japanese Penetration of Korea, 1895–1910*, Berkeley, CA: University of California Press, 1995.

——, 'Japan's Informal Empire in China, 1895–1937: An Overview', in Duus, Peter *et al.* (eds), *The Japanese Informal Empire in China, 1895–1937*, Princeton, NJ: Princeton University Press, 1989, pp. xi–xxix.

Esherick, Joseph W., *The Origins of the Boxer Uprising*, Berkeley, CA: University of California Press, 1987.

Eskildsen, Robert, 'Of Civilization and Savages: the Mimetic Imperialism of Japan's 1874 Expedition to Taiwan', *American Historical Review*, Vol. 107, No. 2 (February 2002), pp. 388–418.

Fairbank, John K., and S. Y. Teng, 'On the Ch'ing Tributary System', *Harvard Journal of Asiatic Studies*, Vol. 6, No. 2 (June 1941), pp. 135–246.

Fairbank, John K. (ed.), *The Chinese World Order: Traditional China's Foreign Relations*, Cambridge, MA: Harvard University Press, 1968.

Ferguson, Niall, 'Public Finance and National Security: the Domestic Origins of the First World War Revisited', *Past and Present*, No. 142 (February 1994), pp. 141–68.

Fogel, Joshua A., 'To Reform China: Naitō Konan's Formative Years in the Meiji Press', *Modern Asian Studies*, Vol. 16, No. 3 (1982), pp. 353–95.

——, *Politics and Sinology: The Case of Naitō Konan (1866–1934)*, Cambridge, MA: Council on East Asian Studies, Harvard University, 1984.

——,*The Literature of Travel in the Japanese Rediscovery of China, 1862–1945*, Stanford, CA: Stanford University Press, 1996.

—— (ed.), *Late Qing China and Meiji Japan: Political and Cultural Aspects*, Norwalk, CT: Eastbridge, 2004.

—— (ed.), *The Role of Japan in Liang Qichao's Introduction of Modern Western Civilization to China*, Berkeley, CA: Institute of East Asian Studies, University of California, 2004.

Fujimura, Michio 藤村道生, *Nisshin sensō* 日清戦争 (The Sino–Japanese War), Tokyo: Iwanami shoten, 1973.

Gaimushō gaikō shiryō-kan Nihon gaikō-shi jiten hensan iinkai 外務省外交史料館日本外交辞典編纂委員会, *Nihon gaikō-shi jiten* 日本外交辞典 (A lexicon of Japanese diplomatic history), Tokyo: Yamakawa shuppansha, 1992.

Gluck, Carol, *Japan's Modern Myths: Ideology in the Late Meiji Period*. Princeton, NJ: Princeton University Press, 1985.

Gollwitzer, Heinz, *Die Gelbe Gefahr: Geschichte eines Schlagwortes. Studien zum imperialistischen Denken* (The Yellow Peril: the history of a catchphrase. Studies on imperial thought), Göttingen: Vandenhoeck und Ruprecht, 1961.

Gong, Gerrit W., *The Standard of 'Civilization' in International Society*, Oxford: Clarendon Press, 1984.

Hara, Takeshi 原剛, 'Gunji-teki shiten kara mita Nisshin sensō' 軍事的視点からみた日清戦争 (The Sino–Japanese War from a military viewpoint), in Higashi-Ajia kindai-shi gakkai 東アジア近代史学会 (ed.), *Nisshin sensō to Higashi-Ajia sekai no hen'yō* 日清戦争と東アジア世界の変容 (The Sino–Japanese War and the transformation of East-Asia), Tokyo: Yumani shobō, 1997, Vol. 2, pp. 89–101.

Harrell, Paula, *Sowing the Seeds of Change: Chinese Students, Japanese Teachers, 1895–1905*, Stanford, CA: Stanford University Press, 1992.

Harootunian, Harry D., 'The Functions of China in Tokugawa Thought', in Akira Iriye (ed.), *The Chinese and the Japanese*, Princeton, NJ: Princeton University Press, 1980, pp. 9–36.

Hashikawa Bunzō 橋川文三, *Jungyaku no shisō: Datsua ron igo* 順逆の思想－脱亜論以後, Tokyo: Keisō shobō, 1973, pp. 78–153.

Hata, Ikuhiko, 'Continental Expansion, 1905–41', in Peter Duus (ed.), *The Cambridge History of Japan*, Vol. 6: *The Twentieth Century*, Cambridge, New York: Cambridge University Press, 1988, pp. 271–314.

Hatsuse, Ryūhei 初瀬龍平, "Datsua ron' saikō 「脱亜論」再考' (Reconsidering the 'Datsua ron'), in Hirano Ken'ichirō 平野健一郎 (ed.), *Kindai Nihon to Ajia: bunka no kōryū to masatsu* 近代日本とアジア-文化の交流と摩擦 (Modern Japan and Asia: cultural exchange and conflict), Tokyo: Tōkyō daigaku shuppan-kai, 1984, pp. 19–41.

Hirakawa, Sukehiro, 'Japan's turn to the West', in Marius B. Jansen (ed.), *The Cambridge History of Japan, Vol. 5: The Nineteenth Century*, Cambridge: Cambridge University Press, 1989, pp. 432–98.

Hiratsuka, Kentarō 平塚健太郎, 'Kuga Katsunan to Minami-Afurika sensō' 陸羯南と南アフリカ戦争 (Kuga Katsunan and the South African War), *Gendai-shi kenkyū*, No. 48, (February 2002), pp. 1–19.

Ho, Ping-Ti, 'Weng T'ung-Ho and the "One Hundred Days of Reform"', *Far Eastern Quarterly*, Vol. 10, No. 2 (February 1951), pp. 125–35.

Hoare, J. E., *Japan's Treaty Ports and Foreign Settlements: The Uninvited Guests*, Sandgate, Folkestone: Japan Library, 1994.

Hobsbawm, Eric, *The Age of Empire*, New York: Vintage Books, 1989.

Hook, Glenn D. et al., *Japan's International Relations: Politics, Economy and Security*, 2nd edn, London: Routledge, 2005.

Howard, Richard C., 'Japan's Role in the Reform Program of K'ang Yu-wei', in Jung-Pang Lo (ed.), *Kang Yu-wei: A Biography and a Symposium*, Tucson, AZ: University of Arizona Press, 1967, pp. 281–312.

Howland, D.R., *Borders of Chinese Civilization: Geography and History at Empire's End*, Durham, NC and London: Duke University Press, 1996.

Hsu [Hsü], Immanuel C.Y., 'Late Ch'ing foreign relations, 1866–1905', in John K. Fairbank and Kwang-Ching Liu (eds), *The Cambridge History of China*, Vol. 2: *Late Ch'ing, 1800–1911*, Part 2, Cambridge: Cambridge University Press, 1978, pp. 70–141.

Huang, Fu-ch'ing, *Chinese Students in Japan in the Late Ch'ing Period*, translated by Katherine P. K. Whitaker, Tokyo: Tokyo Press, 1982.

Huffman, James L., *Creating a Public: People and Press in Meiji Japan*, Honolulu: University of Hawaii Press, 1997.

Ichimata, Masao 一又正雄, *Nihon no kokusaihō-gaku o kizuita hitobito* 日本の国際法学を築いた人々 (The people who built Japanese international legal studies), Tokyo: Nihon kokusai mondai kenkyū-jo, 1973.

Iguchi, Kazuki 井口和起, 'Nichiro sensō' 日露戦争 (The Russo–Japanese War), in Iguchi Kazuki 井口和起 (ed.), *Nisshin Nichiro sensō* 日清日露戦争 (The Sino–Japanese and the Russo–Japanese War), Tokyo: Yoshikawa Kōbunkan, 1994, pp. 75–96.

Ikei, Masaru, 'Japan's Response to the Chinese Revolution of 1911', *Journal of Asian Studies* Vol. 25, No. 2 (February 1966), pp. 213–27.

Ikle, Frank W., 'The Triple Intervention: Japan's Lesson in the Diplomacy of Imperialism', *Monumenta Nipponica*, Vol. 22, No. 1–2 (1967), pp. 122–30.

Iriye, Akira, *Pacific Estrangement: Japanese and American Expansion, 1897–1911*, Cambridge, MA: Harvard University Press, 1971.

——, ed., *The Chinese and the Japanese: Essays in Political and Cultural Interaction*, Princeton, NJ: Princeton University Press, 1980.

——, 'Japan's drive to great power status', in Marius B. Jansen (ed.), *Cambridge History of Japan, Vol. 5: The Nineteenth Century*, Cambridge, New York: Cambridge University Press, 1989, pp. 721–81.

——, *China and Japan in the Global Setting*, Cambridge, MA: Harvard University Press, 1992.

——, 'Chinese-Japanese Relations, 1895–1990', in Christopher Howe (ed.), *China and Japan: History, Trends, and Prospects*, Oxford: Clarendon Press, 1996, pp. 46–59.

Ishihara, Michihiro 石原道博, 'Mindai Chūgoku-jin no Nihon-kan' 明代中国人の日本観 (Ming Chinese views of Japan), *Rekishi kyōiku* Vol. 8, No. 1 (January 1960), pp. 44–51.

Itō, Teruo 伊藤昭雄 (ed.), *Ajia to Kindai Nihon: Han-shinryaku no shisō to undō* アジアと近代日本：反侵略の思想と運動 (Asia and modern Japan: anti-invasionist thought and action), Tokyo: Shakai hyōron-sha, 1990.

Iwakabe, Yoshimitsu 岩壁義光, 'Nisshin senjihō-ka no zainichi Chūgoku-jin mondai' 日清戦時法下の在日中国人問題 (The legal problem of Chinese residing in Japan during the Sino–Japanese War), in Higashi-Ajia kindai-shi gakkai 東アジア近代史学会 (ed.), *Nisshin sensō to Higashi-Ajia sekai no hen'yō* 日清戦争と東アジア世界の変容 (The first Sino–Japanese war and the transformation of East-Asia), Tokyo: Yumani shobō, 1997, Vol. 2, pp. 207–42.

Janku, Andrea, *Nur leere Reden: Politischer Diskurs und die Shanghaier Presse im China des späten 19. Jahrhunderts* (Just idle talk: political discourse and the Shanghai press in China in the late nineteenth century), Wiesbaden: Harrassowitz, 2003.

Jansen, Marius B., 'Ōi Kentarō: Radicalism and Chauvinism', *Far Eastern Quarterly*, Vol. 11, No. 3 (1952), pp. 305–16.

——, *The Japanese and Sun Yat-Sen*, Cambridge, MA: Harvard University Press, 1967.

——, 'Japanese Views of China During the Meiji Period', in Albert Feuerwerker, Rhoads Murphey and Mary C. Wright (eds), *Approaches to Modern Chinese History*, Berkeley, CA: University of California Press, 1967, pp. 163–89.

——, *Japan and China: From War to Peace, 1894–1972*, Chicago, IL: Rand McNally College Publishing Co., 1975.

——, 'Konoe Atsumaro', in Akira Iriye (ed.), *The Chinese and the Japanese: Essays in Political and Cultural Interaction*, Princeton, NJ: Princeton University Press, 1980, pp. 107–23.

——, 'Japan and the Revolution of 1911', in John K. Fairbank and Kwang-Ching Liu (eds), *The Cambridge History of China, Vol. 2: Late Ch'ing, 1800–1911*, Part 2, Cambridge: Cambridge University Press, 1980, pp. 339–74.

——, 'Some Continuities in Meiji Views of China', in Yue-him Tam (ed.), *Sino–Japanese Cultural Interchange: Aspects of Literature and Language Learning*, Hong Kong: Institute of Chinese Studies, University of Hong Kong, 1985, Vol. 3, pp. 243–56.

——, *China in the Tokugawa World*, Cambridge, MA: Harvard University Press, 1992.

Kamachi, Noriko, 'The Chinese in Meiji Japan: Their Interactions with the Japanese before the Sino–Japanese War', in Akira Iriye (ed.), *The Chinese and the Japanese: Essays in Political and Cultural Interaction*, Princeton, NJ: Princeton University Press, 1980, pp. 58–73.

——, *Reform in China: Huang Tsun-hsien and the Japanese Model*, Cambridge, MA: Council on East Asian Studies, Harvard University, 1981.

Kano, Masanao 鹿野政直, *Fukuzawa Yukichi* 福沢諭吉, Tokyo: Century Books, 1967.

——, *Shihon-shugi keisei-ki no chitsujo ishiki* 資本主義形成期の秩序意識 (System consciousness in the formation period of capitalism). Tokyo: Chikuma shobō, 1969.

Karl, Rebecca E., and Peter Zarrow (eds), *Rethinking the 1898 Reform Period: Political and Cultural Change in Late Qing China*, Cambridge, MA: Harvard University Asia Center, 2002.

Katō, Yōko, 'Japanese Perceptions of China and the United States, 1914–19', translated by Roger Brown, in Sven Saaler and Viktor Koschmann (eds), *Pan-Asianism in Modern Japanese History*, London, New York: Routledge, 2007, pp. 67–81.

Keene, Donald, 'The Sino–Japanese War of 1894–95 and its Cultural Effects in Japan', in Donald Shively (ed.), *Tradition and Modernization in Japanese Culture*, Princeton, NJ: Princeton University Press, pp. 121–75.

——, 'Characteristic Responses to Confucianism in Tokugawa Literature', in Peter Nosco (ed.), *Confucianism and Tokugawa Culture*, Princeton, NJ: Princeton University Press, 1984, pp. 120–37.

——, 'The Survival of Chinese Literary Traditions in the Meiji Era', in Yue-him Tam (ed.), *Sino–Japanese Cultural Interchange: Aspects of Literature and Language Learning*, Hong Kong: Institute of Chinese Studies, University of Hong Kong, 1985, Vol. 2, pp. 75–90.

Kim, Key-Hiuk, *The Last Phase of the East Asian World Order: Korea, Japan, and the Chinese Empire, 1860–1882*, Berkeley, CA: University of California Press, 1980.

Kita, Hiroaki 北博昭, *Nitchū kaisen: Gun-hōmukyoku bunsho kara mita kyokoku itchi taisei e no michi* 日中開戦－軍法務局文書からみた挙国一致体制への道 (The beginning of the Sino–Japanese War: the road to the national unity system as seen from documents of the Army Legal Affairs Bureau), Tokyo: Chûô shinsho, 1994.

Kleinschmidt, Harald, *Das europäische Völkerrecht und die ungleichen Verträge um die Mitte des 19. Jahrhunderts* (European international law and the unequal treaties in the mid-nineteenth century), Tokyo: OAG Gesellschaft für Natur-und Völkerkunde Ostasiens Tokyo, 2007.

Kobayashi, Kazumi 小林一美, *Giwadan sensō to Meiji kokka* 義和団戦争と明治国家 (The Boxer War and the Meiji state), Tokyo: Kyūko shoin, 1986.

Komiya, Kazuo 小宮一夫, *Jōyaku kaisei to kokunai seiji* 条約改正と国内政治 (Treaty revisions and domestic politics), Tokyo: Yoshikawa kōbunkan, 2001.

Kong, Xiangji 孔祥吉, and Murata Yūjirō 村田雄二郎, *Han wei ren zhi de Zhong-Ri jiemeng ji qita: Wan-Qing Zhong-Ri guanxi-shi xintan* 罕為人知的中日結盟及其他

一晩清中日関係史新探 (A little-known Sino–Japanese alliance and other matters: new studies on the history of Late Qing Sino–Japanese relations), Chengdu: Boshu shushe, 2004.

Kowner, Rotem (ed.), *The Impact of the Russo–Japanese War*, London: Routledge, 2007.

—— (ed.), *Rethinking the Russo–Japanese War, 1904–5*, Vol. 1: *Centennial Perspectives*, Folkestone, Kent: Global Oriental, 2007.

Koyama, Fumio 小山文雄, *Kuga Katsunan: 'Kokumin' no sōshutsu* 陸羯南：「国民」の創出 (Kuga Katsunan: creating 'the nation'), Tokyo: Misuzu shobō, 1990.

Kreiner, Josef (ed.), *Der Russisch-Japanische Krieg (1904/05)* (*The Russo–Japanese War, 1904/05*), Göttingen: V&R unipress, 2005.

Kunaichō 宮内庁 (ed.), *Meiji Tennō-ki* 明治天皇紀 (Record of the Meiji Emperor), 12 vols, index, Tokyo: Yoshikawa Kōbunkan, 1968–77.

Kuroki, Morifumi, 'The Asianism of the Kōa-kai and the Ajia Kyōkai', in Sven Saaler and Viktor Koschmann (eds), *Pan-Asianism in Modern Japanese History*, London, New York: Routledge, 2007, pp. 34–51.

Kwong, Luke S.K., *A Mosaic of the Hundred Days: Personalities, Politics, and Ideas of 1898*, Cambridge, MA: Harvard University Press, 1984.

Langer, William L., *The Diplomacy of Imperialism*, 2nd edn, New York: Alfred A. Knopf, 1965.

Lee, Sophia, 'The Foreign Ministry's Cultural Agenda for China: The Boxer Indemnity', in Peter Duus *et al.* (eds), *The Japanese Informal Empire in China*, Princeton, NJ: Princeton University Press, 1989, pp. 272–306.

Li Qizhang 李啓彰, 'Nisshin shūkō jōki seiritsu katei no sai-kentō' 日清修好条規成立過程の再検討 (A re-examination of the negotiation and ratification process of the Sino–Japanese Treaty of Amity), *Shigaku zasshi*, Vol. 115, No. 7 (2007), pp. 65–82.

Li Shaojun 李少軍, 'Bojutsu henpō: Nihon o mohan to shita Chūgokujin' 戊戌变法一日本を模範とした中国人 (The Hundred Days Reform – the Chinese modeling themselves on Japan), *China 21*, Vol. 9 (May 2000), pp. 225–40.

Li Tingjiang 李廷江, *Nihon zaikai to kindai Chūgoku: Shingai kakumei o chūshin ni* 日本財界と近代中国一辛亥革命を中心に (The Japanese business world and modern China around the time of the Chinese Revolution 1911), 2nd edn, Tokyo: Ochanomizu shobō, 2003.

——, 'Zhang Zhidong and his Military Advisors: a Preliminary Analysis of Modern Japan's China Policy', translated by Douglas Howland, in Joshua Fogel (ed.), *Late Qing China and Meiji Japan: Political and Cultural Aspects*, Norwalk, CT: Eastbridge, 2004, pp. 39–61.

Liao, Longgan 廖隆幹, 'Bojutsu henpō-ki ni okeru Nihon no taishin gaikō' 戊戌变法期における日本の対清外交 (Japan's China policy during the Hundred Days Reform), *Nihon rekishi*, No. 471 (August 1987), pp. 68–84.

Lin, Mingde 林明德, 'Qing-mo Min-chu Riben zhengzhi dui Zhongguo de yingxiang 清末民初日本政治对中国的影響' (The influence of the Japanese political system on Late Qing and early Republican China), in Yue-him Tam (ed.), *Sino-Japanese Cultural Interchange: Aspects of Literature and Language Learning*, Vol. 3, Hong Kong: Institute of Chinese Studies, Chinese University of Hong Kong, 1985, pp. 187–99.

Loftus, Ronald, 'The Inversion of Progress: Taoka Reiun's *Hibunmeiron*', *Monumenta Nipponica*, Vol. 40, No. 2 (Summer 1985), pp. 191–208.

Lone, Stewart, *Japan's First Modern War: Army and Society in the Conflict with China, 1894–95*, Basingstoke: Macmillan, 1994.

Lu, Yan, *Re-understanding Japan: Chinese Perspectives, 1895–1945*, Honolulu: Association for Asian Studies and University of Hawai'i Press, 2004.

Marutani, Yoshinori 丸谷嘉徳, *Kuga Katsunan kenkyū* 陸羯南研究 (Studies on Kuga Katsunan), Tokyo: Keisō shobō, 1990.

Maruyama, Masao, 'Fukuzawa Yukichi no 'Datsua ron' to sono shūhen' 福沢諭吉の「脱亜論」とその周辺 (Fukuzawa Yukichi's Datsua ron and its context), *Maruyama Masao techō* 丸山真男手帳, No. 20 (January 2002), pp. 1–42.

Masuda, Tomoko 増田知子, 'Nisshin sengo keiei' 日清戦後経営 (The postwar management after the Sino–Japanese War), in Inoue Matsusada 井上光貞 *et al.* (eds), *Nihon rekishi taikei* 日本歴史大系 (An outline of Japanese history), Tokyo: Yamakawa shuppan-sha, 1987, Vol. 4, pp. 732–58.

Masuda, Wataru, *Japan and China: Mutual Representations in the Modern Era*, translated by Joshua A. Fogel, Richmond, Surrey: Curzon, 2000.

Matsuoka, Bunpei 松岡文平, 'Reimei-ki rōdō kumiai undō no tokushitsu: "Rōdō sekai" to Chūgoku zakkyo mondai' 黎明期労働組合運動の特質－『労働世界』と中国人雑居問題 (The characteristics of the early labor movement: the magazine *Rōdō sekai* and the Chinese mixed residence problem', *Shisen* 48 (1974), pp. 15–32.

Mayo, Marlene, 'A Catechism of Western Diplomacy: The Japanese and Hamilton Fish, 1873', *Journal of Asian Studies*, Vol. 26, No. 3 (May 1967), pp. 389–410.

McWilliams, Wayne C., 'East Meets East: the Soejima Mission to China, 1873', *Monumenta Nipponica*, Vol. 30, No. 3 (Autumn 1975), pp. 237–75.

Mehl, Margaret, 'Private Academies for Chinese Learning (*Kangaku juku*) in the Meiji Period', in Joshua A. Fogel (ed.), *Late Qing China and Meiji Japan: Political and Cultural Aspects*, Norwalk, CT: Eastbridge, 2004, pp. 87–107.

Mehnert, Ute, *Deutschland, Amerika und die 'Gelbe Gefahr': zur Karriere eines Schlagwortes in der Großen Politik, 1905–1917* (Germany, America and the 'Yellow Peril': the career of a catchphrase in international politics, 1905–17), Stuttgart: Frany Steiner Verlag, 1995.

Meienberger, Norbert, *The Emergence of Constitutional Government in China (1905–1908): The Concept Sanctioned by the Empress Dowager Tz'u-Hsi*, Bern: Peter Lang, 1980.

Metzler, Mark, *Lever of Empire: the International Gold Standard and the Crisis of Liberalism in Prewar Japan*, Berkeley, CA: University of California Press, 2006

Miwa, Kimitada, 'Fukuzawa Yukichi's 'Departure from Asia': A Prelude to the Sino–Japanese War', in Edmund Skrzypczak (ed.), *Japan's Modern Century*, Tokyo: Sophia University and Charles E. Tuttle, 1968, pp. 1–26.

Morohashi, Tetsuji 諸橋轍次, *Dai-Kanwa jiten* 大漢和辞典 (Chinese-Japanese character dictionary), '13 vols, Tokyo: Taishūkan shoten, 1955–60.

Müller, Gotelind, 'Chinesische Perspektiven auf den Russisch-japanischen Krieg' ('Chinese perspectives of the Russo–Japanese War'), in Maik Hendrik Sprotte, Wolfgang Seifert and Heinz-Dietrich Löwe (eds), *Der Russisch-Japanische Krieg 1904/5: Anbruch einer neuen Zeit? (The Russo–Japanese War 1904/5: the dawn of a new era?)*, Wiesbaden: Harrassowitz, 2007, pp. 203–39.

Nagai, Michio, 'Herbert Spencer in Early Meiji Japan', *Far Eastern Quarterly*, Vol. 14, No. 1 (November 1954), pp. 55–64.

Najita, Tetsuo, and H.D. Harootunian, 'Japanese revolt against the West: political and cultural criticism in the twentieth century', in Peter Duus (ed.), *The Cambridge*

History of Japan, Vol. 6: The Twentieth Century, Cambridge, New York: Cambridge University Press, 1988, pp. 711–74.

Nakai, Kate Wildman, 'The Naturalization of Confucianism in Tokugawa Japan: the Problem of Sinocentrism', *Harvard Journal of Asiatic Studies*, Vol. 40, No. 1 (June 1980), pp. 157–90.

Nakashita, Masaharu 中下正治, *Shinbun ni miru Nitchū kankei-shi: Chūgoku no Nihon-jin keieishi* 新聞にみる日中関係史：中国の日本人経営紙 (Sino–Japanese relations as seen through newspapers: China's Japanese-run newspapers). Tokyo: Kenbun shuppan, 1996.

Narsimhan, Sushila, *Japanese Perceptions of China in the Nineteenth Century: Influence of Fukuzawa Yukichi*, New Delhi: Phoenix Publishing House, 1999.

Nish, Ian, 'Japan's Indecision during the Boxer Disturbances', *Journal of Asian Studies*, Vol. 22, No. 4 (1961), pp. 449–61.

——, *Japanese Foreign Policy, 1869–1942: Kasumigaseki to Miyakezaka*, London: Routledge and Kegan Paul, 1977.

——, *The Anglo–Japanese Alliance: The Diplomacy of Two Island Empires, 1894–1907*, 2nd edn, London: Athlone Press, 1985.

——, *The Origins of the Russo–Japanese War*, London: Longman, 1985.

——, 'An Overview of Relations between China and Japan, 1895–1945', in Christopher Howe (ed.), *China and Japan: History, Trends, and Prospects*, Oxford: Clarendon Press, 1996, pp. 23–45.

——, 'China and the Russo–Japanese War', *International Studies* (STICERD, London School of Economics), 2004, pp. 1–16.

Nishida, Taketoshi 西田長寿, *Meiji jidai no shinbun to zasshi* 明治時代の新聞と雑誌 (Newspapers and magazines in the Meiji era), Tokyo: Shibundō, 1961.

Notehelfer, F. G., *Kōtoku Shūsui: Portrait of a Japanese Radical*, Cambridge: Cambridge University Press, 1971.

Nozawa, Yutaka 野沢豊, 'Chūgoku kakumei, Roshia kakumei e no shisō-teki taiō 中国革命 ロシア革命への思想的対応' (The intellectual response to the Chinese and the Russian Revolution), in Furuta Hikaru 古田光, *et al.* (eds), *Kindai Nihon shakai shisō-shi* 近代日本社会思想史 (A history of modern Japanese thought on society), Tokyo: Yūhikaku, 1971, Vol. 2, pp. 39–69.

Nyūsupâku ニュースパーク (Nihon shinbun hakubutsukan 日本新聞博物館) (ed.), *Shinbun manga no me – hito seiji shakai* 新聞漫画の眼-人 政治 社会 (People, politics and society as seen through the eyes of newspaper caricatures), Yokohama: Nyūsupâku (Nihon shinbun hakubutsukan), 2003.

Ōba, Osamu 大庭修, *Edo jidai ni okeru Chūgoku bunka juyō no kenkyū* 江戸時代における中国文化受容の研究 (Studies on the reception of Chinese culture in the Edo period), Tokyo: Dōhōsha, 1984.

Obinata Sumio 大日方純夫, 'Jiyūminken-ki no higashi-Ajia jōsei ninshiki: "Marumaru chinbun" manga no sekai o yomu' 自由民権期の東アジア情勢認識 －『団団珍聞』漫画の世界を読む－ (The perception of East Asian conditions during the Jiyū minken era: reading the world of *Marumaru chinbun*'s caricatures), *Bunka kokusai kenkyū* (Tōkyō toritsu tanki daigaku), Vol. 1 (February 1997), 29–45.

Oguma, Eiji, *A Genealogy of 'Japanese' Self-Images*, translated by David Askew, Melbourne: Trans Pacific Press, 2002.

Oh, Bonnie B., 'Sino–Japanese Rivalry in Korea, 1876–85', in Akira Iriye (ed.), *The Chinese and the Japanese: Essays in Political and Cultural Interaction*, Princeton, NJ: Princeton University Press, 1980, pp. 37–57.

Ōhama, Tetsuya 大濱徹也, *Shomin no mita Nisshin-Nichiro sensō* 庶民の見た日清日露戦争 (The people's view of the Sino–Japanese and Russo–Japanese War), Tokyo: Tōsui shobō, 2003.

Oka, Yoshitake, 'The first Anglo–Japanese Alliance in Japanese public opinion', in Sue Henny and Jean-Pierre Lehmann (eds), *Themes and Theories in Modern Japanese History: Essays in memory of Richard Storry*, London: Athlone Press, 1988, pp. 185–93.

Okabe, Yasuko 岡部泰子, 'Shōden Hinohara Shōzō' 小伝日原昌造 (A short biography of Hinohara Shōzō), *Fukuzawa techō* 福沢手帳, No. 110 (2001), pp. 12–30.

Okamoto, Shumpei, *The Japanese Oligarchy and the Russo–Japanese War*, New York: Columbia University Press, 1970.

Onogawa, Hidemi 小野川秀美, *Shin-matsu seiji shisō kenkyū* 清末政治思想研究 (Studies in Late Qing political thought), Tokyo: Misuzu shobō, 1969.

Osterhammel, Jürgen, *China und die Weltgesellschaft: vom 18. Jahrhundert bis in unsere Zeit* (China and the international society: from the eighteenth century to the present), Munich: C. H. Beck, 1989.

——, 'Vielfalt und Einheit im neuzeitlichen Asien' (Unity and Diversity in Early Modern and Modern Asia), in Osterhammel (ed.), *Asien in der Neuzeit, 1500–1950: sieben historische Stationen* (Asia in Early Modern and Modern Times, 1550–1950: seven historical chapters), Frankfurt a.M.: Fischer Taschenbuch Verlag, 1994, pp. 9–25.

Ōuchi Chōzō 大内暢三, 'Konoe Kazan-kō to Tōa dōbun shoin' 近衛霞山公と東亜同文書院 (Prince Konoe and the Tōa dōbun shoin), *Shina*, Vol. 25, No. 2/3 (February 1934), pp. 143–47.

——, 'Kazan-kō no bunka hatsuyō' 霞山公の文化発揚 (Prince Konoe's promotion of culture), *Shina*, Vol. 25, No. 2/3 (February 1934), pp. 179–85.

Owada, Hisashi, 'Japan, International Law, and the International Community', in Andō Nisuke (ed.), *Japan and International Law: Past, Present and Future. International Symposium to Mark the Centennial of the Japanese Association of International Law*, The Hague: Kluwer 1999, pp. 347–78.

Paine, S. C. M., *The Sino–Japanese War of 1894–1895: Perceptions, Power and Primacy*, Cambridge: Cambridge University Press, 2003.

Patrick, Hugh T., 'External Equilibrium and Internal Convertibility: Financial Policy in Meiji Japan', *Journal of Economic History*, Vol. 25, No. 2 (June 1965), pp. 187–213.

Peattie, Mark R., 'The Japanese Colonial Empire, 1895–1945', in Peter Duus (ed.), *The Cambridge History of Japan*, Vol. 6: *The Twentieth Century*. Cambridge, New York: Cambridge University Press, 1988, pp. 217–70.

Peng Zezhou 彭沢周, 'Kō Yūi no henpō undō to Meiji ishin' 康有為の変法運動と明治維新 (Kang Youwei's reform movement and the Meiji Restoration), *Jinbun gakuhō*, Vol. 30 (March 1970), pp. 149–93.

——, 'Itō Hirobumi to Bojutsu henpō' 伊藤博文と戊戌変法 (Itō Hirobumi and the Hundred Days Reform), *Rekishi-gaku kenkyū*, No. 406 (March 1974), pp. 17 – 29.

Pollack, David, *The Fracture of Meaning: Japan's Synthesis of China from the Eighth through the Eighteenth Centuries*, Princeton, NJ: Princeton University Press, 1986.

Pyle, Kenneth B., *The New Generation in Meiji Japan: Problems of Cultural Identity 1885–1895*, Cambridge, MA: Harvard University Press, 1969.

——, 'Early Meiji Conservatism', in Marius B. Jansen (ed.), *The Cambridge History of Japan*, Vol. 5: *The Nineteenth Century*, Cambridge, New York: Cambridge University Press, 1989, pp. 674–720.

Reynolds, Douglas R., 'Training Young China Hands: Tōa Dōbun shoin and its Precursors, 1886–1945', in Peter Duus, Ramon H. Myers and Mark R. Peattie (eds), *The Japanese Informal Empire in China, 1895–1937*, Princeton, NJ: Princeton University Press, 1989, pp. 210–71.

——, *China, 1898–1912: The Xinzheng Revolution and Japan*, Cambridge, MA: Harvard University Press, 1993.

Rose, Caroline, *Interpreting History in Sino–Japanese Relations: A Case Study in Political Decision-Making*, London and New York: Routledge, 1998.

——, *Sino–Japanese Relations: Facing the Past, Looking to the Future?* London: Routledge, 2005.

Saaler, Sven, 'Pan-Asianism in modern Japanese history', in Sven Saaler and Viktor Koschmann (eds), *Pan-Asianism in Modern Japanese History*, London, New York: Routledge, 2007, pp. 1–18.

Said, Edward, *Orientalism: Western Conceptions of the Orient*, London: Penguin Books, 1995.

Sakai, Tadayasu 酒井忠康, and Shimizu Isao 清水勲 (eds), *Nisshin sensō-ki no manga* 日清戦争期の漫画 (Caricatures of the Sino–Japanese War period), Tokyo: Chikuma shobō, 1985.

Sakayori, Masashi 酒寄雅志, 'Ka'i shisō no shosō' 華夷思想の諸相 (Aspects of Sino-centric thinking), in Arano, Yasunori 荒野泰典 *et al.* (eds), *Ji-ishiki to sōgo rikai* 自意識と相互理解 (Self-consciousness and mutual understanding), Tokyo: Tōkyō daigaku shuppankai, 1993, pp. 27–58.

Sakeda, Masatoshi 酒田正敏, *Kindai Nihon ni okeru taigai-kō undō no kenkyū* 近代日本における対外硬運動 (Studies on the strong foreign-policy movement in modern Japan), Tokyo: Tōkyō daigaku shuppan-kai, 1979.

Sanetō, Keishū 実藤恵秀, *Chūgoku-jin Nihon ryūgaku-shi zōho* 中国人日本留学史増補 (A history of Chinese students in Japan, enlarged ed.)., Tokyo: Kuroshio shuppan, 1970.

——, *Nitchū hi-yūkō no rekishi* 日中非友好の歴史 (The history of Sino–Japanese unfriendly relations), Tokyo: Asahi shinbunsha, 1973.

Sasaki, Takashi 佐々木隆, *Media to kenryoku* メディアと権力 (The media and power), Tokyo: Chūō kōron shinsha, 1999.

Sato, Kazuki, '"Same Language, Same Race': the Dilemma of Kanbun in Modern Japan', in Frank Dikötter (ed.), *The Construction of Racial Identities in China and Japan: Historical and Contemporary Perspectives*. London: Hurst & Co., 1997, pp. 118–35.

Satō, Yoshimaru 佐藤能丸, 'Ozaki Yukio bunshō no 'Kyōwa enzetsu jiken' no nazo' 尾崎行雄文相の「共和演説事件」の謎 (The mystery of the 'Republican Speech Affair' involving Education Minister Ozaki Yukio), *Nihon rekishi*, no, 682 (March 2005), pp. 37–39.

Schmitt, Carl, *Der Begriff des Politischen: Text von 1932 mit einem Vorwort und drei Corollarien* (The concept of the political: the text of 1932 with a preface and three corollaries), 7th edn, Berlin: Duncker & Humblot, 2002.

Schöllgen, Gregor, *Das Zeitalter des Imperialismus* (The age of imperialism), fourth revised edn, München: R. Oldenbourg Verlag, 2000.

Schrecker, John E., 'The Reform Movement of 1898 and the Meiji Restoration as Ch'ing-I Movement', in Akira Iriye, *The Chinese and the Japanese: Essays in Political and Cultural Interactions*, Princeton, NJ: Princeton University Press, 1980, pp. 96–106.

Schwartz, Benjamin, *In Search of Wealth and Power: Yen Fu and the West*, Cambridge, MA: Belknap Press, 1964.

Seifert, Wolfgang, 'Japan Großmacht, Korea Kolonie – völkerrechtliche Entwicklungen vor und nach dem Vertrag von Portsmouth 1905' (Great power Japan, Korea the colony – developments in international law before and after the Portsmouth Treaty 1905), in Maik Hendrik Sprotte, Wolfgang Seifert and Heinz-Dietrich Löwe (eds), *Der Russisch-Japanische Krieg 1904/5: Anbruch einer neuen Zeit? (The Russo–Japanese War 1904/5: the dawn of a new era?)*, Wiesbaden: Harrassowitz, 2007, pp. 55–82.

Shibahara, Takuji 芝原拓自, 'Taigai-kan to nashonarizumu 対外観とナショナリズム' (Views of foreign affairs and nationalism), in Shibahara *et al.* (eds), *Taigai-kan* 対外観 (Views of foreign affairs), Tokyo: Iwanami, 1991, pp. 458–534.

Shillony, Ben-Ami, 'Friend or foe: the ambivalent images of the U.S. and China in wartime Japan', in James W. White, Michio Umegaki and Thomas R. H. Havens (eds), *The Ambivalence of Nationalism: Modern Japan between East and West*, Lanham, MD: University Press of America, 1990, pp. 187–211.

Shimura, Toshiko 志村寿子, 'Bojutsu henpō to Nihon: Nisshin sensō-go no shinbun o chūshin to shite' 戊戌変法と日本－日清戦争後の新聞を中心として (The Hundred Days Reform and Japan in Japanese newspapers after the Sino–Japanese War), *Tōkyō toritsu daigaku hōgaku zasshi*, Vol. 6, No. 2 (March 1996), pp. 253–90.

Shinobu, Seizaburō 信夫清三郎 (ed.), *Nihon gaikō-shi 1853–1972* 日本外交史 (A history of Japanese foreign policy, 1853–1972), two vols, Tokyo: Mainichi shinbunsha, 1974.

Shunpo-kō tsuishō-kai 春畝公追頌会, *Itō Hirobumi den* 伊藤博文伝 (The life of Itō Hirobumi), three vols, Tokyo, Hara shobō, 1970.

Söderberg, Marie (ed.), *Chinese-Japanese Relations in the Twenty-first Century: Complementarity and Conflict*, London: Routledge, 2002.

Spence, Jonathan, *The Search for Modern China*, New York, London: W.W. Norton, 1990.

Sprotte, Maik Hendrik, Wolfgang Seifert and Heinz-Dietrich Löwe (eds), *Der Russisch–Japanische Krieg 1904/5: Anbruch einer neuen Zeit? (The Russo–Japanese War 1904/5: the dawn of a new era?)*, Wiesbaden: Harrassowitz.

Steinberg, John W. *et al.* (eds), *The Russo–Japanese War in Global Perspective: World War Zero*, two vols, Leiden: Brill, 2005/7.

Sugano Tadashi 菅野正, 'Giwadan jihen to Nihon no yoron' 義和団事変と日本の輿論 (The Boxer Incident and Japanese public opinion), *Hisutoria* No. 44/45 (June 1966), pp. 26–50.

——, *Shinmatsu Nitchū kankei-shi no kenkyū* 清末日中関係史の研究 (Studies on Late Qing Sino–Japanese relations), Tokyo: Kyūko shoin, 2002.

Takahashi, Hidenao 高橋秀直, *Nisshin sensō e no michi* 日清戦争への道 (The road to the Sino–Japanese War), Tokyo: Tōkyō sōgensha, 1995.

Takamura, Naosuke 高村直助, 'Nisshin senji, sengo no zaisei to kinyū' 日清戦時戦後の財政と金融 (Financial policy and the money market during and after the Sino–Japanese War), in Inoue Matsusada 井上光貞 *et al.* (eds), *Nihon rekishi taikei* 日本歴史大系 (An outline of Japanese history), Tokyo: Yamakawa shuppan-sha, 1987, Vol. 4, pp. 789–814.

Takeuchi, Yoshimi 竹内好 (1963): 'Ajia-shugi no tenbō' アジア主義の展望 (A survey of Asianism), in Takeuchi Yoshimi (ed.), *Ajia-shugi* アジア主義 (Asianism), Tokyo: Chikuma shobō, pp. 7–63.

Tanaka, Masatoshi 田中正俊, 'Shinfutsu sensō to Nihon-jin no Chūgoku-kan 清仏戦争と日本人の中国間' (The Sino-French War and Japanese views of China), *Shisō* 思想, No. 512 (February 1967), pp. 14–34.

Tanaka, Stefan, *Japan's Orient: Rendering Pasts into History*, Berkeley and Los Angeles: University of California Press, 1993. *) not cited?*

Tao, De-min, 'Nishimura Tenshū's Journey to the Yangtze Basin in 1897–98', *Sino–Japanese Studies*, Vol. 4, No. 1 (October 1991), pp. 28–43.

Tashiro, Kazui, 'Foreign Relations during the Edo Period: Sakoku Reexamined', *Journal of Japanese Studies*, Vol. 8, No. 2 (Summer 1982), pp. 283–306.

Teng, Ssu-yü, and John K. Fairbank (eds), *China's Response to the West: A Documentary Survey*, Cambridge, MA: Harvard University Press, 1979.

Toby, Ronald P., 'Reopening the Question of Sakoku: Diplomacy in the Legitimation of the Tokugawa Bakufu', *Journal of Japanese Studies*, Vol. 3, No. 2 (Summer 1977), pp. 323–63.

——, *State and Diplomacy in Early Modern Japan: Asia in the Development of the Tokugawa Bakufu*, Stanford, CA: Stanford University Press, 1984.

Tōyama, Shigeki 遠山茂樹, 'Fukuzawa Yukichi no keimō-shugi to Kuga Katsunan no rekishi-shugi' 福沢諭吉の啓蒙主義と陸羯南の歴史主義 (Fukuzawa's enlightenment thinking and Kuga Katsunan's historicism), in Uete Michiari 植手通有 (ed.), *Kuga Katsunan shū* 陸羯南集, Tokyo: Chikuma shobō, 1987, pp. 484–94.

Tsiang, T. F., 'Sino–Japanese Diplomatic Relations, 1870–94', *Chinese Social and Political Science Review*, Vol. 17, No. 1 (April 1933), pp. 1–106.

Tsuruta, Kei 鶴田啓, 'Kinsei Nihon no yotsu no "kuchi"' 近世日本の四つの「口」 (The four 'portals' of Tokugawa Japan), in Arano Yasunori 荒野泰典 *et al.* (eds), *Gaikō to sensō* 外交と戦争 (Diplomacy and war), Tokyo: Tōkyō daigaku shuppankai, 1992, pp. 297–316.

Uchikawa, Yoshimi 内川芳美, 'Jūkyū seiki kōhan-ki no sekai to Nihon no kokusai hōdō' 19世紀後半期の世界と日本の国際報道 (The world in the late nineteenth century and international news coverage in Japan), in Kokusai nyūsu jiten shuppan iinkai, Mainichi komyunikêshonzu 国際ニュース事典出版委員会, 毎日コミュニケーションズ (eds), *Gaikoku shinbun ni miru Nihon* 外国新聞に見る日本 (Japan as seen through foreign newspapers), Tokyo: Mainichi komyunikêshonzu, Vol. 2 (1990), pp. vi–xi.

Uete, Michiari 植手通有, 'Taigai-kan no tenkai' 対外観の転回 (Shifting paradigms in Japanese views of foreign affairs), in: Hashikawa Bunzō and Matsumoto Sannosuke (eds), *Kindai Nihon seiji shisō-shi* 近代日本の政治思想史 (A history of modern Japanese political thought), Tokyo: Yūhikaku, 1971, Vol. 1, pp. 33–74.

Uno, Shun'ichi 宇野俊一, 'Itō Hirobumi to Ōkuma Shigenobu' 伊藤博文と大隈重信 (Itō Hirobumi and Ōkuma Shigenobu), in Takeuchi Yoshimi 竹内好 and Hashikawa Bunzō 橋川文三 (eds), *Kindai Nihon to Chūgoku* 近代日本と中国 (Modern Japan and China), Tokyo: Asahi shinbunsha, 1974, Vol. 1, pp. 37–54.

Valliant, Robert B., 'The Selling of Japan: Japanese Manipulation of Western Opinion, 1900–905', *Monumenta Nipponica*, Vol. 29, No. 4 (Winter 1974), pp. 415–38.

van Gulik, R. H., 'Kakkaron: a Japanese Echo of the Opium War', *Monumenta Serica* 4 (1939/40), pp. 478–545.

Varg, Paul A., 'The Foreign Policy of Japan and the Boxer Revolt', *Pacific Historical Review*, Vol. 15, No. 3 (September 1946), 279–85.

——, 'The Myth of the China Market, 1890–1914', *American Historical Review*, Vol. 73, No. 3 (February 1968), pp. 742–58.

Vincent, R.J., 'Race in International Relations', *International Affairs*, Vol. 58, No. 4 (Autumn 1982), pp. 658–70.

Wagner, Wieland, *Japans Aussenpolitik in der frühen Meiji-Zeit (1868–1894): die ideologische und politische Grundlegung des japanischen Führungsanspruchs in Ostasien* (Japan's foreign policy in the Early Meiji period, 1869–94: the ideological and political foundations of Japan's claims to hegemony in East Asia), Stuttgart: Franz Steiner Verlag, 1990.

Wakabayashi, Bob Tadashi, 'Opium, Expulsion, Sovereignty: China's Lessons for Bakumatsu Japan', *Monumenta Nipponica* 47.1 (Spring 1992), pp. 1–25.

Wang, Shuhuai 王樹槐, *Wairen yu wuxu bianfa* 外人與戊戌变法 (Foreigners and the Hundred Days Reform), Taibei: Jinghua yinshuguan, 1965.

Watanabe, Hiroshi 渡辺浩, *Higashi Ajia no ōken to shisō* 東アジアの王権と思想 (Confucianism and After: Political Thoughts in Early Modern East Asia), Tokyo: Tokyo daigaku shuppansha, 1997.

——, 'Shisō mondai toshite no "kaikoku": Nihon no baai' 思想問題としての「開国」－日本の場合 (The 'opening of the country' as an intellectual problem: Japan's case), Park Choong Seok 朴忠錫 and Watanabe Hiroshi 渡辺浩 (eds), *Kokka rinen to taigai ninshiki: jūshichi jūkyū-seiki* 国家理念と対外認識17–19世紀 (The concept of the State and the perception of foreign countries: seventeenth to nineteenth century), Tokyo: Keiō gijuku daigaku shuppan-kai, 2001, pp. 281–329.

Wasserstrom, Jeffrey N. (ed.), *Twentieth Century China: New Approaches*, London: Routledge, 2003.

White, John A., *The Diplomacy of the Russo–Japanese War*. Princeton, NJ: Princeton University Press, 1964.

Whiting, Allen S., *China Eyes Japan*, Berkeley, CA: University of California Press, 1989.

Wippich, Rolf Harald, *Japan und die deutsche Fernostpolitik 1984–1898: Vom Ausbruch des Chinesisch-Japanischen Krieges bis zur Besetzung der Kiautschou-Bucht: ein Beitrag zur Wilhelminischen Weltpolitik* (Japan and German Far East policies: from the outbreak of the Sino–Japanese War to the occupation of Kiao-chow: a study on Wilhelminian *Weltpolitik*), Stuttgart: Steiner Verlag, 1987.

—— (ed.), *'Haut sie, dass die Lappen fliegen!': Briefe von Deutschen an das japanische Kriegsministerium während des chinesisch-japanischen Krieges 1894/95* ('Beat them to pulp!': German letters to the Japanese War Ministry during the Sino–Japanese War, 1894/95), Tokyo: OAG Gesellschaft für Natur-und Völkerkunde Ostasiens Tokyo, 1997.

Wong, Young-Tsu, 'Revisionism Reconsidered: Kang Youwei and the Reform Movement of 1898', *Journal of Asian Studies*, Vol. 51, No. 3 (August 1992), pp. 513–44.

Yamaguchi, Kazuyuki 山口一之, 'Kenseitō naikaku no seiritsu to kyokutō jōsei 憲政党内閣の成立と極東情勢' (The emergence of the Kensei-tō cabinet and the political situation in the Far East), Nihon kokusai seiji gakkai 日本国際政治学会 (ed.), *Nihon gaikō-shi kenkyū (Nisshin/Nichiro sensō)* 日本外交史研究（日清 日露戦争）(Studies on the diplomatic history of Japan: the Sino–Japanese and the Russo–Japanese War), Tokyo: Yūhikaku, 1962, pp. 87–101.

——, 'Kuga Katsunan no gaiseiron: Meiji 31 – 33-nen' 陸羯南の外政論－明治三十一年～三十三年 (Kuga Katsunan's opinions on foreign policy, 1898–1900), *Komazawa shigaku*, No. 27 (March 1980), pp. 1–26, No. 28 (March 1981), pp. 1–30.

——, 'Kuga Katsunan no gaiseiron: Giwadan jihen to zengosaku' 陸羯南の外政論－義和団事変と善後策 (Kuga Katsunan's views on foreign policy: the Boxer Incident and its settlement), *Komazawa shigaku*, No. 35 (May 1986), pp. 3–50.

Yamamoto, Shigeki 山本茂樹, *Konoe Atsumaro: sono Meiji kokka-kan to Ajia-kan* 近衛篤麿：その明治国家観とアジア観 (Konoe Atsumaro: his views on the Meiji state and Asia), Kyōto: Minerva shobō, 2001.

Yamamoto, Taketoshi 山本武利, *Kindai Nihon no shinbun dokusha-sō* 近代日本の新聞読者層 (Newspaper readership in modern Japan), Tokyo: Hōsei daigaku shuppan-kyoku, 1981.

Yamane, Yukio 山根幸夫, 'Bojutsu henpō to Nihon: Kō Yūi no "Meiji ishin" haaku o chūshin ni shite' 戊戌変法と日本：康有為の「明治維新」把握を中心にして (The Hundred Days Reform and Japan: Kang Youwei's grasp of the 'Meiji Restoration'), in *Kindai Nihon to Chūgoku* 近代日本と中国 (Modern Japan and China), Tokyo: Yamakawa shuppansha, 1976, pp. 1–36.

Yasukawa, Junosuke 安川寿之助, *Fukuzawa Yukichi no Ajia ninshiki: Nihon kindaishi-zō o toraekaesu* 福沢諭吉のアジア認識：日本近代史像をとらえ返す (Fukuzawa Yukichi's perception of Asia: re-understanding the image of modern Japanese history), Tokyo: Kōbunken, 2000.

Zachmann, Urs Matthias, 'Imperialism in a Nutshell: Conflict and the "Concert of Powers" in the Tripartite Intervention, 1895', *Japanstudien* 17 (2005), pp. 57–82.

——, 'Blowing Up a Double Portrait in Black and White: The Concept of Asia in the Writings of Fukuzawa Yukichi and Okakura Tenshin', *positions: east asia cultures critique*, Vol. 15, No. 2 (2007), pp. 345–68.

——, 'Guarding the Gates of Our East Asia: Japanese Reactions to the Far Eastern Crisis (1897–98) as a Prelude to the War', in Rotem Kowner, *Rethinking the Russo-Japanese War, 1904–5*, Vol. 1: *Centennial Perspectives,* Folkestone, Kent: Global Oriental, 2007, pp. 13–30.

Zarrow, Peter 'Late Qing Reformism and the Meiji Model: Kang Youwei, Liang Qichao, and the Japanese Emperor', in Joshua A. Fogel, *The Role of Japan in Liang Qichao's Introduction of Modern Western Civilization to China*, Berkeley, CA: Institute of East Asian Studies, University of California, 2004, pp. 40–67.

Zhai Xin 翟新, *Tōa dōbunkai to Chūgoku: kindai Nihon ni okeru taigai rinen to sono jissen* 東亜同文会と中国　近代日本における対外理念とその実践 (The Tōa dōbun-kai and China: the ideology and practice of foreign relations in modern Japan), Tokyo: Keiō gijuku daigaku shuppan-kai, 2001.

Zhang, Weixiong 張偉雄, *Bunjin gaikō-kan no Meiji Nihon: Chūgoku shodai chūnichi kōshi-dan no ibunka taiken* 文人外交官の明治日本－中国初代駐日公使団の異文化体験 (The Meiji Japan of literati diplomats: the foreign culture experience of the first Chinese diplomatic mission to Japan), Tokyo: Kashiwa shobō, 1999.

Index

"the strong eat the weak" 24 (Fukuzawa)

pan-Asianism source (2007) Saaler & Koschmann, eds., 187n.94

gashin shōtan "sleeping on firewood and licking bile" 37-38

illustrations needed Knockfuss painting 44

jakuniku kyōshoku (see index)

logic y imperialism   FY p41   Icuga katsunan 84; post 100 Days 121 "duty"

meiji ß transfer speed   103± (No ø Herald 1894), 104 KYw

Sources Zhai Xin 『TVK文中囯』 (2001)
         Saaler, Sven on Pan-Asianism in ß (2007)